THE FATE OF
THE FOREST

V

THE FATE OF THE FOREST

DEVELOPERS, DESTROYERS AND

DEFENDERS OF THE AMAZON

SUSANNA HECHT

AND

ALEXANDER COCKBURN

VERSO

London · New York

First published by Verso 1989
© 1989 Susanna Hecht & Alexander Cockburn

Verso
UK: 6 Meard Street, London W1V 3HR
USA: 29 West 35th Street, New York, NY 10001-2291

Verso is the imprint of New Left Books

British Library Cataloguing in Publication Data

Hecht, Susanna
The fate of the forest: developers, destroyers and
defenders of the Amazon.
1. South America. Tropical rain forest ecosystems
I. Title
II. Cockburn, Alexander, 1941–
574.5'2642'098

ISBN 0–86091–261–2

US Library of Congress Cataloging-in-Publication Data

Hecht, Susanna B.
The fate of the forest: developers, destroyers, and defenders of
the Amazon/Susanna Hecht and Alexander Cockburn.
p. cm.
Includes bibliographical references.
ISBN 0–86091–261–2
1. Deforestation—Amazon River Region. 2. Forest conservation—
Amazon River Region. 3. Rain forest ecology—Amazon River Region.
4. Amazon River Region. I. Cockburn, Alexander. II. Title.
SD418.3.A53H43 1989
333.75'0981'1—dc20

Typeset by BP Datagraphics Ltd, Bath, Avon
Printed in Great Britain and the USA by Courier International Ltd

To Ilse Wagner Hecht who raised me in exile, and who encouraged, cajoled and financially supported much of the research herein described; also to my grandfather Hans Hecht who wrote paeans to coffee and monkeys on an Amazon he never saw.

S.H.

To Patricia Cockburn who traveled through the Ituri rainforest of the eastern Congo in 1937, making a language map for the Royal Geographical Society, and to her sister Joan Arbuthnot who was a *garimpeira* and would-be *aviadora* on the Barima river in Amazônia in 1931.

A.C.

Contents

Maps

Acknowledgements

Susanna Hecht and Alexander Cockburn would like to thank Haripriya Rangan and Junko Goto, students of rural development in UCLA's Planning Program who superintended the production and bibliography of this book; Wendy Hitz and Shiv Someshwar, who did bibliographic research in UCLA's impressive library of books on Brazil and the Amazon; Mark McDonald, whose research skills appear in many forms in this volume; Michael Kiernan and Michele Melone who prepared maps; Richard McKerrow who supplied research from New York; Frank Bardacke who supplied the title; Mike Davis, the initiator; Colin Robinson, Anna Del Nevo, Lucy Morton and Charlotte Greig, all of Verso, who pressed forward under a demanding schedule. Among those who made special efforts to make material available to us were Marianne Schmink; Jim Tucker; Alfredo Wagner; Anthony Anderson; Barbara Weinstein; Donald Sawyer; Michael Small; John Richard; Kent Redford; Alberto Rogério da Silva; Hercules Bellville.

For general collaboration our thanks to Wim Groeneveld and Letitia Santos, of Porto Velho and Fazenda Inferno Verde; Darrell Posey; Peter May; Ailton Krenak; Osmarino Amâncio Rodrigues.

Susanna Hecht has been researching the Amazon for more than a decade. Over that period she has received personal, intellectual, and financial support from many. The following bodies have provided assistance: the National Science Foundation; Wenner-Gren Foundation; the University of California Academic Senate; UCLA International Studies and Overseas Program; Resources for the Future; Man and the Biosphere; World Wildlife Foundation (through *Projeto Kayapó*). This book was written in part with funding from the MacArthur Foundation. Valuable institutional support came from the Museu Goeldi in Belém; EMBRAPA; the Nucleus for Higher Amazon Studies (NAEA) of the Federal University of Pará, CEDEPLAR in Belo Horizonte. Acrean work was carried out under the auspices of FUNTAC, and Gil Siqueira, Jorge Ney and the *Conselho Nacional dos Seringueiros*; IEA and Marie Allegretti; the Environmental Defense Fund (EDF) and Steve Schwartzman and Bruce Rich. The Graduate School of Architecture and Urban Planning (GSAUP) at UCLA, patient with erratic schedules, provided a supportive institutional home. Several people gave moral support to Hecht over the years: John Friedmann;

Edward Soja; and especially Michael Storper, who tolerated the frequent absences and disruptions that such research requires. His kindness and criticisms were indispensable. She would like to thank those scholars whose ideas and examples, and later, friendship, inspired her to take on the Amazon and its debates: Robert Goodland, Pedro Sanchez, Alain de Janvry, Hilgard Sternberg. A special thanks also to those who were there from the beginning: Judy Carney, Marianne Schmink, Barbara Weinstein, Anthony Anderson, Stephen Bunker, Darrell Posey, Donald Sawyer.

Finally, thanks to the graduate students who provided a lively intellectual climate: Jacque Chase, Roberto Monte-Mor, Mark MacDonald, Shiv Someshwar, Wendy Hitz, Michael Kiernan, Michele Melone, Carlos Quandt, Brent Millikan, Ted Whitesell, Mark Freudenberger, George Ledec.

The plants shown in plates 8, 9, and 10 were drawn by Cecilia Rizzini and originally published in *Useful Plants of Brazil* by Walter B. Mors and Carlos Rizzini, Rio de Janeiro 1964. They are reproduced here by kind permission.

The photographs of Percival Farquhar and of the skeletons in an Amazonian mausoleum (plates 18 and 31) are reproduced from *The Last Titan* by Charles Gauld, Stamford 1964, with permission.

Plates 1, 3, 5, 7, 17, 22, 23, 26, 27, 28, 29, 31, 34, 37, 38, 39, 40, 42, 43, 44, 45 and back cover illustrations copyright © Alexander Cockburn.

Plate 3, Alexander von Humboldt's head, was sculpted by David d'Angers and may be seen in the Musée David d'Angers, in Angers.

It is entirely impossible in the Amazon to take stock of the vastness, which can be measured only in fragments; of the expansiveness of space, which must be diminished to be appraised; of the grandeur which allows itself to be seen only by making itself tiny, through microscopes; and of an infinity which is meted out little by little, slowly, indefinitely, excruciatingly. The land is still myster-ious. Its space is like Milton's: it hides from itself. Its amplitude cancels itself out, melts away as it sinks on every side, bound to the inexorable geometry of the earth's curvature or deluding curious onlookers with the treacherous unifor-mity of its immutable appearance. Human intelligence cannot bear the brunt of this portentous reality at one swoop. The mind will have to grow with it, adapting to it, in order to master it. To see it, men must give up the idea of stripping off its veils.

EUCLIDES DA CUNHA
1904

The Forests of Their Desires

Taking a close look at what's around us, there is some kind of harmony. It is the harmony of overwhelming and collective murder. . . . We in comparison to that enormous articulation, we only sound and look like half-finished sentences out of a stupid suburban novel. . . . And we have become humble in front of this overwhelming misery and overwhelming fornication, overwhelming growth and overwhelming lack of order.

WERNER HERZOG, *Burden of Dreams* 1984

It is for this that the region is so beautiful, because it is a piece of the planet that maintains the inheritance of the creation of the world. Christians have a myth of the garden of Eden. Our people have a reality where the first man created by god continues to be free. We want to impregnate humanity with the memory of the creation of the world.

AILTON KRENAK, KRENAK INDIAN AND LEADER OF THE INDIGENOUS PEOPLE'S UNION OF BRAZIL 1989

The destruction in the Amazon forests is not unique. It happens elsewhere, in Central America, in the Congo Basin, in Southeast Asia, but without provoking the same tumult and consternation. What imbues the case of the Amazon with such passion is the symbolic content of the dreams it ignites. The prolixity that so overwhelmed Herzog poses a challenge that has fired the greed of generations of exploiters. It has also inspired the most heroic struggles to resolve the fundamental question underlying the destiny of the world's tropical rainforests: what is the relation of people to nature, how do people perceive the obligations of this relationship?

The mystery that is part of the Amazon's allure is not merely a function of the region's immensity and of the infinitude of species it contains. It is also the consequence of centuries of censorship, of embargoes placed on knowledge and travel in the region by the Spanish and Portuguese crowns, of the polite silences of the religious orders during the Amazon's colonial history. Spanish law in 1556 directed that judges ''shall not permit any books to be printed or sold which treat of subjects relating to the Indies without having special license by the Council of the Indies''. The chronicler-naturalist had to face the Inquisition, the Council of the Indies, the king and the Pope – a daunting set of reviewers – before he could publish his findings. Knowledge was accumulated, then kept under lock and key.[1] The Portuguese were determined that Brazil remain subordinate to their eastern possessions. Royal edicts tried to impede even the first steps towards economic development. The colonial council permitted only the cultivation of ginger and indigo where sugarcane could not grow, thus hoping to protect the markets for their Asian spices. Until the end of the eighteenth century it was forbidden to breed mules or embark on almost any form of manufacture beyond the preparation of crude cotton stuffs for domestic consumption. Intellectual life was equally retarded by royal command. In 1707, the Portuguese viceroy closed a printing press in Rio and forbade others to be opened. The stifling of internal growth was matched by suspicion of foreigners, who were refused permission to own land in the country, or even to reside there.

In part this was due to the fact that many of the region's explorations were carried out by boundary patrols and Jesuits whose superiors had ample economic and political reasons to keep information about the region quiet. Only in 1867, after much national and international pressure, did Dom Pedro II, emperor of Brazil, approve the law authorizing steam navigation in the Amazon. The newly independent state maintained a discreet silence about the region through the latter part of the nineteenth century, until the rubber boom and the demands of commerce with the world made such mystery impossible. Even today, great tracts of the Amazon are periodically designated as zones of national security, and entry without the government's permission denied.[2]

With such silences came fantasies, of marvels unimaginable, of gold and diamonds, of political utopias, of Indians variously amenable or savage beyond belief. Early explorers, vastly outnumbered by the native inhabitants, viewed them as exotic and probably dangerous. As slavers began to penetrate the region, flotillas of natives increasingly menaced travel. Subsequent adventurers justified their slaving forays, proscribed by king and church, as the only possible recourse in the face of cannibalism. Here as elsewhere, the First World was projecting onto its victims the horrors it had itself engendered. The so-called *tropas de resgate* (rescue missions) plied through the far Amazon reaches raiding tribes and claiming that, as prisoners of other tribes, the Indians they seized faced certain death by cannibalism or other heathen forms of torment. As Portuguese slaves at least they would live, after a fashion, with the added benefit of receiving Christian salvation. The immense disruptions of native populations reflected the rampages of slavers on the Atlantic coast, slavers on the rivers, and missionaries everywhere. To avoid destruction, the indigenous people began to migrate through the neighboring territories, and intertribal warfare often ensued. The world the explorers called unfinished was above all a world becoming emptied of its original inhabitants, as imported diseases and social disruption prompted a demographic collapse unmatched in the history of the world. Some 200,000 Amazonian Indians remain today, as against

the six to twelve million inhabitants of the Amazon in 1492. More than a third
of the tribes extant in 1900 have passed from this earth.[3]

A WORLD UNFINISHED

The disordered world that so perturbed Herzog has been the one evoked by
explorers for five hundred years. As they set their feet for the first time on the
banks of the Napo River, or gazed on the pre-Cambrian rise of the Guiana Shield,
they conceived they were seeing a world unfinished, only half minted from the
hand of the Creator, a demi-Eden in which men could still be gods.

The early expeditions, either military or religious, marched to the ends of the
forests taking with them imperial naturalists and chroniclers to bring back documentation of a new world and to complete Adam's task of naming its plants and
creatures. In 1535 the first natural history appeared. By Oviedo, it was a text on the
natural and general histories of this new world. It was followed by similar scholarship, such as Acosta's treatise on the natural and moral history of the Indies. These
relatively elevated works were nothing compared to the seamen's and slavers'
tales. Even the Amazon female warriors[4] and golden kings of the chroniclers were
tame in comparison to the exotic creatures that inhabited wayfarers' lore.

In the wake of these reports came boats plying the rivers in search of slaves and
the products of the great forests. The exploiting impulse was in part economic, to
determine who would have the rights to the unfinished Eden, but it was mostly
military. The European monarchs and ecclesiastical empires vied for a toehold in
forests whose prospective riches would swell treasuries depleted by war. Plants
used for drugs, for dyes (like indigo), for flavorings (like cacao and vanilla),
medicinal plants like sarsaparilla, maritime provisions like turtle oil, and salted
meat from wild game moved down the waterways, while missionaries and military
men forged up them in search of unsaved souls, a labor supply, and uncharted
lands.

The presumption that they were encountering natural chaos fired the ambitions
of the invaders. That luxuriant and treacherous space was seen as "the virgin soil
which awaits the seed of civilization", as Baron de Santa-Anna Néry put it.[5] Out of
chaos could come order, mere space could come into the reach of human history
and the realm of profit. Almost five hundred years later, construction magnates
from São Paulo driving the Kalopálo Indians from their ancestral lands, or ranchers
in northern Mato Grosso incinerating trees and species to create degraded pastures, similarly proposed that they were setting themselves the virtuous task of
subduing raw, unprofitable nature in the cause of order and utility.

PORTUGAL WINS THE AMAZON

No sooner had the New World been discovered than the Old World began to fight over it. In 1493, Rodrigo Borgia, Pope Alexander VI, brokered an agreement between Portugal and Spain that the former take control of all territory west and the latter all territory east of the longitude running through the Cape Verde islands. A year later Castille-Aragon and Portugal signed the Treaty of Tordesillas in which the dividing line was moved 370 leagues to the west and the New World was formally claimed. The interest of the Portuguese was to keep the Spanish out of the south Atlantic, where their islands of Madeira and Cape Verde were important and productive sugar colonies and where, further east on the African littoral, they were positioned to control the market in gold, slaves and other harvests. For their part, the Spaniards dreamed of mercantile bonanzas of oriental silks and spices, and a direct route to the East Indies by which they could circumvent the tightly controlled eastern Arab trade routes and the lock on Mediterranean trade maintained by the Venetians. Thus, a quarter of a century before Cortez and his conquistadores laid low the Aztec Empire, most of Brazil fell under formal control of the Portuguese, whose overriding imperative was to secure this vast space before someone else claimed it. And other claimants stood ready: the French, Dutch and Germans moved along the eastern coast and entered Amazônia via the Guianas, seeking a footing for trading outposts and possible colonies.

Thus was born the dream of Manifest Destiny: the Amazon as the venue for national aspiration. This dream has fired all the nations bordering the Amazon. Even as Pedro Teixeira roamed the headwaters of the Amazon in 1638, back in Belém his Governor, Geraldo Noronha, trembled in fear lest the Dutch or French attack the feeble Portuguese garrison. For their part, the Spanish viceroys of Quito and Lima, while greeting Teixeira with the pomp and graces appropriate to a conquistador, found his arrival in the upper Amazon profoundly disturbing, especially when he planted frontier markers in the name of Philip IV, "King of Portugal". Forts and missions sprang up in the confluences and important tributaries of the rivers, as invaders from Holland, Britain, France, Portugal, Spain, and the Holy Roman Empire scrambled to control the watersheds, and the precious medicines, woods, and slaves each would surrender. Rag-tag battalions of a handful of Europeans and their hundreds of captive Indian rowers, half-breeds and guides, played cat-and-mouse with each other in the hinterlands. Portuguese detachments coursed through the Amazon in an attempt to staunch the flow of northern European goods from the French, Dutch and the British, and to hamper the expansion of the meddlesome Spanish missionaries. Military topographers and engineers kept a firm eye on the flows of commerce and an open ear to the gossip from upstream.[6]

THE DREAM OF THE GOLD KING

Of all the myths pervading the history of the Amazon, El Dorado is the most hypnotic. In its original form it referred to a king with wealth so vast that each day he was anointed with precious resins to fix the gold dust decorating his body. The chronicler Oviedo recounts how the famous conquistador Pizarro who triumphed over the Inca, Quesada the conqueror of Colombia, and Sebastian Ben Alcazar the conqueror of Quito, not sated by such victories, all hankered for more gold and glory through the capture of the king and his possessions. In 1540, inflamed by this vision, Gonzalo Pizarro, brother of the conqueror of Peru, decided to launch an expedition with Francisco de Orellana to conquer the lands of El Dorado and the cinnamon forests. With four thousand Indians, two hundred horses, three thousand swine, and packs of hunting dogs trained to attack Indians, the expedition made its way laboriously through the tropical forests on the east side of the Andes. Hapless forest tribes encountering this army faced an inquisition. When they denied knowledge of the kingdom of El Dorado, they were promptly tortured as liars, burned on *barbacoa*, or thrown to the ravenous hounds. As the expedition descended the Coca watershed towards the Napo river, their provisions – and their Andean Indian bearers – gave out. Swimming the horses across streams became increasingly tiresome. Disheartened and starving, Pizarro ordered the construction of a raft, sending his second-in-command Orellana ahead to find food. Orellana and his fifty companions never returned. Instead they became the first white men to descend from the headwaters to the mouth of the Amazon. Incensed by the treachery of Orellana and frustrated in his attempts to seek out the kingdom of El Dorado, a furious Pizarro made his return to Quito.

Pizarro's was but the first of many attempts to capture this mythical kingdom and its resplendent ruler. The two became conflated as the story of El Dorado continued to fire the imagination, becoming more fabulous with each retelling. In 1774 an Indian described to the Spanish Governor, Don Miguel de Centurion, the features of the kingdom of El Dorado: "a high hill, bare except for a little grass, its surface covered in every direction with cones and pyramids of gold ... so that when struck by the sun, its brilliance was such that it was impossible to gaze on it without dazzling the eyesight." The myth of El Dorado also entered a more populist vein among the petty goldminers and less noble *bandeirantes* – rough-riders of Portuguese imperial expansion from the south, São Paulo. In seeking those magic mountains of emeralds and gold the luck of a poor man might change, and he could become master of the earth, beneficiary of a world unfinished, and therefore of a world in which such strokes of fortune were not absurd.[7]

Both Portuguese and Spaniards were inspired by the entrancing stories of Orellana's chronicler, the Dominican monk Gaspar de Carvajal, who described the gold ornaments circling the wrists and waists of natives he had encountered. Tantalizing tales of inland Inca trading routes, where gold and silver were bartered cheerfully for iron, raised the hopes of the sons of the Portuguese Empire. The *bandeirantes* were no less interested than the rulers of the Grão Pará territory at the mouth of the Amazon.

By 1727 the Paulista *bandeirantes*, standard-bearers of the larger project of conquest, had discovered gold in the southern flanks of the Amazon. The region around Cuiabá, worked by black slave labor since the Indians nearby could not tolerate the toil and had either fled or died, saw river craft and mule trains arrive with jerky and manioc, then depart downriver, and on through savannah and forest, bearing their precious cargo. South from the Guianas, north from the Brazilian Shield, down from the Andes, and up from the river's mouth, rushed adventurers obsessed with these dreams of sudden wealth.[8]

The *bandeirantes* were not only the archetypal frontiersmen, but also forerunners of the booty seekers who coursed across the region ever after, intent upon bringing undiscovered riches to light and untapped labour to heel (usually in the form of slaves), bestowing upon nature the first kiss of the *mission civilisatrice*. Sometimes financed by the state, such booty seekers were the scouts and pioneers of national integration. In a certain sense, the *bandeirantes* represented the coarse delirium of pioneering empire. The naturalists of the Enlightenment represented the first attempts to focus and direct the disordered exuberance of the pioneers, and here the hunt for El Dorado matured into its rational economic expression: development.

BOTANY IN THE SCIENCE OF EMPIRE

From Francis Bacon came the concept that scientific knowledge meant power over nature. Newton's fundamental triumph had been to show that the complexity of the world could be deciphered and understood; the inference was that the confusion of the nether colonies could be unraveled and deeper truths revealed. The eighteenth century saw numerous explorers entering the Amazon, but usually their function was surveying of boundaries, the staying of Spanish and other incursions, or the importation of the Christian God. The first "true" scientific exploration was launched in 1736. The French Académie des Sciences, intent upon resolving some of Newton's theories regarding the size and shape of the earth, mounted an expedition to the Amazon. The party contained one of the Amazon's most famous visitors, Charles Marie de la Condamine, traveling with ten other "natural philosophers". La Condamine's journey differed from earlier ones in that it was sponsored by a scientific institution and in principle concerned the accumulation of pure knowledge; but his botanical descriptions of plants had very practical consequences, and changed the region forever. Rubber, quinine, curare, ipecac, and copaíba oil made their entrance into European history, first as exotica and minor trade novelties, and later as the basis for substantial economic enterprises.

In the last year of the eighteenth century the great naturalists Alexander von Humboldt and Aimé Bonpland traveled to the Amazon under the aegis of the Spanish monarch Carlos IV. Von Humboldt's exploits piqued the curiosity and imperial interest of the European monarchs. King Max Josef of Bavaria sent Karl von Martius and Johann von Spix on a similar mission of enquiry. The naturalists collected their specimens assiduously and displayed great zeal for cartographic description. This remitting of huge botanical collections to the herbaria of Europe, along with detailed discussions of the development potential of these regions, became a leitmotif for other naturalists following in their wake. Such eagerness to collect and to measure sparked fears – always near the surface – about foreign plans to occupy the region. As one Brazilian government agent said sourly of von Humboldt, "I never saw anyone measure so carefully land that was not his."[9]

Of course such botanical pioneers were not heedless of the economic consequences of the natural riches that lay before them. Richard Spruce, who spent some seventeen years of his life in the Amazon, often ardently expressed the wish that Amazônia had fallen into British hands. "How often have I regretted that England did not possess the Amazon valley instead of India!" Spruce lamented. "If that booby James had persevered in supplying Raleigh with ships, money and men until he had formed a permanent establishment on one of the great American rivers, I have no doubt but that the whole American continent would have been at this moment in the hands of the English race!" Failing this, Spruce was determined to bring the Amazon to India. Via commissions from Clements Markham of the India Office, he was easily persuaded to provide the British colony with quinine seeds. To calm malarial fevers rife in Asia, these trees were duly planted in Kandy in 1860. The quality of the quinine produced was mediocre, and this attempt to break the Southeast Asian quinine monopoly, dominated by the Dutch (who had also taken cultivars from the Amazon) failed. In contrast, the later British shipments of rubber seeds to Kew were immensely successful, promoting the commercial development of rubber in Southeast Asia and altering forever the history of tropical economies. These shipments of quinine and rubber seeds were masterminded by Clements Markham who, as an agent for Joseph Hooker, the director of Kew Gardens, organized the collection of tropical germ plasm to the greater glory of Her Majesty's colonies.

In contrast to the robust *bandeirantes* who were spurred by gold and imperial favor, the nineteenth-century naturalists – Humboldt, Darwin, Bates, Wallace, Martius and Spix – expressed a more genteel version of what is now called, in the jargon of development economists, natural resources assessment. While their goals were sensibly scientific and descriptive, their researches were funded by the state, or by the sale of collections to fuel the acquisitive lust of nineteenth-century museum curators. Kew Gardens was founded in 1760 as part of the Linnaean classificatory frenzy of the century, but economic motives stimulated the continuing collections. In contrast to the botanical garden of today, which is essentially an amenity for the contemplation of nature and gazebo architecture, these nineteenth-century gardens were Research and Development facilities for the propagation of germ plasm, subsequently shipped to the appropriate colonies. To take the case of Great Britain: behind a botanist like Spruce stood the agent representing Kew Gardens (in this case Clements Markham); behind Kew Gardens stood the Colonial Office; behind the Colonial Office the tropical experiment station, with all parties eager to turn the Amazon's natural riches to the economic advantage of the British Empire.

LOST EDENS

In the heirs and assigns of Romanticism the Amazon stirred another set of dreams, as the relict of a world otherwise lost, the last remaining outpost of Eden. As Humboldt – whose report of his voyage to South America electrified Europe – explained, ''When nations wearied with mental enjoyment behold nothing in refinement but the germ of depravity, they are flattered with the idea that infant society enjoyed pure and perpetual felicity''. Here was Rousseau's view of the noble savage in harmonious relation with his brethren and nature in a world of primal innocence beyond the taint of commerce, industry and history, and free, as the naturalist Alfred Russel Wallace put it, ''of the thousand curses that gold brings upon us''.

In this version of pastoral, nature is benign, and as man draws closer to it the more virtuous he becomes. Only the ravages of the industrial revolution could have provoked such a reversal of the traditional European view of man's relation to nature, his need to master its harshness and – on the prescription of ecclesiastical literature – to rise above natural brutishness.

Much of the nineteenth- and early twentieth-century writing on this lost Edenic world decried ''civilized excesses'' and contrasted these with the virtues of the natural state. In his humanity and wholeness the noble savage could guide others to the true and the beautiful. This vision was celebrated in a thousand pastorals, in the ecstatic descriptions of the Amazon by nineteenth-century naturalists such as Wallace, who with Darwin developed the central concepts of evolutionary theory, spending his active years searching out the world's most remote places and his old age traveling on the passport of spiritualism to the worlds mankind had lost. In a memoir of his fourteen years in the Amazon, Wallace invoked the perfection of life in an Indian village. He lauded the free physicality, ''the growth that no straps or bonds impede'', the free-striding nobility, the lack of artifice. Although civilization has rewards, its fruits are not shared by all, while the delights of the forest are held in common.

Virtually every decade has seen such heirs of Rousseau discover the Amazon anew. The tribes frolic in their innocent beauty, have the leisure to appreciate life, and are attuned to the deeper verities of human existence. Tropical exuberance honors moral perfection.

It is no surprise that nineteenth-century romanticism should have infused many of the writings of British naturalists. What is less known is the florescence of these ideas in Brazilian society. With the publication of Antônio Gonçalves Dias's trilogy *Cantos*, the first volume of which was published in 1847, the infusion of romantic ideals into the newly liberated colony began. Gonçalves Dias was a young man from northern Maranhão, an area rich in the syncretic lore of *caboclos* (back-woodsmen), black slaves, and Indians, not far from the last rallying places of several indigenous nations such as the Tembé, the Timbira and the Guajajara. Maranhão had always enjoyed richer cultural ties with France than with Portugal, and the ideas of the Enlightenment were eagerly greeted in this northern province. Having once been a French outpost Maranhão had never entirely forgotten its heritage. European culture, fused with native experience and sensibility, produced a work of great brilliance and passion. A fluent Tupi speaker, Dias's poetry was rich in native cadence and the rhythmic phrasing of Tupi words. In his luminous poetry, with its glorification of the Indian warrior, the native blood flowing through the veins of virtually all Brazilians became a source of pride rather than shame.

The poems inaugurated "Indianist" literature which honored the vigor of the tropics and their inhabitants, the youth of the New World as against Old Europe. Gonçalves Dias offered not just a critique of Europe and its ways, in particular the excesses of human exploitation and misery in the surge of the industrial revolution, but also an ideological counterweight to racist and condescending European views of Brazilians and indeed other colonial or ex-colonial peoples. Other Indianist writers produced military epics such as that on the "Tamoio Confederation" by Gonçalves de Magalhães, which addressed the resistance to the Portuguese invasion at Rio de Janeiro. José de Alencar, another Indianist, wrote moving descriptions of indigenous life and infused his diction with native words. His works decry the contamination and destruction of native peoples and their values by corrupt European contact. His most famous work *Iracema*, an anagram of America, movingly describes the process of destruction and oppression of native peoples through their polluting contact with the civilized world. The Brazilian anthropologist Darcy Ribeiro, a recent heir to this long tradition, wrote in 1978 the hugely popular *Maíra*, the story of a Swiss girl who abandons a frivolous existence for the natural wisdom and tumultuous sexuality of the "Mairún" tribe.

Between Chateaubriand and Ribeiro are scores of similar *educations sentimentales*. In 1916 people rushed to buy W.H. Hudson's novel *Green Mansions*. It created a world in which troupes of fauna disport beneath the forest canopy, witness to doomed love between natural woman and civilized, destructive man. Mirroring this contrast is the woman's rich forest versus the arid savannahs and cities of the man. In his famous novel of a tropical Shangri-la, *The Lost Steps*, published in 1968, Alejo Carpentier described the odyssey of a Latin sophisticate who voyages to the upper Orinoco and there discovers a lost world and its earth mother – Eve – constrasting sharply with his own soignée mistress. Combining the essential elements of this genre, Peter Matthiessen's *At Play in the Fields of the Lord*, published in 1965, describes the collision of adventurers and men of God with a native group, and the passion that arises between an Indian woman and the North American narrator. The love proves fatal. The narrator's kiss transmits the disease that destroys her tribe and signals the fateful irruption of the outside world. To discover Eden is to destroy it. Love leads to death. By the very tales we tell we doom the natural tropical world we love and its inhabitants.

These versions of pastoral have not been limited to prose or poetry, as uncountable folios of forest photography attest. With the coming of the nature documentary – which traces its origins to Walt Disney's dispatch of film units to the Third World in the late 1940s to capture for his cartoonists the movement of wild animals[10] – Eden was born again, and became the *élan vital* of genteel television.

Pastoral inhabits the foothills of tragedy (except in Disney, which represents man's most determined effort yet to divest nature of the tragic element) as Claude Lévi-Strauss saw so well in his great travel work *Tristes Tropiques*:

> Journeys, those magic caskets full of dreamlike promises, will never again yield up their treaures untarnished. A proliferating and overexcited civilization has broken the silence of the seas once and for all. The perfumes of the tropics and the pristine freshness of human beings have been corrupted by a busyness with dubious implications, which mortifies our desires and dooms us to acquire only contaminated memories. . . . Our great Western civilization, which has created the marvels we now enjoy, has only succeeded in producing them at the cost of corresponding ills. . . . The first thing we see as we travel round the world is our own filth, thrown into the face of mankind. So I can understand the mad passion for travel books and their deceptiveness. They create the illusion of something that no longer exists but still should exist, if we were to have any hope of avoiding the overwhelming conclusion that the history of the last twenty thousand years is irrevocable. There is nothing to be done about it now; civilization has ceased to be that delicate flower which was preserved and painstakingly cultivated in one or two sheltered areas of a soil rich in wild species which may have seemed menacing because of the vigour of their growth, but which nevertheless made it possible to vary and revitalize the cultivated stock.

Writing in 1955 of his travels in the interior of Brazil in the early 1930s, Lévi-Strauss echoes the melancholy of Henry Thoreau and Margaret Fuller gazing upon the remnants of destroyed native North American society almost a century before. History is indeed irrevocable and the Amazon and its inhabitants are among its victims.

NATURE'S PRESERVE

There is another romantic vision of the Amazon that excludes man altogether and proposes a world whose lineaments reflect only the purity of natural forces, freed entirely from man's despoiling hand. Here is the "virgin rain forest" of a thousand scientific articles, a concept also sprung from Romanticism. For Goethe and Thoreau, both of whom were excellent naturalists, nature was the mirror of the divine. Through its contemplation one could more fully penetrate the mysteries of the human soul. Their approach was born from a rigorous natural science infused with animism. The signposts on this path gestured to transcendentalism, a critique of the spiritual, social and environmental consequences of industrialism, a critique also of conventional Christianity. For the tropical world the preoccupations of the transcendental scientist provoked two important consequences. First, there was the perception of divine nature as virgin, unmodified by human action, and thus meet for virtuous contemplation. Here was the genesis of the idea of national parks in the tropics, construed along the lines of parks in North America whose entire focus was shaped by the transcendental inclinations of John Muir, the founder of Yosemite National Park. Thus have many First World conservationists approached the endangered Amazon with the proposed therapy of making it an Eden under glass. The second consequence was the pure scientific exploration of the region's ecology, inspired by a view of the Amazon as an enormous, unsullied laboratory for the scientific contemplation and classification of nature.

Such were the visions and the myths engendered in the First World's contact with the Amazon. Each has had powerful consequences, has provoked pillage at one extreme and at the other a pastoralism that can be as anti-human as any bulldozer. But in each instance, mythic projections and the fantasies of explorers, freebooters, missionaries, builders of empire, naturalists, Romantics, and transcendentalists, have imposed upon the Amazon preconceptions that have exacted a heavy price: a refusal to permit the Amazon to tell its own story. And if a region is denied its true history how can its future be honestly discussed?

NOTES

1. For obvious reasons, the Portuguese and Spanish crowns were nervous about the flow of knowledge about their holdings in Latin America. The rationale for censorship was national security. Published information could only help alien interests, possible invaders, and undesirable entrepreneurs. Gonzalo Fernandez de Oviedo y Valdes, known as Oviedo, wrote the first major report on the New World, *História General y Natural de las Indias*. Oviedo was royal chronicler of the Spanish Empire, and spent thirty-four years sorting through all reports on the New World, its inhabitants and natural resources. His great work was published posthumously in 1535 and in a very limited edition. Acuna's report of his return voyage with Teixeira, *New Discovery of the Great River of the Amazons* 1641, which was

greatly prized by Clements Markham, was suppressed by the Spanish King. Details of such suppression of knowledge are to be found in A.C.F. Reis, *A Amazônia que os Portugueses Revelaram* 1954, or E. Goodman, *Explorers of South America* 1972, or D. Sweet's thesis "Rich realm of nature destroyed" 1978. The interdiction of manufactures and the orientation of the colonial economy can be found in several excellent histories of Brazil: C. Boxer, *Golden Age of Brazil, 1695–1750* 1962, S. Buarque de Holanda, *História Geral da Civilização Brasileira* 1960–, Furtado, *Formação Econômica do Brasil* 1963, and Santa-Anna Néry, *The Land of the Amazons* 1901.

2. The designation of areas of *Segurança Nacional* is derived from the 1967 Brazilian constitution, which permitted the federal government to intervene in states where there were "cases of grave disturbances of the public order" or areas of special interest to national security. Thus border zones, zones of political unrest, zones of certain economic resources and zones of military experimentation were placed under the control of the military. Traditionally, mayors of these municipalities were under the direct control of the military. In the early 1980s, the brilliant Amazonian journalist, Lucio Flávio Pinto pointed out that the state of Pará barely controlled any of its own land, since areas on either side of Federal highways, mining zones, GETAT (Grupo Executivo do Araguaia-Tocantins) and GEBAM (Grupo Executivo do Baixo Amazonas), areas of land conflict and even revolutionary movements, were beyond the reach of state government. The major area of national security in Amazônia today is the *Calha Norte* zone where a 4,500 mile swath follows the international border and major mineral finds.

3. There is a vigorous and almost violent debate over the population size in the Amazon at the time when white pioneers first arrived. Carvajal described flotillas of canoes, and more than 60,000 warriors coming to meet the Orellana expedition and his account evokes an almost continuously settled river bank. About a century later Acuna describes devastated river bank settlements. These populations were then ravaged by slavers, inter-tribal

warfare, devastating disease, and the onslaughts of colonial troops and the Cabanagem revolt. These chronicle accounts were dismissed for many years until Pierre Clastres suggested in 1973 that they could indeed serve as important sources on numbers of native populations and posited a population close to 4.5 million. The usual technique to ascertain populations involves extrapolation back from current tribal numbers, or making estimates based on the resource endowments of the region, mission accounts, and military control efforts (cf. J.H. Hemming, *Red Gold*, 1978). Others, such as Denevan in his *Native Population of the Americas in 1492* 1976, argued that different zones in the Amazon had different productivities and potentialities for population, given different forms of agriculture. He posited a population level closer to 5 million. With the growing body of information on indigenous agricultural productivities and land use technologies, and more archaeological effort in Amazônia, it is likely that precontact numbers will be pushed upward from the modest 2–5 million inhabitants, to levels approaching 15 million.

4. Orellana was the first traveler to claim that his journey had been impeded by savage Amazon women, marshaling these fair-haired Amazons as an excuse for his failure to return to the aid of Pizarro. Walter Raleigh made the same claim to account for his failure to bring back gold from the Guianas. In his *New Discovery* 1641, Acuna gave a lengthy account of Amazon women living atop Tacamiaba, bearing children to the Guacaré and disposing of the sons. La Condamine spread such stories further. The Baron de Santa-Anna Néry suggests in *Land of the Amazons* that such accounts stemmed from travelers who saw Indian women helping their men in battle. Chroniclers then fused such tales into a tradition of folklore stretching back to Herodotus's tales of the Amazons in his *Histories*. The etymology of the name could either be *A-mazon*, "without a breast" in Greek; or *Ama zona*, "joined with a belt" in Greek. The former was the preference of Diodorus of Sicily, who claimed that such warrior women had

their right breasts removed to make it easier to use weapons such as bows. But classical vases and bas-reliefs in the Capitoline museum show the Amazons to have been in mutilated in no such way. Néry seems to prefer the second etymology which he traces to a conquering race of women in Africa "who fought in pairs, bound together not only by oaths, but by belts". Thus did First World fantasies tarnish the name of the world's largest river, even as the fantasists murdered the inhabitants.

5. The opening chapter of Santa-Anna Néry's *Land of the Amazons* begins, "Brazil is a gift of the sixteenth century offered by chance to the future."

6. The continual battle for economic and military control of the region is discussed in a number of important works. Among the most famous is George Edmundson, "Dutch trade in the basin of the Rio Negro" in the *English Historical Review* 1904; and Fr. S. Fritz, *Journal of the Travels and Labours of Samuel Fritz between 1686–1723* 1922. Detailed, excellent accounts of the various aspects of the economic domination of the Indians is to be found in John Hemming, *Amazon Frontier* 1987. D. Alden, *Colonial Roots of Modern Brazil* 1973, Buarque de Holanda, *História* 1960, S.E. Gross, *The Economic Life of the Estado do Maranhão e Grão Pará* 1969, F. Kieman, *The Indian Policy of Portugal in the Amazon Basin, 1614–1693* 1954.

7. Don Miguel de Centurion's Indian story is from Hemming, *Amazon Frontier* 1987, who himself has a full discussion of El Dorado in his volume, *The Search for El Dorado* 1978. The incorporation of El Dorado into popular culture and myth is described in Ana Luisa Martins, "História dos Garimpos de Ouro no Brasil" in G. Rocha, ed. *Em Busca do Ouro* 1984, and D. Cleary, "Anatomy of a Gold Rush", Ph.D. thesis, University of Oxford 1987.

8. The *bandeirantes* and the whole *bandeira* movement has its origins in São Paulo. Many of the Luso-Indian offspring of the Portuguese Paulistas, alienated from Indian cultural roots and also, despite their Portuguese sires, denied the benefits of white society, sought wealth and glory through adventurism. Well stocked with *mestizos*, the *bandeirantes* could also be the second or more adventurous sons of the local nobility. A *bandeira* refers both to a flag, in this case that of the Portuguese crown, and a raiding party. Always interested in precious metals, but entirely pleased to make do with native slaves, their attacks on Spanish missions not only advanced the Portuguese geopolitical cause, but also supplied the slave market with the "domesticated" Indians who resided in them. El Dorado maniacs, numerous *bandeiras* set forth to the north to seek the land of treasure. One of the most famous expeditions was that of Antônio Raposo Tavares, who in 1647 with 1,200 men made one of the earliest descents of the Guaporé-Madeira river, explored the Rio Negro and finally arrived in Belém. Under a secret charge from the Portuguese crown, his mission was to reconnoitre and to seek out precious metals, and to claim these western lands for the Portuguese domain. Others like Pero Domingues led expeditions down the Araguaia to the Tocantins. He was followed by other such as Cristóvão Lisboa, Luís Figueira and Antônio Ribeiro. Combining devotion to both the crown and precious metals, Bartolemeu Bueno da Silva discovered gold on the lower flanks of the Rio das Mortes in Mato Grosso, in about 1725. Fernão Paes de Barros shortly thereafter also found gold at Cuiabá and at the headwaters of the Guaporé.

The most exhaustive studies of the *bandeirantes* are Affonso d'Escragnolle Taunay, *História das Bandeiras Paulistas* 1954, Buarque de Holanda, *História Geral* 1960, and Richard Morse, *The Bandeirantes: The Historical Role of the Brazilian Pathfinders* 1965.

9. Alexander von Humboldt, *Personal Narrative of Travels to the Equinoctial Regions of the New Continent During the Years 1799–1804* 1815.

10. Richard Schickel, *The Disney Version* 1968.

TWO

The Realm of Nature

The very signs also from which we form our judgement are often very deceptive; a soil that is adorned with tall and graceful trees is not always a favorable one, except, of course for those trees.

PLINY, *Natural History*

Amazônia is still the last unwritten page of Genesis.
In Amazônia, extraordinary and visible changes result from the simple play of the most common physical forces. Even under the most dry topographical aspect, there is no way to fix this land in definitive lines. Every six months, every flood is like a wet sponge that passes over a poorly done drawing – it obliterates, modifies, or transforms the most firm and salient traces.

EUCLIDES DA CUNHA, *Um Paraíso Perdido* 1906

Differing in their purpose, the explorers, naturalists and boundary parties were united in their awe of the complexity and diversity of the tropical forests through which they journeyed. The nineteenth-century naturalists remarked constantly on the region's richness, but then went on to deplore the poor use made of these natural resources. Whether trained naturalist, navy man or simple adventurer, all unfailingly observed that the richness of the land contrasted mightily with the poverty of its people, the self-same poverty being blamed on the indolence and ineptitude of the region's occupants. No small vituperation was levied against Amazonians: Henri Coudreau, one of the most knowledgeable explorers of the southern Amazon tributaries, and a fanatic advocate of Aryan superiority wrote: "the only way to occupy this region would be to establish white colonies". Even the brilliant Baron Alexander von Humboldt felt that the indolence and inferior civilization of the native populations reflected the generosity of the environment: "The degree of civilization bears an inverse relationship to the fertility of the soil and beneficence of the nature that surrounds them".

It occurred to few visitors that the biological exuberance they so much admired might set serious limitations on the forms of agriculture that they hoped to encourage. The orderly parade of European agriculture was quite at variance to the jumbled fields of mixed crops that they surveyed with such approbation. Walter

Bates, another nineteenth-century naturalist who was an entomologist by training, at least noticed animal pests and suggested that these might hamper productivity. Bates focused on marauding parrots plaguing rice fields, the inevitable and highly destructive incursions of the leafcutter ant, and the ravenous rats in the cacao storehouses. But his reaction was to reiterate the wail raised time after time in the literature of Amazônia, that if only the locals would carry out agriculture in the proper – that is, European – way, then things would be different.[1]

The luxuriance of the tropics consistently deceived new arrivals. They imagined the rich forests sprang from fertile soils and they were utterly wrong. Amazon forests exist on soils that are, by temperate zone standards, mostly poor. The rapidly growing and weedy vegetation, and great diversity of insects, pests, and pathogens make tropical agriculture a formidable task, and one where European models of land use – the sweep of fields composed of one species – are extraordinarily difficult to sustain. From the attempts of the most humble peasant to the most arrogant entrepreneur, the history of this type of agricultural approach is written in failure. People not native to the region regularly found their ambitious plans thwarted in the collision between their visions and the reality of the Amazon itself. Their tropical Eden was more refractory than they had supposed.

Amazônia appears in the popular imagination as a vast green swath of forest, mostly flat, stretching without interruption from the foothills of the Andes to the Atlantic Ocean, unvarying in its geology and superficial appearance. In fact the terrain through which the Amazon river system flows is of immense variety. Some soils are exceedingly rich, others so poor that they are essentially bleached sand. In the regions of what the naturalist Spruce called "the dead rivers" – the Rio Negro drainage – the forests are almost silent, vegetation stunted, and the waters themselves stained almost black by the humic acids. Elsewhere, where richer soils occur, as in southeastern Pará, forests abound with wildlife, and the earth is a purplish red. There are also huge areas of wetlands. Large expanses of the Amazon Basin support native savannah. In sum the Amazon is continental, almost the size of the United States, and embraces a profusion of different climates, geologies and living worlds.

THE GEOLOGY OF AMAZÔNIA

Gaze down at the Amazon region as a whole and grasp the differing geologic and biological rhythms of the region. We are basically looking at a funnel which drains some six million square kilometers, with its wide end at the Andes, butting into Colombia to the northwest and then curving down in an enormous semi-circle through Ecuador, Peru and Bolivia. This funnel gradually narrows as the great tributaries fall to the Amazon plain or *planície* and swell the river-sea as it heads towards the Atlantic through the narrow end of the funnel at Belém. To the north and south of the funnel respectively lie what geologists call the Guiana and the Brazilian Shields. The pre-Cambrian formations are some of the oldest land surfaces on the planet, part of the young world's first continent Gonwanaland, formed some hundred million years ago. Their waters also flow into the basin, and large areas of the shields are cloaked in lush forests. The contact points between the shields and their Tertiary or younger sediments in the basin are clearly expressed in the rapids and falls that churn the waters where they meet.

The contours of the Amazon are thus expressed in a few basic geological forms: the rising Andes – the source for most of the sediments in the basin – and the crystalline pre-Cambrian shields that encircle the huge sedimentary basin. The basin itself is composed of two basic landforms: the *terra firme*, or uplands which are of Tertiary or Pleistocene age, and the *várzea* or floodplains. The land in the basin is made up of low plateaux and rounded hills.

In its earlier incarnation the Amazon flowed west to the Pacific, in a channel between the two great shields. Access to the Pacific closed when the Andes rose some forty million years ago, creating a sluggish lake. The river, now blocked by rising rock, shifted its flow to the Atlantic, carrying with it the rich sediments of the new range, and began to shape the outlines of the basin as we see it today.

Now view the Amazon again from an Andean perch : the river lies roughly on the equator, its tributaries on the left rising in the northern hemisphere, while those feeding the river from the right rise in the southern hemisphere. From the mouth of the Amazon upriver about 2,000 miles, the land gradient rises by only about 300 feet.

THE CAMPINA FORESTS

Gaze north where the waters of the Rio Negro flow down from old rocks of the Guiana Massif of Brazil, Venezuela, and parts of the foothills of the Colombian *cordillera*. These waters drain through the famous white sand soils, highly eroded sediments derived from the Guiana Shield and almost devoid of plant nutrients such as phosphorus, nitrogen and potassium. The extremely low fertility of these soils produces a vegetation known locally as *campina* forests, at odds with common conceptions of the tropical forest but which comprises one of the largest vegetation formations in Amazônia. The color accents of the *campina* forests are of muted grey, ochre, and rust. Compared to other Amazonian forests, *campinas* are not particularly rich in species. The leathery leaves and open forests bear little

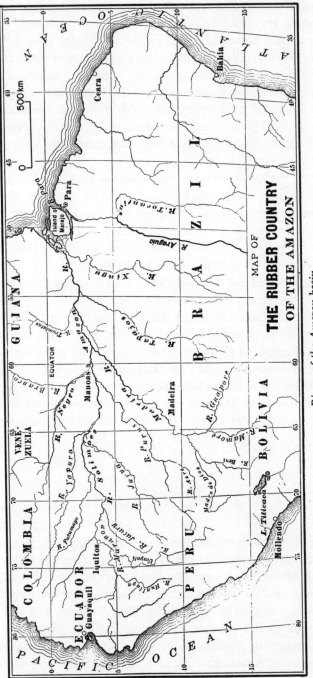

MAP OF

THE RUBBER COUNTRY

OF THE AMAZON

Rivers of the Amazon basin

resemblance to what one normally thinks of as Amazonian vegetation. Lichens that look like puffy corals grow on the ground. In conditions so inhospitable to growth, the lichens, amongst nature's hardiest organisms, flourish in the forest's under-story, capturing the paltry nutrients in the rain water and fixing them in their tissues. Tree branches bear beautiful orchids, but the overall landscape bears no relation to the trees and over-arching canopy of Hollywood set designs for the jungle. In these forests one walks upon a thick, springy mat of leaf litter, some-times a yard in depth, quite uncharacteristic of other parts of the Amazonian forest where such layers of litter barely exist. The mat stays thick because the insects and micro-organisms which would otherwise break down the leaves into chemical elements for reabsorption by plants are deterred by the chemical composition of the leaves, which include many tannins and humic acids.[2]

This area of the Amazon sees an average of some ten feet of rain a year, more than double the rate for the moist northeastern United States. The rains seep through the litter mat and then, darkened by the acids and tannins, run rapidly through the sandy soil, down the streams or *igarapés*, and eventually into the Rio Negro itself, which Orellana described as being "black as ink".

From the headwaters of the Rio Negro travelers can reach the Orinoco drainage of Venezuela by way of the Casiquiare Canal. When this natural access between the Orinoco and Negro basins was first described by La Condamine, the French Académie des Sciences was stunned. It meant that the Orinoco, the Amazon, and portage-links from the Guaporé to the Paraguay and thence Plate river drainages, formed a vast network of fluvial transport, connecting the major river systems of the whole continent. La Condamine was repeating a tale of the Jesuit friar, Roman, who was ascending the Orinoco when he encountered Portuguese slavers from the Rio Negro. At the end of the eighteenth century Humboldt had explored this 220-mile fluvial link between the two major river systems. The swift-flowing canal may have been the result of crustal dislocations, but at high water the Negro is able to divert as much as a quarter of the upper Orinoco waters.[3] Today in the distant backwaters of the Negro's tributaries, goldminers and the Yanomami Indians struggle over the future of important parts of its watersheds, just as Dutch and Portuguese adventurers battled to control it more than three hundred years ago.

As one ascends the Negro, its major tributary river bearing its opposite name, the Rio Branco (literally the white, or clear river), drains large areas of the Brazilian Shield. About 250 miles from the mouth of the Branco begin the rapids of Carac-araí, stretching for nearly thirteen miles. Once passed, the forest recedes, and the Branco-Rupinuni savannahs, more than 25,000 square miles in size, stretch into the horizon. The slightly undulating terrains and poorly developed stream systems prompt sheet flooding, and in the wet season this open savannah turns to flood-land. In high flood the headwaters of the Branco and Negro systems abolish dis-tinctions between land and water and between watersheds, and such watery junctions have served in the past to provide what one geographer has called the most "significant cultural thoroughfares" in South America.[4] There mingled languages, commodities, and cultures flowed from one watershed to the next, linking the Orinoco and the Essiquibo with the Amazon.

THE RIVERS OF THE ANDES

Move now to the center of the western and wider end of the funnel and see the Putumayo whence Roger Casement in 1912 brought reports of savagery and enslavement that had destroyed 80 per cent of the indigenous people in that part of the Amazon. Navigable more than eight hundred miles above its mouth, it passes through no rapids at all. The Putumayo rises in the Colombian and Peruvian Andes, and indeed marks their shared national border before it enters Brazil, where it bears the name Içá. The Içá meets the Solimões, as the Amazon river is named before its cloudy waters mix with the dark waters of the Negro. Rich in the sediments of the younger Andean chain, the Putumayo and sister rivers to the north and south, the Caquetá and the Marañón, descend into the Amazon Basin. Year after year in the rainy season, they flood and deposit their alluvium on their banks. Known as *várzeas*, these became among the richest agricultural sites in the basin, cherished by cultivators since man's arrival in the Amazon. Here annual crops, orchards of palms and fruits, faunal harvests of turtle, lake fish and aquatic birds nourished indigenous tribes such as the Omágua and the Mayoruna, who flourished so mightily that when Orellana floated down out of Ecuador, his scribe Carvajal noted that their settlements extended almost continuously for hundreds of miles along the river's banks.

Swollen with rich Andean sediment, these rivers – the Putumayo, along with the Juruá and the Purus to the south – make and remake their floodplains with each rainy season, meandering interminably as they open and shut new canals, reinventing the landscape. As we head west up from the flat plains the landscape becomes increasingly rich. The torrential rains from the moist air masses rising from the basin and colliding with the Andes swell torrents that carve new channels and wipe out old features with each year, just as da Cunha described. Such a dynamic environment creates conditions for exceptionally high biological diversity and impressive forests. A naturalist conducting a survey can find as many as five hundred different plant species in one forest patch, move ten miles away and find as many species again, with scant overlap between the two. The same is true of insects. Here then, are some of the Amazonian forests of popular imagination, although these forests are of medium stature by the standards of the Amazon basin.

But even within this region, though the forest may appear uniform, we are in fact confronting a mosaic of different types of forest, in the same way that oak and maple forests in Michigan may stand in close proximity to each other yet shelter and sustain different arrays of animals and plants. No example of this phenomenon is clearer than in the differences between the great Juruá and Purus rivers which rise in the Andes south of the Putumayo and are famed for their rubber trees. Often called the "twin" rivers because of their similar character, the Purus and the Juruá sluggishly meander through vast lowlands of lakes and flooded forests, uniform in width for more than a thousand miles. Unlike most Amazonian rivers, every twist in their courses carries a place name or small hamlet that bears witness to the frenzied rubber trading of the past. Yet in spite of the similarities of the two rivers there are dramatic differences in their botanical composition. The upper Juruá for example, the most famous river for rubber in Brazil, has thick *Hevea* (rubber tree) stands but virtually no Brazil-nut trees, whereas on the Acre river, the main affluent of the Purus, the forest is rich in both.[5]

THE WORLDS OF THE MADEIRA, TAPAJÓS AND ARAGUAIA

To the south and east, on the lower side of the funnel, we enter the area bordered by Bolivia and drained by the Brazilian Shield. To the west is the Beni beginning almost at La Paz and draining the thick lowland forests of Bolivia; then, eastward, the Mamoré also draining lowland Bolivia and flowing into the Guaporé. The Guaporé begins its descent into the Amazon in the savannah zones, not far from the Pantanal, the enormous, swampy dish which harbors one of the world's richest assemblages of fauna and divides Brazil and Bolivia for several hundred miles. The Beni, Guaporé and Mamoré all converge on the Madeira. The Madeira flows northeast across the forested plains before joining the Amazon about nine hundred miles from the Atlantic Ocean. Like the other great southern tributaries, the Tapajós, the Xingu, and Araguaia, the Madeira rises in the open *campo* and scrub forests of the Brazilian Shield in the Mato Grosso *planalto*, some 2,000 feet up. The headwaters meander through the *planalto* in the narrow veins of forest, interspersed with open savannah and scrubbier forests – the beautiful *cerradão*. As they slowly carve through the landscape, the streams leave the long, dry seasons behind for more humid climates. Their courses swell, and the landscape becomes a patchy mosaic of upland forest, grassland, and palm savannah. Then these waters course down from the shield into cataracts, spectacular and deadly. The Madeira has more than two hundred miles of rapids as the river swirls down the geological gutter marking the contact point of the shield with the sedimented basin. The Madeira's back forests were famed for their rubber, while its caving banks nourished an early industry in tropical cedar, as the drifting logs for which this river is named were dragged ashore and sawn. The middle Madeira is known for its mahogany, tropical cyprus, and cherry wood trees, less profuse in the watersheds to the west. Arising from sources both in the Andes and, via the Guaporé, in areas close to the shield, the river carries a burden of sediments and at the delta where it meets the Amazon an island 125 miles long has formed. This island, called Tupinambaranas, was a former haunt for slavers and pirates.

Move east again to the Tapajós river valley. The Tapajós, a clear water river, meets the Amazon at Santarém. Archaeological sites near the confluence have produced some of the most exquisite pottery, of a delicate beauty rarely matched elsewhere in South America. The area was once heavily populated by the Tapajós, wiped out over 250 years ago. Theirs were the tribes able to "field 60,000 bows".[6] They left only their name and pottery as they passed from this world.

The landscape at the confluence of the Tapajós and the Amazon reminded the nineteenth-century botanist Spruce of "an English pleasure ground" with small trees, flowering shrubs, cashews bearing their red and yellow fruits, interspersed elegantly among grassy swards. Descending the Tapajós, one gradually leaves behind the open forests and *campinas* for vistas more characteristic of classic Amazonian forest, and indeed, the Tapajós was an important area for products such as sarsaparilla, copal oil and, later, rubber. The river extends deep into the Brazilian Shield, flowing more than six hundred miles to the south. These forests become sparser as one rises on the shield to the *cerradão*, transitional forests and open savannahs.

Miles to the east the next great tributary, the Xingu river, known today primarily for the Indian reservation in its southern reaches, has had a quieter history than most of the other large rivers of the region. Once the stamping ground of Jesuit missionaries, it remained relatively unexplored until the 1880s. The Xingu became part of history at the end of the nineteenth century when the young German anthropologist von Steinen made his expedition. Plodding north by oxen caravan from the Mato Grosso *planalto* through savannah and scrub forest, the party stumbled into the Xingu's headwaters. The upper reaches of this river erode a "bevelled sediment-covered surface that has been likened to a 'feather duster', providing the local Indians with more than 1,000 miles of stream channels".[7] At high water these rivers are easily navigated by the bark canoes of the region, and in the past offered a meeting ground for virtually all the major Amazonian linguistic groups – the Tupi, Gê, Arawak, and Carib. Von Steinen could barely believe his good fortune. The Indians were less pleased. Many Indian groups had fled to the sanctuary provided by the falls and rapids on one side, and the protection of the *cerradão* and *campo* on the other, viewed with economic indifference by most of the earlier adventurers. The confusing maze of streams peopled with numerous and different tribes, some among them such as the Txukahamêi and the Suyá renowned for their belligerence, discouraged exploration. The river route from the Mato Grosso to the Amazon was more easily navigable via the Madeira and the Tapajós.

East again, the Araguaia river begins its course in Mato Grosso. Almost due west from the town of Cuiabá, begins the Rio das Mortes, the "river of the dead", so named because across its *cerradão* and gallery forests lay Indian territory from which few whites ever returned. This Amazonian Styx is the westernmost tributary of the great Araguaia whose clear waters flow through an immense diversity of vegetation. The most notable feature is the huge island of Bananal, a swampy grassland swarming with game. The Araguaia flows through the mahogany, Brazil-nut and rubber forests, and now increasingly, through landscapes degraded to pasture along its bank, one of the most exquisite waterways in the world.

BROKEN WATERS

With knowledge of the fundamental contours of the whole region, one can anticipate the adventures and reverses of a thousand voyages of the nineteenth and twentieth centuries. In volumes of reminiscence of travelers venturing up any of these rivers – the Madeira, Xingu, Tapajós, and Araguaia – draining out of the Brazilian Shield, or of those intrepid pioneers facing the Rio Branco, the Negro, and the Uaupés, one encounters time and again the same joys and sorrows. Through the first few hundred miles, voyagers happily recount easy days on the majestic lower rivers, broad and unobstructed, flanked by *várzea* forest and agricultural settlement. Then comes irritated and increasingly desperate prose as the travelers confide to their journals the first, almost imperceptible, sharpening rise of terrain towards the shield, mirrored league after league in cataracts, reaches of rapids, broken waters, swirling pools; all of them sources of exhausting portage, cargo loss, and death by drowning. Week after week – for more than 220 miles in the case of the Madeira – cataracts and rapids break the bravest heart until, up at last on the shield, the travelers would once again find broad reaches of easily navigable water and easy movement between the great river drainages, before the water becomes too shallow for anything but small canoes.

History followed geography. Below the cataracts traders would scour the forests, in the early days seeking slaves, and then later, when a *mestizo* and detribalized population had emerged on the banks, plying the rivers for provisions and for their yields of sarsaparilla, cacao, rubber, copaiba oil, indigo, and vanilla. Here competition between traders could take place. Above the cataracts many indigenous tribes sought refuge from formal slavery or debt peonage and tried to reconstruct their shattered cultures. There they would often find themselves plunged into bitter intertribal warfare against Indian groups similarly displaced. But cataracts also served to winnow out the entrepreneurs, and as a rule, those who survived the cascades could enjoy commercial monopoly of the region beyond the rapids. And of course, those who controlled the rapids also controlled prices.[8]

On the lower Amazon itself, up until the city of Santarém so savored by Spruce and Bates, travelers and their sailing ships could work the tides and the trade winds. But upriver, navigation in the days before steam required scores of men poling and rowing against the currents. No cataracts impeded their journey for thousands of miles until they reached the very foothills of the Andes. Ocean-going vessels could easily make their way to Iquitos in Peru. This western tier, beyond the range of tides, amidst the treacherous channels, islands and side lakes of the great river, was contested political terrain, with Spain facing east toward the advancing Portuguese.

THE MULTIPLICITY OF SPECIES

Euclides da Cunha, the brilliant geographer and journalist who served on the Brazilian-Bolivian survey team after the Acrean wars of 1898, once exclaimed that the Amazon was ''the last unwritten page of Genesis''. No other area in the world contains such a profuse variety of living things. Until recently, scientists had estimated the number of species on the planet at an enormous, yet comprehensible, one and a half million. But during the last decade, the entomologist Terry Erwin's studies of the diversity of beetles on a single tree suggests a far greater number. Erwin noted that while working in the forest canopy his team had identified more than 3,000 species of beetle within only five plots of twelve square meters each. Extrapolating from these studies, he calculated that, based on the overall numbers of tree and insect species, there were on earth more than thirty million species of insect alone. These estimates are contested and the generally accepted limit for all species on the earth is around five million. In fact, no one knows even within orders of magnitude the number of species, but at least half of any number in the accepted range can be found in the drainage systems of the Amazon. A tree can carry many species peculiar to it alone, and each region, at least in its insect fauna and flora, shares few species with other areas in the Amazon. Thus, over small distances in Ecuador, only 10 per cent of the insects of one plot were found in the next. In Manaus, forests fifty miles apart shared only 1 per cent of their species.[9]

New species evolve in two ways. The first is by polyploidy, the multiplication of the number of chromosomes in organisms. This can occur with already existing species or, in hybrids, with two species. Thus the original modest ear of corn becomes the larger and more luscious polyploids of recent human history. This form of chromosome multiplication results from spontaneous mutations or through hybridization, and is a central characteristic of the human domestication of plants. The second, and perhaps here more relevant process, allopatric speciation, involves geographic isolation and thus the divergence of organisms from similar stock as they adapt to differing environments. Geographic isolation and competition are central to Darwin's theory of the origin of species, and explain his fascination with the finches of the Galapagos which, while stemming from similar genetic forebears, varied subtly from island to island in the archipelago.

Polyploidy can happen in one generation, but allopatric speciation is more time-consuming. For many years, one body of theory has stressed what are called "equilibrium models" in accounting for tropical diversity. The underlying world view here proposes that ever higher diversity is the consequence of stability both in geological time and in the communities of organisms. Populations are widely distributed, and those subpopulations separated by great distances begin to evolve along separate paths in the benevolent environment of warm temperatures and abundant rainfall. Thus diversity is a function of a long history in benign conditions where the ecological interactions of competition, coevolution and predation produced finer and finer separations of distinct species and thus their innumerable representatives in the tropical lowlands.[10] In contrast to the tumultuous changes in the northern hemispheres – the advance and retreat of glaciers that drove many species to extinction as climates altered and habitats shrank – tropical forests remained unperturbed by larger forces, continuing quietly to evolve millions of species. This, in the jargon, is the "available time" hypothesis. In this conservative perception of the natural economy, changes are slow and almost imperceptible. The measure here is of time's slow footfall, in the rhythm of a slowly eroding mountain. Many of the proponents of this view derive their inspiration from the nineteenth-century Scottish geologist, Lyell.

A central premise of the "available time" hypothesis is that the tropics remained unaffected by glaciers. But though these areas may not have felt the direct onslaught of a glacier, there is evidence of considerable climatic turbulence, expressed in changes in sea level, temperature and rainfall, which would have forced changes in the distribution of species inconsistent with the stately decorum of the "equilibrium model".[11]

Against such conservative natural economy is posed a world of constant and rapid transformation: the "non-equilibrium" models. Here is an evolutionary environment inflected by forces great and small, from geological upheaval and climatic catastrophe to the chance fall of a single tree which may bridge a stream, open up the forest floor to light. In this world of calamities, the diversity of species in the forest reflects the constant "fine grain" disruptions of falling trees creating light gaps and new environments, randomly killing trees and thus creating a landscape of patches of different ages where such events constantly changed the rules of the game, and where competitive exclusion could never entirely holds sway. This is no primeval forest where species and communities evolve at a stately pace, but rather one in which rapid change takes place: 25 per cent of the trees can die in a period of only fifteen years.[12]

In trying to explain why Amazônia has so many species, biogeographers, botanists and ecologists began to search for explanations at different historical scales, and infer ways in which allopatric speciation could occur. With new data on the impacts of long-term climatic changes, the idea that the Amazon had been insulated from Pleistocene events cannot now be sustained. The work of Jürgen Haffer and Ghillean Prance led to the formulation of the "refugia" theory to explain the number of species and their distributions in Amazônia. This view argues that during the glaciations of the Pleistocene phase ten thousand years ago, abrupt changes in the hemispheric climate turned large areas of the Amazon into savannah; however, some parts – in the Andean foothills, always well-watered, or in more eastward regions whose contours drew rainfall – remained moist. Drier expanses of savannah separated these "islands" of tropical forests. Geographically isolated from one another, distinct species evolved. When moister epochs occurred, the forest recaptured the more arid lands. The "refugia" theory first explained several curious features of Amazon forests: how one genus might have several similar species growing adjacent to each other, or co-dominant in the same habitat. This challenged the theory of competitive exclusion, which argues that where similar species inhabit the same area, one will dominate. The theory also explained the striking discontinuities in the distribution of species in the Amazon.

In his essays on Amazonian palaeo-ecology the biologist Paul Colinvaux challenges the "refugia" theories associated with Haffer and Prance, now curator of Kew Gardens. The origins of species diversity have become the subject of renewed debate. Colinvaux contests the "refugia" hypothesis on the basis of several forms of data and concentrates on endogenous disturbance – tree falls, flooding, local catastrophic events – to a far greater degree. He isolates as many as five kinds of disturbances or events that have enhanced diversity, maintaining that climatic change affected the region in a different way.

One of the central proposals of the "refugia" theory is that the moist Andean foothills served as sanctuaries during dry episodes in the Pleistocene age. Data from palynology – the study of pollen deposited in lake sediments in order to determine the vegetation patterns of the past – suggests that the Andean foothills were much colder, perhaps by as much as 10 to 15 degrees Fahrenheit. The prevalence of the pollen of cold tolerant species in the western Amazon basin argues, says Colinvaux, for the advance of more robust Andean species down into what is now tropical habitat.

Flooding has particular importance in explaining diversity of species in the Amazon both at the level of major historical catastrophes and in annual flooding of landscape and vegetation. It has affected Amazonian environments and species diversity in several ways. During the Cenozoic and interglacial periods of the Pleistocene age the sea level rose, and the broad river courses may have become so large that they isolated, to degrees not seen today, some animal and plant populations on archipelagos and islands. This helps explain differences in flora and fauna in the various watersheds today. At an intermediate level, the hundred-year or two-hundred-year flood provides the kind of catastrophic event that obliterates mature vegetation and reduces it back to bare ground. Colinvaux next presents considerable evidence that at least once in the last two hundred years, lowland forest in the main western drainages was disrupted by very extensive floods caused by increased rainfall in the Andes. In the western Amazon more than a quarter of the land surface is even now being reworked by changing river courses.

Nothing could be more contrary to the vision of the forest primeval, unchanged until the axe and firebrand of modern times. Colinvaux reckons that "possibly a quarter of the forests of the whole region has been destroyed by flowing rivers within no longer than a few tree generations and that probably more than a tenth of the entire western forest is disturbed so frequently as to be kept in early successional stages". Finally, the annual flooding drives the insect fauna that inhabit these forests toward the canopy or other *terra firme* habitats. These are already full of other species, so as these new part-time inhabitants arrive, selection pressures, such as competition and predation, accelerate and impinge on these populations.

The range of disturbance on both long- and short-term scales gives the landscape an instability that may be crucial in the evolution of its diversity. As da Cunha wrote, "every flood is like a wet sponge that passes over a poorly done drawing. It obliterates, modifies, or transforms the most firm and salient features". In addition, the seasonal climates in the northern and southern parts of the basin are subject to severe drought cycles and flooding, with consequent effects on the diversity of organisms. Finally, upland forests have been subject to wildfires for almost four millennia, many caused by human intervention.[13]

Just as the fantasies visited upon the Amazon by the pioneers and naturalists governed their observations and behavior so too do the scientific models described in these pages have practical consequences. Those whose view of the Amazon is informed by the idea of an ur-forest, stable since the beginning of time with man as a late interloper in the natural epic, tend to take a catastrophist attitude to any form of human intervention. Their solution to the destruction of the forest tends to the creation of large set-asides: natural preserves from which man is excluded. Thus for example the Tropical Rain Forest Action developed by bodies including the United Nations Environmental Program and the World Resources Institute recommends a vigorous forest conservation policy that "will set aside substantial areas of remaining tropical forests as ecological reserves to be protected from all forms of encroachment". The same is often true of those whose palaeo-ecology rests on the notion of refuges.

In the conservation model based on the "refugia", areas of especially high diversity are protected and essentially become evolutionary museums. Extrapolating from theories of island biogeography the conservationists suggest that about twenty parks, located in areas of high diversity and suitably buffered, would be capable of safeguarding about 20 per cent of the species in the Amazon. Quite aside from the fact that this accepts extinction of the other 80 per cent, these reserves are once again Edens under glass from which the local populations are excluded, denied any role in the sustaining of the ecosystem. With very few exceptions – such as the Cuyabeno Park in Ecuador and Kuna Indian Park in southern Panama (essentially native reserves coupled with "adventure tourism") – few conservation areas incorporate local populations, an approach which can be traced back to John Muir's Yosemite National Park which inaugurated its career with the expulsion of the Miwok Indians who had previously made their homes there.

Overlooked in virtually all the accounts of the distribution of species and the structure of forests is the role of humanity. There is in fact a growing body of knowledge on how indigenous and local populations manage their natural resources and sustain them over time. Amplified by the dynamic view of the region's ecological history, described above, this knowledge permits an understanding of the forest as the outcome of human as well as biological history, and hence the view that humans can continue to make their history in the forest, sustaining and sustained. Thus is the Amazon extricated from the fantasies of the *bandeirante*, the romantic, the curator and the speculator.

MAN-MADE NATURE

Unsurprisingly, the areas that supported the densest native populations were those that had experienced the most productive natural disturbances – the floodplains. Here were fertile sediments, new oxbow lakes teeming with game and fish, water-saturated land where productive palms could flourish in good soils, excellent planting areas for the annuals and tree crops of native agronomy. In the early years, explorer after explorer "opening" an area to the European consumers of his adventures wrote effusively of the agricultural productivity of the ample populations thronging the shores. When Herndon, Bates and Wallace trekked through similar areas of the Amazon in the nineteenth century, they saw detribalized Indians and half-breeds engaged in what they viewed as deficient agricultural practices. The Amazon of the great native populations – the societies with rich pottery that rivaled the craftsmanship of the Inca, the vast interregional trading networks of salt, seeds and medicines – was purged from memory. As populations fled, died or were enslaved, the banks and interiors of the great rivers became mute green walls, revealing little of their history. The agricultural bounty of native production gave way to the paltry yields of the white man's plantations. The vision of the Amazon forest as a purely biological entity began to hold sway.

Travelers today, as over the last four centuries, believe they are observing "natural" forest, but this forest is most likely the product of human decisions of the past and even today. *Caboclos* in the Amazon's estuary have developed intensively-managed systems to provide timber, palm hearts, palm fruit, cocoa and rubber for local and international markets. *Ribeirinhos*, those who dwell along rivers near Iquitos in the Peruvian Amazon, create complex cultivation strategies, orchards of fruit and food trees. These modern resource managers use techniques derived from indigenous practice. Virtually all the crops are native. In a *caboclo* or *mestizo* backwoodsman still reside centuries of accumulated knowledge.[14]

Wherever one turns, the landscape almost invariably bears the imprint of human agency, starting with fire. Charcoal has been found in numerous areas when soil pits are dug. Many of these ash deposits are the outcome of natural fires, but the use of burning by Indians as part of agricultural and forest management cycles is very well documented. Pot shards are found extensively throughout the basin. The existence of Indian "black earths" – kitchen midden, rich in organic matter and residua from earlier occupation – have been found in innumerable upland sites from Colombia to the mouth of the Amazon.[15]

The impact of human activity on the biogeography and structure of plant and animal communities in the tropics has been given short shrift by many biologists and agronomists, but the fact is that there are vast tracts of forests created by man. Those of the babassu palm cover hundreds of thousands of acres on the eastern and southern flanks of the basin. Such palm forests, initially viewed as natural, are now clearly discerned and documented as the consequence of human action. Large areas along the rivers that again appear to be natural *várzea* forest are the consequence of careful choices. Indeed much of the Amazon's forests may very well reflect the intercessions of man.

Research in several areas of Latin America, such as Janice Alcorn's landmark study on the Huastec, suggests that the range of interventions in forest ecosystems is much greater than has been realized. Both *caboclos* and native peoples planted and protected forest species. In perhaps the longest running study of natural resource management by native people, the North American anthropologist Darrell Posey has been able to document substantial amounts of forest manipulation by the Kayapó Indians, with direct planting of useful species, such as *Caryocar guinanensis* – the Piqui tree – and upland plantings of *Euterpe* palms in the forest's under-story. He also suggests that they have been active in reforesting open grassland areas. The Kayapó have shifted plant material – valuable medicinals, ritual plants and other useful species – to locations that are easier to reach. They have described to Posey how they have collected germ plasm over a region roughly the size of western Europe and planted it in areas of interest to them. They place plants along trekking trails, in forest gaps, in camping sites, in favored hunting areas, and near gardens. These produce "resource islands", areas of useful plants not necessarily located close to the village but important to the larger human community and regional ecology. These fruit and food plants also serve to attract and maintain populations of wild animals, a highly prized food source for the Kayapó.[16]

Traditional Kayapó lands were about the size of France, so a more spacious view of their agricultural systems should replace the parochial concept of tropical forest cultivation localized only in the agricultural field. Indeed numerous scholars have shown that after "abandonment" agricultural fields remain sites of planting and manipulation within forest areas. Studies throughout Latin America increasingly suggest that rural populations are actively manipulating numerous vegetation types well beyond the agricultural sites, showing once more that our concepts of agriculture may be entirely deficient for understanding the basis of resource management and production by peoples.

The portrayal of native peoples as Rousseauian creatures of the forest has served several functions. It has permitted a view of them as children, incapable of wise decisions or the exercise of adult responsibilities. Until recently the official Brazilian view is that they are wards of the state, unable to participate in political life. To perceive native peoples as stone-age remnants who lie in the same relationship to nature as a tapir or a deer has made it easy to claim that these peoples' contribution to modern societies amounts to little. The enormous economic contribution to the First World of their domesticated plants has been disregarded. These peoples are accomplished environmental scientists and, contrary to patronizing supposition, indigenous groups have been involved in market activities for decades. Many native economies have been shaped by such market pressures and have often adapted well, at least enough to keep the forest and many features of their societies intact.

The eyes of the intruders saw the forests as primeval and empty. They missed the innumerable trails and portages, just as they missed the trading networks of the upper Xingu, or the salt routes that extended from the Atlantic to the Andes, or the connection between Central America and the Amazon via the Orinoco to the Casiquiare to the Rio Negro. The focus of traditional anthropology on the "primitive" and its emphasis on tribal forest inhabitants fostered the illusion of sparse settlement, and made it appear that a few Indians in a state of nature were the region's only occupants, along with some tough backwoodsmen, flotsam of the long past rubber boom. But more than two million people make their living in the forest through forms of petty extraction.[17] The patronizing eye sees nothing of this and the image of the forest as a wild biological entity secluded from human intervention remains, making it easier to envisage forest clearance as the only rational form of development. And so the forests began to fall and shrouds of smoke covered the Amazon.

NOTES

1. The contrast between the intoxicating growth and density of the vegetation and the poverty of populations was also summed up by Bates: "[it is] nonchalance and laziness alone which prevent people from surrounding themselves in edible luxuriance." This tone echoes through the volumes of observers, from Agassiz to Wallace, journeying through the Amazon. The themes of the laziness of locals and the under-utilization of resources has its corollary: if they can't do it properly, European colonists can. As Henri Coudreau, in his ineffably racist manner, noted in his *Voyage au Tocantins-Araguaia* 1897, "the Aryans will have tamed the Equator; but the Indians will have contributed almost nothing to the result. . . . It will not be long before nothing remains of these wandering hordes but their lands, now widowed. But these lands will always be there, beautiful, rich, and

only awaiting men of good will.'' José Palacios, a Bolivian surveyor for the Madeira-Mamoré railroad ended his report with the words, ''the immense territory which we occupy is best suited for foreign immigrants.'' Maury, Herndon's cousin, head of the National Observatory in Washington and Amazon-booster, was eager to establish a ''New South'' near Santarém. In this light the prospectuses of the Farquhars, Fords and Ludwigs in Amazonian development take on a familiar ring.

2. Thorough discussions of the Rio Negro are provided by H. Klinge, ''Podzol soils'' in H. Leut, ed. *Atas do Simpósio Sobre a Biota Amazônica* 1967. A. Anderson's 1981 review essay on *campinas* in Amazônia is an excellent survey of the literature. For a stimulating theoretical discussion see D. H. Janzen, ''Tropical blackwater rivers'' in *Biotropica* 1974. A major research station – São Carlos do Rio Negro – is located near *campina* vegetation and much of the research carried out there focuses on the ecological dynamics of this vegetation. See C. F. Jordan, *Amazonian Rain Forests* 1987, the edited volume that summarizes this research.

3. An excellent review of Amazonian geomorphology and hydrology is provided by H. O. Sternberg, *Amazon River of Brazil* 1975.

4. See Sternberg.

5. Surveys of Amazonian vegetation formations can be found in several articles. The venerable classic is that of Ducke and Black, published in 1953. The collaborations of João Murca Pires and Ghillean Prance also supply excellent reviews. Also see G. Prance, *Biological Diversification in the Tropics* 1982.

6. See Sternberg.

7. See Sternberg.

8. Robert Murphy's classic *Headhunter's Heritage* 1960, describes in fine detail the impact of the rapids on the trading relations of the Mundurucu. The Madeira river above the rapids was also the monopolized realm of one or two traders who managed to control commerce with little generosity. Barbara Weinstein, *The*

Amazon Rubber Boom 1983, also provides insight into the control of trading networks.

9. T. Erwin, ''Tropical forest canopy: the heart of biotic diversity'', in E. O. Wilson, ed. *Biodiversity* 1988. This excellent and accessible volume sums up much of the current data and debate on the issues of biodiversity. The now classic paper where Erwin does his calculations is in the arcane *Coleopteristists Bulletin* 36(1).

10. For an elegant overview of the theories of tropical diversity prior to the explosion of disturbance hypotheses, there is none better than H. Baker, ''Diversity in the tropics'', *Biotropica* 1, 1972.

11. Evidence for climatic change in the Amazon rests on pollen studies of cones from permanent lakes which provide a general pattern of the vegetation of the past, studies of geomorphology of the basin and sediment deposition at the mouth, and climate simulation models. The 1987 *Quaternary Science Reviews*, where P. Colinvaux's ''Amazonian Diversity in Light of the Paleoecological Record'' appears, supplies good summary papers on tropical climate changes during the last ice age and reviews a wide variety of data. Another useful volume is G. Prance, *Biological Diversification in the Tropics* 1982.

12. These are the results of a long-running study in Belém by Mourca Pires, one of the most distinguished Amazonian botanists. The results are in accordance with others in many areas in the humid tropics. Probably the best known analyst is Gary Hartshorn whose pioneering research helped redefine the nature of tropical forests. See ''Neotropical Forest Dynamics'', in *Biotropica* 12(Supp.), 1980.

13. Buck Sanford and his colleagues at São Carlos were early analysts of the role of fire in formal Amazonian ecology, but anthropological accounts of the use of fire are found in the historical literatures (Coudreau, von Steinen, Tastevin) and current observers of native land-use practices (see for example Hecht and Posey, Denevan and Padoch). The geographer Carl Sauer was one of the most eloquent apostrophers of the role of fire in native land management. Recent studies by

Saldarriaga and West show the widespread occurrence of fire in *terra firme* zones.

14. The study of "manipulation" of succession by indigenous and peasant populations is the subject of several current edited volumes: D. Posey and W. Balée, *Resource Management in Amazônia* 1989, W. Denevan and C. Padoch, *Swidden Agroforestry* 1987. Geographically broader volumes that focus on similar themes include J. Browder, ed. *Fragile Lands of Latin America* 1989, A. Anderson, ed. *Alternatives to Deforestation* 1989, and M. Altieri and S.B. Hecht, eds. *Agroecology and Small Farm Development* 1989.

15. See N. Smith, "Anthrosols and human carrying capacity in the Amazon", *Annals of the American Association of Geographers* 70 1980.

16. The diversity of resource management carried out by the Kayapó is documented in numerous papers cited in the bibliography. Many other studies illustrate their extensive interventions. See R. Hames and W. Vickers, *Adaptative Responses of Native Amazonians* 1984.

17. Petty extraction refers to forms of renewable resource extraction carried out by peasants or others. It can involve the extraction of animals as well as plants. Petty extractionists rely on portfolios of activities – agriculture, livestock production, wage activities, as well as commerce, and this is a central feature of most Amazonian rural economies. For more detailed discussions of extraction see S. Hecht, A. Anderson, and P. May, "The subsidy from nature", *Human Organization* 47(1), 1988; S. Hecht and S. Schwartzman, "The good, the bad, and the ugly", submitted to *Interciencia* 1989.

THREE

The Heritage of Fire

There was no remedy, nor shredded herb
Nor draught to drink nor ointment, and in default
Of physic their flesh withered, until I
Revealed the blends of gentle medicines
Wherewith they arm themselves against disease.
And many ways of prophecy I ordered,
    . . . and augury by fire,
For long in darkness hid, I brought to light.
Such help I gave, and more . . .
Prometheus founded all the arts of man.

AESCHYLUS, *Prometheus Bound*

The nature that preceded human history no longer exists anywhere.

KARL MARX, *Grundrisse*

The Amazon forests are no strangers to fire. Dig almost anywhere on the uplands and, a few feet down, you will probably find traces of charcoal. The fires that coursed for thousands of years have been the consequence of both natural and human agency. At the height of the dry season a lightning strike can start a fire, or grasslands burst into flame through spontaneous combustion of the hot leaves and dry grasses. Native tribes today, as they have in the past, set fire to grasslands, to savannahs, to downed forests destined to be agricultural plots. They use fire to control pests in orchards, suppress weeds, flush game, and reduce snakes close to trails. Tribes such as the Kayapó have shamans steeped in fire rituals, and hand down a complex taxonomy of fire: when to use it, how to attain the desired degree of heat, how to master it, how to produce the desired quality of ash, whose uses are not only agricultural but also ritual and medicinal.

Fire is integral to indigenous cosmology.[1] In Bororo shamanism, the powerful *bope* - the mediators of disruption, of the periodic efflorescence of the land, of the cyclic waves of births among animals, of the menstrual cycle - are closely associated with fire. The *bope*'s intercessions are revealed in chaotic disruptions. All natural transition has moments of violence, but underlying the chaos is an inherent reliability. The *bope* are the harbingers of fire, disruption and transformation, but they also sustain the consistent repetitions of birth and renewal.[2]

Fire is essential to the management of humid tropical forests for human purposes. Only an American generation brought up on the ursine caveats of Smoky the Bear would find anything odd about this. Foresters in the United States have long recognized the importance of fire in maintaining the vigor of temperate forests and in providing suitable habitats for wild life. More than a million acres of forests in the southeastern US are regularly managed with controlled burning which, if properly handled, controls some tree pathogens and improves the food and habitat for wild and domesticated animals. Foresters in the Mediterranean climate of California similarly use fire to provide better forage and habitat for deer and game fowl, and to avoid catastrophic wildfires.[3]

The issue in the rainforest is not fire itself, but its purposes. Does its use in a particular instance inhibit regeneration, diminish the diversity of species and waste nutrients, or is it part of a process through which this diversity is enhanced, nutrients recaptured in new vegetation, and regeneration encouraged?

As we have seen, with the exception of the rich sediments carried down from the geologically young Andes and deposited along the *várzeas* – floodplains – of the white water rivers or in the outcroppings of fertile soil in the uplands, most of the soils of the Amazon are highly weathered and not very fertile. The action of warm temperatures and rainfall generally exceeding 120 inches a year, on surfaces that are old or eroded to begin with, has removed most of the nutrients from the soil, making them deficient in phosphorus, nitrogen, potassium, calcium, magnesium and many micronutrients.

These highly weathered soils are acid. In agriculture not employing acid-tolerant strains, satisfactory production is difficult if not impossible. Add afflictions such as poor drainage, erosion and aluminum toxicity to the list and it turns out that only about 7 per cent of Amazonian soils lack major constraints to conventional agricultural production.[4]

On the whole, Amazonian soils have a very low "cation" exchange capacity; even when these soils have nutrients applied to them in the form of fertilizers or ash, they are unable to retain them to any useful degree because hydrogen, hydrous oxides or aluminum ions occupy the spaces in the soil where bases such as calcium or potassium could be held. This combination of low-exchange capacity and high rainfall means that soil nutrients are very easily leached. Thus, soils are less like nutrient storage areas and more like channels connecting rainfall that lands on surfaces with river drainages. Yet many Amazon forests boast more than 250 metric tons of living material per acre. Given such conditions, one of the central problems for research in the postwar period has been the difficulty of explaining the paradox of how very large amounts of living material can exist on a substrate of impoverished soil in the Amazon.

HOW THE FOREST LIVES

In the early 1960s came the beginnings of an answer, courtesy of the cold war, when the US Atomic Energy Commission asked itself what would to happen to forests in the event of nuclear war or major accident in a nuclear reactor. To satisfy their curiosity they turned to Puerto Rico and to Howard Odum, a systems ecologist.

For three months a patch of government-owned forest in El Verde, Puerto Rico, was bombarded with gamma rays. As the forest withered under this simulation of planetary holocaust, Odum led his team of young scientists to analyze the wounded ecosystem and from this study to deduce the structure and the functions of the forest. Thus began the first comprehensive inter-disciplinary study of a tropical forest. The experience launched a cohort of tropical ecologists who, over the next generation, have had enormous influence in the North American study of tropical systems. One of the central contributions was developed by Carl Jordan who analysed nutrient cycling and the mechanisms by which tropical forests maintain themselves on shoddy soils.

Even today the way tropical rainforests concentrate and cycle elements is not completely understood. But some of the dominant features of the forest that permit this cycling can be isolated. The plants in a temperate-zone forest draw nutrients up from the soils. In tropical forests the nutrients are derived from and exchanged within the living forest and its litter, and held in the tissues of living organisms rather than in the soil. These "store houses" include plants, animals, and micro-organisms as well as plant litter that decomposes swiftly. With poor soils that allow nutrients to leach rapidly, a large proportion of nutrients must be held in the living tissues lest they be drained off and thus lost to the ecosystem. So efficient is the retention and recycling of nutrients under these conditions that when the chemistry of clear water rivers is tested, the water is comparable to slightly contaminated, de-ionized water.[5]

Structural features such as shallow rooting depths, where most of the roots are found within the first foot of soil, permit rapid capture of nutrients deposited by rainfall or nutrients in leaf litter. In some forests, like those of the Rio Negro where soils are particularly deficient, 99 per cent of the radioactive calcium and phosphorus sprinkled on the forest floor to test nutrient uptake was immediately absorbed by the root mat and never even arrived at the mineral soil. The configuration of branches and leaves can also favor the capture of nutrients before raindrops even reach the ground. Some kinds of lichens, algaes and plant epiphytes (plants that grow on other plants, such as many bromeliads and orchids) are able to "scrub" nutrients from rainfall and even fix nitrogen on leaf surfaces. There are also physiological adaptations that improve the plants' tolerance to adverse conditions such as high levels of soil aluminum or low levels of soil nutrients like phosphorus. Adaptations include those that prolong the lives of leaves and reduce the nutrients needed to replace damaged leaves. Thus, the leathery leaves found in many Amazon ecosystems conserve nutrients by lowering their susceptibility to insect attack and the leaching of nutrients. High levels of secondary chemicals that make tropical leaves tough, unpleasant or poisonous to eat may also deter predatory animals or insects. These secondary compounds are characteristic of tropical forests, and also the reason why so many drug plants are derived from them. Indeed latex is just such a form of defense for *Hevea brasiliensis*, the rubber tree.

Finally there are the interactions, associations and symbioses so important in the nutrient economy of tropical forests. Plants need nitrogen, which makes up 80 per cent of the atmosphere, but they also require a mediating agent to convert it into a form they can use. The agent can be bacteria – rhizobia – that often exist in symbiosis with plants like legumes, which make up one of the largest plant families in the Amazon. Algae living on the surface of leaves of the forest canopy are able to capture from the atmosphere elements such as sulphur which are otherwise rare in the forest's nutrient economy. Perhaps one of the most important symbioses in tropical forests are those involving mycorrhizal fungi, which are particularly important in the cycling of the most critical element in tropical forest ecosystems, phosphorus. These fungi surround the roots, their filaments or hyphae extending upward to leaf litter and thus effecting a direct transfer of nutrients from the litter to the roots below. At least as important are the enzymes associated with the mycorrhizae that make scarce phosphorus more available from the soil where it is tightly held in chemical bonds.

Each type of forest has a different balance of mechanisms. The *campina* forests of much of the Rio Negro drainage incorporate virtually all of them to an extreme degree because these forests grow from the worst soils in the Amazon, and each nutrient element is correspondingly precious. Forests on more fertile sites are not under such extreme pressure to conserve nutrients, although, in general, tropical forest ecosystems are far more parsimonious with their nutrient budgets than most temperate zone equivalents.[6]

DESTRUCTION AND RENEWAL

When the vegetation of a forest area is destroyed, either by natural forces or by human hand, the process of land recovery – succession – begins. If the land is completely denuded, a predictable set of plant types appear: first come the mostly shade-intolerant species of herbs, grasses and fast growing trees. When a gap appears in a forest through a tree fall, seedlings already established on the forest floor and stump sprouts, as well as heliophilic plants that colonize open ground, contribute to the initial vegetation. These fast-growing and light-loving species are usually referred to as successional vegetation. Successional communities involve interactive change; as the initial plants grow, they change the habitat; the early conditions favored by the fast-growing trees, herbs and grass are modified as they grow, making it shadier, changing the nutrients available to the ecosystem as a whole, and under most conditions, rendering many in the first generation less able to survive in the new environment of their own creation. As succession proceeds, several things happen: the site becomes home to a larger number of animals and plants; species become longer lived; the forest itself becomes larger – that is, it has more ''biomass'', or living material; and nutrients released by the destruction of the forest are recaptured.

The mechanisms by which succession occurs in the tropics involve the colonization of open areas by airborne propagules, or seeds carried in by animals, the regeneration of stump sprouts, the rapid growth of already established seedlings when given adequate light, germination of forest seeds already in the soil, and even the initiation of new symbioses with mycorrhizae and other micro-organisms. Plants and seeds must also avoid being eaten, and here the environmental diversity in a forest gap or swidden plot is most helpful for ''hiding'' them from their predators, both at the site of the new opening and in the patchy landscape that includes forest and successional vegetation of different ages.

However, there is a vulnerability inherent in the mechanisms sustaining this tight cycling of nutrients designed to overcome the constraints of the poor fertility of the soil. When the forest itself is destroyed, and the means of cycling nutrients are impaired, the fertility elements are easily flushed away in torrential rains if the mechanisms of regeneration – succession – are thwarted. Unless new plants efficient in taking up these soil nutrients are in place, the consequence of destruction is not only a degraded ecosystem, but one in which the biological elements of recovery are absent. Nutrients have been leached away and the biological means of recuperation may be irrevocably damaged.[7]

On September 28, 1987, a satellite of the National Oceanographic and Atmospheric Administration (NOAA) documented more than 5,000 individual fires in the Amazon. They stretched in an arc from southern Acre through Rondônia and Mato Grosso, up through the state of Pará to Belém, with sputterings along the road from Manaus up to the gold boom town of Boa Vista in the state of Roraima. Smoke and particles were so thick in the atmosphere that pilots could not land on the Amazon's radar-less airstrips. The images of these fires shocked the world. President José Sarney was prompted to make his speech on the Amazon, in which he vowed to develop a coherent environmental policy for the forest. By presidential decree he prohibited burning in the entire region.

But what were those fires?

INDIAN LESSONS: ASHES AND LIFE

In most sustainable agricultural systems in the Amazon and indeed throughout the Latin American tropics, fire has an integral and sensible role in making the land productive for human use.[8] Fire is coupled with activities that compensate for its potentially destructive effects. Forests are cut at the beginning of the dry season, in April or May, depending on location. Indigenous peoples such as the Kayapó use a number of biological indicators such as the flowering of particular trees, migration of animals, and astronomy as signals for the beginning of the cutting period. Logs are then left to dry until late August or September when the fires are set. The period of burning is carefully monitored by shamans with particular skills in fire management. The flowering of the Piqui tree, the constellations and movements of fish dictate the ritual cycle that culminates in carefully timed burning. Fires are set with prudent attention to weather and timing so that they burn thoroughly the small and moderate trunks and lianas, but still remain under control. Weeks prior to burning, the Kayapó women who own the fields plant varieties of sweet potato, manioc, and yam that begin to sprout almost immediately after the fires have cooled, thus quickly initiating the agricultural succession. They then plant short-cycle crops such as corn, beans, melons, and squash that rapidly cover large areas, along with longer-cycle crops that can be harvested anywhere from six months to two years after the planting. In their use of short-cycle, light-tolerant species that gradually give way to woody fruits, the principles of succession are maintained. The grasses, corn, the fast growing vines, the squashes, sweet potatoes and melons all mirror the types of plant families found in early succession. The role of the weedy *solanum* is taken on by their domesticated cousins – peppers. Domesticated beans mimic the wild vetches and legumes. The ubiquitous euphorbia of successional vegetation find their analogs in manioc.[9]

The Kayapó also gather charred branches and debris, and set a second fire, called *coivara* in Portuguese, which provides particularly fertile ''hot spots'' within the field. Sweet potatoes which thrive on the potassium from ash are continuously planted and replanted on these open sites. To prevent soil compaction women till and loosen the soil with their machetes. Around the perimeters of the field, ash and branches will once again be piled and burned. Here, yams – to be harvested several years hence – are planted with papayas, pineapples, the *urucu* tree (the source of a beautiful red body paint and an excellent food coloring, annatto), and other useful ritual, medicinal and food plants. The Kayapó prepare food in the fields, and their cooking fires and ash are moved around so that fresh nutrients from the ashes are distributed where necessary.

In areas where sweet potatoes are regularly grown, harvested and replanted, the Kayapó set harvest residue aflame to supply nutrients to the new crops, to reduce pest problems on the younger plants and to control weeds. Most unusual is the practice of the Kayapó of burning substantial portions of the crop field while their crops are still on the ground. Many of the cultivars – the types of crop plants – are fire tolerant, and the Kayapó practise a form of highly specific, controlled ''cool'' burns, so that seed stocks in the ground, and the root crops on which their subsistence is based, are not destroyed by fire. When the plot ceases to be a central area for the production of root crops it will become a source of perennial crops and of game. By planting shrubs and trees which provide fruits of interest to wildlife, the secondary successional stages become "animal gardens".

What the Kayapó are doing can easily be interpreted within the terms of First World science. The Kayapó stimulate forest succession in their fallows by making sure that their agricultural sites incorporate the necessary elements to recuperate forests, which are often as valuable to them as the agriculture. This includes the creation of suitable environmental conditions and the manipulation of successional processes themselves. In tropical forests, as we have seen, most of the nutrients are held in the plants themselves. To make these nutrients available for crop growth the forest must be cut and burned. In natural fires and native agriculture, seeds already in the ground or crops planted prior to or immediately after the burn begin to grow almost as soon as the ground has cooled. Thus plants begin to take up the available nutrients rapidly and store them in their tissues. The rapid uptake of nutrients by plants that root to different depths and have life cycles of different lengths mimics what happens in plant succession in the tropics. Short-lived plants are gradually replaced with longer-lived species. The soil is not compacted because it is carefully worked, always has a cover of vegetation and is thus protected from rainfall – which is the main agent of soil compaction – so that forest seedlings can establish themselves fairly easily. The relatively small size of the plots (although some Kayapó ceremonial agricultural sites can be more than two hundred acres in size) results in a microclimate that is influenced by the forest surrounding it. The parching conditions so characteristic of Amazonian pastures are not found in these indigenous agricultural zones. Moreover, animals and seeds from the adjacent forest can easily arrive in the field.

Manipulation of the fallows is central to the process of forest regeneration. The forests that arise from "abandoned" agricultural plots are only as "natural" as European mixed orchards with sheep browsing underneath the shade. The Kayapó work the fallow in several ways: by weeding out some plants, protecting others such as palms, planting particularly cherished trees and shrubs, transplanting, pruning, and fertilizing them with bones, ash and mulch. They carry out these activities at different intensities, but they always enhance the regeneration process through the introduction of species whose seeds and seedlings may have been destroyed in the burning. This fosters species and spatial diversity in the plot, thereby helping to confound the seed and seedling predators. Also, by planting and protecting plant species whose fruit are eaten by animals, they attract into the plot a diversity of wildlife and game.

About three-quarters of all tropical forest trees have fleshy fruits. A Tembé Indian conversing with the anthropologist and ethnobotanist William Balée informed him that nearly 90 per cent of the fruits produced by trees in a two-and-a-half acre plot in Maranhão were consumed by game animals. The Kayapó also plant more than sixteen species that bear fruits enjoyed not only by them but also by game. Scholars like Kent Redford who focus on wildlife interactions have demonstrated that nine out of eleven favored game animals and the seven most favored game birds eat fruit, and that more than sixty genera of fruit-bearing plants consumed by game are to be found in the Amazon gardens. Planted fruit trees are likely to attract more game into the fields which in turn introduce seeds of other fruit or forest trees through their droppings.[10] Making gardens attractive to wildlife is an essential part of the recuperation process.

Thus do agriculture and fallow management ensure that rich and useful forests will follow cultivation. In comparison with natural succession, indeed, this manipulation can increase the diversity of species on a given site. Study after study has shown that even when tribes move these sites are anything but abandoned.[11]

ASHES AND DEATH

In contrast to such judicious regenerative systems we find, at the opposite extreme, a very different consequence of most of those fires seen raging on that September day by the NOAA satellite. Hundreds and sometimes thousands of acres at a time are put to the torch. Large crews of landless men who roam the Amazon in search of any kind of labor are mustered by contractors – the *empreiteiros* – to clear the tracts for a dollar a day plus food. Alternatively, two D8 tractors with a 40,000 kilo chain slung between them churn through the old growth dragging it down, ready to be fired at the end of the dry season. The huge dimension of the area and the ignorance of fire management by those consigning the acreage to flame prompts a firestorm. The heat is so intense that the fires often break into standing forests, particularly those which have already been damaged by the removal of valuable timber.[12] Into the air spew thousands of tons of carbon, and the uprush causes turbulence and eddies of smoke thousands of feet up. The sky turns a dirty ochre and a soft ash mingles with the dust from the unpaved roads, giving the people on whom the powder settles a spectral aspect, and the landscape itself the patina of death. Deforestation in the Amazon now approaches an exponential rate, with increasing millions of acres of forest reduced to dust each year.[13]

When the rains finally begin, small aircraft hover and buzz over the charred landscape spraying down tons of grass seed, colonial guinea grass, brachiaria, and even sometimes a legume or two. In a few months this landscape will be a lush tangle of grass, root stumps and vagrant seedlings of all kinds, but still unsuitable for grazing. The next year what is called the "fire of formation" – *fogo de formação* – will be set. Its purpose is to reduce plants competing with the grasses for space and nutrients. The following year come the floppy-eared zebu cattle, glossy white bovines, humped and agile, which were the pride and vehicles of the Hindu god Shiva.

The grasses do well only so long as the nutrients burned out of the forest remain available to them. The exotic grasses are from Africa and evolved in the somewhat richer soils of the African savannahs. But they are soon overwhelmed by secondary brush, known in the Amazon as *juquira*, the bastard offspring of forest and pasture. The grasses face the double strain of ardently browsing cattle much preferring them to the coarse brush, and the increasingly inhospitable terrain leached of its nutrients by rains. The brush, adapted to local conditions and usually with far deeper rooting systems, begins to make the pastures almost useless as grazing lands. At this point the rancher may attempt to control the brush by drenching it with herbicide, the most popular of which is Dow Chemical's Tordon, whose active chemical 2,4,5T (dioxin), was known as Agent Orange in the Vietnam War. Less expensive is the strategy of sending work crews through to chop down the brush, let it dry, and once again to set it aflame.

This pattern of burning every couple of years, combined with constant replacement of a diverse system by feeble monocultures of exotic grasses, rapidly exhausts the soil, often beyond regeneration. The soil becomes compacted, increasingly less accessible to germinating seedlings and at times almost anaerobic. The pasture's microclimate is hot and dry, some 10–20 degrees fahrenheit above that of the forest, and is thus extremely difficult for forest plants to colonize and survive in. Seed in the soil, stump sprouts and seeds wafted in from adjacent forest are destroyed in the constant burns. Mycorrhizae and other micro-organisms may not be able to tolerate the changed habitat, especially because they often grow only with particular plants. Thus within the pastures themselves the means of regeneration are destroyed. Since these pastures are inhospitable to the fauna that might carry seeds from within the forest, only those species of plant whose seeds are airborne become available. These form a very small proportion of forest propagules. Such seedlings as do survive exist in a more or less uniform habitat where both seed predators and herbivores can easily find their victims. Once established, plants are then subject to the ravages of one of the most voracious predators in the Amazon, the leafcutter ant.

The consequences of this disastrous application of fire can now be seen across thousands of square miles of the Amazon where more than half the area cleared is abandoned to useless scrub. Fire, as suggested by both Aeschylus and Amazonian cosmology, is the origin of all the arts of man, but here it is unmanaged, clumsy and brutal in its application.

And the colonist small farmer, the villain of numerous accounts of forest pillage – what of his use of fire? The total area that colonist agriculture captures in Brazil is extremely small in comparison with the pasturage of the ranchers who seize 90 per cent of all land that ends up cleared of forest. There is no such creature as the typical Amazon small farmer or colonist. The forest farmers come from different places, have different levels of capital, of agricultural knowledge. They have different ambitions. Clearly peasants are responsible for some of these fires; peasants also speculate on land and clear for pasture. This range means that the use of fire and the care of the 220-acre plots varies enormously. Colonists from within the Amazon are more likely to use fire judiciously and to turn their agricultural plots to something in the nature of a successional orchard, in the pattern of indigenous forest reconstruction. Colonists who turn their plots to monocultures such as rice and pasture areas are more likely to engage in destructive burning.

Most of the lands cleared in the Amazon for whatever reason will sooner or later end up as pasture. These tall forests can tolerate a great deal of disturbance and still recover so long as such disturbance has spared pollinators, seed dispersal agents, and habitats suitable for the germination and establishment of seeds. A variegated landscape of forests of different ages and different successional patterns is more diverse than a single-age forest, however venerable. But the kind of destruction practised over the last quarter century impedes regeneration; the impacts are not confined to the cleared land, but are regional and global and extend through time.

FIRE AND WATER

From fire we must now turn to its complement, water. Anyone who has watched rainwater sluicing down a barren slope, eroding lands, and swelling into destructive torrents, can readily appreciate the role of forests as essential mechanisms for flood control. As one might expect, the forests of the Amazon play an indispensable role in the water economy of the region, buffering the flow of the streams and rivers and the very rainfall that nourishes them. But the destruction inscribed in the degraded pastures can be seen too in the *igarapés* or streams that so charmed the nineteenth-century naturalists. Travel in the region, and it is not long before one hears old-timers lament silt-clogged river beds and streams, once perennial, that now dry up for half the year.

The crisis in the region's hydrology affects not only the smaller streams, but also the riparian ecology of the larger river systems. In the Amazon semi-annually flooded forests, covering some fourteen million acres, sustain an important part of the region's fish, and these fish, many of which are the relics of the world's primal seas before the oceans became salt, form, with root crops, the basis of the Amazonian diet. Generations of natives have grown up savoring the flesh of the tambaqui, tucunare, pirarucu, pacu and surubim. Commercial over-fishing has reduced the availability of these fish for the poor; shippers now corner the commercial catch for Manaus, Belém, São Paulo and the international market. By the mid 1980s, 90 per cent of the Belém catch was exported.[14] This attrition of stocks has been made worse by changes in the ecology of the *várzea*.

A large proportion of Amazonian fish get most of their food during the rainy season by browsing on the fruits and litter of the submerged forest floor (thus assisting also in seed distribution). The gradual rise in water level and slow acceleration of currents during high water (as much as 50 to 60 feet higher than the dry season low) allow fish to swim beyond the river channels, low waters and sparse feeding opportunities of the dry season into the adjacent *várzeas*. But ravaged watersheds generate currents and turbulent waters that sweep rapidly through the river channels and forests, making it far more difficult for this essential browsing to occur. Instead of a leisurely grazing season the water's rapid rise and fall, and the increasing turbidity, truncate the necessary feeding period.

The effect of forests on ground water is only one dimension of their influence on Amazonian hydrology. The forests themselves recycle much of the rainfall that nourishes them. About half the rains that fall in the Amazon are derived from water vapor from the Atlantic ocean. The remaining 50 per cent of the moisture falling to earth is generated from what hydrologists call the evapo-transpiration of the forest itself. When rain falls on the forest, it is absorbed by trees, evaporated off leaves and other surfaces, and transpired by the metabolism of the forest itself back into the atmosphere. Every traveler in the Amazon has seen, at sun-up, the wispy tendrils of white vapor condensing above the forest canopy. What they are admiring is the operation of an endogenous climate.[15]

The conversion of vast areas of tropical forest into pasture promises to change regional climates drastically. Fire which leads in the short-to-medium term to degraded scrub, also prompts a degraded climate of parched drier air instead of the moist breezes of former times, and since the climates of adjacent regions depend on movement of some of this moist air out from the Amazon basin, people in central Brazil and the Andean *planalto* are increasingly likely to find themselves searching the sky for rain.

THE GREENHOUSE EFFECT

As midwesterners in the United States sweltered in the summer of 1988 and plowed their desiccated grain fields under, the question of the "greenhouse effect" became a topic of popular discussion and political debate. The phrase refers to the gradual global heating of the atmosphere, thought to stem mainly from additions of carbon dioxide derived primarily from the burning of fossil fuels. Solar radiation first strikes the earth's surface in short waves, and is reflected back as long wave infrared radiation into the atmosphere where the build-up of carbon dioxide absorbs some of the radiation and re-radiates the remainder within the atmosphere, causing the atmosphere to grow warmer, with far-reaching effects on the movement of air and water currents that control the climate of the planet. Other "greenhouse gases", like methane, affect the atmosphere in ways that also augment the atmospheric warming and now roughly equal the impact of carbon dioxide.[16]

Combustion of petroleum products in the First World provides most of the carbon dioxide, methane, nitrous oxides and chlorofluorocarbons going into the atmosphere, but Third World energy use and deforestation contribute to the ever-increasing amounts. One index of the changing situation is the rising curve of complaints from satellite photo-analysts that they are unable to get decent dry-season shots of the Amazon anymore, because of the great clouds of smoke and particulates hanging over large parts of the forest. The reasons for this pall are quite clear when one examines the numbers of fires and the consequent contributions of particulates and "greenhouse" gases. Compton Tucker and his colleagues at the Goddard Space Flight Center have monitored the numbers of fires during the burning period of July through September 1987 in a quadrant from 6.5 to 15.5 degrees latitude and 55 to 67 degrees west longitude, an area that includes Rondônia and western Mato Grosso; i.e., that of the most severe burning on the Amazon flank. What they have shown is that more than 8,000 fires burn each day during the burning season. Factoring in the average duration of fires, Tucker's group arrived at a total of 240,000 fires over the season. On the average each fire belches out some 4,500 metric tons of carbon dioxide, 750 metric tons of carbon monoxide and more than 25 metric tons of methane. By the end of the burning season more than 10 million metric tons of particulates have darkened the sky.[17]

Scientists quarrel a great deal about the contribution of Amazonian carbon dioxide to the global carbon economy. The debates have much to do with the structures of their computer models and the way that they view carbon flows between the atmosphere, vegetation and the oceans. About one third of the carbon dioxide spewed into the atmosphere from worldwide tropical deforestation and associated burning is thought to stem from the Amazon, which provides about 85 per cent of the Latin American contribution.[18] Approximately 10 per cent of the global atmospheric contribution of carbon dixide comes from the area examined by Tucker and his colleagues.

The accretion of carbon dioxide in the atmosphere is not irreversible. Plants grow by taking carbon dioxide from the air, via photosynthesis, and converting it in their plant bodies into various forms of hydrocarbons. Growing forests take up large amounts of carbon dioxide, and tall, high biomass forests are major storage areas of carbon dioxide. But repeated burnings on the new pastures destroy growing organisms and thrust the incinerated carbon from their bodies back up into the atmosphere. In place of a 300–600 metric ton forest storing and absorbing hydrocarbons, we now have a scrubby, degraded succession of between 10 and 20 metric tons per hectare, thus reducing the area available to store carbon. This is, moreover, a system whose ability to regenerate a forest is in question.

PATHS OF DESTRUCTION IN THE AMAZON

There is some uncertainty about the dimensions of the greenhouse effect and the impact of tropical deforestation on climate. But there is nothing speculative about the extinction of species. The destruction of the Amazon forest is a biological catastrophe on the order of that which made dinosaurs raw material for natural history museums.

Consider first the extent of this destruction. There are wildly varying estimates both of the areas deforested and the rate at which the destruction is occurring. A prudent reckoning suggests that there is now from 8 to 10 per cent less of the Amazon forest than there was a hundred years ago.[19] In 1975 a little under seven million acres of land in the Brazilian Amazon had been altered from its original forest cover. By 1988 more than 40 million acres of forest had been destroyed.

Take a map of Amazônia and find the town of Rio Branco, in the far northwestern state of Acre. Then trace a path east along the road BR 364 through the state of Rondônia, where close to 17 per cent of the forests have been cleared, crossing through northern and central Mato Grosso. Here is where rates of deforestation are highest in Amazônia. At Barra do Garças turn north on BR 158, past the Rio das Mortes and into the Araguaia drainage. Here the rivers bear the names of Indian tribes, the Suyá Missu, the Xavante, the Tapirapé. Following BR 158 we pass through a region where some of the largest ranches in all of Brazil are found, huge rangelands, some exceeding more than a quarter of a million acres, and carrying on their placards names of the great industrial and banking consortia and corporations of Brazil, as well as some of their multinational partners – the big Brazilian bank BCN, Bordon Meat Packers, Aracruz are the more obvious – in the Fortune 500 roster. Pass north through northern Mato Grosso and into Conceição do Araguaia and we come upon the Volkswagen ranch, Manah fertilizers and the names of some of Brazil's most prominent land magnates: the Lunardelli family, Ariosto da Riva. The area is now the purview of huge ranches, gold rushes, and voracious timber exploitation.[20] These ranches of northern Mato Grosso and southern Pará, along with several timber operations, were the largest recipients of tax breaks and federal subsidies when, back in the 1960s, the military junta sweetened the pot for big investors from southern Brazil.[21] To the north are Redenção, lumber mills, gold merchants, the Kayapó Indians, terrible land hunger. North again through seemingly unending degraded pasture is the Serra do Carajás, home to the largest iron ore deposits in the world. On either side of the road in this region are landscapes degraded in the search for property and profit, as we approach the realm of iron and gold.

Following the course of the Rio Vermelho – the Red River – a mere stone's throw from the Serra Pelada we arrive at the largest gold strike thus far in the Amazon, indeed the largest open pit gold mine in the world. Since the first strike here about a decade ago the pit has been excavated by an army of *garimpeiros*, workers of placer mines, and their helpers, with the metal-bearing ores hauled up the steep walls of the pit in five-liter cans, in a scene reminiscent of Brueghel's Tower of Babel. A few hours' drive north from here and we are at Marabá, where the waters of the Tucuruí dam practically lap at the banks of the city. Day after day the sawmills process for fine cabinetry Brazil-nut trees whose harvests formed the wealth of Marabá's former masters. Now a burgeoning supply area and industrial center, Marabá is the major city on the rail line connecting the waters of the Tocantíns with the sea, at the harbor city of São Luis. As the train, loaded with iron ore from Carajás, heads east towards Açailândia, a future smelting site, it passes close to an area known as the Bico do Papagaio – the parrot's beak – in the state of Goías. This area between Marabá and Açailândia has seen some of the most intense land conflict in the entire Amazon. Everywhere we drive the old forests have gone, visible only as a distant green scratch on the horizon. Açailândia is now the town designated as the largest center of charcoal production for pig iron from the smelters using the ore from Carajás. Feeding the furnaces will require at least 450,000 acres of forest a year, to turn high-value ore into low-value pig iron, all in the effort to snatch the paltry added value of a low-grade industrial product. The enterprise is cost effective only if the value of the forest itself is calculated at zero.[22]

At Açailândia turn north and follow the Belém-Brasília road, the so-called Estrada da Onça – Highway of the Jaguar – which, begun in 1960, was the first major road artery through Amazônia, connecting it to the new Brazilian capital in the south. Once a source of ridicule, it has thoroughly transformed its environs and is now mainly a zone of ranches with some cash-crop fruit farms – mostly owned by the Japanese – that appear as one approaches Belém. Born of President Getúlio Vargas's vision first expressed in the late 1930s of the March to the West, it has solidly defined the development patterns of the Amazon for the last thirty years.

Had we turned west at Marabá we would have embarked on the Trans-Amazon highway toward Altamira through Itaituba, another gold zone, then down BR 230 back toward Porto Velho and Rondônia. All along here deforestation follows the road. Northwards towards Belém and the Amazon's mouth, the same story unfolds. With each road comes forest destruction on each side, and as these trees fall, several species are extinguished each day.

THE EXTINCTION OF THE SPECIES

No one knows how many species have disappeared with every mile cleared. But we do know the ways in which extinctions of species are accomplished.

Most obvious is elimination of an organism through direct destruction: the undocumented rare species of tree that have never been classified, the incinerated insects that lived on that tree. Then there are those species lost when their habitats are destroyed: an unusual orchid that evolved on trees on the iron-rich soil of the Serra do Carajás has no alternative site on which to colonize. Loss of a pollinator or a seed-dispersal agent can spell extinction for some species. Thus, though the plant lives for a while, its role in the history and future of evolution is gone. The flames may spare areas where rare organisms still exist, but the organisms that remain are the living dead. All the resources necessary to sustain a breeding population, like habitats, pollinators and seed dispersal agents, are gone. With every acre burned, some species see their numbers contract until offspring of the breeding survivors become vulnerable to genetic disabilities, or chance events, a disease or a single storm that can wipe out a population forever.

Systematic hunting or extraction of a particular species may lead to its demise. The rosewood tree, desired for its aromatic oil for perfumery, has been so rapaciously extracted from the forest that now it has virtually disappeared. Nineteenth-century travelers such as Herndon reported the collection of millions of turtle eggs to supply the trade in turtle ''butter''. Canoes were filled with eggs, which were then crushed underfoot, removing any embryonic turtles. Water was then poured on this fetid mess, and the canoe left in the sun. The oil was then skimmed off and sent to markets.[23] Carvajal was most impressed – as were many others – by the vast swarms of these creatures whose numbers choked the rivers near the breeding beaches. But incessant hunting has resulted in the near extinction of this species.

The cases of the rosewood trees and the turtles are exceptional. They were so economically important – and in the case of turtles, so ubiquitous – that we have some indication of their previous abundance. For most of the species that are lost, we have no record of how abundant they were, of what they meant to life on this earth, or what they might have contributed to mankind.

The flames of the Amazon forest, captured in a thousand photographs, are fueled by the vaporizing DNA of the world's evolutionary heritage. Unknown plants and insects may touch our hearts less than the whales or jaguars, but in the long run they might have been be more useful to people and central to the functions of their ecosystems in ways that we cannot imagine. At the present rate, many of them are dead for the rest of history, extinguished by fire, mercury, dioxin, and the loss of the agents of their survival, whether a pollinator, a dispersal agent, a particular type of soil, or a particular tree.

There are moral and religious arguments as to why species should not be rushed into extinction. But most people, in the end, respond to practical pleas. Amazonian forests provide the germ plasm for an international trade in products valued at billions per year. The rather modest port of Manaus alone exports over a billion dollars of Amazon products, materials produced out of the domesticated and wild germ plasm of the forest.[24] The contribution of Amazonian germ plasm to world trade includes cacao, palm hearts, *guaraná*, Brazil nuts, rubber, chicle, babassu oil, fish, manioc, cashew and coca. With coca the global annual value of Amazonian germ plasm easily exceeds one hundred billion dollars a year.[25]

The genetic constituent of most crop plants throughout the world is extremely narrow and requires a regular input of varieties to improve the stocks most widely in use. As more than 80 per cent of the world's food supply depends on less than two dozen species of plants and animals, the loss of their wild ancestors and their hybridizing cousins can reduce the viability of these crops even as mankind comes increasingly to depend on them. Both for short-cycle and perennial crops it is essential to preserve not only the habitat of the wild relatives, but also the agricultural systems in which they were domesticated and through which their cultivar diversity is maintained. The Tikuna Indians on the Rio Negro have more than hundred cultivars of manioc adapted to different soil types, different tolerance to the onslaught of pests, and which produce tubers of differing characteristics.

The Tikuna grow these cultivars in a variety of environmental conditions and experiment with different crosses between the strains. Perennial crops such as cocoa, rubber, fruit trees, fibers, oils and fruit-producing palms are likely to play a more important role as agroforestry systems loom larger in the world's food economy. Their manipulation of perennial species occurs in the secondary successional phases when agricultural plots are allowed to regenerate and when fruit and other trees are planted into the succession. Forest species may produce useful crosses with domesticated trees. No agriculture is static and constant experimentation with cultivars is as characteristic of the native agronomist as of the most seasoned crop geneticist working in the International Center for Tropical Agriculture in Colombia. Destroy native cultures – so many have been destroyed – and the world loses the knowledge that has taken several millennia of Amazonian history to evolve. This knowledge cannot be reconstructed from shards any more than our dynamic agronomy could be regenerated if all the books, laboratories, experimental fields, seeds and most of the agronomists were destroyed. Agriculture requires living cultures, working with all the elements of their agronomy: the particular environment, the cultivars, the ways people talk about agriculture, their rituals and lore. Amazonians evolved the science that provided the world with some of its most useful and valuable species. These systems and the crop germ plasm they evolved can only be effectively conserved in the context of traditional agriculture.

TOMORROW'S LOSSES

William Balée, an ethnobotanist based in Belém, has recently shown that the Ka'apor Indians in western Maranhão, the northeast Brazilian state bordering on the Atlantic south of Belém, name and use 94 per cent of the plants in a given sample area of about two and a half acres. Comparative studies with several other groups also show that at least 50 per cent of the species are regularly used by forest populations.[26] But indigenous peoples are not the only repository of this knowledge. Those working with *caboclos*, petty extractors and river populations have discovered that these people also influence the structure and production of forests, and have a profound knowledge of the wide range of forest species they regularly use. This is not merely arcane folkloric knowledge. Many of these plants and fruits form the basis of vibrant local economies. *Açaí* fruits, *umari, pupunha, massaranduba, cajú bravo*, and *uxi* may not strike the gastronomic chords of most First World people, but they are the basis of economies that partially sustain thousands of forest inhabitants near cities like Belém, Manaus and Iquitos. Increasingly, evidence from many studies – carried out in the floodplains of Peru by Padoch and Peters, the Belém estuary by Anderson and his colleagues, studies of rubber tappers by Hecht and Schwartzman, and of the babassu palm by May, Anderson and Hecht – show the broad use of natural forest resources in providing a sustainable living, and also afford an insight into the diverse ways in which people use forests to make their living without destroying them. These harvests of the forest are often undervalued by being couched purely in the language of subsistence. While extractive products contribute importantly to such subsistence, they also form part of the regional economy in these products and even serve international markets. Relegating their role solely to one of subsistence is like dismissing the economic significance of California orchards, or of regional French markets in game or mushroom. Other scholars, such as ethnopharmacologist Elaine Elizabetsky, show the rich medicinal traditions elaborated by the *caboclo* and other backwoods populations, in which there is also a brisk herbal trade.

The biological diversity of these tropical forests have made the Amazon a particularly important source of medicine. Hundreds of examples crowd onto the shelves of First World pharmacies, drugs that owe their origin to the medical acumen of Amazônian shamans who have guided botanists through their pharmacopoeias: the so-called *drogas do sertão*, or drugs of the backlands. Since the sixteenth century, the Amazon has been the focus of searches for drug plants. The *drogas do sertão* were the economic foundation of the Amazonian economy for centuries. These gardenings from the forest were the first stimuli for its occupation, as the cravings for sarsaparilla, ipecac, *guaraná*, quinine bark, fueled early incursions up the tributaries. Native medicines include cures against animal toxins such as snake bites and wasp stings, anti-worm medicines, natural insect repellants (a common feature of the pigments used in body painting), anti-inflammatories of various kinds, contraceptives, abortifacients, anti-convulsives such as *cissus sicyoides*, muscle relaxants such as curare and emetics like ipecac. There are also anti-malarial and anti-fever drugs such as quinine, and also powerful psychotropic drugs such as datura, virola, coca and yage. Seventy per cent of the plants known to have some kind of anti-cancer compound are indigenous to the lowland tropics. While most of the drugs derived from tropical sources in First World commerce concentrate on the few important ones, such as Mexican yam which is used in the production of steroids, the potential of these plants still remains largely unexplored and untested for commercial markets.

The needs of civilization change. By the late nineteenth century vulcanized rubber was one of the staple materials of industrial civilization. A hundred years earlier the rubber tree, *Hevea brasiliensis*, was a minor curiosity whose "caoutchouc" was noted by La Condamine. The insecticidal effects of rotenone derived from *Lonchocarpus* were of little interest twenty-five years ago. Outside the Amazon, the Madagascar rosy periwinkle flower, *Vinca*, attracted little attention until the most widely used cure for childhood leukemia was discoverd to lie in the periwinkle. The flower, source of vincristine and marketed as oncovin, is now the basis of a $100-million-a-year industry.

While the Madagascar periwinkle was not used in folk medicine, about three-quarters of the major drug plants in international commerce are put to the uses first devised by folk doctors and shamans at the point of their original collection. The medicinal plants of tomorrow and the genetic basis of our foods and fibers will be gone if their source has been eradicated by the D8 tractors on BR 364. The cultures that nurtured, observed, and used these plants are being annihilated, the native and folk curers along with everyone else exiled to urban slums, wasting away their talents as they keep body and soul together as unskilled labor.

On the matter of extinction Erwin has written:

> Our generation will participate in an extinction process involving perhaps 20 to 30 million species. We are not talking about a few endangered species in the Red Data books, or the few forbish louseworts and snail darters that garner so much media attention. No matter what the number we are talking about, whether one million or twenty million, it is massive destruction of the biological richness of the earth.[27]

The thought is eloquent but should be amplified. The extinction is not only of nature but of socialized nature: what is also being exterminated in the Amazon is civilization.

NOTES

1. There are themes associated with fire in the cosmology of many Amazonian tribes, ranging from those of uncontrolled nature to that of disciplined civilized ritual. A common subject is the destructiveness of untamed fire and its association with a myth common to many groups in Amazônia – the "Great World Fire" – where huge areas and many societies are destroyed. Intermediate between utter lack of control and destruction is the association of fire with heat, sex and procreative rhythms, menstrual cycles and births. Here fire and heat trigger the mystery of creation.

   In the myths that elaborate the origins of fire for human use there are several sub-themes. First, the disruption of natural order: fire comes to the hands of men through deceit, theft or death, and thus the knowledge of fire, according to Lévi-Strauss, results in a fall from grace and loss of immortality. Next, fire is often associated with domesticated plants which require it for both their cultivation and preparation. Finally, with fire comes weaponry or ritual musical instruments, artifacts that are most distant from nature and are used to control it through ritual and action.

   In the myths of many Gê tribes such as the Kayapó, Apinagé and Crahó, fire was stolen from the jaguar, who was not even left with an ember. A young boy hunting macaws in the forest becomes stranded and is rescued by the jaguar who takes him home, where the boy tastes cooked meat for the first time. The jaguar's pregnant wife glowers at the boy, but agrees to treat him well. The jaguar sets off to hunt, leaving the boy to chew happily on roast tapir, but his noisy eating so irritates the jaguar's wife that she shows him her formidable claws and bares her enormous teeth at him. The boy flees in terror to the jaguar hunting in the forest, who tells him that should his wife threaten him again, to shoot her with the jaguar's bow and arrow. When she threatens him again, the boy shoots her and runs to tell the jaguar who sends him back to his village, warning him to be careful and avoid the call of the rotten wood. On hearing the boy's description of the ambrosial taste of cooked meat, the villagers become extremely eager to get fire, and assuming the form of animals, set forth to the jaguar's abode to steal it from his hearth. In some versions of this myth, sweet potatoes, manioc, bananas and cotton are also stolen from the hearth to enrich their diet of raw meat and rotten wood, and to replace their rough palm clothing with finely woven fibers of cotton. While the villagers returned with the fire, many birds sought to protect forests and fields from burning, picking up the sparks that flew up in the air or fell to the ground. Several were burned while doing so, which is why some birds are known to have feet, legs and beaks the color of flame. The accoutrements of civilization, the bow and arrow for hunting and agriculture, come with the acquisition of fire. For a listing of all variants of this myth see Johannes Wilbert, *Folk Tales of the Gê* 1984.

In the case of the Barasana in the Uaupés of Colombia described by Stephen Hugh-Jones, *The Palm and the Pleiades* 1987, it is Yurupary – or the Manioc Stick Anaconda – who obtains fire from the underworld. Anaconda uses this fire to kill his brother Macaw, and is then himself burned to death. His bones become the charred logs of a manioc garden and his body gives rise to cultivated plants. After Yurupary has been burned survivors plant seeds in the ash, including those of the Paxiuba palm from which ritual musical instruments are made.

2. C. Crocker's book *Vital Souls* 1985, provides

an account of shamanism unmatched in eloquence. Our discussion of Bororo shamanism is based on his account.

3. See *Fire in Mediterranean Ecosystems* by the Pacific South West Experiment Station, published at the University of California Press, Berkeley in 1987.

4. T. Cochrane and P. Sanchez, "Land Resources", in S. B. Hecht, ed. *Amazônia* 1982, provide a useful table summarizing the constraints of Amazonian soils. Their table is given below.

Main Soil Constraints in the Amazon under Native Vegetation

Soil Constraint	Million Hectares	Per cent of Amazon
Phosphorus deficiency	436	90
Aluminum toxicity	353	73
Drought Stress	254	53
Low Potassium Reserves	242	50
Poor Drainage/Flood Hazards	116	24
High Phosphorus Fixation	77	16
Low Cation Exchange Capacity	64	13
High Erodibility	39	8
No Major Limitations	32	7
Slopes of over 30 per cent	30	6
Laterite Hazard if Subsoil Exposed	21	4

5. See Fittkau, Junk, et al, "Substrate and Vegetation in the Amazon Region", in H. Dierschke, ed. *Vegetation und Substrat* 1975.

6. The preceding discussion is based largely on the work of the San Carlos team. For more technical detail see C. Jordan, *Nutrient Cycling in Tropical Forest Ecosystems* 1985.

7. See various articles by Uhl and his colleagues in the bibliography. Uhl has carried out more long-term studies of succession and recuperation in Amazônia than anyone else.

8. See for example Nigh and Nations 1980, Alcorn 1983, Denevan and Padoch 1987, and Posey and Balée 1989.

9. See the various articles by Posey cited in the bibliography. The fire discussion comes mainly in Hecht and Posey 1989.

10. The ways by which people manage animals in tropical ecosystems has not been widely studied. Kent Redford and his associates provide particularly useful insights. Redford's paper with Robinson 1987, "The Game of Choice", and with Klein and Murcia 1989, "The Incorporation of Game Animals into Small Scale Agroforestry", are highly recommended for further readings on the subject.

11. D. Irvine in Posey and Balée, eds. *Resource Management* 1989. See also the volume by W.M. Denevan and C. Padoch *Swidden Agroforestry* 1987.

12. C. Uhl and R. Buschbacker, "A Disturbing Synergism" 1985. See bibliography.

13. *Alteration of Forest Cover –
1975, 1978, 1980 and 1987 by State*

State	Area Altered in 1000s of hectares			
	1975	1978	1980	1988
Amapá	15,2	17,0	17,0	57,1
Pará	865,4	2,244,5	3,391,3	12,000,0
Roraima	5,5	14,3	14,3	327,0
Maranhão	294,0	733,7	1,067,1	5,067,0
Goiás (Tocantins)	350,7	1,028,8	1,145,6	1,950,0
Acre	116,5	246,4	462,6	1,950,0
Rondônia	121,6	418,4	757,9	5,800,0
Mato Grosso	1,012,4	2,835,5	5,329,9	20,800,0
Amazonas	77,9	178,5	178,5	16,579,0
Amazônia Total	2,859,2	7,717,1	12,364,2	59,892,1

Source: IBDF/INPE 1988.
With more refined techniques the total area deforested is now placed at 8–10%.

14. M. Goulding, *The Fishes and the Forest* 1980.

15. See various publications of Salati in the bibliography.

16. S. Schneider, "Greenhouse Effect: Science and Policy", in *Science*, 243: 771–779. 1989. R.E. Dickinson, ed. *Geophysiology of Amazônia* 1987. G. Prance, ed. *Tropical Forests and The World Atmosphere* 1986.

17. Y. Kaufman, C. Tucker and I. Fung: *Remote Sensing of Biomass Burning in the Tropics*, NASA/GSFC/GISS Code 640, 1989.

18. See McConnell in Dickinson.

19. Two main groups in the US are tracking satellite images of deforestation in the Amazon. One is at Wood's Hole, Mass. and the other is at the NASA/Goddard Space Flight Center in Maryland. The following is from Malingreau and Tucker's 1988 paper, *Ambio*. "Disturbance" refers to areas where activities associated with subsequent forest conversion – road building, mining, clearing for agriculture, etc., are taking place.

"Disturbance and deforested areas in the Southern Amazon region as measured from AVHRR 1-km data as of September 1985. The deforested and disturbance areas presented in this table were extracted from the data presented in figures 2 and 3. No percentage of state-wide deforestation is given for Mato Grosso because the figures are only from the phytogeographical Amazon portion of this state.

1. ACRE
Area of territory	152,589 km^2
Area of disturbances	30,061 km^2
Area of deforestation	5,269 km^2
% of territory deforested	3.45%

2. RONDÔNIA
Area of territory	243,044 km^2
Area of disturbances	86,808 km^2
Area of deforestation	27,658 km^2
% of State deforested	11.38%

3. MATO GROSSO
Area of territory	881,001 km^2
Area of disturbances	148,893 km^2
Area deforested	56,646 km^2

4. TOTAL
Area of disturbances	265,762 km^2
Area deforested	89,573 km^2
	(−34% of disturbance areas)."

20. The Brazilian Amazon's main source of timber are the states of Pará and Rondônia, and the impact of their exploitation has been substantial. In 1976, wood harvests from the Amazon accounted for about 14% of Brazil's total production but had increased to 44% by 1986.

21. The SUDAM package involved fiscal incentives of several types, such as:
    1. Capital grants of 75 per cent of the implementation costs;
    2. Tax holidays of more than fifteen years on corporate holdings if the money was used for projects in the Amazon;
    3. Subsidized credits with several years grace period that resulted in negative interest rates because inflation vastly exceeded the interest;
    4. Duty-free heavy machinery imports;
    5. A low tax rate holding;
    6. Land concessions or land sales at nominal prices.
    These resulted in delirous capital gains. The details of the fiscal incentives are outlined in Mahar, 1979, 1988; Hecht, 1982, 1985, and et al. 1988, and Browder, 1988.

22. This is derived from the studies commissioned by the Superintendent of Amazônia on the economics of iron ore. Also see SEPLAN 1988a, Plano Diretor da Estrada Ferroviária Carajás, Fearnside 1986, and Bunker 1989.

23. See Herndon 1854; also Smith 1979.

24. Prance 1989, personal communication.

25. This is based on FAO global trade statistics and the US Drug Enforcement Agency estimates of the global cocaine trade.

26. See for example Clay 1988, Posey and Balée 1989, Denevan and Padoch 1988, Altieri and Hecht 1989.

27. Terry Erwin, ''The Tropical Forest Canopy: The Heart of Biotic Diversity'' in E. O. Wilson, ed. *Biodiversity* 1988. The discussion in this section is also based on the work of Plotkin, Farnsworth, and Myers whose articles can also be found in *Biodiversity*; N. Myers, *The Primary Source* 1984, E. Elizabetsky and R. Setzer, ''Caboclo Concepts of Disease'', *Studies in Third World Societies* 1985. See also Posey and Santos 1985, Gottlieb 1981, Mors and Rizzini 1966, and Balandrin et al. 1985.

FOUR

The Amazon Prospectus

From its mountains you may dig silver, iron, coal, copper, quicksilver, zinc, and tin; from the sands of its tributaries you may wash gold, diamonds and precious stones; from its forests you may gather drugs of virtues the most rare, spices of aroma the most exquisite, gums and resins of the most useful properties, dyes of hues the most brilliant, with cabinet and building woods of finest polish and most enduring texture. Its climate is everlasting summer, and its harvests perennial.

MATTHEW MAURY, Amazon booster, 1850s

The region is a welter of putrefaction, where men die like flies. Even with all the money in the world and half its population it is impossible to finish this railway.

THE [BRITISH] PUBLIC WORKS COMPANY, 1873

What is now called the environmental destruction of the Amazon is merely the latest surge in a long epic of annihilation. The dynamics of the region will remain a mystery to us unless we can reconstruct and understand the ways that markets have been perceived, resources captured, and labor exploited over the years.

Today, it is easy to see from the air to see the long rents in the forest where trees have been torn out to make way for roads and pasture. Smoke hangs over the Amazon from July to October. The waters of a hundred tributaries of rivers such as the Tapajós and Araguaia, once crystal clear, are fouled with mine-silt. But other more ancient wounds are invisible now, or harder to decipher. They are registered not so much as scars upon a landscape but as absences from it. The history of the Amazon's exploitation resonates mournfully in the names of tribes now extinct, shards of polychrome pottery made by peoples now long gone, petroglyphs on the rocks of cataracts marking sanctuaries for tribes who in the end did not escape. Today the tracks of the Madeira-Mamoré railroad rust in the forest and the ancient locomotives stand a little comically in their yard overlooking the great bend in the Madeira below the Santo Antonio cataract. Yet the railroad's construction cost thousands of lives. Its collapse in 1912 rocked the stock exchanges of Europe and ruined more than one great fortune. On the upper Guaporé there still exists a *quilombo* – hideout – for runaway slaves, where their descendants still reside. More than 150 years ago, African slaves who had been brought to the horrors of the Cuiabá gold mines managed to escape there. Secondary jungle now reclaims the neat huts and plantations of Ford's Belterra beside the Tapajós. In the shabby town of Labréa, at the mouth of the Purus, it is not unusual to come upon finely-wrought iron work in the style of the Belle Epoque, imported from France during the rubber boom. Tantalizingly, the past offers itself up.

Exploitation of the Amazon has always been couched in the rhythms of violence, of capture, of obsession. The exigencies of the environment, the chronic labor shortage and allure of easier fortunes to be snatched from the treasures of the forest have always threatened to overwhelm the feeble pulse of agriculture. The grand families of Belém yearned for the dignified stability of agricultural empires to rival the sugar estates of the Northeast, the pastoral fortunes of Recife, but their wealth was amassed from products dragged out from the forest by slave or peon overseen by their younger sons or their *criados* – the bastard offspring of the master of the house – raised to be loyal servants and foremen. For decade after decade, agricultural ambitions expired as both labor and capital chased off upriver on yet another extractive jaunt: for quinine bark, sarsaparilla, vanilla, chocolate, indigo, and of course rubber. This was a mercantile and bureaucratic elite in the traditional style of the Portuguese empire, set in its ways down the centuries. Hopes that Amazônia would gracefully submit to the paradigms of development and shun the raffish temptations of extraction survived into the 1950s when the Superintendency for the Valorization of Amazônia – the initial postwar development agency for the Amazon – proclaimed that the region's vulgar past would finally be extinguished and it would become a cornucopia of respectable crops. This had been anticipated by the effusive boosterism of Matthew Maury, who in the mid-nineteenth century had told the North American public that Amazônia could sustain two crops of rice and four of maize each year and that "the country drained by the Amazon would be capable of supporting ... the population of the whole world".

POMBAL'S STRATEGY FOR AMAZÔNIA

Entrepreneurs may furnish the stuff of legend in the Amazon, but at various times the state has attempted to set the agenda. The region rang with the exploits of marauders, *bandeirantes* and men of God, but in 1750, with the Treaty of Madrid, Spain ceded its Amazon up to the junction of the Madeira to the Portuguese crown under the principle of *uti possedetis* (whoever has it, holds it). The Spanish, distracted by continuing hostilities with the British crown, scarcely realized they had yielded nearly a thousand miles of river and millions of acres with all the treasure contained therein.

First on the agenda was assertion of sovereignty over the forest tracts. The Vargas regime's imperative of "The March to the West" in the 1930s merely echoed earlier imperial compulsions. The aims of the empire's masters in 1750 prefigured those of the Brazilian generals who seized power in 1964, and there are intimations of the present blueprints for the Amazon in those eighteenth-century schemes.

The Portuguese empire feared encroachment by the Spanish, the Dutch and the British. The generals of the 1960s had memories long enough to recall the frontier wars in Acre and the prospective land grab of an international consortium at that time. Next came consolidation of the state itself. How to undertake the exploitation or development of what was, after all, over half the national territory? The Marquis of Pombal was so concerned for the Amazon's role in the Luso-Brazilian empire that in 1777 he sent his brother Xavier de Mendonça Furtado to govern the states of Maranhão and Pará. Letters passed from Pombal in Rio or Lisbon to his brother in Belém, fretting constantly round the question of why the province was in such decay and yielding so little income to the coffers of the state.

The language of Rousseau was recruited to pragmatic concerns. Pombal pronounced the Indians abused and decreed that they be accorded all the privileges and rights of Brazilian citizens, freed from slavery, peonage, or church tutelage. His purpose was twofold. Freed from the religious yoke, the Indians would become loyal subjects of the crown and standard bearers of its sovereignty. The national territory required citizens, and the immense territories now ceded to Portugal would be impossible to "occupy", given the sparse Portuguese population. Natives, as "free citizens", could fill this land and make *de jure* occupation *de facto* by their humble existence. Pursuing this logic of national integration, Pombal was a vigorous advocate of miscegenation and promulgated decrees against the persecution of *mestizos*.

Virulently hostile to the Church, he thus struck a mortal economic blow at the Church's holdings, since Indians formed its workforce and in the missions were, in the words of Pombal's brother, "condemned to the hard yoke of perpetual captivity". Mission or "descended" Indians worked on Church holdings but were made available as wage laborers to settlers. Pombal viewed the region's economic stagnation as the outcome of Jesuit monopoly of labor and prime lands and so devised a labor allocation system meant to free this otherwise captive workforce. This system was known as the *Diretório*, the Directorate, and under its auspices each Indian village would have a director to allocate its labor and oversee and tithe a portion of its production to the crown.

Pombal looked to an Amazônia peopled by detribalized and acculturated Indians and *mestizos*. Alongside the smaller farms of this yeomanry providing food and fibers to sustain the slave economy, which could theoretically turn to the

Directorate villages for extra labor, he envisioned huge sugar, cotton, coffee and cacao plantations worked by African slaves. His grand strategy for the Amazon, if expressed in today's idiom, was the promotion of an agrarian proto-capitalism based on export plantation agriculture and sustained with food grown by small farmers.

In a move echoed almost two hundred years later by the generals, Pombal decided that the region needed the stimulus of state-backed economic expansion. Seeking to emulate the East India Company, he created the *Companhía Grão Pará e Maranhão*, to stimulate and monitor trade throughout the region. He handed out concessions, encouraged private investors and provided galleons to guard the Companhía's Atlantic fleet from piracy. Incentives and allurements to agricultural enterprise were provided. The Companhía, a parastatal company, would underwrite and subsidize various agricultural undertakings, provide tax holidays, promote individual entrepreneurship through special concessions, even guarantee prices. Both dealing in and providing credit for African slaves, the Companhía would also provide transport for the region's trade items and its flotillas would sail under state protection. This supply-side approach to regional development concentrated on overcoming the problem of capital constraints and uncertain transportation, enticing investors into the productive activities of the region.

One of the first acts of the generals after they siezed power in 1964 was to form a latterday *Companhía Grão Pará*. In its modern guise it was called the *Superintendência de Desenvolvimento da Amazônia* (SUDAM) – the Amazon Development Agency – which in like manner via its development bank, BASA, provided tax holidays, concessions, subsidies and investment funds for large holdings on which the entrepreneurial future of the Amazon would be based.

THE LABOR PROBLEM

Pombal's vision was strikingly modernist in its notion of how development might work. The essential ingredients in such strategies usually include an ample labor force, a yeoman class to buffer or absorb threats of social and political disruption from a landless "dangerous class" below, allurements to the entrepreneurial spirit in the form of monopolies, concessions and military escorts for their galleons. Such were Pombal's hopes in Rio and Lisbon. In Belém, where his brother was charged with administering this strategy, the outlook was more confused. There was as always, in Amazônia, the labor problem, and Pombal's labor strategy was to have far-reaching effects. The Companhía might attract entrepreneurs and stimulate trade but without labor this capital could not advance development. "Free" labor allocation was the charge of the Directorate.

In Pombal's program, state-appointed directors replaced Jesuit control of Indian labor. Under the new system each Indian village was under the control of a director who would advise the Indian chief and organize their collecting expeditions, agricultural production, labor corvées and labor rentals to settlers or the state. Through their lock on native labor, directors became masters of fiefdoms and under a chronically short labor economy were constantly cast into temptation's path for they could profit from their charges in several ways. Directors were paid no salary, but granted one-sixth of the value of the products and services of the village as their living; they therefore swiftly perceived that they could garner more wealth by sending the villagers off on extractive expeditions than from the production of rice, beans and manioc. Such long absences removed able-bodied men from the agrarian labor pool, undermining the pastoral dreams of Pombal. Directors could also profit from unofficial sales of the production to *comissários volantes* – roving traders – who began to ply the rivers. These informal transactions held a certain charm since the entire value, not just one-sixth, could be captured by the director. Thus, the Directorate system offered strong incentives to apply the natives to work that could directly benefit the director of the village, and since the director's charges had little idea of the monetary system they could naturally be cheated of their share.

The availability of labor for settlers was undermined by another provision in Pombal's system. Those who wanted to rent Indians were required to put up the entire Indian wage in advance. Such mandatory deposits made it virtually impossible for any small settler to use native labor. The inevitable followed, in the form of a rapidly accelerating labor monopoly by those with capital resources, the large plantation owners and men with booming extractive businesses. Again, it was possible to strike illegal bargains with the directors in order to assure a favorable allocation in the very competitive labor environment.

Under a variant of corvée labor and the Spanish *mita* system, the Indians were also allocated to state projects. Crown officials continuously depleted the labor pool by their endless demands for the human infrastructure necessary to mount their military enterprises: boatmen, bearers, provisioners and guides. Forts had to be reared, palisades planted, and ditches dug. The military-colonial complex found itself calling upon the labor directors with increasing urgency. Initially the Indians preferred government service to the vagaries of employment by settlers. But as the labor shortage deepened, they or at least their directors were able to strike more advantageous bargains in the private sector. The final result was that large owners, directors and the state controlled labor and resources. Smaller settlers either went "native" amid much contempt, or became *comissários volantes* – the beginnings of the mobile traders (*regatão*), and middlemen (*marreteiro*), who moved goods through the region untaxed and untrammeled by the crown. Here in the petty mercantilism of the thriving "black market" of scarce goods and isolated population, directors could make a few extra milreis, and settlers otherwise doomed began the development of the form of commerce that so characterized the region during the rubber period. Some of the great *aviador* houses which handled the rubber trade had their beginnings in the modest *comissários*.

The executives of Pombal's plan found themselves confronting an ever-shrinking force for several reasons. Those pressed into military service and dispatched on prolonged expeditions often died or deserted. Disease took a constant toll, striking with particular force after the *Companhía Grão Pará e Maranhão* began regular imports of slaves from West Africa. With no sanitation, no quarantine of the slaves, and no in-built resistance, Indian populations reeled under the blows of one pestilence after another. Under such conditions, many Indians preferred to escape to Belém or upriver rather than remain trapped in their villages, drafted to one labor detail after another by the state, by directors, by large growers or by slave masters. Labor for agriculture remained as unavailable as it had always been.[1] *Mestizos*, however honored in Pombal's hopes for miscegenation, similarly fled to Belém and esconced themselves along the estuary. There, freed from the tyranny of the directors, Indian and *mestizo* swelled an urban force of increasingly fractious laborers, no longer the wards of either Jesuit fathers or the Pombaline state.

Pombal's program came to grief on other familiar shoals: his brother handed monopoly concessions to his cronies and even such prizes as Jesuit ranches with their half million head of cattle on the island of Marajó, the proudest emblems of the colony's husbandry, were appropriated for state ranches and promptly turned over to a handful of well-placed social parasites whose real enthusiasms were far removed from any productive stewardship of these assets, as attested by the spiralling decline of the Marajó livestock industry in the nineteenth century.

The flourishing colony of Pombal's plan was undermined in part by the intensity of his own anti-Catholicism. He believed that the poverty of the colony could be explained in good measure by the exactions of the Society of Jesus. In Pará his brother was fortified in these suspicions by unscrupulous parties coveting the possessions of the Church and therefore greatly exaggerating the fortunes that were supposedly being remitted to Rome. Not for the last time in the Amazon the expectations of treasure vastly outstripped the reality. The Jesuits were expelled and the Church stripped of all important assets and economic potential, but the upheaval had no particularly benign cauterizing consequence. At the end of the day the only outcome of the Directorate's initiative was the creation of a class of free laborers and *caboclos* with a distinctive syncretic culture, insufficient in number for agricultural development, but ready for the next historical stage in their destiny – debt bondage – associated with the extractivism which reached its apogee in the great rubber boom.

So far from repelling the menace of any dangerous classes by a sedate yeomanry, Pombal seeded a legacy of explosive social discontent which erupted in the early 1830s in the famous Cabanagem revolt, when an alliance of forest peoples, exploited Indians, impoverished *caboclos*, and fugitive slaves from the *quilombos* could no longer endure the economic monopoly and oppression of the oligarchs and, as shall later be described, rose up in fury.

The Portuguese empire remained resolute in preventing Amazônia from presenting any challenge to the production of sugar and other commodities in southern Brazil. As the strategists of the empire conceived it, Amazônia's comparative advantage lay in the *drogas de sertão*, dyes, woods, cacao and medicines. But all the while a new extractive trade was already emerging in Pará, on the island of Marajó, up the Jari river and down the Tocantins.

THE RISE OF THE RUBBER TRADE

It is often supposed that the rubber trade in the Amazon did not attain any significance until the late nineteenth century, and scarcely any presence in world markets until Charles Goodyear discovered accidentally in 1839, and patented in 1844, the means whereby rubber, when combined with sulphur in the presence of heat, could be chemically stabilized in a process to which Brockedon applied the pleasing name "vulcanization" in 1842. But in fact, by the 1750s, not long after La Condamine reported in 1745 to the Académie des Sciences that he had seen "cahuchu", as he originally heard the Quechua native word in Peru, army boots and knapsacks were being sent to Belém from Lisbon to be waterproofed. Even Dom José, king of Portugal, dispatched his boots to Pará for this purpose. By 1768, Macquer had learned how to make rubber tubes and catheters. A year later, the chemist Priestley was erasing pencil marks with what the English then called India-rubber. Men were lofting themselves in rubber-coated balloons by 1785. By 1811 Champion was waterproofing materials for the French army, and a year later Baron Schilling used a rubber underwater cable to explode a mine in the Neva. Already by 1800 Belém was exporting rubber shoes to New England, with this trade reaching 450,000 pairs by 1839.[2]

A rubber factory making ladies' garters began production in France in 1803. By 1813 Clark was taking out patents on inflatable beds and pillows treated with rubber. The first British industrial factory for making rubber goods – awnings and pumps – opened for business in 1820. Charles Mackintosh found that naphtha added to rubber could make a waterproof coating for cloth, and patented his discovery in 1823. By 1827 a rubber hose had put out a fire on Fresh Wharf, London. The first rubber factory in the United States opened in Roxbury in 1828.[3] Given the associations of the words "rubber goods" it should be added that contraceptives made from rubber first seem to have entered commerce in the 1840s, after Goodyear's discovery.[4]

The consequences of the rubber trade upon Amazônia were predictable. Any zeal for patient agriculture diminished rapidly as rubber grew in importance and the infant trade began to shape labor and property rights.

The essential structure of the extractive industries in rubber, gold, and other forest products remained unchanged for over a hundred and fifty years. There were two familiar and constant constraints: scarcity of capital and of labor. The threads of investment and exploitation came together in Belém and to a lesser extent in Manaus. Here were the great commercial houses, financed initially by British capital, extending upriver to its outermost reaches a chain of credit and dependencies which ended in the shack of the isolated *seringueiro* (rubber tapper) or *caboclo* (backwoodsman).[5] On their debt peonage the entire structure reposed. The links from these shacks went directly to the trading post – *barracão* – where the rubber tappers bought their supplies on credit at grossly inflated prices and to which they sold their *peles* or balls of latex for a mere pittance in the form of goods. In this classic expression of unequal exchange flowered the extravagant fortunes of the rubber barons of Manaus and Belém, and of the principals' mercantile houses. The links in the chain could either be simple or extended, through *seringalistas*, river traders or commercial traders, but the balls of rubber always ended up in the warehouses of the trade houses – the *aviadores* – and thence to the export houses who were the agents for purchasers in New York and Liverpool.

There was very little state sponsorship or intervention in this network, which ironically had its origins in the small *comissários volantes* that emerged from the settlers' desperation during Pombal's Directorate. The state made no attempt to regulate the trade, well-known for extortions and cruelties, beyond its two concerns, which were levying export taxes at the port of Pará – that is, Belém – and ensuring that national sovereignty would not be eroded by international consortia – no idle fear, as we shall see. The state financed a few public works to assist in the export trade and to make Belém more congenial to its own nouveau riche and to the international businessmen who had increasing occasion to visit or to lodge there.

As the boom began to crest in the late nineteenth century it was already too late for rubber-based industrial development in the Amazon basin. The artisanal shops of fifty years before, producing rubber goods for export, were overwhelmed by the highly mechanized factories of the United States and Europe. Rubber shoe producers in Boston – in the heart of the industrial northeast – preferred to make their own latex-related commodities rather than import finished work of uneven quality from Brazil. The state of Pará belatedly mounted incentives for industrial development, but by the 1890s the damage had been done. There were machine shops in Belém to service river transport, which after all played a crucial role in the trade and was a real source of income, but there were no shops for the manufacture of processed rubber goods to compete on the international market. This told the story. In the crisp phrase of Barbara Weinstein, one of the best historians of the boom, "Pará earned a much-deserved reputation for producing what it could not consume and consuming what it could not produce." In both cases the beneficiaries were the captains of industry in the developed world and the local mercantile elites. Belém, one journalist lamented in the local Belém paper in 1895, had become "an emporium for foreign manufactured goods".

THE WORLD'S COVETOUS GAZE

Aside from levying taxes on exports, the state – first the Portuguese empire, then the Brazilian – was concerned with consolidating sovereignty, and with good reason. The naturalists and explorers who roamed through the Amazon throughout the nineteenth century often had as compromised an agenda as the anthropologists of a later date transmitting their findings on Indian groups to construction firms and government agencies. Only seven years after the *Savannah* had made the first steam-assisted crossing of the Atlantic from Georgia to Liverpool in 1819, North American entrepreneurs tried to send a steam boat up the Amazon to the borders of Peru. It was wrecked en route and steam boats did not make a successful appearance on the river system until the Brazilian government, headed by Dom Pedro II, subsidized the Amazon Navigation and Commercial Company organized by Baron de Mauá, with backing from British and Portuguese capital. Its steamers were in business by 1853 and operated for twenty years until the British bought out the line in 1873.

The most famous survey of the navigability of the Amazon was done in 1849 by two US Navy officers, Lieutenant Lewis Herndon and Midshipman Lardner Gibbon. Herndon's brother-in-law was Matthew Maury, the leather-lunged booster of free trade with the Amazon and of the desirability of its settlement. Maury, a native of Virginia and at one point head of the National Observatory had an overtly political agenda, crying:

> Let the slaves of the South be sold to the planter of the Amazon. The slaves of the South are worth 15 hundred million. Their value is increasing at the rate of 30 or 40 million a year. It is the industrial capital of the South. Did ever a people consent to sink so much industrial capital by emancipation or any other voluntary act?

Maury, who published a series of enormously influential articles on Amazônia in *The National Intelligencer* under the *nom de plume* "Inca", held the view common to nineteenth- and indeed twentieth-century First Worlders that the Amazonians were a shiftless bunch, incapable of developing their region. "She has arrayed herself," he said of Brazil, "against the improvement and the progress of the age, and she has attempted by intrigue so to shape the course of events that she might lock up and seal with the seal of ignorance and superstition and savage barbarity the finest portions of the earth; and if free men were to keep their silence the very stones would cry out."[6] Mme. Agassiz, accompanying her husband on his famous voyage, noted also that the hope for the region lay in colonization, "when the banks of the Amazons will teem with a population more vigorous than any it has yet seen – when all civilizations will share in its wealth, when the twin continents will shake hands and Americans of the North come to help the Americans of the South in developing its resources". Mr. Agassiz felt that 300 million people could clearly abide in the region.

Herndon's orders came not from Maury but from the US Navy, which requested him to explore the entire watershed of the Amazon, with regard to navigability and also to the terrain's possibilities in "the field, the forest, the river, or of the mine". He was also required to bring back any specimens or seeds he thought might do well on American shores. His report was finally published in 1854, three years before its author died in a storm off Cape Hatteras, going down with his ship and a cargo of gold bullion. However, his paeans to the wealth of the Amazon basin (and, it should be added, to the beauty of the region's women), aroused great excitement. Among those who resolved to set forth at once to make his fortune was a young man of twenty-one who read Herndon in Keokuk, Iowa, and took particular note of the navy man's account of coca, to which he attributed miraculous powers.

Mark Twain wrote later in his essay *The Turning Point in My Life:*

> I was fired with a longing to ascend the Amazon. Also with a longing to open up a trade in coca with all the world. During months I dreamed that dream, and tried to contrive ways to get to Pará. In New Orleans I inquired and found there was no ship leaving for Pará. Also that there had never *been* one leaving for Pará. I reflected. A policeman came and asked me what I was doing, and I told him. He made me move on, and said that if he caught me reflecting in the public street again he would run me in.... On my way down [the Mississippi], I had made the acquaintance of a pilot. I begged him to teach me the river, and he consented. I became a pilot.

And so Mark Twain embarked on the river that led him to Huck Finn and Tom Sawyer. With different shipping schedules, he might have ascended the Amazon and the Madeira.

RAILWAY TO EL DORADO

The civil war in the United States distracted attention from Amazonian possibilities but only for a season. One of that war's veterans was the soldier, journalist, and speculator George Church. He turned his attention to a reach of the Amazon which had recently acquired allure to the international entrepreneur.

By the 1850s the world's thirst for rubber had sent prospectors through more than 11,000 waterways making up the Amazon, looking for unclaimed swaths of rubber trees. The early arrivals seized huge territories. Particularly desirable were the lands that lay at the meeting of Brazilian and Bolivian territory, defined by the Madeira and its tributaries flowing in from the south – the Abuna, the Beni, the Mamoré, and the Guaporé. The valleys of these drainages and their interconnections with the headwaters of the Purus and the Juruá included the richest *Hevea* forests in the whole Amazon basin. But there were tremendous impediments to efficient exploitation. Scarcely three miles above where Porto Velho now stands beside the Madeira – at the old town of Santa Antonio – began a series of no less than nineteen cataracts and rapids formed by the meeting of the Brazilian Shield and the Amazonian *planície*. For more than 250 miles the river was un-navigable. Boats hauled up and down in exhausting portages only made three round trips a year. Straddling this waterway were the immense holdings of three rubber barons, the most notorious of whom was Nicolau Suarez, working his holdings with Caripuña Indians who were, in all but the formal sense, slaves. Suarez was not only the master of more than twelve million acres of rubber lands. He also ruled the rapids and could exact whatever tolls he desired.

Beyond these territories lay Bolivia and in La Paz the businessmen of that land-locked country dreamed of easy passage for their products on a railroad that circumvented not only the rapids but the extortionate tolls of Suarez. The age of railways had already dawned in Latin America. By the end of the 1850s tracks were being laid all over the continent and for the Bolivians rail and river passage down the Amazon presented a most desirable exit for yields of quinine bark from the forests of the Andean foothills, and from the enormously productive rubber holdings at the head of the Purus and the Juruá. In these watersheds they were then the masters of what later became the Brazilian state of Acre.

In this excited state they were addressed by George Church, who was later to announce to his North American readers that Bolivia was the ''Garden of the Lord''. Church persuaded them that a 225-mile railroad, running just to the east of the rapids on the Mamoré and Madeira to Santo Antonio, was feasible. Bolivia and Brazil approved the plan. Church raised one million seven hundred thousand pounds sterling in bonds backed by the Bolivian government, and thus set up the Madeira-Mamoré Railway Company.

In 1872 his first crew of British engineers arrived and advanced upon disaster. Their boats sank. Caripuña Indians attacked. Fever-wracked crews tried to escape their lot by plunging through the forests. After less than a year, the project was all over. In London, the Madeira-Mamoré stock plummeted from 68 to 18 points on the exchange. Told of the bankruptcy of their project, the remaining workers hastened downriver, leaving tools and equipment behind to rot and rust. Despite a harsh post-mortem by British financial assessors (who were told by the contractors that ''the region is a welter of putrefaction where men die like flies. Even with all the money in the world and half its population it is impossible to finish this railway''), George Church was irrepressible. He took himself to Philadelphia, a city beset with unemployment after the panic of 1873, which reached out to seize the glittering prospects that Church so eloquently unfurled. It was said that no less than 80,000 men applied to the offices of the contracting engineers P. T. Collins for the privilege of traveling to the heart of the Amazon. On January 2, 1878, the first complement of engineers, workers, construction materials, and even coal, set sail. Doubtless, the prospect of a railway line with no chunk of coal within thousands of miles also sent a shiver of pleasure through the spines of Pennsylvania coal mine owners, envisaging exports.

The frightful working conditions soon provoked discontent which expressed itself in conflicts between the Irish, German and Italian workmen. Incensed by Collins's higher wages to Irish and German workers, the Italians went on strike. One evening, seventy-five of them slipped off through the forest, heading for Bolivia. They were never heard from again. Another group of three hundred disheartened workers made off with a few canoes and floated downriver some sixteen hundred miles to Belém, where they arrived ragged and penniless.

Labor was in short supply. Rubber barons were already urging the *aviadores* in Manaus and Belém to send them fresh tappers, in part to capture new terrain and in part to replace the Indian tappers who had either died or fled. In a migrant pattern that has lasted till today, workers from the endemically drought-stricken Northeast moved west. Five hundred of these Cearaense workers arrived for jobs on Church's railroad and promptly began to die from yellow fever. By 1881, when the Brazilian government closed the project down, more than five hundred of the 1400 initial workers were dead. Much of the line had been surveyed, twenty-five miles graded, and four miles of track actually laid. An engine named after Church even pulled some work cars over a few hundred yards of this exiguous track,[7] before ingloriously jumping the rails.

THE LORDS OF ACRE

Consumed with the urgency of overcoming their geographic seclusion as a land-locked nation, the Bolivians had been evolving other schemes to reach the Atlantic waters. Crucial to all their designs was free passage down the Amazon, and in the irrepressible Maury they found a willing ally. Like the Bolivians, Maury thought it eminently just that the waterways of the Amazon Basin should be internationalized. As a geographer he had conceived the notion that natural forces linked the Amazon Basin to the Mississippi delta, given that the swirl of currents and winds offered easy passage between the two. This natural link could be consolidated with the ties of beneficial trade. The Brazilian government viewed any notion of free trade or free rivers with profound suspicion.[8] They feared with good cause that the sparse inhabitants lining the shores of Brazil could be easily seduced by foreign infiltration, surrendering their nationality and ties of the Portuguese language, which was often not their own since many river populations at this time were detribalized Indians, often happier speaking their own tongues or the *língua geral*.

However, the president of Bolivia, Belzu, was enchanted by Maury's ideas and yearned to bring them to instant consummation. He was what was described in that era as a rough diamond, of whom the refined Rio diplomat Duarte Ponte Ribeiro said sourly, "a soldier who had his home in the barracks or the brothel, who never appeared in decent society, and who never opened a book".[9] Belzu also offended Brazil's sense of propriety by threatening to shoot its commercial attaché in a public square in La Paz, thus prompting the prudent envoy to flee the capital. Such diplomatic humiliation was not unique in La Paz. Church later liked to tell friends of the *caudillo* Mariano Melgarejo, who gave him his railroad concession in 1869. Wearied of the complaints of a British envoy, Melgarejo lifted the skirts of his mistress and ordered the Briton to kiss her bare bottom. When the diplomat refused, Melgarejo had him paraded on an ass, facing backwards. Queen Victoria and her prime minister Palmerston ordered Bolivia's capital to be bombarded. Told that it was out of gunboat range, they satisfied themselves merely with erasing Bolivia from British maps.[10]

In January of 1853, arguing that free ports made free rivers, President Belzu decreed that the ports of the Bolivian tributaries of the Madeira[11] were open to international commerce and put up a $10,000 prize, a vast sum in those days, for the first foreign ship to tie up at a Bolivian port. This affront to Brazil's sovereignty demanded immediate response and the Brazilian government predictably answered Belzu's challenge with its view that both river and shores were under the dominion of the nation in which they were to be found.

The Bolivians were more interested in the principle of free passage, to move their goods through the Amazon rather than around the Horn. Neither Bolivians nor Brazilians had much sense of the immense potential value of their resources in the headwaters of the Purus, Juruá and the tributaries to the Madeira; the area was conceived as *terra incognita*. In 1866, both parties signed the Treaty of Ayacucho which drew between them an international boundary of great geometrical simplicity – a straight line west by northwest from the Beni to the headwaters of the Javari, whose geography was unknown. This omitted any recognition of political economy and thus of which country was capturing *de jure* the resources which had hitherto been held under the principle of *uti possedetis*. Bolivia had acquired sovereignty over the territory of Acre.[12]

This feat of diplomacy had no immediate consequence, but by the 1880s Acre was becoming one of the most commercially desirable stretches of territory on earth. At the signing of the Ayacucho treaty, the Purus only had some 240 houses on its banks. By 1877, the rising price of rubber and the particularly disastrous drought of that year in the Northeast impelled a tumultuous migration of up to 100,000 Cearaenses up the rivers, assisted directly by *seringalistas* or even by the *aviadores*. By 1887, Antônio Labre, *seringalista* and latterday *bandeirante*, noted that 500,000 kilos of rubber drained down the Acre/Purus, and that 10,000 souls could be found there.[13] Rubber was now integral to First World industrial development, and some 20 per cent of all the rubber revenues of the Amazon basin already stemmed from Acre and the Madeira drainage. With immense fortunes at stake, intrigue began to enmesh the priceless territory.

As the lands became more valuable, boundary commissions coursed through the upper Amazon trying to find the headwaters of the Javari. Of more nationalistic than legalistic bent, Colonel Taumaturgo of the Brazilian Frontier Commission of 1896 nervously observed that Brazil would lose the best portions of its territory and its "rivers that give the largest portion of rubber exports ... extracted by Brazilians".[14] The area rang with Brazilian surnames, and if a straight line between 10.20 latitude and the Javari at 7.10 latitude were taken, these lands would fall into Bolivian hands. Moreover, many of the landholders were awaiting definitive title from the Brazilian state. In a move that incensed Taumaturgo and the local populace, the Brazilian minister Dionysius de Cerqueira, based in Rio de Janeiro, informed the Bolivian envoy José Paravacini that Brazil still recognized Bolivian claims to Acre, even though conflicts in the surveys needed to be resolved. Paravacini felt that the results of further surveys would probably not favor Bolivia, and hence urged, indeed partook in, immediate occupation of the contested territory.

Bolivia yearned to see the line drawn on paper in the Ayacucho treaty assume material form in customs revenues and taxes. Its leaders fretted at the fact that the tappers and traders now flooding into their new territory were indubitably Brazilian and scarcely respectful of Bolivia's sovereign rights. For its part Brazil angrily rejected proposals that Bolivia start establishing customs houses and imposing tolls. As Paravacini set up the Bolivian port of Puerto Alfonso near the rubber estate of Lua Nova, local rubber barons looked askance. In a land where the main recourse was "Article 44 of the legal code" meaning rule by the gun (the reference is to the 44 Winchester), Paravacini's schools "for both sexes" and chapels were poor counterweights to his alarming statement that Puerto Alfonso and the rivers of the Acre, Purus and Iacó would be open to "the merchant fleets of nations friendly to Bolivia from the point where are found customs and storage houses to the limits of navigation". These were fighting words, especially since the discoverers of the great rubber estates now needed to petition Bolivia for the formalization of their concessionary rights. For people whose "desperate craving for fast riches in order to get out of the line of fire more quickly", and "profiteers of all stripes and speculators of all persuasions",[15] the formal niceties of the Bolivian bureaucracy were met with anger and increasing insubordination. The Bolivians sought to interdict all arms in the area.[16] The trading houses in Manaus and Belém assumed a predictably pragmatic posture. The local seringalistas and the aviadores of Manaus, already profiting greatly from the Acrean seringais, had the most practical reasons to support resistance to Bolivian demands, whereas their rivals in Belém hoped that if Bolivians assumed real control of the area they could make their own arrangements and prise loose the grip of the aviadores of Manaus. In any case, Belém was reluctant to see anything disrupt the lucrative flow of latex. Thousands of miles to the north, geo-strategists in Washington and robber barons in New York gazed at their maps of the Amazon and pondered how to turn the situation to advantage. Thus began the famous Bolivian syndicate.

THE BOLIVIAN SYNDICATE

The colonial charter company was one of the prime vehicles whereby imperial governments could undertake the administration and development of resources far from their shores. In exchange for grants and concessions, charter companies would carry out basic colonial administration, and the state would receive various portions of the revenues for a predetermined period of time, while infrastructure and administration would be the purview of the companies. Model charter companies of that time included the British South African Company, the German East Africa Company, and the Belgian Congo Company. A nation claiming an area would subcontract its administration and economy to a large firm which would raise international capital as well as receive initial funding from the nation claiming sovereignty.

Avelino Aramayo was a visionary Bolivian capitalist who saw the immense relevance of this form of economic exploitation to the *terra incognita* of the Bolivian Amazon. The rights of the Aramayo charter company were vast, and before its story ended, it implicated the names of the greatest capitalists of the day – Vanderbilt, Astor, Morgan – and the great diplomats, Hay, Baron von Richthofen, Nabuco.

The Aramayo charter was straightforward. The syndicate, based in New York, would have fiscal administration of the Acrean territory, the exclusive right to levy taxes, exact customs, tolls, and land rents in conformity with Bolivian law for thirty years. It had the right to use force to secure its privileges. No less than 60 per cent of the profits on the initial capital of 500,000 pounds sterling would go to Bolivia, and the rest to the syndicate. The syndicate could buy any land in Acre not claimed by others under Bolivian law. Mineral rights would be ceded to the syndicate. The syndicate would construct or subcontract the development of roads, ports, telegraphs, and other crucial infrastructures. The syndicate had rights of free navigation and could, at its discretion, grant navigation concessions. It would study ways of uniting the Acre river by rail with the rivers Orton and Madre de Dios.

Backed by powerful banking interests, the US Rubber Company, Metropolitan Life, and other shareholders aligned their fate with the Bolivian syndicate now called the Whittlesey-Aramayo Company. The Bolivians dissembled about the nature of the charter, but in essence, Acre was to become an American colony, in fact if not in name.

In the *seringais* of Bom Destino and Caquetá, José Carvalho and a few other disgruntled Acreans chafing under the exactions of Bolivian customs houses and Bolivian domination began their seditions and sent a missive to the delegate pointing to a "large popular movement against Bolivian authority". Descending the Acre river at five in the morning, Carvalho leapt ashore at Puerto Alfonso, demanding an audience with a sleepy Bolivian consul Santivanez, and declared, "Consul ... I come before you in the name of the people of this river and the

Brazilian people to notify you to abandon this place because we no longer tolerate the government that you represent.'' Taken aback, the consul demanded, ''And who is the leader of this movement?'' Carvalho replied vehemently, ''No one! We all lead this movement.'' Thus began the Acrean revolt. The manifesto of Carvalho's conspirators stated:

> The Brazilian people . . . notify you to abandon your illegal government in this terri-
> tory . . . tamed, inhabited, and today defended by thousands of Brazilians . . . . The
> people of this state have been extremely tolerant in the face of this shameful con-
> dition, sanctioned it is true by a disastrous Brazilian [foreign] minister . . . the passion
> of our will, so patriotic and so just, does not permit long argument. . . . This posses-
> sion [of Acre by Bolivia] is an insult to our sovereignty . . . we notify you to withdraw
> your government from this territory as soon as possible, because this is the over-
> arching will of the people of this municipality.

On May Day 1899, the proclamation of liberation was handed to the consul. On May 3, 1899, the consul left Acre. Paravacini, realizing his consul had fled, awaited salvation from the North.

THE ACREAN REVOLUTION

In March of 1899, the *Wilmington* of the US Navy tied up at Pará, and Chapman Todd stepped ashore to render greeting to the governor there. He spoke eloquently of the ''love which dignifies the human species'' but his real mission was to carry a secret agreement from Paravacini, the Bolivian diplomat eagerly awaiting him, to the US government. With momentous folly the Bolivian then asked Luis Galvez, a young journalist working for the *Província do Pará* to translate the Spanish docu-ment to English for him, assuming that Galvez's Hispanic ancestry would ensure his discretion. He misjudged his man. Galvez studied the document with incred-ulity. Its seven clauses spelled out a tremendous conspiracy. The United States would urge Bolivia's diplomatic cause upon Brazil; would provide Bolivia with all appropriate military assistance; would press Brazil to grant free passage through its customs and rivers of all shipping and products coming from the ports of Bolivia; would defend Bolivia's rights to this free transit; would receive a 50 per cent discount on all taxes on North American goods shipped to Bolivia; would receive for ten years, 50 per cent of all customs revenues on rubber shipped down the Amazon from Bolivia; would pay the cost of war between Bolivia and Brazil; would be granted about a third of Bolivia's Acrean holdings for colonization. An outraged Galvez hastened to his newspaper and published the document forthwith. But his sensational disclosure aroused no great excitement in Belém, whose commercial houses had, as we have seen, their own reasons for complaisance towards any plot hatched between Bolivia, the McKinley administration and the Bolivian syndicate, which included a relative of Teddy Roosevelt, later to travel with Rondon through the region and nearly perish.

Galvez was Spanish by birth, cosmopolitan by nature, and, in the phrase of Tocantins, adventurer by action.[17] He was also a revolutionary. "I am working in Belém," he stated, "on everything related to the palpitating question of Brazil-Bolivia sovereignty, and I am in complete agreement with the Acrean revolutionaries. . . ." He then continued on to Manaus and embarked on the revolution. Two million kilos of rubber came from Acre. Manaus as well as Belém swam in gold, and the governor, Ramalho Junior, was not disposed to see it evaporate. Dispatched with twenty men and a shipment of arms upriver under the pretext of scouting for rubber estates, Galvez appeared in late June at a *seringal* a few minutes' north of Puerto Alfonso where the Central Revolutionary Junta was esconced. In the political void created by the Bolivian consul's eviction and by Brazilian indifference, they agreed that the Brazilian nation had not responded to the Acrean pleas, and had thus forfeited sovereignty. They therefore founded the independent State of Acre, sometimes termed the Republic of Poets. On July 14, 1899, 110 years after the storming of the Bastille, telegrams were sent out to heads of state proclaiming Acre as an independent republic founded on the principles of the French Revolution. Amidst cheers, Galvez became president.

The wealth of Acre could not, however, be left to the devices of a few romantics. In La Paz, Manaus and Belém the counter-revolution was forming. Local *aviadores* and powerful politicians made their arrangements. In a coup d'état Galvez was replaced by the merchant Souza Braga, and banished to Fortaleza. Meanwhile, the Bolivians resolved to retake Puerto Alfonso. But a new champion soon emerged in the form of Plácido de Castro, a *gaúcho* and second son from Santa Catarina who had come to Acre to make his fortune as a *seringalista*. He had cut his teeth on many military actions, and was skilled in training and disciplining rough men. A man of blood rather than poetry, he was infuriated at the arrogance of the Bolivian syndicate, despoilers in his view, of the humanity of Acreanos. A *caudillo* in spirit and not given to egalitarian views, he still favored an independent Acre, given the spineless response of Brazil towards the invaders. He toured the region with a simple injunction to each of his fellow *seringalistas*: give me men or die. He proved adept at guerrilla warfare and after some months the Bolivians were in full retreat. Acre was Brazil's for the taking.

Plácido de Castro was ambushed in 1908 as a result of a quarrel with other *seringalistas*.[18] As President of Acre he had favored independence but was persuaded that its future would be best secured as part of Brazil. Rio Branco's skills were now displayed in the negotiations that produced the treaty of Petrópolis in 1903. He studied charts and stipulations of the treaty of Ayacucho and performed topological calculations tolerable only to a defeated army. Fifteen million hectares of Bolivian territory – Acre, the richest rubber-producing land in the world – would now pass permanently into Brazil's possession for a consideration of $2 million to pay off the Bolivian syndicate and a pledge by Brazil to finance final construction of the Madeira-Mamoré railroad. The Bolivians bowed to the inevitable. The treaty of Petrópolis was signed on November 17, 1903, and a statue of Plácido was raised in the central square of Rio Branco, where it can be admired to this day.[19]

The schemes of the Bolivian syndicate were not forgotten in Brazil, and help to explain why the notion of "internationalization"of the Amazon, put about by some North American and European politicians today as one solution to the crisis of deforestation, has a particularly sinister tone.

NOTES

1. Excellent discussions of the Directorate and the colonial economy in general can be found in D. Alden, "Economic Aspects of the Expulsion of the Jesuits from Brazil", in H. Henry and S. Edwards eds., *Conflict and Continuity in Brazilian Society* 1969; MacLachlan's 1973 articles, "Indian Labor Structure in the Portuguese Amazon", and "The Indian Directorate: 1757-1799" 1972; M. Morner, *The Expulsion of the Jesuits from Latin America* 1965; as ever, Hemming's *Amazon Frontier*. Parker's "Cabocloization in Amazônia: 1615-1800", is a very good summary. A more detailed discussion of the early mercantile history of Amazônia can be found in Manoel Barata's classic *A Antiga Produção e Exportação do Pará* 1915. A rigorous review of the Companhía Grão Pará e Maranhão documents is to be found in Manuel Nunes Dias, *Fomento e Mercantilismo: a Companhía Geral do Grão Pará e Maranhão (1755-78)* 1970.

2. See Warren Dean, *Brazil and the Struggle for Rubber* 1987. See also Santa-Anna Néry's *The Land of the Amazons* where he notes that long before La Condamine noted the use of cahuchu (Gallicized as caoutchouc), "Father Manoel da Esperança ... had found it in use among the Cambebas Indians" and he "called it they say by the singular name of seringa. Having remarked that these intelligent savages used it to make bottles and bowls in the form of a syringe, the good Father called to his aid his figures of rhetoric, and devised the name of seringa for the substance which served for the fabrication of these articles

for domestic use. Thence came the name of 'syringers' or 'seringueiros' by which the extractors of the milky sap are still known in Amazônia, and that of seringais given to the places where they extract this product by incision." Also see H.H. Edwards, *A Voyage up the River Amazon* 1847, and D. Kidder, *Sketches of Residence and Travels in Brazil* 1939. Also A.C.F. Reis, *O Seringal e O Seringueiro* 1953.

3. See P. Schisrowitz and T.R. Dawson, *History of the Rubber Industry* 1952.

4. It is tempting to trace the etymology of the word "condom" to La Condamine, since his name was associated with the importing to Europe of rubber artifacts. But the condom was not only in use by the seventeenth century, being then made of animal gut or fish membrane, but was specifically referred to by that name. There has been prolonged debate on what precisely was the name's derivation, with various proposed etymologies being traced by William E. Kruck, in his thoroughly researched monograph, "Looking for Dr. Condom", University of Alabama 1982. Kruck decided that an etymology from a "Dr. Condom" or "Conton" or "Condon" who supposedly supplied contraceptives to Charles II, cannot be sustained and that "the man and his act of invention ... are a myth". Kruck concluded that no one etymology was satisfactory. The word "Condum" first appears in print in 1706 in a poem by John Hamilton, second Baron of Belhaven. Belhaven had voiced fears about

Scotland's union with England. As a result of the debate over the twenty-five articles of the Union in 1706, a pamphleteer, employed by the Crown to promote the pro-union view among the Scots, wrote a poem rebutting Belhaven's alarm. Belhaven's response to this rebuttal, "A Scot's Answer to a British Vision", included mention that one perturbing result of the union would be increased sexual activity in the civilized land of the Scots because of the use of condoms. Belhaven wrote:

> Then Sirenge and Condum
> Come both in request,
> While virtuous Quondam
> Is treated in jest.

Apparently Belhaven was referring to Argyll's entry to Parliament and his mistaken use of the word, "Quondam". He first gives the correct name of the instrument, "condum", and then rhymes it with Argyll's malapropism saying that such an item would make mockery of Scottish decorum of past times, of quondam.

The use of the word "sirenge" does not indicate that Amazonian rubber goods were prospectively part of a licentious English assault on Scotland at the start of the eighteenth century, since "syringes", not made of rubber, had already been used in medicine and in attempts at contraception. As we have seen, an early European visitor to the Amazon applied this word, derived from Greek, to one of the rubber artifacts used by the Amazonian Indians, thus giving rubber the generic Portuguese name of *seringa*. The relevant histories are silent on the rise of the rubber syringe as a contraceptive device.

The first "Condom Revolution" occurred after Goodyear invented the vulcanization process in 1839 and patented it in 1844, making it possible to produce rubber condoms with relative cheapness. By the early 1900s, rubber condoms were widely available. However, it is reckoned that three-quarters of them were defective and the quality of many deteriorated within three months. While condoms became common, they were condemned as immoral and also dangerous by doctors.

In the 1930s, the second technological revolution occurred when the "latex" process was developed, making condoms from liquid latex instead of crepe rubber. The use of liquid latex and the introduction of automatic machinery made the condom even cheaper and in the early 1930s it came to light in an American Circuit Court of Appeals that one American manufacturer, Youngs Rubber Corporation Inc., sold 20 million in one year to druggists and doctors. Latex also improved the quality of condoms.

5. How was the rubber actually collected? The tapper would rise before dawn and, armed with tapping ax, gun and tin cap, walk the forest paths from one rubber tree to the next on his particular round. With a little ax (much later a knife), he would incise the bark and the latex would drip into a cup fixed below. Returning two or three hours later he would collect the latex in a can and return to his shack. There he would eat manioc, beans, and maybe dried beef and start to smoke the latex. He would make a fire of oily *urucuri* palm nuts and place over this a funnel – originally of clay, later of sheet iron. Then winding a bit of coagulated rubber round a paddle he would dip this in the can of latex and then dry it over the smoke, repeating the process until a large ball, or *pele*, of smoke-blackened rubber had formed. Sometimes *seringueiros* would adulterate their *peles* with manioc or sand, or increase their weight by adding wood or stones. The rubber would later be graded in Belém as "fine hard Pará", or semifine, "entrefina", or coarse, "sernambí".

6. M. F. Maury, *Valley of the Amazon: The Amazon and the Atlantic Slopes of South America* 1853. Maury was not the only North American to dream of exporting the economic relations of the Old South. In the late 1850s the filibuster William Walker, briefly president of Nicaragua, introduced slavery, partly as an effort to get southern backing for his enterprise.

7. J. Fred Rippy gives a succinct account of railroading in the Amazon in his book *Latin America and the Industrial Age* 1944, including some amusing material about Maury and Church. See also Manuel Rodrigues Ferreira, *A Ferrovia do Diabo* 1987.

8. Herndon in his Report, recounted how the Brazilian commander at the post he came upon after crossing the border from Peru, insisted that he give up his own boat and sail in Brazilian timber, thus maintaining the law – which remained in force till 1875 – that no foreign vessel could sail on Brazilian waters. Herndon was also careful to travel lightly, with a small party and trivial arms, so that the United States could not be accused of mounting an expedition. See William Herndon, *Exploration of the Valley of the Amazon*, edited by Hamilton Basso 1952.

9. See José Antônio Soares de Souza, *Um Diplomata do Imperio* 1952, and the *Pró Memória de Duarte Ponte Ribeiro* 1852.

10. See Charles Gauld, *Last Titan* 1964.

11. The Trinidade, Exaltação, Loreto, Renenvaque, Chimoré, Guarany, Coroico, among others.

12. The language of this treaty became the source of much contention, and Baron Rio Branco's ingenious solution eventually legitimized the return of Acrean territory to Brazil. The language of the 1867 treaty was as follows: ''From this river [the Beni at its confluence with the Madeira] will follow the frontier with a parallel line drawn at its left margin at the latitude 10.20 until it arrives at the source of the Javari.'' A safeguard was added in the case that the Javari did not reach the latitude of 10.20. This exception became, in the end, the war horse on which Brazilian claims were later fought. The addendum stated that, ''If the Javari has its sources to the north of the east-west line, it will follow the frontier from the same latitude with a straight line seeking the principal origin of the Javari.'' The debate over a straight line linking the two rivers or parallel lines became central to the conflicts later on. The central point was that if an *oblique* line connected the Madeira and the Javari, the drainages of the Iacó, Acre, upper Purus and Juruá would be gained by Bolivia. If the frontier line remained parallel to the 10.20 latitude, then Brazil would hold the spectacularly rich Acrean territories. As can be deduced from any effort to find this line on a map, no one really knew where anything was, which the Baron sensibly realized. A good account of these matters can be found in Leandro Tocantin, *Formação Histórica do Acre* 1961. See also Ferreira Reis, *O Seringal e O Seringueiro* and Craveiro Costa, *A Conquista do Deserto Ocidental* 1940.

13. See Antônio R. Pereira Labre, *Itinerário da Exploração do Purus ao Beni* 1887.

14. Taumaturgo de Azevedo, *O Acre* 1897. This volume of Taumaturgo's voyages of demarcation and diplomatic correspondence include many sarcastic comments on the spinelessness of the Brazilian diplomatic corps, as well as his dry exchanges with his Bolivian counterpart, José Pando.

15. José Carvalho, *A Primeira Insurreição Acreana* 1904.

16. Paravacini was concerned with any scheme that would swell Bolivian coffers. He sought succor from the clergy. Father Leite of the diocese of Labréa would not only undertake the sacred offices, but would also serve as an agent in administering a state-run ''life insurance'' firm. As forms of indulgence, rubber tappers would pay the curate for his blessings to ward off disasters. This was yet another in a series of vexations that grated the nerves of Brazilian settlers.

17. See Tocantin, *Formação Histórica do Acre*.

18. Plácido de Castro's death shows how little justice has changed in Acre. Dr. Nilo Guerra presented proof to the army that a group of ''individuals, publicly and notoriously known to have the most salient desire to murder Plácido de Castro, among them the names of Alexandrino José da Silva, Luiz Paulo e Antônio . . . the same that by day armed with rifles challenged with insults who would align themselves as friend or ally of Col. Plácido. Ambushed later on the Rio Acre, Plácido uttered his last words: ''Death is a phenomenon as natural as life. He who knows how to live will know how to die. I only lament that having had so much occasion for glorious death, these 'heroes' have shot me in the back.'' See Cláudio de Araujo Lima, *Plácido de Castro* 1973.

19. This was not the last time that Baron Rio Branco was involved in cartographic

uncertainty. ''That geographer-statesman failed in 1906–11 to clarify the exact location of the Juruena River from Gen. Rondon's surveys. This weakened the title of the American-owned General Rubber Co. to a huge tract of rubber forest. Rio Branco allowed Generoso Ponce, who violently seized the governorship of Mato Grosso, to steal the 33,000 square-mile concession by arbitrarily renaming the Juruena. The result was that the company invested in Asian rubber plantations, helping destroy Amazônia's one-product economy.''
Charles A. Gauld, *The Last Titan*.

The Rainforest.

Indian sketched by Midshipman Gibbon who accompanied Lieutenant Herndon on a voyage of exploration down the Amazon, under orders from the US government to determine the navigability of the Amazon basin and the ''character and extent of its undeveloped commercial resources, whether of the field, the forest, the river or the mine''. By the time of Herndon's trip the Indian population had already been decimated. Three centuries earlier Orellana's party had marveled at the extensive indigenous population established along the rivers.

Alexander von Humboldt.

Karl von Martius.

The Botanical Garden in Rio de Janeiro.

Richard Spruce.

The great naturalists and explorers of the eighteenth and nineteenth centuries catalogued natural resources and remitted important materials and advice to their sponsors in the Old World. ''How often have I regretted that England did not possess the Amazon valley instead of India!'' Spruce lamented. Botanical gardens played an important role in shifting plants of economic significance throughout the tropics. The garden in Rio was no different, as exotic plants from all over the tropical world were kept and acclimated there. Architectural fancies often obscure the important economic function these gardens had in earlier periods.

Brazil-nut tree.

Hevea brasiliensis, *the rubber tree.*

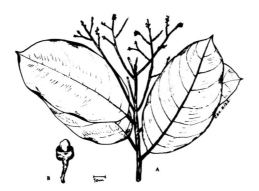

Aniba rosaeodora, *the rosewood tree, almost driven to extinction because of its oil.*

Jutaicica, Hymenaea courbaril, *much prized for its resin.*

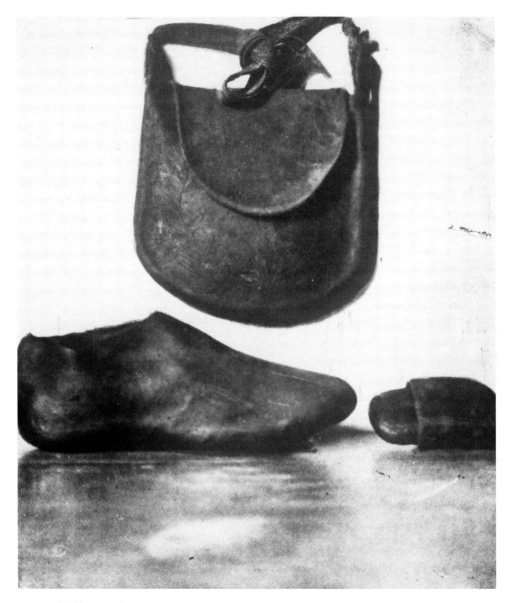

Rubber articles made by Indians on the upper rivers of the Amazon basin. By the 1750s army boots were being sent to Belém from Lisbon to be waterproofed. By 1839 Belém was exporting 450,000 pairs of rubber shoes a year to New England.

Indians enslaved on the Putumayo, on the rubber estates of the Peruvian Julio Arana, whose practices were exposed in Roger Casement's report published in 1912.

Yellow fever, malaria and other diseases wrought a fearful toll on outsiders seeking to exploit the Amazon's resources. These men were part of a medical team on site during construction of the Madeira-Mamoré railroad.

Turn-of-the-century Brazilian newspaper cartoon of the Bolivian Syndicate, a group of US tycoons including J. P. Morgan and a nephew of Teddy Roosevelt, which with the connivance of the McKinley administration schemed to gain control of the territory of Acre, then the richest rubber-producing area in the world.

Plácido de Castro, who led his fellow citizens of the Republic of Acre in driving out the Bolivians, thus foiling the syndicate. Plácido then agreed that Acre should become part of Brazil.

"Descalçou o par de botas mas nos custou muito caro." (Charge de Kalixto *in* "Correio da Manhã" 21-11-1903)

"We got out of those boots but it cost us a lot." Newspaper cartoon showing Baron Rio Branco and fellow Brazilians amid discussions that ended with Brazil indemnifying Bolivia for the latter's eviction from Acre.

FIVE

Magnates in the Amazon: Between Boom and War

The fear sometimes expressed that the rubber produced in the Amazon district will one day suffer when a substitute is found for it, or that the production will decline or disappear, is apparently quite groundless. Experiments made in other parts of Brazil, in Africa, Mexico and other places have not so far been very encouraging, notwithstanding that the trees planted have been treated with all the care and attention that experience could suggest. Nowhere does it appear that climatic conditions are to be met with equal to those of the selva of the Amazon for the growth of this remarkable product, where the rubber tree seems to thrive even better when left to itself than when any cultivation is attempted. Expert opinion all points to the Amazon rubber being undoubtedly an exclusive product, which need not fear the competition of any rival.

THE AMAZON STEAM NAVIGATION COMPANY, *The Great River* 1904

Things have not gone forward so well as they should have.

CARL LARUE TO HENRY FORD, FROM
FORDLÂNDIA PLANTATION 1930

The final crescendo of the great rubber boom had – as all booms do – a hypnotic effect. In the year 1906 the state of Pará exported just over 11,500 pounds of rubber. The boom had in fact reached its peak, though the crash did not come until 1910. The seeds transported by Wickham were now maturing in plantations in Ceylon, Malaya and the Dutch East Indies.[1] But in Manaus and Belém and in the investment houses of London and Paris optimism continued unbounded, paralleling the indifference of the *Californian* to the distress flares and rockets its crew could see being sent up by the crew of the sinking *Titanic*, news of which disaster reached Porto Velho almost at the precise moment the Madeira-Mamoré railroad was completed. As a report later said, the men on the *Californian* could not comprehend the possibility of disaster.

In fairness it should be said that not all were insensible of approaching peril. In that same year of 1904, the newspaper *A Província* was fretting about British progress with its plantations in Ceylon and Malaya, denouncing the local Pará elite for its "extractive mentality". The journalist, Ignácio Moura, warned that the Amazon's lead in rubber production was under threat and that something should be done.[2]

It was in this same year that Percival Farquhar first stepped onto the shores of Brazil.[3] In the long history of fatal ambitions for Amazônia nourished by North American businessmen, the names of Henry Ford and Daniel Ludwig leap readily into mind, yet Farquhar's hopes and, in the period of his triumph, his reach were much greater. At his apogee in 1912 he had a paper fortune worth $25 million and in that year controlled much of the economic activity of Brazil, in railroads, ports, river traffic, utilities and cattle ranching. The "Farquhar Trust" was a staple of nationalist execration and in popular apprehensions his name was synonymous with foreign capitalist plots to loot Brazil.

The object of these animosities was a Pennsylvania Quaker whose father had made a fortune exporting agricultural machinery. Farquhar was briefly a member of the New York state legislature at the start of the 1890s, being a Cleveland Democrat representing the old "hourglass district", including the Bowery and Gramercy Park in Manhattan. He was noted also in Albany as the only member of the Tammany machine to have a valet.

While Plácido was wearing down the Bolivians in the Acrean war, Farquhar was successfully joining battle with competitors from Cuba to capture enormously lucrative concessions for railroads and utilities following the withdrawal of Spain from its old dominion. His genius, evident in these struggles, lay in conceiving large schemes which his forthright manner and optimistic temperament rendered irresistible to the great financiers of the day. He had call on enormous pools of capital in Toronto, London, Paris and Brussels, and it was really only the outbreak of the First World War that finally destroyed his access to these markets.

In 1904 Farquhar had been considering a bid to bring electrification to Constantinople but was deterred by the fabled corruption of Abdul Hamid II, who also had the disadvantage – from the point of view of an investor in utilities – of regarding electricity as the work of the devil. Farquhar turned his attention to Brazil, and with the backing of Canadian capital, soon gained control of the utilities and tram system of Rio de Janeiro. In 1906 he bought the concession to develop the port of Pará at Belém, which carried a Brazilian government guarantee of 6 per cent interest on the capital, in addition to which the private company would receive a 2 per cent gold tax on all imports. It might have been supposed that Church's failures in the 1870s would have deterred any prudent businessman from involvement in a plan to build the Madeira-Mamoré railroad. But Farquhar was not prudent. In 1908 he bought the concession to build the Madeira-Mamoré, acquiring it for $750,000 in stock from a Brazilian engineer called Joaquim Catramby, who had put in an invincibly low bid when the government first offered the concession. Catramby amassed himself a great fortune in the last convulsions of the rubber boom, shocking Farquhar by boasting openly that he had scuttled rubber cargoes in the Madeira from time to time, since he could realize a greater profit on the insurance than on the sale of rubber.

Farquhar turned once again to his bankers in Europe. So great was his eagerness to get the Madeira-Mamoré concession that he even omitted to require the Brazilian government's guarantee of interest on the capital invested, to the subsequent fury of his French backers. He apparently thought that triumph over the difficulties that had crushed Church would greatly augment his reputation and ease negotiations and funding for his other plans. As he said later, "I hoped the achievement would be my calling card".

TYCOON ON THE AMAZON

Between 1905 and 1912 Farquhar sponsored the investment of $70 million in European capital in his schemes, without ever mustering detached expert opinion on the economic prospects of the Amazon. He himself never journeyed further upriver than Belém, and it was only after the boom ended that he commissioned a journalist, Charles Akers, from *The Times* (and also, it was rumored, from the Secret Service) to make a comparative study of the rubber economies of Amazônia and Asia. The study was pessimistic about the Amazon but Farquhar, to his credit, immediately published it. By 1908 Acre was exporting an annual $20 million worth of rubber and the state of Amazonas another $20 million worth; the federal customs in Manaus and Belém had collected $12.5 million in duties – or so alleged the numbers with which Farquhar reassured himself and his capital suppliers that they were investing in the surest of sure things. The automobile and electrical industries were rapidly expanding. Had not Humboldt himself predicted, a century earlier, that Belém was destined to be one of the world's greatest cities? How could they fail?

Farquhar had immense energy and was every inch a tycoon in the style of the period. In Paris he had a mansion on the Avenue d'Iéna and lived there alone, surrounded by twelve servants. He had a Rumanian fiancée, Cathya Popescu (to whom he was later married for many years) and would ride each morning in stately fashion in the Bois de Boulogne. Visitors would come upon him in a vast paneled office, surrounded by assistants, receiving and dispatching lengthy telegrams in code and constantly on the phone long-distance to London, Brussels and New York. Enormous difficulties confronted Farquhar at every turn. Belém was still notorious for yellow fever and Farquhar's port builders, vulnerable as anyone else, threatened to quit. He therefore imported Dr. Osvaldo Cruz, founder of distinguished institutions of tropical medicine and popularly known as the savior of Rio, to Belém. Cruz successfully eliminated the main mosquito breeding grounds in the area. As Farquhar's men began to push south from the infant town laid out by his engineers at Porto Velho, surveying, breaking ground and laying track, disease – mostly yellow fever, malaria, polio, and beri-beri – took a stupefying toll. In 1908 Farquhar had to hire 15,000 laborers in the course of one year in order to sustain an active working force of 1,000. Later he put up a 300-bed hospital at Candelária and enforced rigorous daily administrations of quinine to his workers.

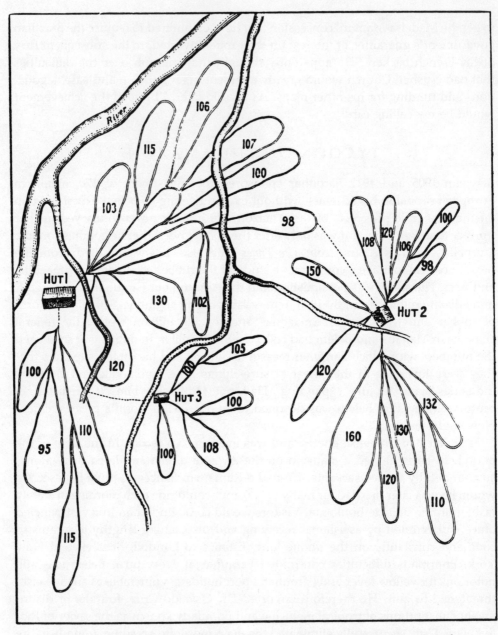

Plan of a seringal, drawn in 1911. It shows estradas, *the number of trees in each, and* seringueiros' *huts. Hut 1 houses 7 men, who work 15* estradas; *hut 2, 6 men, 12 estradas; hut 3, 2 men, 5 estradas.*

On the railroad the monthly payroll was $300,000 and wages were good, but even so there were periods of labor shortage, while the price of rubber soared to $2.50 and even $3 a pound. The *caboclos* and imported workers from the Northeast preferred to try their luck in the *seringais* rather than on the Madeira-Mamoré, which was garnering a reputation as a disease-ridden pest hole. Others were lured by the high wages that Farquhar was paying for his development for the Port of Pará. But the railway pushed forward, southwest to Manoa and the junction with the Abuña, then alongside the Madeira and then the Mamoré to its destination at Guajará-Mirim. In 1911 its cars began accepting Bolivian freight. The 30,000th patient entered Candelária hospital. On April 30, 1912, Farquhar's crews reached kilometer marker 366 and Guajará-Mirim, the same day that the Port of Pará opened. The ceremonial opening took place on September 7, 1912. Farquhar dispatched a golden spike from Paris, duly hammered in by the contractor Albert Jekyll's wife, Grace. The Brazilian president found the journey too demanding and the Bolivian *caudillo* thought it too risky to leave La Paz. The rusty old engine, ''Colonel Church'', was refurbished to make the maiden haul. The railroad had cost $33 million, some $20 million of this being paid by Brazil and the balance by disappointed European investors, most of them French, for the Paris financial markets had long specialized in financing government-backed projects. Farquhar reckoned that 3,600 men died during its construction, though a Brazilian historian, Ferreira Reis, suggests nearly double that number. Later in life Farquhar would compare costs and casualty rates with other such arduous endeavors: Henry Meigg's famous Andean railway built east from Lima in the 1870s cost $115,000 a mile as against the Madeira-Mamoré's $145,000 a mile, but it also cost over 6,000 lives; and the Panama railroad built by North Americans in the 1850s cost 10,000 lives.

FALL OF A TITAN

The Port of Pará and Madeira-Mamoré opened for business amid the collapse of the boom. In short order, rubber exports from Belém had fallen vertiginously, while 220,000 metric tons of food had to be imported for the Amazon. The receipts with which Farquhar hoped to finance his huge debt slowed to a trickle. He had always made inadequate provision of working capital to keep his enterprises going, and the debt loads were so great that years would have to pass before these enterprises paid for themselves. The Amazon fleet which he had bought out from the British in 1909 (by threatening to start a rival company with lower rates) and augmented with fresh, shallow-draught vessels, mostly lay idle in Belém. Nationalist outcries at his enormous holdings, including 60,000 square kilometers of land in Amapá, north of Belém, and land concessions in Mato Grosso, rendered the Brazilian government increasingly less co-operative.

The threat of approaching world war chilled Latin American economies and dried up the supply of capital from Europe. Brazil began to default on its debts, including money owed to Farquhar's concerns. Farquhar remained optimistic despite rapidly declining confidence among such canny associates as the financier Sir Edgar Speyer. The general manager of Farquhar's Brazilian Railway in São Paulo was Frank Egan who, throughout 1912, transmitted to Paris optimistic monthly reports. Bolstered by these tidings, Farquhar continued to acquire huge chunks of his own securities to boost their sagging value, buying on margin and selling off other interests to save his Brazilian enterprises. Early in 1913, while hosting a lunch in his mansion for bankers and friends, an aide, Dewey Brown, brought in a decoded message from Egan confessing that he had been falsifying the true state of the Brazilian Railway and offering his resignation. Farquhar, as he liked to recall years later, realized instantly that he was ruined, but put the cable in his pocket and continued lunch as though nothing had occurred.[4] He tried one last throw, seeking to raise a European loan of $300 million for Brazil, which would thus have been able to satisfy its debts to Farquhar's businesses. But as the clock ticked towards August 1914, the threat of war ruined his plans. Farquhar returned to Rio de Janeiro, where he spent the last thirty years of his long life vainly trying to win concessions to exploit the Itabira iron deposits in Minas Gerais which would rise to great prominence after the Second World War. In 1921 Brazil defaulted on the guaranteed interest payments on the Port of Pará, which was finally nationalized in 1940 along with the river line.

The Madeira-Mamoré lived on for sixty years. By 1912, Bolivia had built a rail link to the Pacific and the Panama Canal was soon opened. In 1919 the British took the line over and managed it until 1931, when the debt-ridden railroad was handed over to the government, which kept it in business until 1972 when it was closed in favour of a new highway, BR 364. Looters descended rapidly upon its assets and the archives in Porto Velho went up in smoke. By 1979 pressure from groups in Porto Velho and São Paulo prompted the government to prohibit further dismantling. Restoration of small portions at both ends of the line began, so that tourists and people could savour at least a small memory of this prodigious enterprise. Certainly the most eloquent testimony on the railroad's behalf was made by one of its former directors, Vivaldo Teixeira Mendes, in 1978, at a ceremony to commemorate its nationalization and its closure:

You, Madeira-Mamoré, were the railroad of the golden rails; you who were the backbone of the territory, you who were the road to hope, you who were the devil's own railroad, you who were sung in prose and verse, you who transformed Porto Velho, you who were the pioneer of civilisation and progress in this region – today your labours cease. The iron monster will no longer cleave the forest with its strident whistle. We shall no longer hear the strident shriek of steel upon steel. The children will no longer see Puffing Billy rush by, and will no longer in their innocence be told to wave goodbye. When all this ceases and your locomotives and wagons are laid to rest, then dear railroad, answer the call to come before the altar of the fatherland, stand to attention and salute the solemn, virile figure, the giant born of nature herself who has lain in a splendid cradle, and say, "Present, Brazil. Mission accomplished!"[5]

PLANTING RUBBER

In the aftermath of disaster, the Amazon faced a future which seemed to hold no prospect – to the elites of Belém and Manaus – of a return to their former high estate. The riches that seemed permanently assured – after all, the rubber revenues had been on a rising curve for a century – were suddenly gone and the governors of the northern states paced their ramshackle mansions wondering how to make ends meet. Even in the days of the boom the aggregate debt of such states exceeded their revenues and now there was nothing to pay for the civil bureaucracies that had swollen in the salad days. Now providing only 5 per cent of global rubber output, the Amazonian economies were prepared to do anything to survive. The governor of Amazonas thought nothing of offering no less than 500,000 square kilometers of state lands to a North American firm in exchange for some extremely vague pledges to develop it. After this ploy was exposed the federal government, anticipating similar initiatives by the military junta forty years later, protested at the potential injury to national sovereignty and sought to impose some administrative and fiscal discipline. For the most part, attempts to bolster the feeble regional economy took the form of state purchases of rubber when prices were low, against release when the market was more favorable. The model was the coffee purchasing schemes devised in São Paulo, but whereas the fluctuation in coffee prices often reflected climatic variations, rubber prices simply faced long decline. Amazonians complained that the union had been proud to claim the north only so long as their rubber trees wept latex and their proud *seringueiros* pushed back the Bolivian invader. Now that the dark days had come, the whole region had been forgotten, as a primitive embarrassment. The Amazonians complained; even threatened to secede. All in vain. Their prices continued to decline and the nation remained indifferent.

Naturally enough, the Amazonians began to consider rubber plantations. Since the largest market in the world was North America and the Amazon lay much closer to this market than did the plantations of Southeast Asia, it was logical to suppose that the Amazonians could simply copy the rubber production methods of British and Dutch colonialism and have the advantage of cheaper freight. This analysis soon found expression in the National Campaign for the Defense of Rubber, launched in 1912. The Campaign produced blueprints for plantations but interest soon waned when it was perceived that it remained much cheaper to cut costs by pursuing wild rubber extraction. The major problem which has so often spelled doom to plantation agriculture, not only in the Amazon, was the toll exacted by tropical nature.

Naturalists in the Amazon had always noted the considerable distance occurring between trees of the same species. Many tropical biologists suppose that this distance is a defense mechanism against diseases and pests otherwise afflicting species that grow closely together. Plants co-evolve with insects and plant diseases and the areas which are their centers of origin usually have a far greater number of these limiting pests. Plantations in these same areas destroy the protection of distance and permit far greater concentrations of the plant's traditional enemies. It was thus with rubber. The *estrada de seringa*, or rubber tapper's path, would take the tapper along a series of trees not less than a hundred yards apart, and thus the desirable quarantining distance between each tree was maintained. As soon as the rubber trees were planted in orderly proximity, disastrous blights immediately struck, none more devastating than *Microcyclus ulei*, the leaf blight of rubber. But once removed from their center of origin and accompanying panoply of pests, the rubber trees could be grown in plantations and thrive in the new and relatively disease-free environment. This is the rule of tropical production. Coffee, originally from Africa, reaches its most productive extension in South America far removed from the diseases of its place of origin in the Ethiopian highlands. Cacao, native to the Amazon, performs best in tropical forest far beyond Amazônia, whether in Bahia or Africa.

Without resistant stock, rubber plantations established in the Amazon itself were doomed to failure, as was evidenced by the disastrous experience of the next major North American investor after Farquhar seeking to extract a fortune from the region.

FORDLÂNDIA

As we have already seen, First World prospectors of the Amazon often felt that the sole impediment to success lay in deficiencies in the work habits and psychology of the locals. James Bryce lamented in 1912 that

> the white part of the Brazilian nation – and it is the only part that needs to be considered – seems too small for the task which possession of this country imposes. How men from the Mississippi would make things hum along the Amazon! In thirty years Brazil would have fifty millions of inhabitants. Steamers would ply upon rivers, railways would thread through the recesses of the forest, and the already vast domain would almost inevitably be enlarged at the expense of weaker neighbors until it reached the foot of the Andes.[6]

A visitor from the US Department of Agriculture, Carl LaRue, remarked in 1924, ''A million Chinese in the rubber sections of Brazil would be a godsend to that country''. In this perspective, the requirements of success were organization, capital and work disciplines of the advanced industrial world or, for that matter, of those vigorously regimented societies in Asia. To these intellectual delusions fell prey the most famous capitalist in the world, Henry Ford.

By 1922 the world glut of rubber was seriously afflicting even the Southeast Asian plantations. Four out of five of them were paying no dividends and a British official commission, known as the Stevenson Committee, recommended restriction in production. World prices rose soon thereafter. By now, world production seemed to be tilting towards a British and Dutch monopoly and since the industrial boom of the 1920s in the United States rested on automobiles which in turn rested on rubber tires, the secretary of commerce, Herbert Hoover, ordered a government mission to look for alternative sources of supply. In due course a group from the Department of Agriculture ascended the Amazon, at that time with the notion of acquiring seeds and developing rubber-tree plantations in the US colonies of Panama and the Philippines. Meanwhile Brazilian envoys, frantic to seduce investment to the Amazon, were making their own approaches to magnates such as Ford and Harvey Firestone. By 1927 Ford paid an entirely unnecessary $125,000, exacted from him by a Brazilian land swindler, Jorge Villares, for the land that Pará would have been eager to give him for nothing. The property, to be called Fordlândia, was two and a half million acres in size and stretched for seventy-five miles along the east bank of the Tapajós, south of Santarém. The state of Pará was happy to forgive the new Ford Company of Brazil taxes for fifty years, with a share in any profits after twelve years. It was essentially the same deal arranged by Farquhar when he was given land in Amapá, and by Ludwig, when he was given two and a half million acres in Jari in 1967.

Soon Brazilians were marveling at the neat company houses, school, sawmill, hospital and other facilities shipped in from Dearborn. A plantation of just under 7,000 acres was started and a deadline for tapping set for 1936. In the interim the sawmill would process and export hard tropical woods felled on the property. It was to be an enterprise in the Ford mould. Ford's industries were characterized by tight linkages with suppliers and rigorous control over labor. Fordlândia was to be a southern extension of the Rouge Plant in Detroit, with its integrated system of production.

Things went wrong from the start. The concessions to Ford became a contentious issue in state politics, and to deflect charges that he had been bribed by agents of Ford, the Governor of Pará, Dionisio Bentes, became unco-operative. The land itself was entirely unsuitable. The arrangements hatched between Villares and his probable North American co-conspirator LaRue had managed to set Fordlândia on some of the most undesirable terrain in the state of Pará, cursed with hills, stony outcrops and sandy soils, all of which were inimical to a successful rubber plantation, making it impossible to mechanize. The hardwoods were soon processed and the sawmill stood idle. Once the canopies of the young trees began to close upon each other, *Microcyclus ulei* struck savagely. In its first five years, there was no one at Fordlândia trained in agriculture or with experience in rubber planting. Its manager, Archibald Johnston, thought that *Hevea* branches, if stuck in the ground, "will take root almost without fail". Ford executives imagined that they would be blessed with an abundance of tractable laborers, thankful for a decent wage and free housing. But Fordlândia's recruits did not care for the rigorous corporate ethic imposed by the proconsuls from Dearborn. They soon protested and mass firings followed. Nor were the North American menus and cultural recipes such as square dancing particularly welcome. Worse still, workers were hard to get, and the Paraense state even discussed the importation of Asians to fill the gap.

Recruitment was hard for several reasons. In an area as remote as Fordlândia, labor was scarce. Many rubber tappers had returned to the Northeast at the end of the boom. Along the main Amazon channel, productive *caboclo* farms coupled with extraction trails required the labor of men who might otherwise be at Fordlândia, to satisfy the needs of the family and the local *aviador*. Small villages continued to exact labor corvées, and family crises or celebrations incurred debts that had to be paid through extractive goods. The tappers and *caboclos* viewed their jobs at Fordlândia as a seasonal enterprise, to be put aside when necessary for other seasonal activities such as planting, harvesting or extractive jaunts into the *selva*. Pay scales at Fordlândia exceeded regional wage norms by a large margin, but many of the workers found the concomitant corporate control not to their liking.

By 1941 the Ford Company of Brazil had 2,723 employees working in its forest plantations, but the writing was on the wall. In 1934 the enterprise had been moved to more favorable terrain at Belterra, further down the Tapajós, but *Microcyclus ulei* struck once again. Disease-resistant grafts and clones were brought in from Sumatra and Liberia in an attempt to beat back the blight. All fifty-three introductions turned out to be susceptible, and no less than twenty-three varieties of insect predators also attacked Belterra. Grafting was labor-intensive and enormously costly. The masters of capital retreated. In 1945, after an overall investment by the company of nearly $10 million, Henry Ford II sold Fordlândia and Belterra assets to the Brazilian government for $500,000.[7]

VARGAS, ROCKEFELLER AND THE "BATTLE FOR RUBBER"

The 1930s were the decade of President Getúlio Vargas, and with the arrival in power of this famous *gaúcho* from the south, there was born for the first time since Pombal a comprehensive strategy for regional development. And if Vargas echoed Pombal, he also presaged the generals of the 1960s. As the artificer of the first Brazilian economic miracle in the late 1930s he well understood the unifying power of his famous slogan "The March to the West"; that is, the integration of Brazil's interior – including the Amazon – into the national destiny as a whole. Fired by dreams of an Amazon dominant in global commodity exchanges and supplying Brazil's burgeoning industrial requirements, Vargas felt that the twin concerns of economic recuperation and integration of Amazônia would be served by the revival of the rubber economy.

The policies of Vargas's *Estado Novo* were argued in "modernizing", authoritarian terms. Vargas saw his opposition as either the old corrupt oligarchs or the rising communist movement marshaled by Colonel Prestes, both of whom threatened his own strategy of entrepreneurial industrial corporatism. In Vargas's view, these oligarchs and communists had only parochial concerns. What the nation required was a professional military and bureaucratic class whose loyalties would be to the state and to an overarching national vision. As war once again drew near, it became plain that with rubber a strategic material, prudent powers would stockpile as much of it as possible. The chemists of the Third Reich were already hard at work seeking a synthetic version, which I.G. Farben would eventually discover and manufacture with the most horrible of all corvées at the Auschwitz complex. Even before the war, Germany was buying almost 80 per cent of the Amazon's rubber. It was also clear – though to Britons implausible – that Japan could menace the rubber plantations of Malaya and the Dutch East Indies.

Vargas and US officials began to nourish their plans. Vargas – himself suspected of favoring the cause of the Axis powers – had a clear object in mind. The Allies' thirst for rubber could be used as a fulcrum to lever millions in development money into the Brazilian economy, accelerating industrialization, re-equipping the military (on whose beneficence Vargas ultimately depended), and invigorating trade. Thus long term benefits could arise from this short-term crisis. However, the efforts and attention on the Amazon would placate the "Integralists" – the Fascist party – whose geopolitical fears about occupation of the Amazon were falling on eager ears. His political agenda for national integration would thus be satisfied. Washington saw its course as one of securing as much rubber as possible, and of neutralizing any tilt in Brazil towards the Axis. Eventually the Board of Economic Welfare and the Inter-American Affairs Agency – in which Nelson Rockefeller was a moving spirit – forged agreement on what would be offered Vargas: $100 million would be made available for the general mobilizing of the Brazilian economy, of which $5 million would be specifically dedicated to the production of rubber, with the Rubber Development Corporation as the officiating agency. The United States would create a rubber credit bank with capital from the US, Brazil, and private investors, and control over the purchase and sale of rubber. The *Banco de Crédito da Borracha* (BCB), was the first real development bank for Amazônia and served as a template for future state lending institutions in the region. It would ultimately be the co-ordinator of exports, supplying the necessary capital for transport, health and labor recruitment. Brazil, after satisfying its own domestic requirements, would export the remainder to the United States at the fixed rate of 39 cents a pound.[8] There would be back-plans for colonization of the Amazon and other forms of credit.

And so the *batalha da borracha* – the battle for rubber – began. Vargas kept his side of the bargain. In charge of obtaining the labor supply for the rubber boom was a crony of Vargas's called João Alberto Lins de Barros. A person of maniacal tendencies and visionary energy, he had been a leader of the Prestes column as it had marched through the backlands in a drive, similar to Mao's "Long March", to inspire the masses to revolution. He became the Co-ordinator of the Economic Mobilization for the Brazilian War Effort and was particularly intrigued with the Amazon dimensions of the program, specifically its labor recruitment.

In 1942 a drought once again parched the Northeast of Brazil. João Alberto proposed that the *flagelados* – the impoverished sufferers of the Northeast – be immediately encouraged to go to Amazônia, and he began to plan for the first government-financed mass migration in Brazil. With characteristic imagination he thought that some 80,000 men could be convinced to move to Amazônia. Recruiters for both the Army and the *batalha da borracha* scoured the back hamlets of the Northeast, promising a future more glorious than starvation at least. João Alberto's view was that if the Prestes column, himself included, could march through the backlands between São Luís and Belém, so could the "rubber army". He set up staging points along the Tocantins river. He was eventually convinced to rethink his approach and a maritime service as well as overland marches were finally mobilized. He also envisioned colonization along with this migration so that a humming agricultural economy might also flower from the patriotic rubber endeavor. He was sharply reprimanded by Nelson Rockefeller, who echoed many an Amazonian businessman. No activities should compete with the urgencies of rubber collection. The *Serviço de Mobilização de Trabalhadores para Amazônia* (SEMTA) was frantically trying to get 50,000 workers to the region in one year. In the end, only about 9,000 were recruited, under misleading conditions that shocked both the US co-ordinator of the Credit Bank, Douglas Allen, and a then unknown Catholic priest – later to become a prominent activist and Archbishop of Recife – Dom Helder Câmara, who urged that SEMTA be disbanded. The cannon fodder in this rubber war were then given a month's training in Belém and sent to the front, delivered once again to virtual peonage at the hands of *seringalistas*. The labor shortage stimulated another influx of capital for recruitment of some $2.4 million for yet another agency that would deliver men to the *seringais*. Promising 16,000 workers, they ended up delivering only 6,000. In an attempt to override the debt peonage system, new contracts between *seringalista* and *seringueiro* stipulated that some food cultivation be allowed, and that 60 per cent of the profits of the rubber sales would go to the worker. Since most *seringueiros* were illiterate, such contracts were easily ignored by *seringalistas* who imposed their usual discipline on fresh bodies from the Northeast.[9]

The continuing inefficiencies in labor procurement culminated in reinstatement of the "free market" system. The Rubber Development Corporation gave over the labor recruitment to the *aviador* houses, which, after all, were long experienced in this sort of activity. Soldiers, one veteran remarked sourly forty-five years later, got their wounds treated in hospitals. In the *selva*, the rubber war workers fought in isolation, and when stricken by disease or mishap, suffered or died alone. Between 1940 and 1945 the region's annual output of rubber rose by 10,000 tons. Once again the remote *seringais* were stocked with fresh recruits from the Northeast, and once again there was an avid market. But when it was all over, nothing had really changed, just as nothing had really changed by the time the Amazon awoke to the aftermath of the boom in 1910. The press-ganged *seringueiros* were abandoned to the forest. There were, however, the new airfields built by the North Americans in joint venture with Brazilians to counter the possibility of Axis powers using secret Amazon landing fields for a sneak attack on the Panama Canal. The indefatigable João Alberto's *Fundação Brasil Central* had tried to incarnate the "March to the West" in a colonization and transport program located at the Araguaia-Xingu area which would link Amazônia with the south. Using the language of patriotic *bandeirantismo*, he tried to get large industrialists from São Paulo to create private companies to develop resources and bring in immigrants, a scheme that fell for a while on deaf ears.[10] There was a development bank now, the BCB, the most recent incarnation of the original strategy of Pombal, but even so, the Amazon began once again to slide to the margins of world history, until the sixties dawned and at last the "March to the West", and to destruction, began in earnest.

NOTES

1. Legends have been woven from the transfer of rubber tree seeds from the Amazon basin for British and Dutch plantations in Southeast Asia. The following summary is closely based on Warren Dean's finely researched account in his *Brazil and the Struggle for Rubber*, Cambridge 1987.

In 1836 La Condamine sent back to France samples of Castilla rubber from Ecuador, where it was called Hévé. He called rubber Caoutchouc. A decade later he found Seringa rubber on the Amazon and confused it with Castilla. In 1775 a French naturalist Fusée Aublet published a description of a rubber tree in the Guianas which he called *Hevea guianensis*, not realising that La Condamine's Hévé tree had nothing to do with his Seringa tree. Finally in 1807 Carl Ludwig Willdenow, director of the Berlin Botanical Gardens, got a specimen of Seringa to which he gave the name *Hevea brasiliensis* in 1811.

The removal of seeds of *Hevea brasiliensis* via London to the plantations of Southeast Asia, thus destroying the Amazon's rubber boom in 1910, happened as follows. A Brazilian, José da Silva Coutinho, had been advocating rubber cultivation to Brazilian authorities in the early 1860s and probably was the person who dispatched *Hevea* seeds to Rio de Janeiro where they were planted in the grounds of the National Museum. In 1867 Coutinho was one of Brazil's representatives at the 1867 Universal Exposition in Paris where, as chairman of the jury that evaluated various types of rubber, he showed that *Hevea brasiliensis* was superior, and even reckoned the costs of plantation production. The jury's findings were published in the official record of the Exposition, and studied with interest by James Collins, curator in Britain of the Pharmaceutical Society. Collins published his own account of rubber forthwith, which aroused the attention of Clements Markham, who a decade earlier had successfully organized the transfer of the cinchona plant from Peru (with the help of Spruce) to India. The transfer and subsequent Asian production of quinine was a turning point in the history of First World penetration of the tropics, since it offered salvation from the malarial mosquito in the various colonial backwaters. In 1870, while working at the India Office Markham began to ruminate on the idea of cultivating rubber trees in Britain's Asian colonies. In 1873 he asked the Foreign Office to request the British consul in Belém to supply *Hevea* seeds, suggesting that help might be sought from Henry Wickham, then residing near Santarém. Wickham had already written to Joseph Hooker, director of Kew Gardens, offering to collect specimens of possible importance.

The first consignment of *Hevea* seeds was actually brought to London in person by Charles Ferris, who had been in correspondence with Collins, and who was paid £5 for 2000 seeds which were planted at Kew. Twelve germinated, of which six were sent to the Botanic Gardens in Calcutta where three were left after a year. None appear to have survived. Wickham, very much down on his luck and sustained partly by the good offices of the exiled Confederate colony living near Santarém, offered to cultivate *Hevea*, the better to send a consignment of seeds. This offer was rejected but Markham told Hooker to inform Wickham that the India Office would buy any amount of *Hevea* seeds from him. By the spring of 1876 Wickham was on the Tapajós, collecting seeds from cultivars inferior to the trees in the Acre and Madeira drainage that benefitted greatly from the longer dry season there.

From Wickham later came increasingly glorious accounts of his fateful transfer of the seeds: his surreptitious collection of some 70,000 seeds; decisive chartering of a British ship, the *Amazonas*, at Santarém, onto which he loaded the baskets of carefully packed seeds, along with himself, his wife and his possessions. With solemn representations from himself and the British consul in Belém that ''delicate botanical specimens'' were being shipped to Kew, the chief of customs at Belém gave permission for the export of the Amazon's most precious asset, the seeds of *Hevea brasiliensis*.

With pertinacious scholarship Dean shows this account to be either suspect or certainly untrue. Wickham's motive was to exaggerate his own resourcefulness and the difficulty of his mission to the point where he would be rewarded by a grateful nation with money and honors, both of which he received in due course, being knighted near the end of his life. In fact he collected the seeds with the permission of the *seringalistas* and almost certainly with the knowledge of the authorities. His story of the chartered ship was fanciful and his mysterious "Baron do S", the chief of customs in Belém, another fiction. At that time there was no prohibition of the export of rubber seeds.

By June 15, 1876, Wickham's seeds were at Kew. On August 9 1,919 of the seedlings were sent to the botanic garden at Peradeniya, in Ceylon's capital, Colombo. Anyone interested in the blindness of bureaucracy should read Dean's account of Markham's desperate efforts to get the India Office to remit to Thwaites, the Peradeniya garden's director, the freight charges without which the shipping company refused to release the seedlings. Markham had to carry the invoice all the way to Louis Mallet, the secretary of state for India, a man of great stupidity who did not realise that with his tranfers of cinchona and *Hevea brasiliensis* Markham was certainly one of the most valuable servants the British Empire would ever know.

From this shipment stemmed most of the genetic stock of *Hevea brasiliensis* throughout the British and indeed Dutch colonies. By 1881 the first experiments in tapping Wickham's stock began at Heneratgoda research station in Ceylon. Plantations were established in Ceylon and Malaya. By the end of the century the Dutch, French and Belgians were all sponsoring plantations in the Congo, Java, Sumatra, Cochin China and Cambodia. By 1907 shipments of rubber from Asian plantations had reached 1,000 tons. By 1910 almost a million acres were given over to *Hevea* plantations in Malaya, with 250,000 acres similarly planted in the Dutch colonies. Dean reckons that by then there were "more *Hevea brasiliensis* growing on Far Eastern plantations than growing wild in the Brazilian Amazon!" The great rubber boom in the Amazon was over. Wickham may have exaggerated the circumstances of his achievement but we should leave him on the kinder note of Dean's final assessment: "For all the amateurism and desperation of his exertions, he had succeeded where dozens, perhaps hundreds, of better-equipped adventurers and even professional botanists had failed. Within thirty years a few basketsful of seeds had been transformed into an agricultural resource of immense consequences in world trade and industry."

The hopes for rubber in the British colonies may readily be gathered from the reflections of Sir Henry Blake, Governor of Ceylon between 1903 and 1907 (and great-grandfather to one of the present authors, Alexander Cockburn). As early as 1894 Sir Henry, then Governor of Jamaica, had been trying to introduce rubber plantations to the Caribbean. The edition of the (London) *Morning Advertiser* for January 15, 1908, carried an account of a speech Sir Henry had made the night before at the Royal Colonial Institute on "Ceylon of Today". After dealing with the two great industries of the island (tea and cocoanuts), Sir Henry Blake said that within the past four years another industry had come to the front that widened the basis of Ceylon's prosperity and bid fair to become the second in value, if not the leading export of the island. In 1903 there were but 11,595 acres planted with rubber. Then came a great rise in the market price, and capitalists realized that Ceylon possessed all the necessary capabilities for the production of so valuable a crop.

Land was taken up in feverish haste, and every officer of the Government who could assist in its survey, settlement, and sale, was devoted to the duty of satisfying the demands of impatient capitalists. In a colony where large numbers of proprietary rights were undetermined the Government was bound to ensure that every title granted to purchasers should be valid and free from claims, and that in many cases this process necessarily involved considerable delay; but the Government did everything in its power to expedite matters, with the result that up to the middle of last year the area acquired and being cleared for rubber was over 120,000 acres, and companies had been formed with an aggregate capital of 700,000*l*.

There were at present at least 140,000 acres planted with rubber in Ceylon which, on the estimate he had adopted, would in six years return annually 14,062 tons. . . . Having regard to the amount of land opened for rubber it was evident that the labour supply must be increased by probably 150,000, and a considerable number of European superintendents and managers would be required. The demand for increased labour came at a time when the competition for Indian coolie labour was intensifying. In the competition Ceylon had a great advantage, for not alone did it lie at the very door of the South Indian recruiting districts, but it was the birthplace and early home of numbers who came and went in the annual movement of coolies.

In 1906 Sir Henry presided over the Ceylon Rubber Exhibition held at the botanic station at Peradeniya, whose booklet for visitors compared plantation rubber with the products of the Amazon, to the great disadvantage of the latter. In 1914 he was similarly president of the Fourth International Rubber Exhibition in London, extolling rubber as the accompaniment of man in all stages from the teat on an infant's feeding bottle to the rubber wheels of a hearse. At this exhibition the North British Rubber Company provided a writing room demonstrating the versatility of the product. As described in *The African World*,

The apartment measures 20 feet by 15 feet. The walls have a rubber material of pleasing appearance. . . . Hard rubber frames surround the pictures. . . . The writing table and other tables in the room, as well as the Chesterfield and the chairs, are made from rubber. . . . The ink stands and even the penholders are entirely of rubber. . . . The window has prettily designed rubber curtains. They are attached to rubber rings and hung on a rubber pole. . . . Another novelty is the rubber tennis court. . . .

Sir Henry was an ardent advocate of rubber pavements, pointing out in one letter published in *The Standard* on October 13, 1915, that the shell-shock experienced by soldiers in the trenches was mirrored by the terrible din of carriage traffic in Britain's major cities ''where the nervous system and brain power of businessmen are gravely affected by the noise of the traffic''.

2. See Wickham. In 1910, Farquhar's employees worried in their in-house sheet, *The Porto Velho Marconigram*, that

plantations in Ceylon and Malaya had expanded to over 300,000 acres. It is often a condescension of history that everyone in the path of approaching disaster was too stupid to see it coming.

3. By far the best source on Farquhar, reflected closely in the following pages, is Charles Gauld, *The Last Titan, American Entrepreneur in Latin America*, published as a special issue of Hispanic American Report, put out by the Institute of Hispanic-American and Luso-Brazilian Studies, under the directorship of Ronald Hilton at Stanford University, in 1964. Gauld's 427 page monograph must be one of the most detailed accounts of an entrepreneur in the history of business scholarship. Based on long hours with Farquhar and his associates, plus much archival research, it is essential reading for anyone trying to understand the mentality as well as the day-to-day practices of the capitalists plunged in Latin American investments at the turn of the century. Gauld's perspective is often that of Farquhar, but such sympathies are clearly visible.

Other sources include some sarcastic passages about Farquhar in Rippy. See also Manuel Rodrigues Ferreira's extensively researched *O Ferrovia do Diabo*; *Madeira-Mamoré: Image and Memory* 1968, an exceptionally beautiful volume of photographs by Marcos Santilli of the old railroad and of survivors who worked on it with accompanying interviews and a useful map.

4. In the etiquette of ruin, Farquhar had strong nerves and impeccable manners, assuming his story was true. For the behavior of Farquhar's old associate, Sir Edgar Speyer, on the day of the Wall Street Crash, in 1929, see Claud Cockburn's memoirs.

5. Vivaldo Teixeira Mendes also said, ''Thus, on July 10, 1972, at 7 pm, when the moon shone brightly in the sky, in this same square twinkling with the lights of five of our locomotives, all of them with a full head of steam, puffing and snorting as if they were eager to depart, or as if they were protesting at the closure, almost the

whole population of Porto Velho gathered to witness the final termination of operations on the Madeira-Mamoré railroad. It was the end, the last chapter in a saga which had begun in the remote past of 1872. . . . The population shed tears, the whole crowd was moved by the incessant loud bellowing of the locomotives." *Madeira-Mamoré*.

6. James Bryce, *South America: Observations and Impressions* 1912.

7. There is an informative account of Fordlândia, and of the internecine corporate warfare there in Dean, *Brazil and the Struggle for Rubber*, though Dean is inclined to discount later problems preferring to stress – as he does in his whole history of the Amazon's post-boom rubber economy – the central importance of *Microcyclus ulei*. Marianne Schmink has a succinct essay on Fordlândia and Ludwig's disastrous project at Jari, in "Big Business in the Amazon", in *People of the Tropical Rain Forest*, eds. Julie Sloan Denslow and Christine Padoch 1988.

8. The native Amazonians would have much preferred the unregulated world price of rubber, since it was once again soaring, and the old glory days had not receded from memory. Vargas did not want his infant industries to be priced out of existence by a clique of Amazonian rentiers. The solution was to provide bonuses for rubber delivery in excess of projections. In 1944 the price in any case had to be adjusted up to 60 cents a pound. These increases in the value of the product were in no way reflected in the quality of life for the labor force.

9. The story of the Battle for Rubber relies on John Galey's unpublished Ph.D. thesis, *The Politics of Development in the Brazilian Amazon, 1940–1950* 1977; Pedro Martinello, *A Batalha da Borracha na Segunda Guerra Mundial* 1988; Dennis Mahar, *Frontier Development Policy in Brazil* 1979. For a political overview of the period see T. Skidmore, *Politics in Brazil* 1967.

10. For a stirring story of João Alberto, see C. Telles, *História Secreta da Fundação Brasil Central* 1946.

SIX

The Generals' Blueprint

Geopolitical truth is like a porcupine. It doesn't know much, but it knows one big thing. And here is the power of geopolitics properly applied. It is robust in perspective, admittedly partial, always incomplete, schematic even, and at times fanatic. In the end it unifies and clarifies, and imposes on complex reality its imperatives, to plan and to act.

GENERAL GOLBERY DO COUTO E SILVA 1957

Amazonian occupation will proceed as though we are waging a strategically conducted war.

GENERAL CASTELLO BRANCO 1964

As the Second World War ended, the forests of the Amazon stretched almost as far as they had two hundred years earlier. Yet within thirty short years the trees had begun to fall; a decade after that, the Amazon had become once more the focus of world concern, just as it had been when Roger Casement publicized the horrors of the rubber boom on the Putumayo in 1912.

By the mid 1980s there was no shortage of explanations as to why the forests were burning. Malthusians argued that hungry peasants and their large families, abandoning mountain farms in the Andes or the drought-stricken Northeast, or pushed by population pressure off the ever more subdivided plots in the South, had flooded into the Amazon. There they were clearing the forest to win some scant agricultural return to feed their burgeoning families.[1]

Others, following Garrett Hardin's famous thesis on the "tragedy of the commons", proposed that the pressures of rising population and market forces on communal land holdings were generating inappropriate and environmentally destructive uses of land.[2] Individual gains were achieved by the environmental degradation of the communal resource, a small cost borne by all. Thus the individual incentive to abuse resources was high, while the penalty for such abuse was low. The solution, according to Hardin, was private property. By making the destroyer

feel the direct consequence of his actions on his property, management of resources would improve, since the costs would be felt by the producer and not by
the community.

Unsurprisingly, many disputed the notion that expanding capitalist property
relations would reduce environmental degradation of commonly held resources.
They protested that it was in fact the incursion of capitalist markets and social
structures that was doing the damage, since the capitalist imperative was to exploit
people and resources mercilessly in the search for profit. In their unlovely jargon,
environmental degradation is merely an "externality", a cost that falls outside of
entrepreneurial calculation, and one that regards the destruction of a forest or
other resources as merely the price of progress.[3]

In this perspective of the Amazon, the exploiters were often seen to be the
international firms of the First World, mostly international mining and timber
consortia, extracting resources and profit and leaving ruin behind them. An associated argument proposed that the exploiters were not necessarily international capitalist firms per se but merely international markets, luring the Amazon into
thriftless production for export, as in the claims for the notorious "hamburger
connection", where the fast-food chains of North America keep costs low by
buying cheap Third World beef raised in cleared forest areas.

Less rooted in history or in nature were analyses stressing that the Amazon had
fallen victim to "inappropriate technology". In this view, peasants from outside
the region apply land uses that may not fit with the local ecologies, or become
maladapted as human densities increase.[4] The implicit view here is that the problems of environmental degradation lie in some faulty technology, which can be
corrected by a technological fix. Others argued that careless policy, or application
of the wrong subsidies to ill-considered development strategies, were to blame. On
this view, poor technologies and planning have produced environmental ruin. In
more recent years a popular charge is that deforestation has been caused by the
debt crisis afflicting the Third World, notably Brazil, since the exactions of First
World creditors have forced Brazil to run down precious resources such as timber
or to clear forests for export products like beef and cacao in order to produce
precious foreign exchange.

Each of these explanations has its matching solution. For the followers of Malthus, the answers to environmental ruin lie ultimately in the rigorous control of
population and, in the short-term, with increases in productivity on the best farm
lands. Hardin's disciples urge pell-mell conversion of communal to privately held
land, along with population control. An analysis stressing the baneful role of
international capital has led, naturally enough, to the conclusion that at the very
least the grip of "international capital" should be prised loose from the Amazon.
Those seeing the burning trees as the result of a faulty match of agriculture to
environment maintain that if unsound agricultural practices have produced
environmental disaster, the answer lies in improved and finely tuned technologies,

whether their advocates were of the agro-ecological or high-input persuasion. Those whose concerns emphasize policy claim that the core problem lies with the encouragement of cattle farming with its incentives such as subsidized credit for pasture, and that reduction of these subsidies would save the day. Those regarding debt as the arbiter of disaster urge stretched terms of repayment and other forms of relief, even repudiation or – in a less drastic mode – some form of "debt for nature" swap.

WHY DID DESTRUCTION BEGIN?

Aside from Hardin's ecstatic vision of the recuperative powers of private ownership, all of these theories have a ring of truth to them. But while their ensemble may help us get a purchase on the dynamics of environmental destruction in the Amazon, each argument on its own has serious deficiencies. Followers of Hardin rushing to condemn communal forms of ownership ignore the fact that virtually all deforestation in the Amazon has occurred on privately held land, or is used to assist in the passage of public land into private hands. Indeed, the Amazon is the site of one of the most rapid and large-scale enclosure movements in history as more than 100 million acres pass from public to private ownership.[5] This transfer exactly coincides with the explosion of deforestation in Amazônia.

The disciples of Malthus overlook the inconvenient fact that although the Amazon forms over 60 per cent of Brazilian national territory, less than 10 per cent of Brazil's population lives there. The region is a net importer of food from southern Brazil and more than half the population within the Amazon region lives in cities. Only six million or so people live in rural zones, of whom two to three million dwell in the forest itself. Most land cleared of forest produces little in the way of food and often was not cleared for that purpose. Migration into the region has much more to do with structural changes in the region of emigration than with population growth. Thus, decline in access to land, as it occurred in the Northeastern states, stimulated emigration. In the case of migrants from the South, the expansion of mechanized agriculture and the flooding of enormous areas of agricultural land forced small farmers out of their holdings. Finally, threat of violence and lack of employment have also expelled farmers from their holdings. Since more than half of all agriculturists in Brazil rely on wage labor as well as cropping for their income, activities like mechanization which reduce rural employment are often as disastrous to peasants as brute expulsion from their lands.[6]

Brazil's is certainly a capitalist economy and one which has been proffered as an exemplar of capitalist development in the Third World. But the Amazon presents some problems for this theory. For example, rubber – the quintessential industrial product – was and is extracted by "pre-capitalist" labor, in that the *seringueiros* have ranged in status from debt peons to petty traders, often in a barter economy.[7] They had control over their own labor in many cases, but the coercion came at the point of exchange. Thus, a product so emblematic of capitalism's economic expansion was supplied by non-capitalist labor in circumstances producing little environmental degradation. An array of similar examples can be marshaled in the extractive sector.

One view particularly popular in the Third World is that international capital, relatively exempt from local or international regulation, has been the prime sponsor of destruction. While environmental degradation certainly is associated with multinational mining interests, their effort is carried out in conjunction with national and parastatal firms which are often themselves multinationals. The "triple alliance" of international, domestic and state corporations requires a more penetrating analysis regarding the role of the state and national elites than is usually offered. Thus, the flow of books on the role of international firms in the environmental destruction of Amazônia, each with its bestiary of ten or twenty firms, overlooks the role and complicity of national elites.[8] In fact the role of international capital in producing deforestation in the Amazon has been relatively minor. The most toxic and widespread form of mining – placer mining for gold – is carried out by artisanal miners. The prime motive for deforestation in the region, clearing for pasture, has been largely entertained by Brazilian capitalists with no connection to transnational sponsors or investors.

The discipline of international markets does produce environmental degradation, particularly for crops like cotton; and historically the export market in turtle oil led, as we have seen, to the Amazonian turtle's virtual extinction. But most timber extraction feeds the domestic requirements of the tenth largest economy in the world: Brazil's. Even Central America, where the "hamburger connection" has been most elaborately argued, exports only about 15 per cent of its beef.[9] The Amazon is a net beef importer. With aftosa – foot and mouth disease – endemic and rife among its herds, Amazonian beef is prohibited from sale on international markets. Brazil does export beef, but its source can be found in the feedlots and intensive production of the southern states of São Paulo and Rio Grande do Sul.

Those perceiving the problem as one of inappropriate technology must explain why one particular technology or another is promoted and prevails, since the ways of producing any crop can take many forms in techniques and social structures.[10] Technologies of production are thoroughly embedded in economic logic and social systems. Without such an explanation, their own solutions end up as failures, inappropriate as the ones they superseded. There are successful agroecological technologies and strategies in the Amazon, agroforestry being the most notable. But why is an indubitably appropriate and sustainable technology such as agroforestry so little in evidence, in contrast to the vast stretches of degraded pasture? The answer must be sought in the national and local economic processes that ravage existing agroforestry systems, and impede, in many cases, the expansion of new ones.

To take "poor policy" as the precipitating factor in deforestation is to see "policy" as something conceived and executed by technocrats secluded from a country's political economy, and is an extraordinarily naive assumption. One constant theme proposed by those urging the "bad policy" approach has been the role of subsidized credit and incentives which create distortions and impel environmental destruction. There is no question but that such credits and incentives have played an important role, but they do not offer an explanation for most of the degradation that one can see in the Amazon. For example, even though credits of all kinds began to dry up in the Amazon after 1980, deforestation increased vertiginously.[11]

Has Brazil's enormous indebtedness to First World banks – higher than any other Third World country – prompted it to over-exploit and destroy its Amazonian natural resources in an effort to satisfy its creditors? It is difficult to substantiate the claim that it has. First, Brazil's exports amount to less than 10 per cent of its Gross Domestic Product. Almost 50 per cent of these exports come from textiles and manufacturing activities. The share of Brazil's primary commodities other than fuels, minerals and metals has plummeted to less than half its levels twenty years ago. These commodities are agricultural, and overwhelmingly reflect the contribution of processed Brazilian soybean and orange juice products, as well as the traditional exports of coffee, sugar and cacao. These hard currency earners – 85 per cent of Brazil's export earnings according to World Bank statistics – are produced almost entirely outside the Amazon. Brazil's aluminum and iron come largely from Amazônia (at Trombetas and Carajás), but face flagging commercial markets.

One of the most dramatic episodes in Brazil's environmental history was the near total destruction of its *araucaria* forests long before its debt became an issue. Wood exports do form an increasing proportion of Amazônia's exports, but so far this reflects depletion of forests in the south of Brazil, in the states of Santa Catarina and Paraná.

It is true, as we have mentioned, that the influx of migrants to the Amazon throughout the 1980s was prompted in part by the expansion of mechanized agriculture, particularly soybean production for export, in South and Central Brazil. The growth of these soybean *latifundia* pushed small farmers off their land, into the cities or to the North. As they sold their land, these small farmers benefited from rising local prices and thus were able to buy larger holdings in the Amazon, portions of which they duly cleared. Thus there is an indirect link to export expansion, but this is not a complete explanation. Indebtedness and the policies urged by the IMF and the First World banks have powerfully contributed to misery in Brazil as a whole,[12] but they have done so by exacerbating, not generating, what was already the most unequal distribution of assets and income in the world.

THE CAUSE OF DESTRUCTION

All these explanations suffer from a common failure to set the degradation of the Amazon over the past twenty years against the political history and political economy both of the region and of Brazil. No effective analyses can ever emerge without an effort to understand the rationales of particular actors, in light of their class positions and economic strategies.[13] The artificers of Amazônia's environmental decline imagined they were pursuing rational courses of action, though such actions set into play forces well beyond the reach of any single solution. Once that political history and that political economy are understood, the genealogy of disaster stands forth. The causes of environmental degradation in the Amazon can be traced to a philosophy and strategy for regional development formulated by the Brazilian military, whose influence in Brazilian and specifically Amazonian policy expanded steadily from the first days of Vargas's *Estado Novo* in 1937. From the aftermath of the Second World War, and particularly after they directly seized power in 1964, the generals set an overall agenda for the Amazon which unleashed the new forces that are today destroying the region.

The generals did not suddenly press their plans upon a region untouched since the "war for rubber". In 1953 an agency known as the Superintendency for the Economic Valorization of the Amazon (SPVEA) was set up, and assigned the duty of elaborating and putting into execution plans for the long-term development of the region. It thus became the Amazon's first major planning body. Three achievements marked the Superintendency's erratic progress towards extinction at the hands of the generals in 1964. Firstly, it enlarged the legal area of the Amazon to include parts of Mato Grosso, Goiás and Maranhão, and with this bureaucratic coup became the planning authority for more than 60 per cent of the national territory; secondly, it took the wartime rubber bank, the *Banco de Crédito de Borracha*, and converted it into a regional development bank with broader concerns; and thirdly, in 1958 it supervised the start of construction of the "road of the jaguar", the Belém-Brasília highway, completed in 1960. Amid cheers of local politicians, contractors and others mustered for the road's inauguration, a so-called "caravan of integration"made its way through the newly opened forest, south down the dirt road (paving was concluded in 1973) along the valley of Tocantins and up onto the *planalto* savannahs to Brasília.

There was much uncertainty about the economic reverberations of the highway, but among those welcoming the opening of this road was the Brazilian military, exultant that, for the first time, the North was accessible by land as well as by air or sea. Less delighted were the indigenous people whose traditional lands had been severally invaded by surveyors, road crews, bulldozers, land speculators and migrants.

Almost overnight the first land boom exploded in the Amazon. Large stretches of so-called *terras devolutas*, or unsurveyed state lands, were transferred to private owners in an immense series of enclosures. Between 1959 and 1963, 13.4 million acres in Pará went from public to private hands.[14] Prefiguring larger horrors to come, a riot of competing land rights, fraudulent land claims and associated uncertainties turned the region into a zone of bloody conflict, giving it a reputation for violence which it retains to this day.

The three contributions of SPVEA were momentous in their long-term effects, and created structures in financing, administration and infrastructure that have survived to this day. Yet these achievements could not extinguish the reputation for corruption and malfeasance that justly clung to the Superintendency from its inception. It had nothing resembling a technical staff; its executives handed out contracts to friends and relatives and advanced relatively little of its admittedly ambitious agenda.[15] Among those watching the Superintendency's antics with disfavor were the generals, who felt that if the Amazon was to be developed in an orderly fashion, the corruption of the SPVEA and the pervasive baneful influence of the self-interested extractive baronies of the region would have to be destroyed. In 1964 their moment came.

GEOPOLITICS AND GENERAL GOLBERY

Geopolitics dominated the intellectual horizons of the generals, as one might expect in a country whose borders had been redrawn or put under pressure since 1750. The twentieth century alone had seen several important territorial treaties. In 1903, the treaty of Petrópolis ceded Acre to Brazil. In 1904 under an agreement brokered by the King of Italy, Brazil lost more than 14,000 square kilometers of territory to British Guyana; and in 1905 Brazil renegotiated its border with Venezuela and did the same in 1907 with Colombia. In 1919, the frontier was redrawn with Peru. These concerns about the military, political and economic consolidation of national territory were, in the postwar period, augmented by fresh anxieties about communist subversion, with consequent redefinitions of the nature of war.

Given the undoubted and well-documented US hostility towards President João Goulart, and the role of the Kennedy and Johnson administrations in engineering his downfall,[16] General Castello Branco's seizure of power is sometimes misconstrued as merely a coup d'état along Bolivian lines. Such a view seriously misunderstands the place of the military within the Brazilian political system, where the military presented itself, and indeed was often perceived, as a professional, uncorrupted, ordered presence within the national political culture which could, in the last resort, resolve contradictions and dictate priorities beyond the competence or purview of civilian politicians.

In the postwar period Brazil began to tear at the seams with immense convulsions: internal migration from country to town, pell-mell industrialization, rapid economic growth, inflation. Amid these convulsions (which in 1954 drove Vargas to the conclusion that suicide was his only political option[17]), the generals took over in 1945, 1954, and 1964 and launched abortive attempts in 1955 and 1961. As the social and political strains increased so did the tempo of military intervention.[18] On March 31, in a nationally televised speech Goulart refused to dissociate himself from attacks on military discipline. Long-nurtured plans for a coup reached their climax. In Minas Gerais, a general told his troops on March 31 they were to march on Rio. On April 1, 1964, Goulart left Rio, flew to Brasília and then on to Rio Grande do Sul. On April 4 he went into exile in Uruguay. The US Ambassador had already on April 1 telegraphed the State Department that "we believe it is all over, with [the] democratic [sic] rebellion already 95 per cent successful". Early on April 2, President Johnson telegraphed the new acting President Ranieri Mazzilli his "warmest good wishes". General Castello Branco was duly proclaimed the new military president in a "revolution from above".

Just one week after the coup, the generals took over SPVEA, purged it of so-called "bad" or "unpatriotic" Brazilians, and placed it under the control of an extraordinary ministry for regional agencies, to be restructured to fit better with the strategies so long pondered by one of their number, General Golbery.

The name of General Golbery do Couto e Silva should have a most prominent place in any history of the Amazon. He was a *gaúcho* who had fought in France in 1940 and then had further training in the United States in 1944 before going, like Castello Branco, to join General Mark Clark's Fourth Army Corps as a member of the Brazilian Expeditionary Force.[19] By 1950 he had become a high-ranking intelligence officer and within a few years was one of those formulating Brazilian military doctrine, as taught in the War College. In 1960 he became Chief of Operations of the General Staff and a year later *chef de cabinet* of the National Security Council. Soon thereafter he retired from active military service, but remained extremely active and was deeply involved in preparations for the coup of 1964, in which year he was named chief of the *Serviço Nacional de Informações* – state security. He went on to be *chef de cabinet* to Ernesto Geisel and João Figueiredo, the generals who ran Brazil in the late 1970s and early 1980s, with Figueiredo inaugurating the *abertura* to "democratization". Throughout the whole period few major political initiatives took place without consultation with Golbery. To his *fazenda* in Rio Grande do Sul both military officers and civilians of all reputable political stripes would repair for *churrasco*, barbecued in the proper *gaúcho* manner.

In his books Golbery outlined a coherent philosophy of action.[20] To have any long-term resonance, policies had to be set in the geopolitical realities of Brazil. With its clusters of population clinging to the coastline from Porto Alegre to Belém, Brazil had ignored the "vast hinterlands waiting and hoping to be aroused to life and to fulfill their historic destiny". In Golbery's view this destiny was the consummation of Vargas's "March to the West". Such a march would kindle the population to a sense of national purpose, and achieve the all-important occupation of empty hinterland and unguarded frontier, exploiting unused resources.

Golbery's political analysis owed a great deal to the German geographer Ratzel, and to the German geopolitical theorists. In Golbery's view, the spatial configuration of Brazil was the fundamental reality of the nation's political life; any development strategy had to confront this physical space. For him, the first task was therefore to conceptualize a "geopolitical framework" from which a long-term development strategy, or "grand strategy", could be articulated and then implemented by specific policies. Geopolitics is the lode star which orients goals and policy. In the Brazilian case, the developed South would serve as the "maneuvering platform" through which geopolitical consolidation of the Northeast, Central West and Amazônia would occur. Such geopolitics, formulated as "grand strategy" were matched with "total war" against internal and external subversion: the cold war optic. Indeed the national security of Brazil demanded the complete integration of economic and military strategy and space, since rapid economic development was mandatory for neutralizing political challenges from the left.

It goes without saying that these notions formulated by Golbery and set forth in the training manuals for officers entering the *Escola Superior de Guerra* – the Brazilian war college – were much influenced by evolving US hemispheric doctrine.[21] The panic prompted by the victory of the Cuban revolution and the flight of Fulgencio Batista in January of 1959 prompted the Kennedy brothers and their entourage to develop a policy both of economic assistance to and close co-operation with the military and police in Latin America, fortifying both their ideology and arsenals of repression. The more publicized aspect of this strategy, embodied in the Alliance for Progress, was the program of economic aid to outflank the challenges from the left.

Within the broader prescriptions of geopolitics, grand strategy, and "total war", Golbery was extremely concrete in his three-phased program in which the Amazon was to play a central part. The first phase was to strengthen integration between the Northeast and the South, and at the same time close off such possible corridors for guerrilla subversion as the valleys of the Tocantins, the Araguaia, and the São Francisco which could funnel insurgency to the "central platform" and the South. The second phase was to redirect colonization in Brazil's southern frontiers to the Northwest (what are today the states of Rondônia and Acre), launching this advance on the Northwest from the "central platform", the area of southern Mato Grosso and Goiás which was "the real heart of the country", and simultaneously integrating this central platform with the politically and economically developed regions to the east and south. The final phase, in Golbery's peremptory prose, was to "advance from a forward base, developed in the Central-West and co-ordinated with an east-west progression following the bed of the great river, to protect certain frontier points and inundate the Amazon forest with civilization".

POLITICS AND THE GENERALS

In early December of 1966, the liner *Rosa da Fonseca* set course upstream from Manaus. On board were generals, businessmen, bankers, industrialists, and planners. In the week-long cruise that followed, the three hundred guests relaxed over appropriate regional delicacies and folkloric entertainment, discussing the implications of the momentous speech they had just heard in Manaus, where on December 3, General Castello Branco had unveiled the long-awaited *Operation Amazônia*, the practical expression of Golbery's "grand strategy" for the Amazon. Though one of the first acts of the generals after seizing power had been to destroy the old Superintendency, SPVEA, it had taken them over two and a half years to lay the plans and develop the structure for Amazonian development.

The attention to SPVEA reflected the weight of Amazônia in the military government's thinking, and the strategic importance that it would have for their overall national economic strategy. Though installed by force – at least the threatened force – of arms, the generals were still necessarily preoccupied with the question of their own legitimacy. That legitimacy could be enhanced by the unifying appeal of a call for national integration under the aegis of manifest destiny, accompanied by the fervent ideology of modernization. *Esto é um país que vai prá frente* – this is a country that is going forward – became their war cry. The generals began to consolidate their political base.

The landed elites were still panicked by Goulart's strong push for land reform. Millions in Brazil were urging the break-up of their enormous estates, and the leadership of the peasant leagues had been increasingly well-organized and determined. To them the generals could offer the safety valve of Amazonian settlement for at least some of these landless millions. The generals also pleased the landlords mightily by destroying, in the most bloody manner, the peasant leagues,[22] simultaneously exciting the applause of visiting Aliança bureaucrats by passing a land reform law known as the Brazilian Land Statute which seemed to follow the prescription of Goulart in requiring that employers pay salaries and health benefits for their rural workers. But the law was mostly symbolic. No effort was made to enforce its social content, and it was seen by peasants as *prá inglés ver* – something to please the foreigners. Its concrete effects, when it was used, undermined the sharecroppers on rural lands, and was one of the factors that in the end contributed to the emergence of *bóias frias*, landless temporary workers in agriculture.[23]

Securing the immediate confidence of the industrial elites by declaring all strikes illegal, the generals swiftly established a solid rapport between entrepreneurial dreams and military goals.[24] As Castello Branco put it, "We seek a sincere dialogue with investors ... the national entrepreneur is the fundamental instrument and the master foundation of the model of economic development we prefer".

For the average worker-consumer in Brazil a central preoccupation was food prices, most particularly the price of meat. Cheap food policies, particularly for beef, were therefore a priority. But Brazil's meat industry had reached a moment of crisis;[25] both domestic and international demand had soared, but traditional producers, the *fazendeiros*, seemed unable to satisfy this demand. This was a failure particularly galling to the generals, since beef exports could generate badly needed foreign exchange and diversify their export sector, as urged by the Alliance for Progress and international organizations. The prospects for the livestock industry in Latin America seemed particularly rosy, but economists argued that the industry needed modernization, one of the main problems being that the limited credit extended to this sector had hampered its growth. One logical strategy for the generals would have been to force modernization, hence improved productivity, on the old *fazendas*, and some effort was made in this direction.[26] But it also suited their purposes to encourage the entrepreneurial and agro-industrial elites to embark on livestock production in the well-watered Amazon where vexatious dry seasons would not hamper animal growth and marketed beef supplies. The 300-year-old history of livestock production on the island of Marajó at the mouth of the Amazon gave the entirely false impression that similar success could be enjoyed in the uplands and new pastures created from forest. There was another constituency that the strategy sought to satisfy: the generals' security concerns. On the maps in their offices the Araguaia and Tocantins valley running south from the mouth of the Amazon at Belém had special significance. Here, in the estimation of the generals, was an artery which could carry the toxins of subversion from the north to the heartland. Further to the north, in the middle of the map, sat Manaus, in isolation and decline. In Golbery's prescription Manaus was to be the pivot of the Amazon. The generals now formulated the strategy that would meld politics with geopolitics along the lines elaborated by Golbery, and this was what Castello Branco finally unveiled in Manaus on December 3, 1966.

Twenty-six years earlier, in October 1940, President Getúlio Vargas had come to Manaus to issue his testimonial to the future role of the Amazon. Vargas had just visited Ford's doomed Belterra plantation on the Tapajós and much admired what he saw, pronouncing it "planned" and "rational". "Nothing," he then proclaimed in Manaus,

> will stop us in this movement which is, in the twentieth century, the highest task of civilizing man: to conquer and dominate the valleys of the great equatorial torrents, transforming their blind force and their extraordinary fertility into disciplined energy. The Amazon, under the impact of our will and our labor, shall cease to be a simple chapter in the history of the world and, made equivalent to other great rivers, shall become a chapter in the history of civilization.

OPERATION AMAZÔNIA

In his speech of 1966 Castello Branco first elaborated some larger objectives, of which the first was regional occupation through "development poles". The concept of "development poles" had originated with François Perroux in the mid 1950s. Perroux had advocated a deliberately imbalanced approach to incentives for development. By showering the target sector (known in the jargon of planners as the "propulsive sector") with any number of tax breaks, land concessions, trade breaks, sweetheart loans and credit, Perroux and his followers believed that "multiplier" effects would duly follow. Industries, services and commerce of all sorts would flower to serve the favored target sector. Overall development would be the happy outcome. The fortunate investor in whatever economic enterprise the growth pole was designed to serve was assured guaranteed profits, which partly explained the exhilaration on the *Rosa da Fonseca*. While the industries clustered around the pole would be subject to the discipline of the free market, the central enterprise would enjoy every economic blessing in the government's competence.[27] Other objectives outlined by Castello Branco included encouragement of immigration and settlement in the Amazon; the creation of a stable, self-sustaining population; development of the infrastructure, particularly paving of the Belém-Brasília highway and construction of secondary roads hooking up to the highway; a commitment to livestock and agriculture, with execrations against extractivism familiar since the days of Pombal; and expanded research into the Amazon's potential in resources such as minerals, timber and fish.

For a year preceding his speech, Castello Branco had mustered a team of five men to assist in the development of this program. Grandly described as "the group for the reformulation of the Political Economy of Amazônia", its numbers included three generals and two businessmen. They were charged with the task of transforming the old SPVEA into a new, lean and professional body, redolent of austere military virtues. The group had also the task of determining how to apply fiscal incentives to stimulate private investors, along the lines elaborated by Perroux. The most intoxicating portion of Castello Branco's oration had been the list of inducements which could now be enjoyed by the entrepreneurs whom he hailed as the regime's most cherished allies. These incentives stipulated that 50 per cent of a corporation's tax liability for up to twelve years could be invested in already existing Amazonian projects, thus allowing taxes to become venture capital. New projects started before 1972 would enjoy a 100-per-cent tax rebate for twelve years. (This tax holiday was later extended to seventeen years.) Next, 75 per cent of the costs of projects in the Amazon would be supplied by the federal government. Special credit lines would be opened at the BASA, the Amazon Development Bank. Finally, existing subsidized credit lines for livestock development would be made available for the Amazonian entrepreneur, including funds for the purchase of land, with grace periods of four to eight years before repayment began, at interest rates of 10 to 12 per cent. The significance of these provisions to the businessmen on the *Rosa da Fonseca* was particularly fortifying. Given the historic rates of inflation, the government was in effect offering enormous amounts of money at negative rates of interest. The businessmen floating up the Amazon that week in December could echo Farquhar, but with far greater truth. It was the surest of sure things.

And so the Amazon's new boom began. Projects flooded the Araguaia-Tocantins region, which was given preferential status as a focus of development. At the same time, Manaus became a free trade zone and export platform, receiving industrial incentives similar to those applied to the livestock sector.

Of the lines of eager entrepreneurs now haunting the *Superintendência de Desenvolvimento da Amazônia* (SUDAM), SPVEA's replacement, more than 60 per cent were from the São Paulo area, and bore the names of its most prominent industrial and agro-industrial enterprises.

Fiscal incentives were not the only exciting dimension of *Operation Amazônia*. Investment in livestock was one of the least risky activities in the region, or so the entrepreneurs saw it. The animals could even walk themselves to the market if necessary, thus overcoming some of the limitations of the precarious transport system. Cattle ranching required little labor and a ready supply of destitute workers could always be contracted from the Northeast for the big deforesting jobs. There was always a clamoring market for meat, and unlike cocoa or other crops, cattle were relatively resistant to the vagaries of tropical ecology. Moreover, as inflation began to pick up, these lands (and the livestock) were certainly an excellent way of diversifying investment portfolios and could serve as a hedge against inflation.

This combination of benefits fired an extraordinary boom in land, whose value rose as much as 100 per cent a year in real terms.[28] Land in the Amazon became a vehicle for capturing incentives, cheap credits, and itself assumed the form of a speculative instrument and an object of exchange rather than being an input into agriculture. Once again the dreams of stable agriculture dissipated in gusts of financial extractivism of a sort undreamed of in the region's history.

In the years that followed Castello Branco's epochal address, investors rushed to the Amazon, as did legions of laborers and squatters, attracted by work on the new roads and the possibilities of a fresh start under a government's blessing. For most of these would-be settlers the difficulty of acquiring land meant that their futures lay more surely in a *favela* on the edge of Belém than a *fazenda*. Amid the irruptions into the eastern Amazon, where Indians fled the advancing bulldozers or were driven from lands by guns, threats and the legal briefs of the *fazendeiros*, and where the *caboclos* watched giant rubber trees crash to the ground engulfed in flames, social tensions in the region became increasingly explosive. Indeed the worst nightmares of the generals began to take shape, provoked by the very schemes they had devised to prevent sedition from flooding down the Araguaia-Tocantins.

Where the large SUDAM holdings were granted titles, the beneficiaries of these titles then had to rely on the state's repressive forces to remove Indians and peasants from their lands. In 1970 the Communist Party, P.C. do B., began a rural *foco* on the border between the states of Pará and Goiás. About seventy guerrillas – in the form of couples and families – militants of the Communist Party, were agriculturalists by day and trained in the forest at night. Discovered by the intelligence service, retribution was swift and thorough. Some 20,000 soldiers trained in counter-insurgency occupied the area, and in the largest mobilization ever carried out by the Brazilian military, hunted down the guerrillas, liquidated them and tortured their sympathizers. The counter-insurgency was successful, and most gratifying to the Brazilian army and its North American advisers, bore many similarities to the US pacification programs in Vietnam.[29]

LAND FOR THE SETTLERS

The message to the generals was quite clear. Their program had favored only the most powerful groups. In an area as huge as the Amazon, it was irrational to deny a few acres to would-be settlers looking for land. From a disposition to satisfy this land hunger sprang the next great program promulgated by the generals – the *Programa de Integração Nacional*, PIN, whose intent was to shift the ideology of Amazonian occupation away from an "economic" to a "social" perspective. Thus the slogans of "Amazônia is your best business" on television and radio were put aside in favor of – *O homem é a meta* – "man is the goal". General Emilio Medici, the military president of the time and a notorious hard-liner, in a well-publicized trip to the drought-stricken Northeast, pronounced himself touched by the suffering he observed and determined to open the well-watered lands of the Amazon from Marabá west towards Porto Velho for settlement. Borrowing a line from nineteenth-century Zionism, he offered to provide "a land without men for men without land".

The construction of a Trans-Amazon highway was announced forthwith. It was to run west from the confluence of the Tocantins and the Araguaia at Marabá, to Itaituba on the Tapajós, and on to Porto Velho. Other projects were announced with less fanfare: a road from Cuiabá, in southern Mato Grosso, running directly north to Santarém, and the *Perimetral Norte*, a highway running just below Brazil's northern frontier. All of these prospective roads bore the imprint of Golbery's geopolitical vision. The Trans-Amazon highway and the road cutting north across Mato Grosso would link his "central platform" with the Amazon, which itself would be linked by the Trans-Amazon to the Northeast, all of which were anchored by the now paved Belém-Brasília "road of the jaguar". The starving Northeasterners would be the agents whereby the Amazon would be "flooded with civilization''. The *Perimetral Norte*, never built but later reborn as *Calha Norte*, was a straightforward geopolitical resource defense.

The PIN had three main consequences. It formalized the military's first foray into colonization, by providing credits for small farmers and, via the National Institute for Colonization and Agrarian Reform (INCRA), by setting up an agency with the power to mediate land disputes and award titles. It also nationalized the *terras devolutas* along federal highways and adjacent to Brazil's northern and western borders, and so unclaimed lands formerly lying within the purview of individual states passed under the control of the federal government.[30] This law, 1.164, representing a rebirth of Goulart's last initiative before his overthrow, vastly increased federal, hence military power. Finally it provided a large line of credit, called PROTERRA, for investment in Amazônia. Initially designed for small farmers, its funds were often appropriated by large landowners.[31]

From the generals' point of view, PIN's logic was clear enough. By establishing federal control over the particularly desirable land running adjacent to the highways it would control or hopefully, at the very least, cool speculative fever. Reality scarcely ratified these hopes. Law 1.164 immediately spawned three separate land markets: a conventional one, where land was bought and sold in response to price signals; an illegal land market based on fraud and land-grabbing; and a government land market which included land grants and concessionary pricing. All of these markets could operate simultaneously in a given area and in some cases involved the same piece of land.

To an optimist the blueprint for what blithe planners in Brasília described as the *faixas*, swaths of ''social occupation'' connecting ''dynamic growth poles'', must have seemed compelling. The small farmers charged with the destiny of flooding the Amazon with civilization would be given land in the swaths running alongsides the highway, while the larger entrepreneurs would be concentrated in the ''growth poles''. Supervising the entrepreneurial sector would be the agencies, SUDAM and the Ministry of the Interior, while the small farmers would be under the aegis of INCRA, this body becoming overseer of lands larger in dimension than the national territories of all but ten countries in the world – some 2.2 million square kilometers.

WHY DID SETTLERS FAIL?

The Trans-Amazon was launched with a public relations campaign laying great stress on the rich earth and vibrant opportunities awaiting the settlers choosing to forge a new future in the Amazon. Protestant ministers exhorted their charges to seek the promised land. The Pentecostal churches saw numerous new congregations stretching across the Amazon, an expectation which turned out to be sounder than the Catholic Church would care to admit. INCRA also offered tangible inducements: transportation to the Amazon and a 240-acre plot for each settler, with sure title, guaranteed credit for the planting of rice, corn and beans; a six-month household subsidy to tide the family over the initial difficult months; and food subsidies as insurance against disaster. Colonists were also promised housing, schools, medicine, transportation and technical assistance. But if the generals were hoping for an Amazonian equivalent to the Oklahoma land rush, they were sadly disappointed. Of the migrants going west, about a third came from the state of Pará, a slightly smaller slice from the Northeast, and a quarter from the South; but though 100,000 were initially expected in the end a far lower number, less than 8,000, committed themselves to the new life. And then, instead of the Jeffersonian yeomen manning the frontier of the generals' dreams, colonist after colonist failed and either trickled back to the cities or tried his luck on new plots further west.

The failure of the vast majority of these small farmers was the subject of furious dispute, for the stakes in the debate were very high. One faction sought the answer in environmental and agronomic factors. Poor tropical soils had doomed settlers from the start. Even if a settler had been lucky enough to get his 240 acres on a patch of rich *terra roxa*, pests would soon take their toll. Large ranchers were eager to press this view, for evidently self-interested reasons. Just one year after the Trans-Amazon settlements began, Reis Velloso, the Minister for the Interior, was arguing that

> until now the Trans-Amazon has emphasized colonization. But the necessity of both avoiding predatory occupation with consequent deforestation and of promoting ecological equilibrium leads us to invite large enterprises to assume the tasks of developing the region.

Those more committed to biological arguments claimed that the carrying capacity of the environment had been exceeded and thus nature had, in a sense, ''collapsed'', carrying the settlers with it. Some agronomists suggested that inappropriate cultivars and even inappropriate agricultural systems had brought the settlers low. Some laid the blame on the personal attributes of the settlers who failed,[32] imputing to them lack of entrepreneurial ability or agricultural skills. Perhaps, some suggested, the problems lay with infrastructure and institutions. The settlers had been dropped in the forest with few ways to market their produce; rain and choking dust made the roads impassable for large periods. Moreover, the precarious transport routes made it possible for middlemen and truckers to impose monopolistic prices.[33] Delays in titling their land had left them without the formal collateral needed to get credit, and they had simply sunk. Furthermore prices that farmers could get for these products were held down by government-imposed ceilings. Even if a peasant's yield was excellent, the return could scarcely cover his costs.[34] In fact, study after study throughout the Amazon has shown that returns to peasant agriculture are often negative. Without the additional income

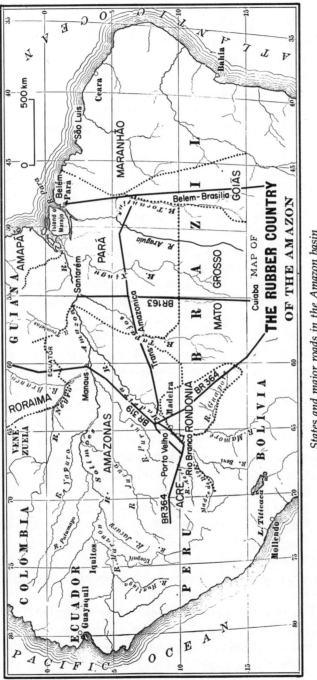

States and major roads in the Amazon basin

111

from wage labor or even petty extraction, small settlers cannot make ends meet.[35]

The motivation of the Minister of the Interior, speaking on behalf of the large entrepreneurs, was obvious. If settlement of small farmers was abandoned, then the lands allocated them could go to large ranches. Indeed Velloso, subsequent to his address, allocated six million acres that had been designated for colonization to large ranchers with the final warning that peasants "carry out the sole, dangerous activity available to them: deforestation and the exhaustion of soil for subsistence agriculture". Of course the most extensive instances of deforestation and soil degradation could be observed, by anyone driving along the Trans-Amazon from Marabá, in the large ranches on either side. Once again, the view that the environment was to blame ignored the political and economic context in which these settlers found themselves. The view of peasants purely as agriculturalists distorted any understanding of their real economic condition. About three-quarters of Trans-Amazon colonists required some kind of wage labor to carry them through. The fantasy of a Jeffersonian yeomanry culling a living from the soil ignored the reality of life along the Trans-Amazon, which was that to get by and keep himself and his family alive a settler needed a job on the side and access to extractive resources ranging from fish to firewood to Brazil nuts to timber. When jobs were gone and extractive resources were depleted, colonists had no option but to pull up stakes.

No study anywhere in the Amazon has been able to show that colonists on poor soils have a higher likelihood of failure than those on excellent ones.[36] Certainly, agricultural techniques could make a difference in the precarious conditions in which the colonists found themselves, but agricultural ability was not the determining factor.

While institutional and infrastructural problems were certainly severe, as they always are in new settlements in frontier areas, the forces that overwhelmed so many settlers were elementary facts of economic life. Settlers arrived with varying capital and credit-worthiness. The better-endowed were able to capture more of the state resources and also snap up the lots of faltering neighbors, thus repeating the familiar rhythm of the Brazilian countryside: consolidation of large holdings, fragmentation of small ones. The land boom also had its consequences for the colonists. Competing land claims, whether from squatters or from large holders claiming usufruct right to immense stretches of land, engendered a turbulent climate of speculative animosity. Peasants with clear titles to their holdings from the state (a rare commodity in the Amazon) could sell such titles for more money than they could earn in five years, a prospect that was often irresistible. Other settlers found themselves facing land-grabbers intent on clearing forest – claiming it through the Brazilian notion of "effective use", an offspring of the old principle of *uti possedetis* – and then promptly selling it. Such confrontations were often accompanied by violence. All areas of either direct or spontaneous colonization in the Amazon have experienced the pressures of speculation and physical coercion.

Large landowners quite simply claimed areas to which the small settlers thought they had titles and drove them off with threats and gunshots. Studies of the reasons for Amazonian migration later showed that as many as one in three colonists abandoned or sold their plots because they were afraid for their lives.[37]

CORPORATE SETTLEMENT

As the generals reviewed their attempt to inundate the Amazon with civilization two years after the Trans-Amazon began, they drew a dour conclusion. "Social occupation" had cost too much, particularly in light of the fact that the Brazilian economic "miracle" of the sixties and early seventies was beginning to sputter. Settlement along the Trans-Amazon was far below initial projections. So the generals, not without some prompting from the Association of Amazonian Entrepreneurs, turned from the complexities of social occupation to simpler balance sheets of large-scale projects, and announced what they now called the Program for Amazon Development (PDAM), invoking the language of the now-beleagured Brazilian miracle, and focusing on capital-intensive development in the areas of Amazônia's "comparative advantage", mining, timber, and of course, cattle. The Minister of Agriculture re-cleared legislation that permitted parcels of over a million acres along the roads to be granted to large entrepreneurs overturning the existing land ceilings. No longer was there talk of flooding the Amazon with the civilizing influence of diligent small farmers. If civilization was to be pressed upon the basin, it would take the form of the historic Brazilian method of occupying large space: the *pata do boi*, the hooves of steers; and those hooves would tread upon degraded pasture. The order of the day was to be export-led development, unhampered by the distracting woes of the small farmer.

To push forward this new strategy, the generals announced the *PoloAmazônia* program, a refinement of *Operation Amazônia*'s development poles, which foretold an Amazon segmented into fifteen enclaves of exploitation where infrastructure and investment would be concentrated and well-subsidized capital-intensive projects would prepare materials for export. These poles also signaled to the entrepreneurs the best sites for speculative gains,[38] with some of the best gains coming in the area of what were known as the "Big Projects".

The "Big Projects" are often cited as a separate phase in Amazonian planning, but they really fall within the purview of the Amazon Development Program and *PoloAmazônia*, with its emphasis on mineral extraction. The *Grandes Projetos* have enormous impact on the short term in that they pull in vast numbers of laborers to carry out arduous construction tasks, and in this light they can be viewed as the keystone of Amazônia's rural employment strategy, although in the end they generate little permanent employment.[39] Their impacts, such as the flooding of forest for dams, mine tailings and deforestation engender the most rancorous environmental debates.

LUDWIG AND JARI

Although not technically a "Big Project" in the purview of development poles, the Jari project was enthusiastically supported by General Golbery. Of all the alliances between government and business, none in the postwar period was better known in the First World than the wood pulp operation on the Jari river launched in 1967 by the North American shipping magnate Daniel K. Ludwig. In scope and expense it far outstripped Henry Ford's attempts to cultivate rubber plantations at Fordlândia and Belterra. But though the scale was greater many of the mistakes were the same. Ludwig's plan, in buying three million acres in northern Pará, west along the Amazon from the island of Marajó, was to raise plantations of fast-growing East India trees known as *Gmelina arborea*, thus meeting an anticipated future shortage of wood fiber. He also envisaged the world's largest rice plantation, along with mining and livestock operations, nicely planned communities for workers, a 2,500-mile network of roads and fifty miles of railroad track.

As with Fordlândia, things went wrong from the start. The bulldozers used for clearing forest also scraped off precious topsoil and most of the seedlings of *Gmelina* failed. Laborers had to be hired to replace the costly and useless bulldozers, landing Ludwig with vastly increased costs and an annual labor turnover rate of 200 to 300 per cent a year. By mid-1970 less than a quarter of the anticipated 250,000 acre plantation had in fact been planted and yields – *Gmelina* did very badly on the sandy soils where it had been foolishly planted – were up to 50 per cent below projections. Meanwhile Ludwig had raised a $250 million loan from the Japanese Import-Export Bank, guaranteed by the Brazilian government through its National Economic Development Bank, to have a pulp mill and wood-fired power plant built in Japan. Amid great fanfare two barges carried this investment from Japan across the Indian Ocean, past the Cape of Good Hope, across the Atlantic and up the Amazon to the Jari river where it was hauled in final triumph into the port of Manguba. But the lag in *Gmelina* production left the pulp mill expensively short of wood to process, and Ludwig had to substitute Caribbean pine, which grew less rapidly. The native timber from Ludwig's vast holding went to fuel the plant to run the mill which eventually turned out pulp made from *Gmelina* mixed with a combination of local trees.

The original vision for the rice plantation was of a highly capital-intensive operation with aerial sowing and spraying. This proved too expensive. The only profitable operation was a kaolin mine from deposits fortunately discovered on the property. By the early 1980s the whole scheme, into which Ludwig had invested about three-quarters of a billion dollars, was in very poor shape. Over his fourteen-year tenure Ludwig hired and fired no less than thirty directors of the project. Whereas Fordlândia in the early 1930s had no botanists or plantation experts at all, Jari had just one researcher. The political context in which the Jari scheme had thrived was now changing and Ludwig could neither get clear title to the Jari property nor a government guarantee with which to back the purchase of a second pulp mill. In 1982 the venerable billionaire had had enough. A consortium of twenty-seven companies, backed by the Brazilian government, bought the pulp project, kaolin operation and the livestock ranch for $280 million.

It was the end of Ludwig's plunge in the Amazon, but Jari continued and by the late 1980s was throwing a longer, more baneful shadow over Amazônia. Amid claims that under more rational management Jari was operating in the black, the development lobby in the Amazon argued that at last large plantation silviculture was a proven success and so the voracious appetite for charcoal of the Carajás pig-iron smelting project could thus be met by plantation fuel. But such claims did not adequately reflect the realities of Jari. The "operating profit" claimed for 1985–86 did not reflect the fact that Jari was sold for a fraction of its original investment and therefore the debt load was also a fraction of what it would be in any equivalent operation. The big income earner at Jari was kaolin, another piece of geological good fortune that an equivalent operation could not expect. Fertilizing of existing *Gmelina* plantations was abandoned in 1982, but would have to be expensively resumed if production was to continue. Labor turnover continued to be high. The ecologist Philip Fearnside, visiting Jari in 1986, showed employees a photograph of 22 technical staff he had taken in 1982 and found that only two of that group remained. Salaries for such staff had fallen as much as 50 per cent since 1980. Fearnside found himself being interrogated about his knowledge of Jari from earlier visits, since the plantation had virtually no institutional memory – a serious deficit on a tree plantation. Also throwing doubt on its supposed profitability was Jari's exemption from income tax and enjoyment of other subsidies.

The fictitious claims for Jari were being applied to the Grande Carajás program, whose plans envisaged 27 enterprises including seven pig-iron plants requiring charcoal, production of which would in turn require 1,680,000 acres of eucalyptus plantations, ten times as large as the managed plantations at Jari. The real losses on silviculture obtained at Jari would soon mainfest themselves in plantations in the Carajás region, whose overseers would therefore continue to destroy native forests in order to save money.[40]

Public colonization programs were temporarily abandoned in favor of growth poles and what could be called corporate colonization.[41] But the generals had now set in motion settlement pressures well beyond their control, and by the late 1970s the Araguaia zone was boiling in land conflict as migrants, land-grabbers, and goldminers fought it out. As social disruption rose in 1980, the entire Araguaia-Tocantins region was placed under emergency military control of the *Grupo*

Executivo de Terras Araguaia-Tocantins (GETAT), the executive group for the Araguaia-Tocantins lands. Here titles could be resolved with military efficiency, and outbreaks between the clergy, peasants and landowners put down with dispatch. Created by decree law 1767 in 1980, GETAT (dissolved under the National Security Council in 1988 with parts of it incoporated into the Greater Carajás Project) had many powers that exceeded those of a land agency. About 113 million acres were under its jurisdiction and it was able to survey, demarcate and distribute lands for the "social and economic recuperation of the region". In its focus on *ad hoc* agrarian reform its purpose has been to resolve short-term tensions that would produce pressures for a more comprehensive agrarian reform. The number and quantity of titles easily outstripped any previous system of titling. In its first four years it gave out thousands of titles to some 12 million acres.

GETAT's strategy was to resettle peasants rapidly when they were involved in conflicts. Predictably the pattern of distribution was terribly skewed, in that 72 per cent of the titles covered only 5 per cent of the lands they distributed, while the 354 titles above 2,400 acres covered 32 per cent of the lands. Among these was a single holding of 960,000 acres. Another disturbing trend however was the speed with which these *títulos definitivos* were trafficked. In those contested lands a definitive title was worth its weight in gold. The titles designed for a peasant patrimony often ended up as "golden handshakes" from big land-holders, and were far more effective in removing peasants in the end than the *pistoleiros* had been. While the army-mediated colonization continued in the eastern Amazon, a new chapter of state-run colonization was opening in the West.

Migrants were heading north from Cuiabá, up the BR 364 (as yet unpaved) to Rondônia. To cope with wave after wave of migrants swelling the Amazon, swarming in on overloaded trucks, the Brazilian government began negotiating with the World Bank for settlement and road building funds. By now the migrants were coming from as far afield as the southern state of Paraná, some forced out by construction of the world's largest dam at Itaipu, others pushed out by the expansion of soybean and other mechanized forms of farming in the southern states. By presidential decree a new growth pole, in Rondônia and northern Mato Grosso, almost the size of France, was established, and $1.5 billion of development funds, more than half from the World Bank, was applied to the pole's purpose, which was to organize the efficient occupation of the area by the civil state, thus avoiding the blood-soaked chapters of the settlement of the eastern Amazon.

HORIZONS OF FIRE

By 1980 military rule was under increasing challenge. General Ernesto Geisel had been unable to halt the plunging standard of living for most Brazilians. The value of the currency evaporated daily, with inflation levels exceeding annual rates of over 100 per cent. By now Brazil's borrowing, which had funded the pharaonic schemes of the generals and their cronies, had engendered huge obligations to First World banks, along with onerous schedules of repayments tied to floating interest rates that translated fluctuations in the US prime rate into extra penalties to Brazil of hundreds of millions of dollars. As the last formal military defender, the noted horseman João Baptista Figueiredo, took office in 1980, the era of untrammeled military rule was drawing to a close. For the first time in twenty-five years there were strikes – initially one by the sheet-metal workers, headed by Luís Inácio "Lula" da Silva; and as the economy lurched from one improvization to the next and inflation bounded forward, there was clamor for direct elections.

In 1980 the reality of the Amazon was far removed from the taut military prospectus drafted by General Golbery a generation earlier. The region was now latticed with migrant trails. Goldminers were rushing to the Serra Pelada, and to placer strikes all along the southern flank of the Amazon, in Pará and northern Mato Grosso. Laborers for the huge construction projects were making their way to Carajás, Tucuruí and along the road project to Rondônia. On the big trucks settlers kept rolling into southern Pará and Rondônia. The forests were now beginning to fall at an ever-increasing rate. The fires of the previous decade had been alarming, but few were prepared for the infernos that blazed on horizon after horizon, from the babassu forests in Maranhão on the Atlantic to the mahogany woods at the Bolivian frontier.

Distracted by mounting economic and political pressures at the national level, the generals now tried to enhance their position by their "Third National Development Plan". Their overall goals were to keep food prices low, exports high, and to control inflation. In contrast to the baton's sweep that visualized *Operation Amazônia*, *PDAM* and *PoloAmazônia*, the Third Plan was uninspiring in its scope. The old preoccupations were still there: the use of tax mechanisms and fiscal incentives to continue the historic mission of Amazônia's integration into the national destiny. By now the blueprint paid lip service to ecological concerns and proffered virtuous phraseology about non-predatory exploitation of natural resources and the desirability of maintaining ecological equilibrium. These guilty homilies were the truest indication of what had happened to the generals' original blueprint.

The final measure of the generals' altered political destiny was the national agrarian reform plan, announced in 1985. Its aim was the distribution of more than a hundred million acres to a million and a half families across Brazil. Legal Amazônia's contribution would involve some hundred thousand square kilometers for 140,000 people. Once again, Amazônia was to emerge, at least on paper, as the safety outlet for irresistible peasant demands for land reform, taking the pressure off the rich developed lands in the South and flooding the Amazon with civilization. While agrarian reform emphasized expropriation in other parts of Brazil, a large portion of the designated land in the North would come from the federal government. The target areas were in the heart of forested Amazônia, in the states of Amazonas and Acre.

The threat of expropriation triggered a spasm of deforestation among property owners, since it was harder to expropriate lands if they were in some notional form of use. Agrarian reform also implied the construction of new roads with concomitant speculation and forest clearance. If the intention of agrarian reform was to give land to the peasants, then the outcome in Amazônia was far from inspiring. Less than 5,000 families were resettled, and in a reform program that proved impotent across Brazil, its performance in the Amazon was the weakest of all. Its main legacy was an accelerated tempo of deforestation.

As Brazil returned to nominal civilian rule under President Sarney, the military still played an extremely powerful role in national politics and particularly in the Amazon, under the zealous eye of General Bayma Denys, chairman of the National Security Council – the post once occupied by General Golbery. Concerned that strategic Brazilian territory just under the northern border was partly given over to Indian reservations, and was furthermore an area of smuggling, the generals wanted to conflate national security and policy towards indigenous tribes. Home to the Yanomami, the largest tribe in Amazônia, whose populations cross several borders, the region was also the outlier of another emerging mineral boom. The Serra de Traira brought at least 20,000 *garimpeiros* into these northern frontier stretches and their porous borders. At this juncture the military suggested that its presence could discipline real or latent conflicts. Among its worries was the politically antipathetic regime in Surinam and the dominance of revolutionaries in the Amazonian reaches of Colombia. Thus the generals would remark that part of their mission was to "put to rest any worries about guerrilla subversion in our territory". With these concerns in mind, the *Calha Norte* project was born.

CALHA NORTE

The *Calha Norte* (literally the Northern Trench) represented the first Amazon program of the "Nova República" of emerging civilian rule. In 1985 the Secretary General of the National Security Council created a working group to elaborate a development plan for the *Calha Norte* zone and the plan was announced in the fall of 1986. The area under its control was vast: roughly 14 per cent of the national territory and 24 per cent of legal Amazônia. Stretching from Tabatinga at the border with Peru to Oiapoque at the border of Guiana, a total of 4,000 miles plus a 100-mile swath inside the frontier would come under the watchful ministrations of the military. Here, 84 indigenous areas, 51 different tribes, 537 mining claims (50 per cent Brazilian, 40 per cent international and 10 per cent state firms), 20,000 goldminers, and land speculators moving up from the Roraima savannahs began to square off. Characterized, in the words of its planning document, "by the rudimentary nature of its productive forms, with a small population, an extensive frontier zone and large indigenous areas [it] inspires one to think of tasks linked to security and development''.

The plan's elaboration was carried out in secret under the aegis of national security. Although Golbery was to die soon after *Calha Norte* began, his shadow hangs over the document. The development program concentrates on three central areas which also carry an ineffable geopolitical ring – the frontier zone, the rivers and the hinterlands. With a caveat about the delicate nature of the project, both domestically and internationally – particularly in light of its reformulation of indigenous policy – it indicated five pressing necessities: an increase in bilateral relations, using the mechanisms of the Amazon pact to combat drug traffic, reinforce international road networks and expand regional consuls; an increase in the military presence in the area (the first phase here was to improve the military installations and transport infrastructure); improvement in the physical establishment of the frontier markings; definition of an indigenous policy appropriate to the area; amplification of the highway infrastructure, acceleration in the production of hydropower, and the integration of development poles as well as provision of more basic social services.

Its specific projects included the development of the *perimetral norte* highway, agricultural projects and colonization on the southeastern zone of the Yanomami territory, and the development of São Paradão hydroelectric plant. With this strip, the generals' first efforts were to improve the shoddy infrastructure of airports and roads. They began to monitor movement of foreigners into these frontier zones and also supervised the movement of Brazilians through the use of identity cards. To better the control of their indigenous charges, they began to promote indigenous colonization, seeking to turn natives into settled Brazilian peasants on the *de rigor* – 240-acre – plots.

UN-NATURAL NATURE

By late 1988 the government of Brazil, now embellished by a civilian president, José Sarney, was under seige by both national and international opinion, and it was getting harder to dismiss protests about the destruction of the Amazon as the mere fabrications of over-heated environmentalists. Conservative bodies like the World Bank and the Inter-American Development Bank were beginning to freeze loans or suspend them, and the environment always seemed to play a role in such decisions. In October 1988, President Sarney convened an inter-ministerial working group to evolve a policy on the environment. Whereas the *Calha Norte* project had been nurtured in secret military counsels, what came to be known as *Nossa Natureza*, Our Nature, was presented almost as an exercise in participatory decision-making. It was promulgated on April 1, 1989.

Some US politicians had been calling for "internationalization of the Amazon" and, to counter this, the *Nossa Natureza* plan was strongly nationalist in tone, stressing that the nation of Brazil would not welcome challenges to its sovereignty. But it was the first time that any Brazilian government had endowed a regional development program with an environmental perspective. The plan put together by Sarney's groups recognized the reality of toxic pollution in goldmining areas, discussed the need to protect the forest from fire and elaborated a program of environmental protection and research. The treatment of this last topic by the working groups of *Nossa Natureza* was of exceptional interest, since the document turned from an assessment of general environmental issues to specific consideration of the effects of environmental degradation on the areas occupied by native communities, populations involved in extractive processes and *ribeirinhos* – dwellers on river banks.

The novelty here was that although Indians had certainly received some attention in government planning, this was the first time that "forest dwellers" and river people had been thus recognized, having been previously invisible to policy makers. *Nossa Natureza* addressed itself to the *garimpeiros*, the miners – thus another group that had hitherto been invisible to the government came into focus. A possible government strategy gradually came emerged: the creation of a number of reserves across the Amazon, allocated to groups such as goldminers, Indians and extractors. In these areas, presumably, property rights and community structures might differ from the corporate occupations outside. For good or for ill, *Nossa Natureza* was proposing an *ejido* system, a series of communal or non-privatized lands such as were distributed in Mexico after the Revolution.

In fact the Mexican experience provided little optimism about this form of holding. Isolated enclaves in the midst of a corporate economy of necessity lead uncertain and difficult lives. Even so, the social and political aspirations of the *garimpeiros*, *ribeirinhos*, rubber tappers and Indians had plainly impinged upon the government's attention. As we shall see, the idea of reserves, recognized in *Nossa Natureza*, had been a battlefield on which men and women – amongst them the leader of the rubber tappers, Chico Mendes – had fought and died. Indeed Mendes's death came on December 22, 1988, just as *Nossa Natureza* was being formulated.

In two other provisions which received much public attention *Nossa Natureza* sounded far more innovative than it actually was, with its temporary suspension of SUDAM's incentives, and its placing of limits on the exports of round logs (as opposed to sawn timber). By that time most of SUDAM's incentive programs were winding down and the export of round logs had been prohibited for years.

Nossa Natureza created national forests in Amapá and Amazonas, national parks in Acre and Mato Grosso, and emphasized the elaboration of several research and conservation units. In addition it placed an emphasis on agro-ecological zoning, an increasingly common buzz-word in environmental planning. The plan paid lip service to the fact that agrarian reform outside Amazônia might staunch the flow of migrants; and that more intensive economic occupation in the Central-West region might deflect the migrant population. The plan also noted that public security in Amazônia ought to be improved.

It was difficult to quarrel with these positions, and equally difficult to take them seriously in light of the *Nova República*'s dilatory agrarian reform. Several colonist surveys already indicated that large percentages of Amazonian migrants had straggled North from the Central South, which was in any case the new center for vast soybean estates. The admonitions about social justice seemed ironic at best. In the Chico Mendes case, only those who had turned themselves in were behind bars, and another rubber-tapper organizer, Osmarino Amâncio Rodrigues, had experienced several assassination attempts. The murder of a socialist representative remained largely uninvestigated, and two days prior to the announcement of *Nossa Natureza* the main rural labour lawyer in Manaus had been shot.[42]

Nossa Natureza was interesting for what it did not say. Migrants were now as invisible as forest dwellers had once been. There was not a word about them. Nor did *Nossa Natureza* address itself to the most venerable activities in the development of infrastructure: the building of dams and roads. This was a considerable omission, since environmental degradation in the Amazon was forcibly expressed in the ongoing rumblings of the Balbina dam project under construction, the proposed Xingu dam and the continuing discussion about the paving and extension of the road to Peru from Rio Branco in Acre. Road building in Amazônia had more than tripled in a decade.

There were in addition some homilies about matching economic development with environmental concerns, but what *Nossa Natureza* made quite clear was that the real Amazonian policy would be covert, or at least undiscussed in public, in much the same manner as the deals made nearly a quarter of a century earlier on the *Rosa da Fonseca*.

THE LOGICS OF DISASTER

Let us return to the question with which we began. Why did the trees suddenly begin to fall? It is clear that the incentives and subsidized credits offered by the generals did play a role in the expansion of livestock, hence conversion of forest into degraded pasture. But the number of entrepreneurs who received them were extremely limited – less than five hundred – and moreover only about 10 per cent of all Amazon holdings used credit of any kind. So incentives and subsidized credit do not, on their own, explain the explosive pattern of deforestation that has occurred.

The generals set up a context in which the struggle for land and the struggle for resources became intense and almost invariably ended in the destruction of yet more forest. Within the context of the larger Brazilian economy, the generals presided over steadily increasing rates of inflation – up to 100 per cent through most of the seventies and eighties. Under these conditions, land served as a hedge against the faltering value of the currency and kept abreast of the rises in cost of living. The rise in Amazonian land values often exceeded the inflation rate. Again, in such conditions of high inflation and general economic instability there was much to be gained from investment in fast plays in stocks, in the overnight currency market, and in land.

Within the regional Amazon economy the rise in the value of land was maintained for several reasons. As natural resource surveys were completed, it was clear that mineral reserves were far more extensive and potentially lucrative than had originally been supposed. Other resources such as timber became increasingly important, owing to the final destruction of the southern Brazilian *Araucaria* forests,[43] and thus this demand began shifting to the North. In the swelling cities low-income consumers increasingly demanded charcoal for cooking. Land values soared because of the commitment of the Brazilian government to expanded road construction, at least within the development pole areas. A well-known formula stated that land near roads had a value from four to ten times greater than more distant parcels on smaller feeder roads. Also contributing to the constant clearing was the fact that the value of land cleared as pasture usually exceeded that of forested land by at least 30 per cent. Finally, at the heart of the pressures for deforestation were the larger battles over land claims, whether by small holder or large. Here the principle was a new version of *uti possedetis*: what is cleared is mine.

A generation earlier the generals had embarked on what they had seen as their historic mission, the geopolitical integration of the Amazon into the economic and political life of the nation. Under a nominal "democracy" (Sarney has both a civilian and military cabinet) the *Calha Norte* project has a reputation as the most secret and authoritarian plan of all. By the time of *Nossa Natureza*, twenty-five years after the generals seized power, and three plans later, billions of dollars had been spent in infrastructural investments in the Amazon. Millions of migrants had trudged into the region. The millionaires of southern Brazil were installed in their great ranches along the Amazon's southern tier. The generals had unleashed forces beyond their control, and now the Amazon faced its apocalypse.

NOTES

1. There are abundant illustrations of this position. Typical is this statement from Gerard Piel, founder of *Scientific American* and a former president of the American Association for the Advancement of Science, the largest scientific professional organization in the United States:

   Destruction of forests is the price being paid for human population growth that is sustained by subsistence agriculture in its historic equilibrium with misery. The fragile soils ... speedily go sterile when the forest is cleared. The farmer thereupon takes his primitive technology deeper into the forest.

   In Ghillean Prance, ed. *Tropical Forests and the World Atmosphere* 1986.

2. Garrett Hardin published his famous article, "The Tragedy of the Commons", in *Science* 1968. His argument may be summarized thus: in the use of common resources all actors try to maximize their individual benefits. With communally owned land an individual can initially derive personal economic benefit from over-exploitative procedures at little personal cost, the adverse consequences being borne by the whole community. In the end the entire communal holding is environmentally degraded. The solution, Hardin argued, was improved population control along Malthusian lines, and privatization of public lands. This thesis was applied by Donella Meadows to the Amazon, and the evocation of Amazônia as "global commons" is still taken seriously.

3. This idea resonates in several bodies of thought. Rosa Luxemburg, for example, argued that the penetration of capital inevitably brought disaster to "natural economies" and a large anthropological literature with an historical orientation has documented this dynamic. Many recent excellent studies have argued that any changes occurring in resource use must be analyzed in more complex terms, examining how access to resources, power and wealth shift within the terms of the local political economy. See for example Michael Watts, *Silent Violence* 1983.

4. See Sanchez and Benetes 1987, Alvim 1982.

5. To give some idea of the rapidity of this process: in the state of Acre, whose area was 75 per cent *terras devolutas* in 1971, 80 per cent of its roughly 33 million acres were transformed into private holdings by 1975 only four years later. The state of Pará transferred some 13.4 milllion acres at the early part of the boom between 1959 and 1963. SUDAM ranch holdings – almost 20 million acres – were transferred to private holders extremely quickly. The state of Mato Grosso and Pará supplied large land holdings to private colonization companies (120,000 acres and up) a process accelerated under Law 1.164 of 1971.

6. For a discussion of factors affecting Amazonian migration, see P. May, *Tragedy of the Non-Commons* 1986. L. Aragon, *Migration to Goiás* 1978, points out that 27 per cent of the migrants he studied fled so as to avoid violence. See also B. Millikan, *Dialectics of Devastation* 1989. Also see the excellent series of studies produced by Donald Sawyer and CEDEPLAR (Centro de Desenvolvimento e Planejamento Regional) on Amazonian migration. For a study of the role of the Itaipu dam in stimulating migration to Rondônia, see C. Quandt, *Case Study: Technical and Social Changes in an Export-Oriented Agricultural Region: Coffee and Soy in Northern Paraná* 1987.

7. Barbara Weinstein makes it a thesis of her *Amazon Rubber Boom*, in seeking to explain why this boom did not transform Amazônia, that "the rubber economy ... is essentially pre-capitalist in its relations of production ... production remained largely under control of the direct producer, with appropriation of surplus occurring at the level of exchange ... it also worked to stifle any developments that might have generated a fundamental transformation in the extractive economy." Ferreira Reis in *O Seringa e O Seringueiro*, Mauro Almeida in *Relaçoẽs do Trabalho nos Seringais do Alto Juruá*, and Roberto Santos in *Economia do Amazonas*, argue essentially the same point.

8. See Peter Evans, *Dependent Development: The Alliance of Multinational, State and Local Capital in Brazil* 1979. Also see

M. Pompermeyer, *The State and Frontier in Brazil* 1979.

9. See Jeffrey Leonard *Resources and Development in Central America* 1987.

10. See Miguel Altieri, *Agroecology* 1987, M. Altieri and S. Hecht, *Agroecology and the Small Farmer* 1989, J.R. Kloppenburg, *First the Seed* 1989.

11. See Figure 1. The provision of credits and incentives has provoked two types of analysis. One is exemplified by the World Resource Institute's studies, which have tended to take the view that subsidies and incentives distort the functioning of the free market and that their removal would result in sounder environmental practices – an approach scarcely borne out by the accompanying graph. Hans Binswanger has produced a concise summary of incentives that contribute to deforestation in his *Fiscal and Legal Incentives with Environmental Effects on the Amazon*, Washington D.C. 1987. Others, such as Hecht and then Browder, have pointed to the political and economic context in which such subsidies have been made.

12. M. Pastor, "The effects of IMF programs in the Third World: Debate and evidence from Latin America, in *World Development*, Vol. 15 (2).

13. For examples of this approach see M. Schminck and C. Wood, "The Political Ecology of Amazônia", in P. Little and M. Horowitz (eds.), *Lands at Risk in the Third World* 1987; S.B. Hecht, "Environment, Development and Politics", in *World Development*, 13, 1985; S. Hecht, *The Sacred Cow: Large and Small Scale Livestock Strategies*, GSAUP Working Paper; Alain de Janvry and R. Garcia, *Rural Poverty and Environmental Degradation in Latin America*, Rome: IFAD 1988, unpublished manuscript; J. Browder, *Logging the Rainforest*, 1986; J. Collins, "Small Holder Settlement of Tropical South America", in *Human Organization*, Vol. 45(1), 1986; B. Millikan 1989; S. Bunker, *Underdeveloping the Amazon*, 1985.

14. R. Santos, "Law and Social Change: The Problem of Land in the Amazon", in Schmink and Wood (eds.) *Frontier Expansion in Amazônia* 1984.

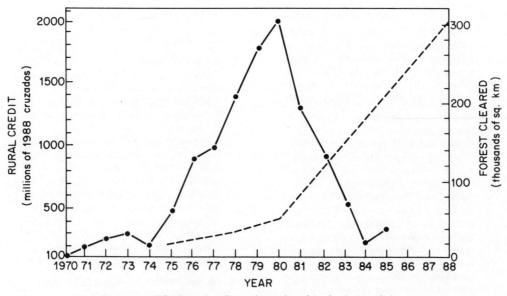

FIGURE 1 *Official rural credit vs. forest cleared in classic Amazônia*

15. For a discussion of SPVEA see J. Galey, 1978.

16. What was the extent of U.S. involvement in the coup that overthrew Goulart? Useful accounts are offered in Phyllis Parker's *Brazil and the Quiet Intervention, 1964*, 1979, and Jan Knippers Black's *United States Penetration of Brazil*, 1977. Three US administrations – Eisenhower's, Kennedy's and Johnson's – watched Brazil's postwar political evolution with increasing trepidation and after April 1, 1964, with relief. The Cuban revolution of January, 1959, vastly augmented fears about communist potential in Brazil, particularly in the Northeast. The Kennedy brothers watched Brazil closely and Robert Kennedy visited Goulart in Brasília in November, 1962, with the express purpose of discussing what the White House viewed as Brazil's "disturbing drift to the left". In this particular meeting, Lincoln Gordon, the US ambassador in Rio, offered to list for Goulart communists in Petrobrás, and the postal and telegraph agency. Both military and economic aid from the US was proffered with clear political objectives, with funds going to states deemed to be politically friendly, and not to the central government. Military assistance and supplies of riot control material for police forces were also dispatched to Brazil's security apparatus in increasing amounts as US unease about Goulart mounted. Economic assistance was predicated on traditional austerity measures and shrinkage of social spending, of a type associated with US government agencies and the IMF.

In the run-up to the 1962 elections in Brazil, the US embassy and regional consulates disbursed several million (about $5 million in Gordon's recollection) to conservative candidates. In that same year Vernon Walters was transferred from Rome to Rio de Janeiro as military attaché. Walters had been translator to Brazilian officers serving in General Mark Clark's campaign as the Brazilian Expeditionary Force, and knew many officers personally, including Castello Branco. Walters later recollected that at the time of his transfer he was told that President Kennedy would not be averse to Goulart's overthrow, if he were to be replaced by a stable anti-communist government. In March of 1964, Ambassador Gordon cabled the State Department calling for increased US military aid to be sent to the Brazilian armed forces, deeming such supplies "essential in restraining the left-wing excesses of [the] Goulart government". By now Chief of Staff General Castello Branco had, probably in February, joined the military conspirators against Goulart and a coup was imminent. At a March 13 mass rally in Rio, Goulart told a huge crowd that he had signed an order expropriating private owners of all land running ten kilometers in from either side of all federal highways, railways and water projects, and was also expropriating oil refineries (all of which were domestically owned). This speech was watched by Castello Branco from his window in the War Ministry and later that evening Branco told Walters that he did not believe Goulart would serve out his term. By the last days of March the US Embassy had informed Washington that a coup was imminent. The US Defense Department readied shipments of oil, gasolene and lubricants to be supplied to the Brazilian armed forces in the event of civil war. Large shipments of shot-guns and other light armament (in an operation called "Brother Sam") were already readied at McGuire Air Force Base in New Jersey. The aircraft carrier Forrestal was ordered to proceed south and stand off Rio Grande do Sul, where it was thought resistance to the military might be fierce.

The coup culminated on April 1, with the State Department filing almost hourly reports to Washington, and with Walters in close touch with Castello Branco. A day later President Johnson was sending a telegram of congratulation to Brazil's new leaders (who had not received any form of constitutional ratification from the Brazilian Congress). Ambassador Gordon, on that same day, sent a message to Carl Hayden, president *pro tempore* of the Senate, describing the coup as "a victory for [the] free world". Thomas Mann, assistant secretary of state for inter-American affairs, said the time had arrived for "sacrifice for all groups including land reform". The US speedily supplied economic aid to Brazil's new leaders.

Phyllis Parker's restrained conclusion is that "[t]here is evidence that U.S. aid further weakened an already weakened central government, not only by witholding assistance from Goulart's government . . . but also . . . through direct dealings with and support of other groups" and "[t]he U.S. was not involved in the execution of the coup only because there was no need to be." Jan Knippers Black asks rhetorically, in her conclusion, "Would those on the right . . . have been willing to risk armed confrontation without the expectation of United States backing? Celso Furtado (the economist) for one doubts it, and so does this author." This is the nub. Both Ambassador Gordon and Military Attaché Walters were continually in touch with Brazilian military officers in the months preceding the coup and at no point warned them that a coup would be viewed with disfavor in Washington. To the contrary. So the generals embarked on a coup knowing that both immediate military aid (up to and including US physical intervention) and long-term economic aid were forthcoming.

In the years following the coup, when it became apparent that the speedy return to democratic civilian rule initially predicted by the US embassy was not occurring, US support for the generals remained constant. (In mid-1989 there was a diplomatic furore in Brazil when an aide to a Brazilian assemblywoman denounced the possible appointment of Richard Murphy as the new US ambassador, saying that while he was under arrest (and tortured) in Recife in 1968, Murphy – serving at the US Consulate at Recife at the time – had come to interrogate him.) In 1971 Senator Frank Church observed that even without counting Peace Corps volunteers, the US had twice as many officials in Brazil, per head of population, as Great Britain had in India when it was ruling that country.

17. Having alienated almost all sectors of society, and with the generals demanding his resignation, Vargas took a revolver from his desk and shot himself through the heart. A farewell note, whose authenticity has been questioned, was immediately published in the press. Asserting that international capital and corrupt national interests were endangering Brazil and injuring the interests of workers Vargas concluded, "I offer my life in the holocaust. I chose this means to be with you always. I gave you my life. Now I offer my death. Nothing remains. Serenely, I take the first step on the road to eternity as I leave life to enter history." See Thomas Skidmore, *Politics in Brazil, 1930–1964* 1967.

18. Alfred Stepan demonstrates this point in great detail in his authoritative *The Military in Politics: Changing Patterns in Brazil*, Princeton, 1971. "Coups could be considered not merely as a unilateral response of an arbitrary and independent military institution acting on behalf of its own institutional needs and ideology, but as dual response of both military officers and civilians to political divisions in the society."

19. The cohort of Brazilian officers serving in the BEF and thus fostering close ties with the US military was later concentrated in the War College, known as the "Sorbonne Group", and was the core of the 1964 takeover.

20. Golbery's philosophy is outlined in two volumes, *Conjuntura, Politica Nacional o Poder Executivo e Geopolítica do Brasil*, Rio 1981, *Geopolítica*, and in various speeches. Geopolitics, for obvious reasons, has always been a popular theme among the generals. See Meira Mattos, *Uma Geopolítica Pan Amazônia*, Rio 1980; Rodrigues, *Geopolítical do Brasil* 1947. Also see M. Alves, *State and Opposition in Military Brazil* 1985. For a more general discussion of the Brazilian military state see A. Stepan's *The Military in Politics* 1971; G. O'Donnell (ed.) *Bureaucratic Authoritarianism* 1979.

21. The Brazilian War College was established in 1949 and by the early 1950s the US Army had exclusive rights to assist in running the College, which was modeled on the National War College in Washington. There was much interchange of officers of the two countries, as well as much US assistance in the provision of materiel and training. See Skidmore.

22. See Joseph Page, *The Revolution that Never Was: Northeast Brazil, 1955–64* 1972. Also Fernando Antonio Azevedo, *As Ligas Camponesas* 1982. Also see the excellent

historical sociology of Luiz Edouardo Soares, *Campesinato: Ideologia e Politica* 1981.

23. J. Martin, *A Milarização da Questão Agraria* 1984, Rio.

24. In the early years of the Castello Branco regime the head of the São Paulo Commercial Association was in fact a general.

25. This was also because the Brazilian "cattle cycle" was in a cyclic low and so owners were holding all animals in order to build up their breeding herds. See S. Hecht, *Cattle Ranching* 1982, and L. Jarvis, *Livestock in Latin America* 1986.

26. See World Bank, Brazil, first and second livestock sector loans, World Bank, Washington DC.

27. For a more detailed explanation see S.B. Hecht, *Development and Deforestation in the Amazon: Current and Future Policies, Investment and Impact on Forest Conversion* 1986.

28. D. Mahar, *Frontier Policy in the Amazon,* 1979.

29. See M. Moreira-Alves, who also points out that the "pacification program" also involved moving peasants to prison camps near towns where they could be kept under surveillance. The most complete account of this episode has been written by the son of an assassinated P.C. do B. member, Vladimir Pomar, in his *Araguaia: O Partido e a Guerrilha* 1980.

30. Along the highway in swaths ranging in depth from 10 to 100 kilometers; along the frontier in swaths of 150 kilometers in depth.

31. See M. Pompermeyer, *The State and the Frontier* 1979. Also see J. Sayad, *Crédito Rural no Brasil* 1984.

32. One detailed study by Emilio Moran, *Developing the Amazon* 1982, argued that settlers who had a more entrepreneurial outlook, and previous managerial experience in managing their own estates, were more likely to succeed. Moran noted the amount of capital and credit-worthiness of those who succeeded or failed.

33. P. Fearnside, *Human Carrying Capacity in the Brazilian Rainforest* 1986.

34. Bunker 1985, Moran 1982.

35. See Susanna Hecht, "Rethinking Colonist Attrition", submitted to *World Development* 1989. Also Hecht, Anderson and May, "The Subsidy from Nature," in *Human*

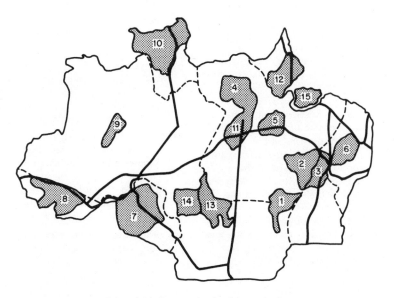

Poles of development in the Amazon basin

Organization 1988. For income studies of peasants, see E. F. Moran and J. Browder, ''Colonists in Rondônia'', presented at the Latin American Studies Association meeting, New Orleans, March 1988. Also see World Bank 1987.

36. See A. Leite and P. Furley, ''Land Development in the Amazon'', in Hemming (ed.), *Change in the Amazon* 1985; E. Moran 1982. This issue is carefully addressed by P. Fearnside, ''Stochastic Modeling and Human Carrying Capacity Estimation'', in Barbira-Scazzochio (ed.), *Land, People and Planning in the Brazilian Amazon*, 1982. Also see B. Millikan, *The Dialectics of Devastation* 1989.

37. See Marianne Schminck's fine article, ''Land Conflict in Amazônia'', in *American Ethnologist*, 1987; S. G. Bunker, *Underdeveloping the Amazon* 1985; B. H. Millikan 1989; S. Hecht, *Contemporary Dynamics of Amazonian Development: Reanalyzing Colonist Attrition* 1989; Alfredo Wagner, *Estrura Fundiaria e Expansão Camponesa*, Manuscript 1987; J. Martins, ''Lutando pela Terra: Indios e Posseiros na Amazônia'', in *Os Camponesas e a Politica no Brasil* 1981; also J. Foweraker, *The Struggle for Land* 1982.

38. The ''growth poles'' in the *PoloAmazônia* project are numbered on map 4. 1: the Xingu-Araguaia, essentially a livestock zone with meat processing; 2: the Carajás, a source of iron ore and gold and later turned into a major regional development pole under the *Projeto Grande Carajás*, which came to dominate 10 per cent of the national territory; 3: the Araguaia-Tocantins, initially livestock, but soon viewed as a major trading area, because of its situation at the crossing of the Belém-Brasília and the Trans-Amazon, and the confluence of the two rivers, the Araguaia and Tocantins. Its importance was later increased by timber extraction and gold mining; 4: Trombetas, huge bauxite deposits; 5: Altamira, on the Trans-Amazon, would become an agriculture and livestock pole to service the mining areas close to it on the Tapajós; 6: the Pré-Amazônia-Maranhense, intended as an agricultural pole, but investment would concentrate in construction of the railroad from São Luís to the Carajás mine; 7: Rondônia, agriculture and livestock; 8: Acre, agriculture and livestock; 9: Juruá, timber extraction, but the area became the center for oil exploration; 10: Roraima, promotion of livestock in areas close to the frontier, and preliminary mining; 11: Tapajós, agriculture and livestock near Itaituba, but soon becomes a thriving gold economy; 12: Amapá, agriculture and livestock in the frontier zone, and manganese mining; 13: Juruena, livestock and agricultural development in an area that later becomes a major goldmining zone; 14: Aripunã, forest research and extraction, and a burgeoning livestock zone; 15: Marajó, livestock, timber and oil exploration.

39. A. T. da Silva, ''Grandes Projetos em implanação na Amazônia'', *Para Desenvolvimento* 1986, (18). As of 1986, indirect stable employment was calculated by da Silva to have produced less than 53,000 jobs for these multi-billion investments. Besides their direct impacts on the environment, they set road building and other processes in motion that increase local rates of deforestation.

40. See Fearnside's excellent series of articles (some of them co-authored) in *Interciencia*.

41. The study of private colonization has been neglected in Amazonian research. The scant information comes from Jim Butler's 1986 Ph.D. thesis on colonists, goldminers and ranchers, which discusses the Tucama project in southern Pará.

42. Given the abyss between action and words, the humorous commentary of rubber tappers on the program provides insight: ''*Nossa Natureza* – Our Nature?'' they laughed, '''you must be kidding. They're talking about *their* Nature, so that's what we call their program, *Natureza deles!*''

43. The lumber exports mentioned earlier in this chapter are derived largely from plantations in the South.

SEVEN

The Furies Unleashed

There among the strangest of civilized people, passing through and pausing to kill trees and men for only so long as it takes to do both, then following other paths where they renew the same anarchy, passing like a devastating wave, and making even more savage the region's savagery ... those disordered adventurers, opening with carbine shots ... new routes for their itineraries.

EUCLIDES DA CUNHA, *Um Paraíso Perdído*

The old blacks, descendants from the Mocambos (the escaped slaves) ... are the keepers of the secrets of the goldfields. The celebrated Agustinho Mafra was the one who had the gift of finding gold. Esterão, his successor, transmitted the secret to Tito, Valério, Alexandre, Tiberio and thus it came down to the living.

R. ALMEIDA, "The Northeast region of Maranhão" 1961

From the sixties until today the entire Amazon has been convulsed by an enormous enclosure movement easily rivaling the conversion of public land to private property in early modern Europe. This enclosure movement drew clear battle lines. On the one side were the generals, the large entrepreneurs whom the generals saw as their natural allies in development, the extractionist oligarchies of rubber forests and Brazil-nut groves who had grown rich on their state leases and debt peons; and the speculators and ranchers. On the other side were people mostly without private property or, if they had property, the incapacity to hold on to it: first, the 200,000 Indians of the Amazon who had ancestral lands but were under relentless attack either by direct appropriation or through constant incursions to seize their valuable minerals and timber. Next, the *garimpeiros*, the workers of placer mines, numbering between some 300,000 and 500,000. In many accounts of the Amazon, these *garimpeiros* are often branded the villains of the story, confronting Indians, sometimes murdering them, polluting their rivers and lands. But these *garimpeiros* are victims too, of hard times and limited opportunities for Brazil's small farmers, and of the harsh fight to survive in the cities. Then there are the extractors – of rubber, nuts, resins, palm products and medicines – gatherers who have been the base of the Amazon economy for five hundred years. More than two million people in the Amazon forests are engaged in the economies of petty extraction; they are often small farmers as well. They have made their livings from intact forests from which they are now being expelled, and which themselves are now being destroyed. And finally there are the settlers; since the sixties some two to three million in number, refugees from economic devastation in the Northeast or the South of Brazil. These are the people drawn to the Amazon by government promises of land and financial backing, those simply forced to migrate or perish, or those just taking a gamble for better times. Indian, *garimpeiro*, extractor and settler have often been bitter enemies in the past, and often still are so today – *garimpeiro* against Indian, Indian against extractor and settler, settler against extractor. But against them all now mustered the generals and their allies as they began to put their plan into execution. Let us now describe the circumstances, logistics and rationale of this onslaught.

The tempi of destruction in the Amazon are varied, and centuries as well as decades must serve as our time scale. In previous epochs agents of destruction included microbes, slavers and metal tools. The means of capturing the great wealth of the Amazon came through control over labor whereas now they stem from control over land. Today, testimony to the accelerating destruction of the Amazon can be found in the constant battles between the surviving native tribes and those who would invade their land, exploit their resources and deny their cultures; in the constant friction between new migrants, old settlers, petty extractors and large landowners; in murderous campaigns waged by large ranchers hungry for pasture and impatient with whatever groups of Indians, rubber tappers, petty extractors or small settlers might stand in their path. It can be found in environmental devastation: burned forests, annihilated species, degraded lands, poisoned rivers, and toxic soils.

CARAJÁ, MUNDURUCU, SUYÁ: THREE HISTORIES OF DESTRUCTION

Virtually from the moment that Pinzón clapped his eyes upon the estuary of the Amazon at the dawn of the sixteenth century, contact with these pale strangers brought disaster upon the native inhabitants. Exploitation of the region compounded the disaster as disease swept through these native populations and as they were pressed into slavery. Few demographic calamities match in the thoroughness of their destruction the destiny of the tribes in the Amazon basin, and today there are more Indian place names than Indians left in Brazil. With these names as witness, and fortified with the fragmented accounts that have survived, a traveler in the Amazon can reconstruct the fates of tribe after tribe, in histories of attrition and annihilation.

When the French explorer Francis de Castelnau traveled down the Araguaia river in 1844, he encountered the Carajá Indians. This tribe dwelt on the banks of the river, and Castelnau applauded their large villages and rich agricultural plantations. The Carajá charmed him. They were beautiful, with excellent crafts of elegant feather work and finely woven cotton. After the corruption he had viewed on his way through Goiás, where native peoples were living in dissolute military outposts, the wholesomeness of the Carajá who lived protected by rapids above and below them was a source of delight. The French expedition marveled at the vibrant ritual life, the large palm straw body masks, the rich use of body decoration and the music and dancing.[1]

Of this tribe only about a thousand people remain today. At contact, the Carajá's numbers were estimated at more than 57,000; now, little remains of them or their dominions except their name. Along the frontier tracts of the Araguaia the Portuguese constructed forts at the confluences of important rivers – Santa Isabel where the Rio das Mortes joined the Araguaia, São João, where the Araguaia meets the Tocantins – or at strategic points near the rapids. Santa Maria, across the river from Conceição do Araguaia was just below the *barreira*, the barrier rapids. These forts were constructed, in the words of one military commander, to "stop gold smuggling, to prevent slaves from fleeing from Cametá [at the junction of the Tocantins and the Amazon] up river to Goiás, and to check the aggressions of the Timbira, Carajá and Apinagé". The Timbira and the Apinagé inhabited the more northerly areas and were forest tribes.

The Carajá were pre-eminently a river tribe, and thus vulnerable to whatever form of disaster might ply these waters. Their proximity to white traders even without evil intention made them the first victims of every epidemic, and they were ravaged by the smallpox outbreak on the Araguaia-Tocantins between 1812 and 1817. The frontier battles further east, along the Tocantins, were brutal in the extreme. Through treachery, tribes like the Timbira were tricked into slavery and dragged off to the slave marts of Belém and San Luís. Others were lured to towns where smallpox was rife. Later in the back forest the disease burned through the native populations. The Araguaia, less directly battered but still under siege, was not punished by direct warfare but felt the effects of intertribal conflicts as those groups on the Tocantins pressed into the Araguaia, as tribes from the south and west pushed into the safer forests and placed pressure on the Carajá. Both natives and whites still sought captives, the legality of the enterprise being of minor interest. Military incursions were increasing as colonist pressures from the east and the south began to mount. In 1813, Xavante and Carajá warriors descended on the garrison at Santa Maria and destroyed it. In attack after attack they disturbed the river trade. Now viewed as hostile, the Carajá, Xavante and Apinagé were subject to constant threats from whites wherever they encountered them. Moreover an extremely fierce tribe called Canoeiros – the canoers – who terrorized large areas of the Tocantins and the Araguaia, were thought by some to have been shock troops

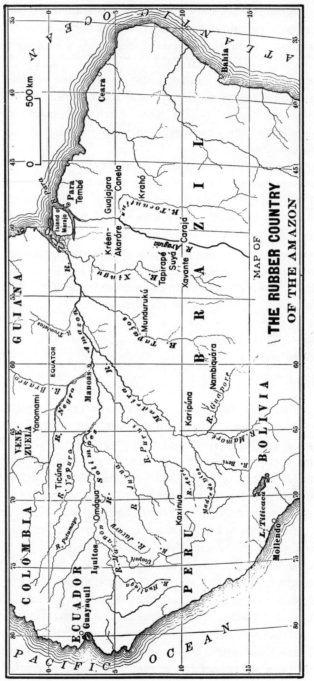

MAP OF

THE RUBBER COUNTRY
OF THE AMAZON

Indian tribes mentioned in the text

of the Carajá who were known as excellent water-masters, unlike many of the forest tribes such as the Xavante.[2]

Some of these stories reflect the Portuguese confusion about what tribe was doing what. Marauding Indians probably blurred into uniformity, all as terrifying as each other. What was clear was that irritations with one tribe could easily translate into brutality against another.

The explosion of the rubber boom, not long after Castelnau's voyage, along the middle Araguaia brought men into the forests near Conceição, and expanded the use of the river as the trade in latex pressed into every conceivable backwater. More docile tribes like the horticultural Carajá entered into trading relations, but were far less integrated into rubber production than local forest tribes or those on the upper Amazon. The gradual incursions of frontiersmen during the middle part of this century scarcely affected them.

The final blow came with the explosion of ranching in the 1970s, and for the Carajá this spelled absolute disaster. Now living on the island of Bananal, the remnant members of the tribe today serve as guides for adventure tourism, and ply their much degraded crafts at local airports.

The name of the Carajá will at least be on the lips of people for the next several centuries, the presumed time it will take to exhaust the mines – 18 billion tons, and about 67 per cent pure – of iron ore. The Serra do Carajás – the mountains of the Carajá Indians – turned out to be one of the richest mineral finds on the planet, with enormous deposits of iron, nickel, copper, bauxite and gold. A two-and-a-half billion dollar railway, financed by the Brazilian government, the United States and Japan, transports about seventy tons of iron ore per railroad car in trains often exceeding one hundred cars. Between the red maw of the mine and the blue ocean at São Luís are the three pig-iron plants, charcoal-fired and therefore destined to increase the cutting in the region by some 400 square miles to 600 square miles per year.[3] Displacing labor for agriculture, a vast army of cutters will hack its way through whatever forest remains there, to provide the raw energy to convert the highest quality ore to the lowest value industrial nuggets. The value of pig iron has dropped by 55 per cent since 1980. As we have already seen, the economics of pig iron is only rational when the energy costs – the forest – are calculated at zero.[4] Up to twenty-five pig-iron furnaces, three cement plants and six metal alloy factories are planned to dot the route of the railway. Their demand for charcoal will exceed 2.5 million tons. All will receive an extraordinary concession package: capital grants of 75 per cent of the development costs of the plants, tax holidays and other encouragements. Though they themselves were not much of a conquering tribe – at least in comparison to groups like the Kayapó – the ghosts of the Carajá will know that their name, at least as a label for the mine, has become all-conquering: the lands devastated have now extended over the territories of their old neighbors and enemies, the Timbira, the Guajajara, and the Canela. After their moment as charcoal, these forests have made the familiar declension to cleared lands and degraded pastures useless to man or beast, as anyone riding the train from Marabá to São Luís can see.

In the 1780s, a powerful force of more than 2,000 Mundurucu warriors pressed east from their homeland on the Tapajós across two watersheds: the Xingu and the Tocantins. Well known as headhunters who always carried their trophies close at hand when hunting or warring, justly feared by the adjacent Mawe, the Mundurucu fell with fury on the settlers of the Rio Capim and Rio Moju not far from Belém, the capital of the Amazon. Incensed by attacks so close to home, the Portuguese hastened to send an expedition of reprisal. Returning to their territories, the Mundurucu were surprised on the Cururu river, near the headwaters of the Tapajós. There, in pitched battle, a thousand of their warriors fell, but they had saved the day. The Portuguese retaliatory expedition was successfully repelled. In the wake of the Portuguese setback, Lobo d'Almada, the governor of Pará, suggested that kindness might succeed where force had failed. Two wounded Mundurucu captured in another skirmish in 1795 were treated humanely and sent back to their tribes in canoes laden with gifts. The returning Indians relayed the message, pointing out that, were the rest of the tribe to supply goods and manioc flour to the whites, they too would be laden with metal axeheads and machetes. Thus began the enduring truce of the Mundurucu with the whites, forging a long collaboration of this tribe with a series of slavers, forest product extractors and rubber barons.

The tribe was populous as well as powerful. In 1819 Martius placed their numbers between 18,000 and 40,000. The loyalty of the Mundurucu was unquestioning, and as agents of the crown, their warring history served them in good stead. They even helped the Portuguese quell the Cabanagem rebellion of the 1830s – a revolt of slaves and *mestizos* against the propertied Portuguese – in the back forest reaches that they knew so well.

Well integrated into European trading circuits and receptive to trading goods, if not to white dominion, the Mundurucu were rapidly swept up in the first wave of the rubber economy. Even in the first half of the nineteenth century, many naturalists and commentators on the Amazon scene noted the role of the Mundurucu as tappers in rubber extraction. In the early 1850s when Bates described them, they were treated with great respect, receiving a return in guns, ammunition and cotton for the loads of rubber they gave to the trader, an appropriate recompense for those who made the Tapajós safe for trade.[5] But only twenty-five years later, others remarked at how strange it was that the former masters of the Tapajós had now become its slaves.

In 1875, Antônio Tocantins wrote about the upper reaches of the Tapajós. He described how the rubber traders would gradually lure the native Indians into debt servitude and then use them to tap the many trees they had claimed. Debt was indeed the main instrument of control, but harsher methods were scarcely shunned. Traders on the upper Tapajós kept the family members of native tappers as prisoners, hostages to be ransomed by the rubber collected by the tapper who thus had no choice where to sell his harvest. Rape of Indian women was standard. A famous case on the Tapajós involved the murder of a rubber trader, Manoel Paes, a baron of 5,000 trees and countless Mundurucu, Mawe and Apiaka Indian collectors. A young Mawe girl, repulsing his advances, shot and killed him. At the subsequent trial a courtroom was held rapt as the girl, lifting her skirts to her thighs to show the marks of her abuse, described the orgiastic scenes that unfolded in the *barracão* – the rubber trading post. In their sadism they easily rivaled the horrors described by Roger Casement in his condemnation of the practices on the Putamayo by agents of the great Peruvian rubber house, the Casa Arana.

One of the main trading posts on the Tapajós where the Mundurucu had traded for more than a century, was the little village of Itaituba. When Tocantins visited Itaituba in 1875 to voyage above the São Luis rapids of the Tapajós, it was already exporting 150,000 kilograms of rubber to Belém. Guaraná, a stimulating flavoring, as well as sarsaparilla and copal oil, also went to Belém and Mato Grosso. These extractive products formed only one part of the economy.

Gold was also to be found in the Tapajós. João de Souza Azevedo, an early explorer *bandeirante*, fired by the lust for gold and the continuing interest in the use of the Amazon tributaries as transport north from the Mato Grosso, began his exploration in 1746 and discovered a major gold deposit. This mine was finally played out, but its memory was never eclipsed. Today, there are more than 186 *garimpos* – placer mines – on the Tapajós producing quantities of gold (more than 10 metric tonnes in some years) that now exceed the production of the Serra Pelada.[6] About eighty-four mines are serviced by the now booming town of Itaituba, which has grown from about 2,000 people in 1970 to more than 30,000 today. These numbers were swollen by the arrival of the Trans-Amazon highway as settlers moved to the region, and by the footloose labor that moved on after construction of the Tucuruí hydroelectric plant, power source for Carajás. But now the central business of the Tapajós is gold.

Gold has always been a very serious enterprise in the Amazon. Since the seventeenth century it has galvanized explorations, rewritten the history of settlements, spelled death for thousands. The role of the state in the New World was initially to manage and regulate the production of precious minerals. The arrogant and the desperate both forged their way into gold fields, the former fired by the legend of El Dorado, the latter by the more humble myth of the Mountain of Martyrs, a mountain of incredible riches inscribed with scenes of the passion of Christ. Brazilian mining has always relied on the men of color, *mestizos* or *mamelucos* who, seeking a "remedy for their poverty", began to pan the rivers for gold.[7]

In Amazônia's past, black and Indian slaves worked the mines along the southern Amazon flanks of Mato Grosso, Goiás and Maranhão. Natividade was worked by some 16,000 slaves, Águas Quentes with 12,000. The Jesuit missionaries used African slaves to work their gold deposits in Maranhão. Today the mines attract men to their pits because of declining rural wages, the marginalization of the smaller farmers, and high unemployment in urban Brazil.

The new Amazonian gold rush began in 1980. The scenes at the Serra Pelada became famous in Brueghel-like photographs showing the sediment being carried up the hill, jerry-can by jerry-can, and then washed in slurry in the lower Tocantins by men drenched in mud, only distinguishable from the substrate because they moved. But the main gold-producing zone is the Tapajós, where more than 60 tons of gold have come out of the earth, and 120 tons of mercury are flushed back into the tropical soils and waters.[8] Here goldminers invade national parks – Indian lands – out of greed and despair. About 85 per cent of Brazilian gold production now comes from the *garimpos*. The placer mines generate almost one billion dollars a year and employ some 500,000 people, according to the Department of Mineral Production.

Today, a century's worth of pressure by adventurers seeking rubber and gold have reduced the Mundurucu who once fielded war parties numbering thousands, to about six villages and some 1,500 souls.[9]

In September of 1884 the German explorer Karl von Steinen was elated when he found yet another tribe on the upper Xingu. From other accounts by Indians with whom Steinen had had dealings in his journey through the Xingu's headwaters, he knew that these people were from one of the terrifying tribes of the Kayapó, the Suyá.

The Suyá had fled from the mounting chaos of the coastal zones and, like other Kayapó groups, had fought their way through to the upper waters where the cataracts might afford some protection. They were concentrated around a tributary of the Xingu called the Suyá-Missu. Most oral accounts of Suyá history record battle after battle with native groups such as the Mundurucu, the Krén Akarore, the Trumai, the Juruena, and the northern Kayapó. The Suyá also remember several devastating epidemics. While von Steinen was commenting on what he considered to be the grotesquerie of their lip disks, the Suyá were assessing him in an even more negative light. Thereafter they were ill disposed to any contact with whites and until 1959 no white man survived an encounter with them. In that year the main body of the Suyá were discovered by aerial reconnaissance and formal contact was carried out with the tribe by the renowned Brazilian anthropologists, the Villas-Boas brothers. The wisdom of the Suyá's national security posture after von Steinen's visit was more than ratified by what followed. The Villas-Boas brothers asked them to consolidate their two villages into a new one, at a new location. In the ensuing move all the older men died from disease.

In the mid sixties the remnant of the Suyá were now advised to move on to the Xingu reservation. Another branch of the tribe, the western Suyá, apparently exhausted from the constant encroachments of colonists and ranchers and years of burned villages and retaliatory attacks, tried to make peaceful contact with the Brazilians, who celebrated the encounter by giving them deliberately poisoned tapir meat. In 1968 the western Suyá were contacted by officials of the Indian Protection Service, SPI.[10] As was common on such occasions when ''wild Indians'' were contacted, reporters were brought along, including one who had influenza. The western Suyá returned to their villages and died in large numbers.[11]

It is only in this light that the story told by one of the great Paulista land speculators – and self-described modern *bandeirantes* – of the Amazon, Herminio Ometto and his partner Ariosto da Riva, sounds relatively benign. Seven years earlier in 1961, the two were searching for land for their large ranching enterprise. At that time the only inhabitants in the area they sought to claim were lodged in one Indian village. Ometto recalled how they won the Indians' confidence in order to steal their land:

> We began by throwing down food and presents from a small plane every day at the same hour: dried meat, brown sugar, red cloth, cheap blankets. We could not give good things. We did all that to deceive the tribe and make the Indians stay in the place where we had thrown down the presents. Meanwhile Teles [his foreman] would open the *piquete* [a cleared survey path and preliminary road bed]. The woodsmen had to open seventy-five miles of virgin forest. Finally they met up with the Indians who had preferred to stay at the spot where the little plane would throw down presents every day.

Two hundred and forty acres of land were reserved for the Indians' use.[12] Three years later they were transferred to a Silesian mission and Ometto named his new ranch the Fazenda Suyá-Missu.

Ometto was almost certainly one of the delighted passengers aboard the *Rosa da Fonseca* and he and his crony Ariosto ended up owning almost five million acres in that region, the largest of the spreads receiving the fiscal incentives promulgated by Castello Branco. Ometto's ranch was more than 1,358,400 acres. More than 60,000 acres had been cleared in a decade. The ranch was finally sold to the Italian agricultural consortium, Liquigás, a producer of industrial chemicals in Brazil, with Liquigás viewing the land as a good means of deferring taxes, for raising cattle and ultimately for speculation in land. In 1974 and 1976 the Fazenda Suyá-Missu was once again granted enormous fiscal incentives.[13]

THE BULLDOZER AND THE CHAINSAW

There are hundreds of ethnographies of other Indian tribes in the Amazon that echo the fates of the Carajá, the Mundurucu and the Suyá. Indeed many of them suffered a worse fate, because the tribe has been extinguished altogether. In 1957 the Brazilian anthropologist Darcy Ribeiro published a report on the condition of Indians in Brazil.[14] Ribeiro demonstrated that between 1900 and 1957 some eighty Indian tribes had been destroyed. During this same period the total numbers of indigenous people had dropped from one million to two hundred thousand. Many of the surviving tribes were on the verge of extinction: deculturated, disease-ridden and in despair. The Amazon basin held most of the remaining Indians – some 140 tribes – and Ribeiro said these too would be extinct unless the Indian Protection Service, SPI,[15] managed to insulate the tribes from advancing national society. It transpired that the buffer SPI had in mind was the graveyard.

By the late 1950s the SPI was filled with corrupt officials inflicting horror on the very people they were meant to protect. In 1967 the Minister of the Interior, General Albuquerque Lima, commissioned an inquiry by the Attorney-General, Jader Figueiredo, which resulted in the publication of a twenty-one volume investigation; among other crimes it found evidence of massacres of entire tribes by dynamite, machine guns and poisoned sugar. The report was followed by a number of private investigations, including one by a French medical attaché, Patrick Braun, who stated that his examination of various Brazilian government files including the Figueiredo Report showed that between 1957 and 1963, tribes in the Mato Grosso had been deliberately infected with smallpox, influenza, tuberculosis and measles, and that tuberculosis had similarly been introduced into the tribes of the northern Amazon in 1964 and 1965. Braun spoke of evidence that the disease microbes ''were deliberately brought into Indian territories by landowners and speculators utilizing a *mestizo* previously infected'' and said that countless Indians subsequently died.[16]

In February 1969, Norman Lewis reported in the London *Sunday Times* that officials of the SPI had joined with ranchers and land speculators in murdering Indians and stealing their lands. Lewis quoted Attorney-General Figueiredo as saying ''It is not only through the embezzlement of funds but by the admission of sexual perversions, murders, and all other crimes listed in the penal code against Indians and their property, that one can see that the Indian Protection Service was for years a den of corruption and indiscriminate killings.''[17] Interior Minister Lima abolished the SPI and set up a new agency called the *Fundação Nacional do Indio* (FUNAI) and promised restitution to the Indians. The following year Lima was gone from politics and the Trans-Amazon highway was announced, with its straight line rolling ruthlessly through Indian lands.

FUNAI was an initial improvement; it could scarcely have been worse than its predecessor. However, its officials were soon evincing corruption and acting as agents for large-scale ranchers, mining consortia, loggers and government road projects. In 1970 the head of FUNAI, Bandeira de Mello, issued several certificates to large-scale livestock operators stating that no Indians lived in the ranchers' area of interest in the Guaporé valley. In fact the area was homeland to the Nambiquara. Bandeira de Mello was always an advocate of pushing highways through Indian reserves as means of bringing progress to otherwise backward folk.

Partly in response to the history of corruption in the agencies meant to serve Indians, law 6001, or the Indian Statute, was passed in 1973 by the Brazilian

Congress. The law provided for the protection of native rights to land, to resources, to community life and to their own cultures. It also indicated that native populations could be removed from their areas by presidential decree and that, in accordance with existing Brazilian law, all sub-surface minerals belonged to the federal union. Mining by the state on Indian lands was therefore entirely legal.

This powerful statute was, however, seen by entrepreneurs as an impediment to their acquisition of land and several campaigns were developed to either overturn or outflank it. In 1978 the Indian Emancipation Decree was promulgated by Rangel Reis, the Minister of the Interior. Reis had been a vehement promoter of livestock in Amazônia. In his formulation, law 6001 and the 1910 Indian protection law were patronizing to native peoples, in that such laws assumed indigenous peoples to be wards of the state. With "emancipation" this relationship of guardian to child would be cast aside and replaced by one in which an Indian would enjoy the same protections of law as any other Brazilian adult. Under the emancipation decree, title to Indian lands would pass from the state to individual Indians who could then dispose of such assets as they felt inclined. Another dimension of the proposed emancipation decree was that activities prohibited by Brazilian law could not be practised by Indians. Indians would therefore be liable to prosecution for traditional practices such as polygamy, nudity, use of hallucinogens and the practice of selective infanticide. The emancipation decree actually became law, but was greeted with such national and international outcry that it had to be revoked.

Another attempt to undermine the Indian Statute took the form of an innovative set of criteria identified by Colonel Zanoni Hausen, to establish "Indianness". Hausen's sixty categories included "primitive mentality", the frequency of use of white clothing, "the Mongolic birthmark", and whether "character identity" was "latent". Such racism also roused uproar and Hausen's schemes had to be abandoned. A more recent attempt to evade the statute involved the generals' proposal in the *Calha Norte* project to settle Indians onto colonist-style plots, under a provision in the Indian Statute that permitted relocation of Indians from national security zones.

Under the new constitution, Indians made several advances. After lobbying by many Indians, their rights required that demarcation and protection of Indian lands should occur in five years, in recognition of their original rights to land for both physical and cultural reproduction. The Constitution in Article 232 states that "Indians, their communities and organizations are legitimate parties capable of suing in defense of their rights and interests." Thus seventy years later, the objectification of an Indian as the ward of the state was struck down. Perhaps the single most significant article is 231, which permits development of energy and mineral resources on native lands only by an act of Congress, and assures Indians royalties from these activities. Whether this hopeful ensemble will really consolidate the native Indians' new rights depends on the dynamics within the Brazilian society itself, as well as their ability to organize effectively. It will also be determined by how well the Indian communities manage the economic forces already unleashed on their territories and in their environment.[18]

Indians have been battling ranchers for almost five hundred years and have been under particularly intense pressure from ranches since the 1960s, not only through direct occupation of their lands but through the explosion in road construction. Federal and state highways have increased at more than 13 per cent a year in Amazônia, from 7,376 miles in 1960 to 15,365 miles in 1984,[19] and this total does not include the vast extensions of private roads built to link up farms, ranches and lumber zones to these highways. The building of roads through "empty" forests usually resulted in surprised surveyors and Indians discovering each other, in mutual dismay. The roads constructed under PIN alone affected ninety-six tribes, more than half the tribes in Brazilian Amazônia, and the further incursions under the auspices of *Polonoroeste* and *Calha Norte* expanded this number close to 75 per cent. When the Trans-Amazon was built, the Parakanã Indians lost 45 per cent of their population within a year of its construction. With the development of the BR 364 and the opening up of areas in the Guaporé valley, the Nambiquara, so admired by Lévi-Strauss and numbering close to 20,000 at the beginning of this century, were reduced to 650 discouraged souls. In the Yanomami territory, the first encounters with road crews reduced the population of the contact villages by some 25 per cent. These preliminaries were merely the overture to the clearing that followed, as forests fell for short-term farms and ranches, as animals fled and were hunted, and as the lumberjacks made their incursions.

In 1986, Kayapó men out on a one-month hunting expedition to supply meat for the major fall naming ceremony discovered four loggers and promptly murdered them. Some observers found this surprising since the Kayapó had long been aware of the lines of logging trucks rolling down the forty-mile dirt road connecting their timber stands to Redenção and the logging mill of SEBA/Azzayp Industria. FUNAI had negotiated highly inequitable timber contracts that paid the Indians $50 per tree and provided a road and potable water system in return for 10,000 trees, each worth between $350 and $500. All summer, logging trucks would line up each night and rumble past for hours. After the predatory attack on southern Pará's mahogany trees by the logging industry and the thriftless use of timber in clearing for pasture, few stands now exist outside native reserves in southern Pará, and the mixed forests where mahogany grew are now transformed to pasture. Now many admire the exquisite mahogany corrals on the ranches in southern Pará. The lust for mahogany has fuelled a spate of legally valid but deeply extortionate contracts between FUNAI, loggers and Indians, which has fed the long simmering fury of tribes against what they and many Indian advocates view as corrupt practices. There are also illegal logging incursions. The desire for this beautiful hardwood has triggered such contracts and invasions in Indian areas in Rondônia, Pará, Mato Grosso and Amazonas.[20] These activities can also erupt in violence. In March of 1988, a massacre of Tikuna Indians occurred in Amazonas while they were

The seringueiro's *cuts on a rubber tree.*

The Madeira-Mamoré railroad, built at the cost of thousands of lives. It was finally closed in 1972.

Percival Farquhar, a genial Quaker and former New York state assemblyman. He had a paper fortune of $25 million in 1912 when he opened the Madeira-Mamoré railroad and the docks in Belém, but lost the bulk of his fortune in the collapse of the rubber boom and the outbreak of the First World War.

The route of the railroad bypassed the nineteen rapids and cataracts on the Madeira and Mamoré rivers and was to give landlocked Bolivia a sure link to the Amazon and world markets.

The southern terminus of the railroad at Guajara-Merim, where the peles, or balls of rubber laboriously collected and coagulated by the tappers (see foreground), awaited shipment by rail and river to Belém and then to the industrial world.

The bend in the Madeira river where Farquhar decided the water was deep enough to found the river town and railhead of Porto Velho. Three miles further upstream the dreaded rapids began.

River-front Porto Velho in 1989, seventy-seven years after Farquhar founded it. The sign says "Read Books ... An Enchanted Universe. The True Origin of Humanity". Underneath is another, later sign reading "The Culture of the Extraterrestrial". On the wall the graffito says "Frank has a cock the size of a burro. Look at it and laugh".

Getulio Vargas, the Brazilian president who called, in the 1930s, for a "March to the West" to occupy the Amazon.

General Golbery, the grand strategist and theoretician of the Brazilian military's plan to develop the region and "flood the Amazon with civilization".

Forest farm in Rondônia flooded by a dam. This settler was doing well until the rising waters forced him and his family to move.

Another settler's farm flooded by the rising water table, caused by the Samuel dam. In the foreground is flooded manioc, also corn stalks; in the middle ground, bananas; in the middle back, at left, is rice; in the background is the levée of the dam itself. This colonist had developed a fine farm with diverse orchard fruits and crops, showing what a resourceful farmer can do. All in vain.

View from a deforested hillside looking down on BR 364, east of Porto Velho. The rising land and farm is run by a failed settler from Pará on behalf of a rancher living in Campo Grande, a thousand miles to the east. At back are waters caused by the Samuel dam.

A varadouro *or trail in the São Luis de Remanso extractive reserve at the end of the wet season. See Euclides da Cunha's extraordinary description of these trails in a footnote to chapter 8. Half the year, transportation is precarious. Until BR 364 came to Rondônia and Acre these* varadouros *and the rivers were the only ways to get around. Most road-building in the Amazon is vigorously resisted by environmental groups, but welcomed by isolated local populations. See Ailton Krenak's remarks about roads in Appendix A.*

Tribe visited   : Tucuna (about 1,000)

Here we had the opportunity of watching the rite of the "hair-plucking" of a virgin, but suspected strongly that this was an organized show laid on for **tourists** by a foreign hotelkeeper, as part of a trip advertised as the "Green Hell Tour". The FUNAI representative seemed to be heavily involved in the organization and appeared to act as the intermediary between the hotel and the Tucuna tribe.

We all agreed that it was shameful and degrading to stoopto the exploitation of human beings in this way and to extract money from tourists eager to witness this kind of spectacle. We also noticed that quite a number of the Tucuna Indians were strongly under the influence of alcohol which had been made available to them by the so-called "civilized" local population, against all FUNAI rules.

6 July

Visit to Aramaça, a large island in the Rio Solimoes, 30 minutes journey by speed-boat from Leticia.

We had heard about this island, and about the Indian lepers who were reported to be living on it, from a number of different sources. After a good deal of time and effort spent in looking for lepers, we at last found three cases suffering from the cutaneous type of leprosy, but they turned out to be caboclos and not Indians.

Page from the report of an International Red Cross Mission to the Amazon in 1970, following international uproar over the treatment of Brazil's indigenous inhabitants.

José Sarney wielding an axe; one of a series done by Brazilian artists on the outside of the wall of the Botanical Garden in Rio de Janeiro.

Victims of fever and cruelty in a mausoleum in an Amazon valley town.

assembled for a meeting; four Indians were dead, twenty-three wounded and ten others shot and missing as they escaped into the forest.[21]

Whether logging occurs on Indian lands, national forests or colonist lots, the timber industry in upland Amazônia is ecologically damaging. Although more than seven hundred promising species in Amazônia have been tested, the Amazonian timber trade concentrates for the most part on about twenty main species. The Amazon has increased its share in Brazilian sawn wood from 14 per cent to 44 per cent in a decade.[22] Amazonian timbering typically extracts one tree per hectare (2.4 acres), and it does so with enormous damage. As loggers move in with roads and skidders they take out a small proportion of the trees, about 3 per cent, and kill or damage more than 52 per cent of those that remain.[23] Forests that are damaged in this way are vulnerable to fires from adjacent lands, thus potentially ruining spontaneous recuperation from smaller trees, seeds and sprouts. Worse still is the genetic erosion of these valuable trees; the best are cut. Called "highlining" in the trade, such selection reduces the possibility of creating excellent "domesticated" lines. The logging roads can also supply the initial infrastructure for the invasions of colonists and ranchers, although logging usually takes place on claimed land and is often seen as a means of financing later investments on it.[24]

MINES AND MERCURY

Timber exploitation is but one recent incursion. Its costs are high, but not as high as the more insiduous and pervasive problem of mining on native lands. As of the summer of 1989 more than 560 applications for *alvarás* (documents that permit prospecting and imply claims) had been approved on eighty-eight indigenous reserves, with an additional 1,685 pending. The applications began in 1983 when President Figueiredo decreed that Indian lands would be opened up for mechanized mining with concessions available to national or international firms. This decree was established in a moment of some panic when Figueiredo was facing the prospect of insurrection at Serra Pelada. The mining firms were furious at being outdone in the lucrative gold rush at the low end by *garimpos*, the small placer mines, and squeezed out at the high end by vast projects like Trombetas and Carajás. The forays into native lands provided substantial new horizons for their actions. But the *garimpos* were always ahead of them.

Goldmining on alluvial lands has a venerable history in the Amazon, with *caboclo* and *garimpeiro* "geologists" proving to be, time after time, more adept at discovering gold than more technologically advanced forms of prospecting.[25] The classic case, of course, is the Carajás, where geologists found iron, but the *garimpeiros* found gold. At least twenty-six gold mines exist on native lands, and though sometimes called "clandestine mines" because they are often illegal, their effects are extremely obvious.

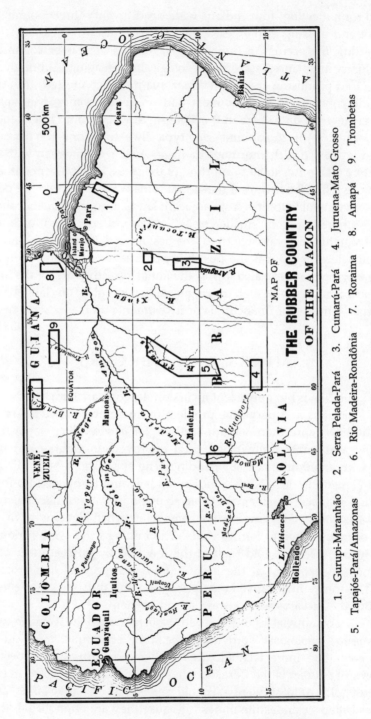

MAP OF

THE RUBBER COUNTRY
OF THE AMAZON

1. Gurupi-Maranhão   2. Serra Pelada-Pará   3. Cumarú-Pará   4. Juruena-Mato Grosso

5. Tapajós-Pará/Amazonas   6. Rio Madeira-Rondônia   7. Roraima   8. Amapá   9. Trombetas

Gold-producing areas of the Amazon basin

The largest and most famous of these is the Cumaru mine in the Gorotire Kayapó reserve. As opposed to the single enormous pit at Serra Pelada, Cumaru is composed of numerous little holdings going up the side streams. The reserve was invaded by 10,000 *garimpeiros* in 1980. The Indians requested government intervention and negotiated for a 10-per-cent royalty on the mine's production. The invasion at Cumaru seems to presage what is now happening in the Yanomami territory. Of more immediate concern is the unfortunate fact that indigenous lands are frequently not demarcated, and, with the discovery of gold, less likely to achieve this desirable status. The ability of the Kayapó to play upon the fear of the *garimpeiros* permitted them to also concentrate and control the *garimpo* activites better. The Kayapó used this money to demarcate their lands, but they may have to pay other serious costs.

The Kayapó have defended their lands fiercely against colonists and ranchers (including an attack on a new *fazenda* in which twenty-one whites were killed) but the allurements and pressures of *garimpos* are more insidious. *Garimpos* can pay for demarcation, for planes, for trucks, for medical care, and for increased autonomy, reducing dependency on the ever problematic FUNAI. But the *garimpos* also bring the threat of more invasion of other rivers and streams as miners seek new strikes. They bring the virulent malaria that has resulted in as much as a 600-per-cent increase in cases of the debilitating fever in the tribes. They pollute the waterways and make the fishing grounds useless. What was once crystal water where women washed and children gamboled has become an oily turgid flow, thick with waterborne diseases, and above all, the more subtle and deadly mercury.

A study carried out in 1988 by the Department of Mines and Energy indicated that Kayapó children, distant from the cesspool of the *garimpo*, now have mercury levels in their blood only marginally lower than in the blood of the *garimpeiros* themselves.[26] Such numbers token an environmental disaster of very great proportions. The toxic properties of mercury have been known since the Middle Ages when the amalgamation process was used for the extraction of silver. This technique involves passing a slurry of the ore over mercury-coated copper plates to which the gold particles then adhere. The gold particles are periodically scraped off, but the remaining mercury mixed in with the gold is removed by distillation, vaporizing into the air.

Wherever it has occurred, the use of mercury has been associated with human poisoning, and the levels of poisoning that are likely to appear in the Amazon promise to eclipse Bhopal or any comparable case of industrial poisoning. The widespread decentralized scale of mercury contamination of the environment and its inhabitants has no historical precedent. What is known about mercury poisoning is the result of a few "hot-spot" exposures in the industrial world. In 1985 one of the authorities on mercury toxicity indicated that some 8,000 cases had been documented worldwide and that some 800 people had died. Clearly uninformed about the Amazonian gold rush, this assessment focused on the famous

Minamata poisonings and a case of food aid gone awry when grain for planting, drenched in mercury to retard fungal growth, was eaten by Turkish people with lethal results.

Mercury contamination can occur through direct contact: inhalation of the vapors, absorption through the skin when handling slurries of mercury and gold, absorption in the intestinal tract when dust-carrying mercury lands on food, or when utensils or hands have come into direct contact with mercury. Every day hundreds of thousands of miners are at risk through such direct contact. Indirect poisoning comes from eating contaminated foods, particularly fish that have been swimming in waters fouled with the heavy metal. Even very small amounts of mercury per day are likely to result in symptoms of chronic mercury poisoning, since mercury penetrates and accumulates in the central nervous system.

What are the symptoms of mercury toxicity? The subclinical symptoms include irritability, difficulty in hearing, kidney problems, insomnia, low fever, manic depressive behavior, loss of memory; in short, a vague set of symptoms that could range from effects similar to a hangover, malaria or any number of minor ailments. In this case, however, the cumulative effects also include madness (hence the mad hatters of the early industrial manufactory and Lewis Carroll), and horrifying birth defects.

Rogério da Silva and his colleagues in Belém have analyzed the blood, urine, and hair of people directly and indirectly exposed to mercury. The data is extremely disturbing: 25 per cent of the Kayapó Indians tested had excessive amounts of mercury. Miners in the Tapajós showed levels of mercury above normal in 37 per cent of the cases.

No one knows for sure how many people have been exposed to mercury poisoning in the placer gold mines in the Amazon, but the National Department of Mineral Production in Belém suggests that there are close to 500,000 *garimpeiros* who are directly involved in mining for gold in the Amazon and who will have been poisoned.[27] Because of the way mercury is absorbed by the ecosystem, there will be many other victims.

Mercury occurs in inorganic and organic forms, but is most baneful when it becomes methylated. This form of mercury is easily absorbed, particularly in the central nervous system. It easily passes through the placenta and disrupts chromosome and cell division at low levels. It also accumulates in parts of the brain. Symptoms of poisoning do not occur right away. Mercury can be methylated by micro-organisms, in fish guts, or in any number of other biological pathways. In the waters of the Amazon, the chemical process known as methylation of mercury (which makes it far more biologically active) is stimulated by metals like iron and manganese, which are common in Amazon waters. Methylation is further enhanced with increased acidity in water, and this unfortunate process may well turn Amazônia's water impoundments into extremely toxic areas. Dams in Amazônia flood living forest, and under water, without air, the decomposing vegetation generates large quantities of humic acids which will probably also accelerate the problems of methylation.

The huge lakes that lie behind these dams are potentially more virulent in terms of mercury than flowing waters. The map of Brazil's current and projected dam projects coincides with chill accuracy with many of its mining areas. Thus the Amapá-Guiana mining zone overlaps with three dams planned for this area. The Tapajós-Alta Floresta mining zones with their venerable mining history could infect the six dams projected for the Tapajós and its tributaries with festering mercury-laden waters and sediments. Southeastern Pará-Altamira-Tocantins-Carajás zones scarred with numerous *garimpos* are supposed to be the site for nineteen dams on several rivers to service the industrial corridor, the ''New Ruhr Valley'' that is planned for the area. The Xingu, Araguaia, and Tocantins rivers will be affected. The Paru-Jari mining zone has seven dams slotted for its water courses. Trombetas, famous for its bauxite mines, also claims thriving placer deposits. The long-term plans envisage four dams there. The environmental impacts of dams are hotly debated, but the implications of these dams as mercury waste dumps are yet more alarming.

Mercury will find its victims in any number of ways, but the most widespread will occur through the food chain. Fish concentrate mercury in large amounts. The Brazilian Department of Mineral Production has tested the fish near several *garimpos* and the waters they inhabit. All the fish tested were over tolerable limits as were 80 per cent of the water samples. When huge shoals of dead fish appeared in the waters of Pará and Mato Grosso in 1985 and 1986, many thought they had been poisoned by mercury. Other wildlife, particularly carnivorous aquatic birds, will also be affected. Even protected areas far from mines will feel the effect of the poisoned water. The Pantanal in western Mato Grosso, perhaps the largest wetlands in the world and home to numerous migratory birds as well as rich local fauna, has already been contaminated, and goldmining occurs in the 2.4 million acre national park on the Tapajós. With active mining already taking place within reserves it surely affects the natives who live there. Havens from mercury are increasingly hard to find, and even areas that have been set aside as areas to be buffered from other forms of encroachment – national parks, wildlife refuges, Indian reserves – feel its consequences. Still more disturbing are the implications of mercury in water impoundments – whether in the large dams already in place or now maturing in the pharaonic imaginations of Brazil's developers.

GOLDMINERS IN THE AMAZON

Who are these *garimpeiros*, some 500,000 in number, working their placer mines throughout southern Pará, along the Tapajós, in the Gurupi, in northern Mato Grosso near Alta Floresta, further north in Amapá, in the Trombetas drainage and in the Carajás? Contemplating such toxic vistas, it is tempting to rail at the *garimpeiros* for the poison they administer the earth, air and water with each golden nugget they extract. In their struggle for gold, they are often on the other side of the battle lines from the Indians, but in fact they have an even more afflicted existence in many cases, since the ranks of *garimpeiros* are swollen with landless or near landless people.

There are numerous stereotypes: the *garimpeiro* adventurer, as vulgar profligate, squandering his fortune on liquor, women, and various extravagances, winding up broke and sober back at the mine; the *garimpeiro* as predator, greedy and undisciplined, the destroyer of the forest. These images, like so many others of the Amazon, reflect the observer. The *garimpeiro*'s isolation, hard work, and hope for a stroke of luck feed these myths; the history of the Amazon is suffused with the hunt for gold, and these myths shield the truths of the *garimpeiro*'s life.

There are many kinds of *garimpeiros* just as there are varied types of *garimpos*, the placer mines on geological terraces or alluvial banks. They range from mine holdings deep in the forest with a few men holding a "cobra fumando" (a "smoking snake", the pump used to blast the sediments and one of the major technical advances) to thousands clambering up and down precarious paths, cutting away at ledges and at the belly of the Serra Pelada. In the official government code, the men are described as miners who work "natural alluvial formations with rudimentary technology and whose productive process is characterized by the individualized nature of the work". Presumably elaborated in a Brazilian mining office, this classification was to serve as the focus for conflict between the labor-intensive *garimpo* methods and the mechanized procedures of the formal mining companies.

Garimpeiros, in the few surveys that have been done of them, are mostly young men between the ages of fifteen and twenty-five. More than half are sons of small farmers. They can also be petty extractors of Brazil nuts and other forest products. They may also be part of the urban informal sector – construction workers or, at the low end of urban formal employment markets, message boys, shop hands, "assistants". Whether rural or urban they are part of the most precarious segments of the Amazonian economy, and life in the *garimpo* offers real hope of social mobility: to be able to buy into a stake and draw status and income from having others work for one. To control one's own labor and work free of onerous foremen – these along with the income are the real advantages of the *garimpo*. Indeed the majority of those who hold claims in areas of the mine began as *garimpeiros* and worked their way up to their current status.

Working a *garimpo* is an occupation that people seek when they are dislodged from the precarious position they occupy in an urban or rural economy. The larger gold fields like the Serra Pelada or the Cumaru will draw people from all over Brazil but the scores of smaller mines capture the desperate from local hinterlands. The *garimpeiro* who might *bamburrar* – strike it rich – has the ability to leave the *garimpo* when needed on the family's farm or for some other reason. In any case the wages he earns exceed by a handsome margin the norms of rural zones. Like petty miners elsewhere,[28] *garimpeiros* may work in the mines to supplement agriculture. For a small farmer ever under attack from internal and external difficulties and from the erratic nature of labor markets everywhere in the Amazon, the *garimpo* is a godsend.[29]

Unlike the Hobbesian social cauldron conjured forth by the government, the *garimpo* is ruled by a complex set of norms and an ideology of independence and solidarity.[30] Every labor form, from grubstaking to sharecropping to wage labor, can be found. Given the context of constant and violent confrontation in the settlement zones, the *garimpo* serves as an important escape valve for the predictable outcomes of the agrarian crisis.[31]

The meaning of the *garimpo* is thus to be found in the agrarian sector. A few statistics help to tell the tale. In a state like Pará, almost 90 per cent of the holdings were on less than 240 acres, the standard colonization lot, and occupied 20 per cent of the area in private hands. They employed 82 per cent of the rural labor force and produced more than 65 per cent of the aggregate value in agriculture. Holdings greater than 2,400 acres gobbled up about 60 per cent of the area in private hands, absorbed about 3 per cent of the labor and produced only 13 per cent of the value in agriculture. While smallholdings were concentrated in areas near Belém and in the estuary zones where smallholders could sell to the city, the large holdings occupied the so-called "empty spaces", areas of forest that were supposedly free of the extractors, *caboclos* and peasants and thus available for the enormous holdings that were encouraged in these areas. No less than twenty-three of the twenty-eight largest landowners in Brazil have their immense estates in Amazônia, covering more than 60 million acres.

FAKE TITLES, EMPTY RANCHES

The Amazon smallholders arise out from two basically different forces. The first are the *caboclos*, the population of backwoods folk formed out of the long history of detribalization, miscegenation, and extraction, from each immigrant wave that left people behind in the region. Making their living from extraction, agriculture, hunting and fishing, this group occupied lands as squatters, renters, sharecroppers, debt peons. Such rights as they have stem from informal arrangements with those who claimed vast holdings from past times through colonial grants and long-term *emphyteusis* rights, that is, usufruct rights granted by the state. These are rights to the exploitation of surface resources such as Brazil nuts, rubber, and so forth. Central to any understanding of the land issue is the importance of the land statute of 1964 which had a provision of "land to the cultivator". If a person could demonstrate effective use – cultivation for a year and a day – then he could claim the holding.

Land titling issues in Amazônia would be hilarious except for the human and ecological disaster they imply. Huge numbers of Amazonian titles rest on shameless fraud. Not only has control over land and titles often shifted between federal and state levels, but legislation and *de facto* policy have had to resolve the conflicts of state appropriation, user rights, user appropriation and protection of property in a context of severe maldistribution of resources and simmering violence. Rights recognized by Brazilian law ranged from the royal *sesmarias*, titles of the seventeenth and eighteenth century whose usage was an extensive as the surveys that defined them were sketchy, to humble squatters' rights. Land offices where archives were housed routinely went up in flames or documents vanished mysteriously. Whole counties would be sold illegally.[32] The confusion and potential both for fraud and for competing claims were enormous.

In principle, under the land statute of 1964 and the usucapion laws of 1980, those who can show that they have occupied the land for five years and put it to productive use can in fact assert legal claim to so-called squatters' rights – *direito de posse*. This issue of user rights of smallholders versus other forms of title became central in the struggles of extractors – rubber tappers, *castanheiros*, Brazil-nut collectors – and small farmers, as large landowners and land-grabbers began to clear forests. The final truth of land claims in Amazônia is in *a lei do mais forte* – the law of the jungle.

In this chaotic situation the government of Mato Grosso issued titles to an area 12 million acres greater than the state. Other states were more niggardly with their titles. The state of Pará, for example, only issued 5,137 titles between 1975 and 1980, this in the full frenzy of Pará's speculation. Authorities connived with speculators. Benidito Tavares, a land speculator in Acre, remarked that one could easily buy any police authority for ten dollars. Throughout the interior of the Amazon lawyers routinely used the *cartórios*, the land registries, as the first line of defense against any accusations of titling irregularities. Zeros were added on holding sizes, signatures forged, pages destroyed, and miracles of geography occurred as rivers changed their courses overnight.

Also characteristic was commercialization of the state rental titles as ownership titles. *Aforamentos* for usufruct rights gave owners access to huge areas for extractivism. In earlier eras, renewal of the rights was mandatory, but in the fifties many of these rights became perpetual. With the explosion of capitalist land markets in Amazônia and chaotic titling, claims to extractive resources over large areas were rapidly commercialized as land claims. These resource claims had been carved out in the last part of the nineteenth and early twentieth century through violence and coercion, and the masters of these lands were those who controled trade in a particular area. SUDAM compounded this problem, since large areas were titled under the ownership of the state with little regard for the existence of previous economic forms or legal arrangements. The total lack of concern towards the distribution of land titles drew the following quip. ''If the government won't give titles, we'll make our own.'' And so they did.

The surest way to claim land and all its rights and obligations was to clear as large an area as quickly as possible. Under Brazilian law, cleared forest land is evidence of effective use and thus fulfills what the agrarian laws term ''the social occupation'' of land, making the person who clears the forest the strongest claimant to a title, and minimizing the probability of later expropriation. ''Effective use'' in Amazônia usually resulted in clearing huge areas of forest for cattle production, often displacing forest dwellers of all kinds, from Indians to peasants. And indeed, cattle pasture, which goes out of production in less than ten years, generated land values that exceeded the value of the forest by 30 per cent.

Overlapping titles and widespread fraud placed more than 12 million acres in the eastern Amazon alone into sharp contest. Time after time the ensuing conflicts pushed long-time inhabitants and migrants into new areas further onto the frontier or even into other countries. Surveys of migrants describe a relentless history of the eviction of people by livestock and colonist attrition ranging from violence to foreclosure.

THE LURES OF LAND AND LIVESTOCK

Throughout the Brazilian Amazon, the expansion of livestock production was intimately linked to the expansion of roads, and a variety of credits ranging from fiscal incentives to subsidized agricultural loans. Control of large areas of land was central to capturing these credits and speculative gains. Land-hungry *grileiros* – land-grabbers – began to roam throughout the Amazon. Livestock became the definitive land use of the Brazilian Amazon, occupying more than 85 per cent of the area cleared. At very low levels of productivity, one animal per 2.4 acres, or one hectare, the costs of raising cattle were rarely met by the selling price. On the other hand, the value of the subsidized credits and soaring land values generously compensated for the risible production performance of the cattle. *Latifundia* covered the landscape, generating the worst structure of land distribution in all Brazil. While the new *latifundistas* waved their fraudulent titles and spread their estates over holdings the size of kingdoms, violent disputes broke out between people who had occupied the sites for decades or, in the case of Indians, millennia. Those who made their livings out of sustainable uses of the forest were pitted against the ranchers and land-grabbers whose fortunes lay in clearing it. Impoverished migrants from southern Brazil, attracted by the dreams of the landed, found themselves embroiled in these conflicts as they too began to try and claim part of these estates through the only means available to them: forest clearing.

In a context of frenzied land speculation, Acre naturally attracted attention. Desperate rubber barons, under-priced land, road development, all created a speculator's dream. In the period between 1972 and 1976 land prices in the state of Acre increased by between 1,000 and 2,000 per cent, and more than a third of the state, nearly 12 million acres, changed hands during this period. Of these, only 81 titles totaling a mere 18,500 acres were formally regulated by the state land agency, INCRA. Wherever the speculative front advanced also appeared pasture. To re-phrase Tacitus, where they made a desert they called it profit.

The creation of pasture required legions of men for the phase in which the forest was destroyed. Afterwards, there were very few jobs. Even ranches highly capi-talized by government subsidy from SUDAM vastly overestimated, by about 60 per cent, the numbers of jobs that livestock would create on their enterprises. Live-stock occupied land and created short-term jobs, but in the end left huge areas cleared of trees and the productive incomes they may have offered in ashes.

The ranches financed by SUDAM were to play a particularly emblematic role in the expansion of livestock in Amazônia. Especially favored and, as we have seen, also richly subsidized, these ranches are only a handful of more than 50,000 enter-prises of all sizes that run cattle in Amazônia. As symbols of the "propulsive" sector of Amazonian rural development the investors received expansive holdings whose average area was just under 60,000 acres, along with several gigantic pro-jects that were greater than 250,000 acres. These projects received nearly a billion dollars in incentives, and their performance was dismal.

The SUDAM ranches had grossly overestimated their productivity, partly because the constraints to production were not well examined and partly because the more ambitious the project, the more bountiful the incentive. On the average they met about 8 to 15 per cent of their projections. About 30 per cent of the large projects were abandoned, while 40 per cent sold nothing. In one survey, only three of these projects were even found profitable. Several studies have shown that livestock in the Amazon is not profitable without subsidies or speculation.[33] More-over, of the 86 projects surveyed, 48 had no regular titles – this in a context of incendiary land conflict.

Using mostly temporary labor, these ranches represented the worst uses of land imaginable in social and economic terms. Almost anything would yield a greater return per acre in comparison, if only the actual value derived from animal produc-tion were to be calculated. The key advantages, of course, were the princely gains to be made through tax breaks, subsidies and selling large chunks of the enormous estates. Many owners managed to start up four or five projects simultaneously, made minor modifications and sold them, promoting a brisk business in the sale and purchase of these expansive holdings. About 20 per cent of these projects were cancelled for improper management. The monopolization of vast lands and con-stant expulsion of settlers and forest dwellers resulted in the SUDAM areas becoming the sites of the most intense violence.

Large-scale ranching and livestock operations in the Amazon along with their baneful effects have dominated discussion, but the highest rates of deforestation currently occur in the state of Rondônia, where colonists and small producers are also intimately involved in deforestation for pasture, which today occupies some 84 per cent of all cleared land. The increase in Rondônia's herds was more than 3,000 per cent in the period between 1970 and 1988. The prevalence of pasture in the context of small farms has received almost no attention.

CATTLE AND THE RATIONAL SMALL SETTLER

Why should livestock figure so prominently in the strategy of small farmers? There are several reasons that pertain to the biological flexibility of the animals and their unusual features within the context of rural and national economies. Cattle, and more generally livestock, have been one of the means of evening out risk in agriculture. To a small farmer debating his strategy, cattle provide an income supplement, in the form of milk or calves, and if, as is often the case in the Brazilian Amazon, there are agricultural disasters cattle can provide a large emergency "lump" of income when sold. They thus cushion the vicissitudes of agriculture. The ability of animals to move between use and exchange values is important for smallholders, as is the ready local market for animal products where beef fetches the highest price of any source of protein, and the highest per kilogram value of any basic food commodity. Cattle provide these market benefits with less labor cost than rice, beans, corn, manioc or tree crops. Unlike crops, animals are capable of transporting themselves. Sale or slaughter of cattle is determined by a household's need or opportunities of the market and not by the biological schedules of crop production which often work against small farmers since everyone brings their main crops to market simultaneously.

Cattle production also extends the economic life of a given cleared area. Sites that have been planted with crops go out of production within three years and are then usually planted with grass. This land is grazed until it becomes choked with weeds or so degraded that no forage will grow. While the productivity of these pastures is among the lowest in the Amazon, they provide marginal return on a piece of land that would otherwise be generating very little for the settler household. This may be a minor increment, but its importance for poor households cannot be easily dismissed, especially since the labor costs are low. In highly inflationary economies, investing in animals is a way in which peasants protect their assets. For people who may not be comfortable with banks and also where interest rates do not keep pace with rates of inflation, such strategies are completely reasonable. Colonization projects have frequently produced credit lines for small-scale producers of cattle. There are obvious benefits in buying a valuable asset with borrowed money whose value is constantly evaporating, while the animal's value exceeds or at least maintains itself at the level of inflation.

The role of cattle as a means of claiming land is well developed for smallholders and follows roughly the same logic as that of large owners. Throughout the Amazon, pasture is the cheapest and easiest way to claim occupation rights. If, as often happens, a peasant household holds a parcel of questionable title, and this land is adjudicated, the larger the cleared area the greater the indemnification if the the peasant is expropriated. As areas that have been cleared for pasture have a value that is about one-third greater than that of the forest, the peasant's ability to speculate with these lands is also enhanced. Among colonists, land speculation and indemnification by the state or larger landowners occurs with some frequency. Finally, given the nature of windfall profits in Amazônia, a lucky strike in the *garimpo* may produce immense surpluses for a rural household. In this case, one of the few means of diversification in the regional economy often involves investing in land with cattle.

Much is made of the symbolism of cattle as items of prestige in Luso-Brazilian culture, and there certainly is an element of pride in emulating the distinction enjoyed by rich landowners and their gleaming white herds. But with or without the symbolic overlay, the diversity of economic ends that can be served by cattle make them very compelling for colonists. Whether these advantages center on their convenience for the household as it struggles along day to day, or in the way livestock can be used within the context of larger economic pressures, cattle have an extraordinary benefit, as against the cultivation of perennial crops, which many consider to be a more appropriate land use. It is not surprising that peasants everywhere clamor for cattle, and are intent on clearing pasture against the day to come when they can add to their humble herds.[34] Livestock reduces risk, protects assets and, being easy to market, extends the life and value of the land parcel with a minimum of effort, since nurture of the cattle is a relatively inexpensive and accessible investment.[35] So for both large and small operators, the advantages of cattle are inescapable. Unfortunately these private benefits have very disastrous public costs in terms of the environment and their implications for the regional economy.

As we have already described, pastures in the Amazon do not remain productive for very long. When forest is cleared for pasture there is a nutrient flush as elements held in the plant material are released to soils; but the soil nutrients decline rapidly to levels below those necessary for maintaining pasture production. The nutrient value of the grasses falls off, and shrubby weeds begin to invade the pasture. Soils become compacted. Clearing the pastures by chopping down the bush, burning and fertilizing can give pastures a new, albeit short lease of life, even though the economics of maintaining pastures versus clearing new ones works against the management of existing cleared land.[36] Thus new areas are constantly being cleared as old ones go out of production. Pastures in the Amazon are degraded and frequently abandoned in just ten years, and these degraded lands are exceedingly difficult to recuperate. Clearing for pasture in the end often condemns land to waste, and more than 50 per cent of the cleared areas have been abandoned.

In terms of regional economies, cattle generate ephemeral employment in the clearing phase, and for brush management, but they do not absorb much labor at any scale of production. This is a private advantage for both peasants and large landowners, but for the regional economy it is a disaster. Livestock generate very little employment. The standard *fazenda* uses mostly temporary labor, and uses about one cowboy for every 3,600 acres cleared. Linkages to other parts of the regional economy are fairly weak. Implements, seed, wire, animal supplements and veterinary products all come from southern Brazil, so the major benefits from these transactions accrue to merchants and transporters, while most of the gains in employment occur in São Paulo. Local urban centers do consume Amazon beef, and some employment is generated in the small slaughter houses and butcher shops, but the bulk of the labor linked to pasture development is in the clearing stage for casual labor. Tax revenues generated from the sale of animals is very low. In the case of the SUDAM enterprises, the ranches produced in taxes about 2 per cent of the value of the incentive money they received.[37]

EXTRACTORS: THE ECONOMIC SINEWS OF THE AMAZON

As ranchers and peasants began to face off against each other, both felling trees to secure holdings, another important segment of the Amazon's population watched with horror as trees crashed to build the fortunes, however ephemeral, of others. In the eastern Amazon, the trees that were carted off to sawmills were Brazil-nut trees – *castanha do Pará* – one of the largest and most beautiful species of tree in the forest. Kayapó and other Indians say that they planted these groves, and *castanha* seedlings can often be seen in their houses, where the germination is carefully supervised.[38] These enormously productive trees are the economic debris of a powerful oligarchy that routinely decorates the society and business sections of the Paraense newspapers. Increasingly, the *castanhais*, the Brazil-nut groves, have been the scene of intense social conflict as public forests were appropriated for private use and those who had access to these groves for decades now found it curtailed. With the building of roads, the lands were being sold off to become speculative instruments. Petty extractors of all kinds found themselves pushed into cities, agricultural colonies and gold mines as part of the foundation of their economic life was torn away. Collectors were either denied access to their traditional harvests, or were physically removed from them, usually with threats of violence. This story is repeated all over the Amazon where extractors and gatherers of all types – rubber tappers, Brazil-nut collectors, babassu collectors – experience a similar fate.

Extraction has always been the most flourishing part of Amazônia's economic life, but until quite recently it was reviled as the drag-anchor on the region's progress. Even as one development program after another crashed in expensive ruins, extractivism of the most diverse sorts sustained a major part of the Amazon's rural population.

What is petty extraction? Put in technical terms, it involves removal of some part of an ecosystem's material for commercial or domestic consumption in a manner that does not threaten the long-term productivity of the resource. It also implies management of the resource, and such management is part of a long tradition of popular knowledge. The Brazil-nut collectors know when to burn under the trees. In the river estuaries the local people weed out various species to favor the spontaneous growth of *açaí* for better production of palm fruits for the local markets and palm hearts for export. The view that extraction is the only way that such collectors make their living ignores the common pattern, which is that petty extractors engage in agriculture, livestock raising and any number of other activities including wage-labor *garimpagem*, commerce and other small-scale enterprises. Extraction is just one in a number of strategies the forest dweller may undertake both for domestic need and for sale. These petty extractors rely mostly on family labor, variants of sharecropping, or upon what anthropologists call "fictive kinships" – appeals for help under the token of some form of familial relationship. Some wage labor is also hired in, and labor exchange, *troca dias*, is also common.

Access to the products – Brazil nuts, palm hearts, rubber, babassu nuts, copaíba and so forth – that are the foundation of the petty economy depend largely on informal agreements about access. An extractor may rent, usually in kind, an area which he can then exploit. He may be a sharecropper, dividing his harvest with the "owner". He may be a debt peon. He may even be earning a daily wage. Only rarely based on a single product, such extractive systems are very flexible, for when the price of one commodity drops, there are others to fall back on.

There is an academic pastoral fallacy about collectors, which holds them to be backwoodsmen whose activities are entirely oriented to subsistence. This condescending vision of an Amazon sheltering millions of rural Calibans is far wide of the mark. Forest collectors have been supplying international markets for almost five hundred years and are also part of lively regional markets. About 30 per cent of rural dwellers in the Amazon would probably define themselves as involved in commercial extraction. Beyond this there is scarcely a rural family in the region that does not support itself in part by extraction.

In the enormous series of enclosures of public lands that have taken place in the Amazon over the past generation the extractor has endured the same abuse as did the peasants of old Europe, themselves also involved in petty extraction, as they were fenced off from their old commons, and flogged or hanged for poaching on the newly enclosed lands.

In the Amazon, such abuse has been fueled by the depredations associated with the rubber boom, ignorance of the actual biological and physical structures of extractive economies, and the invisibility of these economies to outsiders unaware of the diversity of extractive products in their finished form in both domestic and market contexts. Such blindness endorsed the expropriation of lands devoted to extractive activities for competing uses such as livestock and colonist agriculture. This has not only enormously destabilized the rural populations that depend on these products both for domestic and commercial ends, but has interfered with a whole web of petty transporters and processors, which – had the millions of dollars of research and development funds given to large, destructive schemes been allocated to these activities – could have provided the basis for ecologically and economically sustainable rural economies in the Amazon.

This is not to romanticize the life of a petty extractor as one of pastoral delight. By any measure (infant mortality, literacy, and income levels) they are clearly poor people. However, after grim experience in forced migration from their old tapping areas into the *favelas* of Rio Branco, rubber tappers discovered that their real incomes were higher on the *seringal*, in spite of all its difficulties, than as a marginalized *favelado*.[39] Until the late eighties it was not realized that extractive activities, with their associated agriculture, were superior from an ecological and economic point of view to either colonist agriculture or the raising of livestock.

Bureaucrats and planners accustomed to the age-old schemes to civilize the Amazon could dream only of cows and colonists. Thorough studies of the value of these forest products were not even carried out until after 1985 and virtually none of them were done by government agencies devising the economic futures of the region. Economists sitting in their offices in Brasília with little concern for issues of sustainability and with scant knowledge of the Amazon, usually compared the moment of optimum return on livestock raising in the best years of agriculture before the soils had degraded, all this computed in yield per acre, then contrasted this figure with the rather modest returns per acre of the extractors. These calculations never subtracted the income lost from the forest that had now been destroyed.

They also assumed that there was no environmental cost in the conversion of forest to other uses. Cost in terms of lost species can never be calculated, but the cost of recuperating degraded land is known and it is very substantial: more than $110 per acre in fertilizers to revive the pasture sufficiently to sustain a skinny cow; and continued applications of fertilizer are necessary. To get a forest back, according to those who have carried out reconstruction of forests of mixed species of trees, would cost over $3,000 an acre.[40] In the case of rubber tappers at Acre, the returns were calculated and the costs of recuperating degraded land were added in; when these land uses were compared over time it was clear that extractivism was economically and ecologically the better option. Everywhere one turned in the basin, the returns to extractors showed the same basic pattern. Study after study showed that the returns to extraction were greater than those of the land uses that destroy forests.

While there was no question but that the extractors were poor, the problems lay more in the prices they received for their products than in the value of what they generated. Here was no mystery. Those who controlled the commercial systems were rich, and had been rich for a long time. Yet these commercial elites, who had much to lose in the destruction of the forests, were dilatory in their defense of the former basis of their wealth. The reason, once again, lay in the question of land, and in the immense fortunes that could be garnered in land speculation. Since most of the masters of the *seringais* or *castanhais* had paid little or nothing for their land, when it came time to sell they could make extraordinary profits as could those speculating on pasture. To ensure their ability to do so, an essential activity was the *limpeza da área*, that is, clearing the inhabitants off the holding so that it could be bought and sold without the hindering presence of those who had made their lives and livelihoods there. Once lands, regardless of who was found on them, were "cleaned" and titles sold, sale could be more easily "regularized" under state laws. Once regularized, those who certainly had claim to land under the Land Statute of 1964 or the usucapion law of 1985 could be characterized as *posseiros* – invaders – and were thus legally vulnerable to expulsion. This possibility invited the large landowners to evict people in any way possible.

Certainly the simplest way was through intimidation and violence. The suffering, dislocation and hatred engendered by these enclosures and evictions are at least as great as those that fired the European peasant revolts. Violence underlay everthing in Acre, Pará and all over the Amazon. After enduring the attacks of the ranchers, the Indians, settlers and extractors could no longer bear the onslaughts and began to fight back.

NOTES

1. Francis de Castelnau, *Expedition dans les parties centrales de l'Amérique du Sud: Histoire du Voyage* 1850.

2. This discussion is based on V. Hemming, *Amazon Frontier* 1987, H. Baldus *Tribes of the Araguaia* 1960, and Ehrenreich's *Contributions to the Ethnology of Brazil* 1965.

3. See P. Fearnside, "Forest Management in Amazônia", in *Forest Ecology and Management*, 26, forthcoming 1989; A. Anderson, "Smoke Stacks in the Rainforest", submitted to *World Development* 1989; M. Kiernan, *From Forest to Failure*, 1989; S. Bunker, "The Eternal Conquest", in *Report on the Americas*, 23(1), 1989.

4. See A. Anderson 1989, also SUDAM, *Problemática do Carvão Vegetal na Area do Grande Carajás* 1986.

5. R. Murphy, *Headhunter's Heritage* 1960. Hemming 1987.

6. The Tapajós incorporates a placer mining reserve area of some 28,700 square kilometers although the area under *garimpos* in the Tapajós now exceeds 60,000 square kilometers. Gold production statistics are from the Department of Mineral Production.

7. *Caboclos* and other backwoodsmen are still used to locate strikes in Amazônia. Anthropologist Darrell Miller who has analyzed the dynamics of urbanization in the Amazonian backlands records the widespread use of *caboclos* for this task in Itaituba. See his excellent article on Itaituba, "Replacement of Traditional Elites: An Amazon Case Study", in Hemming 1985.

8. These are numbers supplied by R. da Silva, M. de Souza and C. Bezerra, on mercury contamination in Pará, *Contaminação por Mercúrio nos Garimpos Paraenses* 1988.

9. Anthropologists have taken the tribe as an interesting case study of adaptation of a native group to economic pressures, particularly rubber. Their most careful ethnographer has argued that the Mundurucu are on the way to social dissolution and *"caboclization"*. But the affected Indians are not left in social limbo. Rather, they shift their principal bonds of dependency to their already existing relations with the whites and move into the orbit of *caboclo* society.

10. FUNAI, the organization charged with protection of Indians, superseded the scandal-ridden Indian Protection Service, the SPI.

11. For an account of the Suyá, and a discussion of their classification systems and relation to nature, as well as their history, see Anthony Seeger, *Nature and Society in Central Brazil* 1981. Also see J. Hemming, *Amazon Frontier* 1987.

12. For an account of Ometto's acquisition of land in Mato Grosso and southern Pará, see Malori José Pompermayer, *The State and the Frontier in Brazil* 1979. Pompermayer draws on a report in the trade journal *Amazônia*, No. 24, February 1977, which said admiringly of the land-grabber, "It's with men like Ometto that the real conquest of the Amazon began."

13. Herminio Ometto later became head of the lobbying group, the Association of Amazonian Entrepreneurs. One of the Association's members lauded the "mutual understanding" that Ometto managed to forge between entrepreneurs and the government officials of SUDAM as they toured the eastern Amazon and the former lands of the Suyá, the Kayapó and other victims of his land-grabs. One of the items Ometto lobbied these officials for were more "reformulations", that is, refinancing of government-backed projects, with stretched terms of repayment and new and favorable computation of costs.

14. "Culturas e Linguas Indigenas do Brasil" published in *Educação e Ciências Sociais* 1957, and translated and printed in J.H. Hopper (ed.), *Indians of Brazil in the Twentieth Century* 1967. Ribeiro's report and the scandals that led to SPI's replacement by FUNAI are discussed in Sheldon Davis, *Victims of the Miracle* 1977.

15. Set up in 1910 by Rondon, under the maxim, *"Morrer, sé preciso for; matar nunca"* – succumb if necessary, kill never. The Indian leader Ailton Krenak remarked in 1989 that the motto of such services as SPI and FUNAI should be "kill if necessary, die never", *Gazeta do Acre*, March 29, 1989.

16. Braun's findings, as quoted here from Sheldon Davis, *Victims of the Miracle*, were published in *Medical Tribune and Medical News* in New York.

17. As quoted by Sheldon Davis.

18. See M. da Cunha, 1989. Also see "Brazil: Who Pays for Development", in *Cultural Survival Quarterly*, 13(1) 1989.

19. DNER, "A Experiência Nacional no Desenvolvimento Rodivairo da Amazônia", in *Seminario Sobre transporte Rodivairo na Amazônia* 1987.

20. Logging is occurring on the lands of the following tribes: Nambiquara, Cinta Larga, Suruí, Gavião, Arara, Kayapó, Guajajara, Tikuna. Extraction of timber on native lands is technically illegal according to the Indian Statute. The unsupervised and uncontrolled nature of logging would also be illegal under the forestry code. The problems with lumbering on native lands are distributional, in that the wealth often stays with the chief or his clan; the Indians are almost always under-compensated, and violence over distribution can occur. Contact with outside disease also increases. See L. Greenbaum, "Plundering Timber on Brazilian Indian Reservations", in *Cultural Survival Quarterly*, 1989, Vol. 13 (1).

21. The Tikuna number some 20,000, and this event is the outcome of a war with a logger, Castello Branco, and his crews. The killing was a gory replay of a 1985 episode when several Tikuna Indians in the local town were hunted through the city streets, with ten wounded. No culprits were identified.

22. A. Anderson, 1987, Consultancy report to the Ford Foundation.

23. C. Uhl and I. Vieira, forthcoming.

24. The use of timber to finance part of subsequent activities has been documented by C. Uhl and R. Buschbacher, "A Disturbing Synergism between Cattle Ranch Burning Practices and Selective Tree Harvesting", in *Biotropica*, 17, 1985. Colonists also use it to finance part of their activities. See Browder, and Hecht's "Rethinking Colonist Attrition . . .". One of the reasons for the outrage at the private Tucuma settlement project in southern Pará was that the company carted off the woods before the colonists' lots were sold. This triggered fury which eventually culminated in the takeover of the project by squatters.

25. See D. Cleary's fine work, *An Anatomy of A Gold Rush: Garimpagem: in the Brazilian Amazon* 1987. Cleary is preparing a book from his thesis. See also Miller 1985.

26. The Kayapó children have a mean blood level of 4.74 parts per million and working the Cumaru mine upstream have levels of 4.97 ppm. The acceptable upper limit is usually taken as 2 parts per million according to da Silva et al. 1988.

27. This number is based on the estimate that there are 300,000 *garimpeiros* at any given time in the gold fields, but that they rotate out periodically to other activities such as farming, construction and extraction. See R. da Silva et al. 1988.

28. R. Godoy, "Entrepreneurial Risk Management in Peasant Mining: the Bolivia Experience" in W. Culver and C. Greaves, *Mines and Mining in the Americas* 1985.

29. As Marianne Schminck points out in her article "Social Relations in the *Garimpo*", in Hemming, *Change in the Amazon Basin* 1985.

30. This discussion of *garimpagem* is based on the work of Cleary, Schminck, Godoy da Silva et al. 1987, G. Rocha, *Em Busca do Ouro* 1984. M. Baxter, *Garimpeiros of Poxoreo: Small-Scale Diamond Miners and their Environment in Brazil* 1975.

31. See Lucio Flávio Pinto, *Amazônia: No Rastro do Saque* 1980.

32. In a simulation study of livestock economics under various price regimes with and without subsidies and speculation, and with different types of technologies, Hecht et al. 1988, showed that cattle production alone (without credits, no overgrazing, and no land appreciation) was only economically viable under very specific conditions. Overgrazing improved the economic scenario somewhat. See also the excellent studies of Browder, "The Social Costs of Rainforest Destruction", in *Interciencia* 1988.

33. This discussion relies on Gasques and Yokomizo, "Resultados de 20 anos de Incentivos Fiscais na Amazônia", ANPEC 77–85, 1986; Hecht 1982, 1985; Hecht et al. 1988; Browder 1988.

34. If cattle have a rationality for the small farmer but are baneful in their larger consequences, it is not hard to argue similarly with coca production, an important part of the story of the Amazon basin and the future of forests. Livestock is devastating to local economies, doesn't absorb any labor, monopolizes land, marginalizes populations that may have developed sustainable land uses. Coca is well adapted to Amazon conditions. As the economists say, it has a comparative advantage for production in tropical zones, and in fact was first domesticated by the Indians of the upper Amazon. It is well suited to intercropping with agricultural and tree crops. Unlike many perennial crops coca can begin to produce fairly soon. It can be propagated by cutting or seeds, so it is easy to move around. Also, it can be harvested within six months, so there is a good cash crop almost immediately, which for poor peasants is alluring.

Amid the failure and outmigration of colonists in the Amazon basin, the lowest rates are in the coca-producing areas. Coca is profitable enough to pay for inputs like fertilizers, has a high labor demand, creates a lot of local employment, and good pay. Coca producers are not among the world's most exploited labor. In coca-producing areas day laborers are well-paid. This in turn engenders effective local demand for agricultural products, so a reasonable agricultural economy can develop that is fed by demand for foodstuffs for the landless population engaged in coca harvesting. First-stage processing of coca is simple, so local processing and incipient industrialization are possible. It is a model of what a cash crop should look like, and decent money can be made. By contrast, livestock brings in a few dollars an acre; cocoa, maybe $150 to $200 an acre; a short-term crop of maize, maybe $150 an acre. Coca brings between $5,000 and $10,000 an acre. This is the rational peasant speaking. Because local processing is so simple, it is easy to break monopolies in first-stage processing, so local middlemen, local commerce can thrive, with the dreams of Jeffersonian farmers coming true at last.

The problem is that it is illegal. Also, coca is grown in areas that tend to be under control of revolutionary groups and where Mafiosi also roam. The mere presence of these movements means that these areas become the focus of counterinsurgency, often under the guise of drug control. Such areas are, increasingly, zones of violence. Cocaine agriculture is the developmental policy for Andean nations in a very fundamental way. Everything in the coca-producing countries, from right to left, rests on this huge economic base, for the export business from the Andean coca-producing countries is worth $60 billion. The Andean flank of the Amazon basin is run by the coca trade. It creates more jobs and more exports than anything else.

Also in a coca-producing area people whose ambition in life was once to own a mule find themselves having, in their terms, a lot of money. Historically, a peasant invests in land-related things. So one of the factors that has fueled livestock in these areas is superprofits from coca, since there is a dearth of other investments. In the Guaviare, in Colombia, for example, there are 12,000 acres producing coca and 330,000 for livestock.

35. Serrão and Toledo 1988; also see Hecht 1982, 1985, Buschbacher 1986.

36. Gasques and Yokomizo 1986.

37. Stephen Bunker was the first to describe the contraction of nut production with the expansion of cattle, and the process of replacing a stable land use with an ephemeral one. See his "The Impact of Deforestation on Peasant Communities in the Media Amazonas", in *Studies in Third World Societies*, 13, 1982, 45–61.

38. In a recent study carried out in Rio Branco among *seringueiros* in the urban areas and household income formation in the *seringal* showed that incomes on the *seringal* were in fact higher by about 15 per cent. On the *seringal* 61 per cent of the population made over 100,000 cz. versus only 30 per cent in the urban areas; while 40 per cent fell under 65,000 cz. in the cities, only 9 per cent fell under this income level in the *seringal*. See Hecht and Schwartzman, "The Good, the Bad, the Ugly", in *Interciencia*, forthcoming 1989.

39. Henry Knowles, personal communication. Knowles has worked on reforesting degraded sites at Trombetas, and though his work is largely unpublished, he is considered to be among the most knowledgeable practitioners in this area.

40. See Anderson et al. 1985; Padoch et al. 1985; Peters and Boom 1989; Hecht and Schwartzman 1989.

EIGHT

The Defenders of the Amazon

O forest! They cut out your verdant heart.
The grasses, the Brazil nut trees,
the wild beasts already scent the
smell of prison. This we say:
People yearn to be free, so
Who then will be the masters of our history?

SAMBA DO QUINZE

Today I think that we can confess that yes, we bought weapons with the money from the cattle auctions. After the first, in Goiania we bought 1,636 guns. Today we have more than 70,000, one for every man in the Uniao Democratica Ruralista, men who decided to stop being left out of our country's history.

SALVADOR FARINA, Leader of the UDR in Goiás, 1987

Many years later, as he headed towards the outhouse in his back yard and caught the bullets in his chest, Chico Mendes would not have had time to remember Euclides Fernandes Távora, the man on the run from the *polícia federal* who stopped by his home in the forest to talk with him and his father and show him something called a newspaper. Távora agreed to teach the youth to read and write. This was in 1962 and Mendes was eighteen. Each week he would walk three hours through the forest to Euclides's hut for lessons in reading and in the political shape of the world. In the depths of the Acrean forest Chico had met up with Brazil's revolutionary tradition. Euclides had been a follower of Luis Carlos Prestes, an organizer of the lieutenants' revolt of 1924, who had led the famous Prestes Column on a march lasting three years and 14,000 miles through the backlands of Brazil, urging the peasants to rise against the oligarchs and to revive the republic. Euclides joined Prestes when the latter returned from exile in Moscow in 1935, and was with him when they were arrested in 1936. Euclides had escaped from prison, made his way to Bolivia and organized workers' movements there. Now, just an hour from the Bolivian border he had become a rubber tapper. So the Prestes column helped sow the seeds of the rubber tappers' movement.

There were other insurgent memories in the forest where Chico Mendes grew up. Every Acrean knows the story of the insurrection against Bolivia and how noble rubber tappers saved Acre for Brazil. Many of the rubber tappers had roots in the Northeast, and almost every Northeasterner can tell the story of the millenarian leader, Antônio Conselheiro, who led an uprising and established a utopian community, crushed in 1897 after fierce resistance by federal troops in the Canudos campaign that became the basis of Brazil's great epic by Euclides da Cunha, *Os Sertões, Rebellion in the Backlands*. And older Northeasterners from the time of Antônio Conselheiro who had stayed in Ceará or made their way west to the *seringais* in the upper Amazon could not but have heard from passing traders of the Cabanagem, the great revolt of the 1830s that shook the Amazon for almost a decade.

There has been a long tradition of resistance in the Amazon, though none have ever so far achieved the ferocity of the Cabanagem. During the 1830s (though concentrated in the years of 1935 and 1936) 30,000 of the region's sparse population had died in its battles, but in the process and in a strange way, the insurgents achieved their aims. This was the most revolutionary convulsion in a Brazil which in the nineteenth century was fraught with revolt.

The Cabanagem was named after *cabanos*, the landless or migrants who lived in huts near Belém, on the banks of the river or in the forest. Though it started as a battle of political elites it became a rebellion of the oppressed and the dispossessed. Free Indians, harassed by slaving parties in spite of the Pombaline decrees, and Indians already coerced into *de facto* slavery joined the rising, fighting beside people of color and Africans from *quilombos*, those refuges where the slaves had fled. By 1800 there were probably near to two million negro slaves in Brazil[1] as against about a million whites and a million and a quarter *mestizos* and mulattoes. By 1820 the state of Pará had received about 53,000 slaves since 1778[2] and by 1833 may have had 30,000 slaves[3] in a general population, excluding Indians, estimated at only 130,000.

THE REBELLION THAT CHANGED EVERYTHING

Cabanagem initially emerged as a squabble amongst the elites of Pará. On one side was the mercantile and landed elite with monarchist ties and loyalties to Portugal even after independence in 1822; on the other the *nativistas* or *filanthrópicos* who were native-born Brazilians. In the 1820s this squabble was not expected to drift down to the masses, but the conscripted militia marshaled to each side, and the *regatões* began to talk the language of rebellion.

Once fighting had begun, the oligarchs were unable to control the passions which had been seething since stories of the French Revolution and the slave risings in the Caribbean had filtered west and south. The inhabitants of Pará were fired by the language of the Revolution and prompted to action by serious economic differences between the colonial elite on the one hand, the small-scale entrepreneurs on the other, and of course the "proletariat", agriculturalists and extractors. It was not long before this explosive mixture ignited the mass of slaves, indentured Indians, and mulattoes.[4] On January 7, 1835, the *cabanos* went to the barracks, convinced the soldiers to join them and then stormed the prison of Belém before returning to the presidential palace where an Indian, Domingues Onça, in a great moment of retribution, killed the President of Pará. Felix Malcher, one of the leaders of the uprising, was then proclaimed the first *cabano* President of Belém, though still loyal to the Brazilian empire. Disputes rent the *cabano* leaders in Belém but all the while the message of insurgency was speeding across the Amazon and changing relationships of labor if not of property.

In the months and years of upheaval, slaves and semi-enslaved Indians took advantage of the turmoil to escape off the plantations, off the *fazendas* to freedom. The rising spread upriver, past the Madeira, past the Purus and into the headwaters of the Amazon to Tabatinga, at the border of Peru. It was an upsurge which threw together an extraordinary alliance of urban workers, slaves, *caboclos*, peasants and Indians. Its leaders came from the humblest classes and indeed the impetuous Vinagre brothers, amongst the leaders of the revolt, were rubber workers. As might be imagined, the rising was not only widespread but violent and when it was all over, a semi-autonomous labor force prevailed in the region, no longer willing to tolerate direct labor coercions or pressed labor.

The memory of the Cabanagem dwelled painfully in the minds of the propertied classes. The decline of the Directorate and then the Cabanagem had banished irrevocably the old modes of domination, and they were now constantly fearful of fresh uprisings. With much of the agricultural infrastructure damaged or destroyed in almost a decade of unrest, the increase in the number of *quilombos* and the truculent *caboclo* labor faced these elites once more with the old dilemma of the region's economic contours. They yearned for agriculture, where labor was far easier to control. But after the Cabanagem, compliant labor was in short supply since agriculture and extractivism could always provide a living to local people. Thus, in an economy still based on extraction of rubber, nuts, and other forest products, the mode of domination shifted from farm overseer to traders and middlemen forging other bonds of credit and even debt peonage. The region became filled with independent *caboclos*, sustaining themselves from any number of natural resources and establishing petty commercial relations with the river merchants. So the primary means of controlling labor was by the *aviador* and not by the foreman. How the commodity was produced, at what speed, under what conditions, was at first of little concern to these merchants. Their control was maintained by their monopoly of supplies and by personal ties backed by threats of violence. Thus they would restrain the *caboclo* and later the Northeastern immigrant-made-rubber-tapper from exercising his freedom.

On the lower Amazon, where large numbers of free *caboclos* had settled and where larger numbers of traders plied the waters, the bonds of control were of necessity looser. Further up the rivers, past the cataracts or into the deep reaches, oppressive forms of capricious control became more prevalent. Under threats of violence, tappers – either Indians or often single men imported from the Northeast – were forbidden to engage in agriculture or sell their goods to other patrons. Corvée labor was used to maintain the *seringais*, throw bridges across the *igarapés*, clear fallen trees, make ladders, and keep clear the *varadouros*, the trails through the forest. As the tempo of the rubber boom increased, so did the level of coercion.

Yet there was always a limit. The *seringal* was remote, the *seringalista* was one and the rubber tappers many. Even downriver the upper classes found that there were limits to their powers of coercion. Trying to curb the dangerous classes in the decades immediately following the Cabanagem, they sought to resurrect the *Corpo de Trabalhadores* or Workers' Corps, a forced labor brigade enlisting the landless, many of whom were extractors already involved in the rubber trade. The president of Pará announced at the end of the 1850s that the Corpo had been reformed

> for the extremely useful purpose of enforcing obedience and discipline and giving permanent employment to proletarian individuals, and even vagabonds and suspicious persons who showed themselves ready to follow the flag of anarchy, and would undoubtedly have enlisted in the ranks of bandits and rowdies.[5]

But the effort was futile. The hopes of channeling this labor (often landless rubber tappers) into agrarian or infrastructural pursuits evaporated. The state lacked the manpower to police the region, and by then the long wave of the rubber boom was beginning to swell. There was too much money in rubber to waste time worrying about the potential dangers of collectors.

FAILURE OF "MODERN BUSINESS METHODS"

This relative autonomy of the rubber collectors annoyed groups other than the elites of Pará. By the end of the nineteenth century the major foreign importers of rubber were depressed by what they saw as the ramshackle system that brought rubber to their warehouses. The editor of *India Rubber World* declared that a "more intelligent, systematic and economical supervision of rubber gathering" was desirable.[6] Soon well-capitalized foreign firms were trying to replace the *aviadores*, seeking to buy directly from the *seringueiros*, and to impose on them such modern business techniques as rigorous work schedules and wages. There would be no advance credit, as in the baroque dealings of the *aviador*. But it was all a great failure. The *seringueiros* disliked the regimen so dear to the businessmen, just as they would dislike Henry Ford's schedules thirty years later. Since the foreigners did not feel themselves politically powerful enough to emulate the ferocious methods of King Leopold of the Belgians, in his kingdom in the Congo, or indeed the violence of the local *seringalistas*, the *seringueiros* sold their rubber elsewhere. Soon the foreign businessmen gave up and withdrew, foiled by the *seringueiros* in their attempt to transform tappers into salaried workers with less control of the labor process.

Notwithstanding the experience of the foreign businessmen, rubber was produced under conditions ranging from slavery of the sort experienced by the Indians on the Putamayo, to conditions, near Belém, of small independent production in a sort of echo of our old friend the Jeffersonian farmer. Even so, most rubber tappers were – and often still are – involved in coercive forms of labor control which duly provoked resistance.

Resistance can take many forms, from elementary subversion of the exactions of the *barracão* by putting rocks or sand in the rubber, thus getting a greater return for less labor, to selling the balls of rubber clandestinely to other dealers with the hope of getting a better price or establishing greater independence. The *seringueiro* might take an advance from the *patrão* and make off. Ultimately he might kill the *seringalista*, and even in 1982, reports of the murder of a *seringalista* on the Juruá served as a cautionary tale.[7] Something as basic as cultivation of his own food could be an act of resistance by the *seringueiro* because it lessened control over him. The degree of control of the *seringalista* and the degree of independence of the *seringueiro* were fought out on the terrain of subtle exactions, covert denials, flexible negotiations and the threat of violence. These depended on a range of factors conditioned by location, historical moment and temperament. Like the forms of landlord tribute in European peasant societies, the nature of exaction and producer obligations were constantly being redefined.[8] For his part the *patrão* forbade with threats or actual violence, during the height of the boom and even today in many "traditional" *seringais*, the cultivation of plots precisely because it increased the independence of the *seringueiro*.

Historically, the battles revolved around the degree of dependence – whether the rubber tapper could grow food, whom he could sell to – and over the terms of trade, the price the *seringueiro* got for his raw materials versus the price he paid for the supplies he needed to keep going. In the upper Amazon cash *per se* was of little interest. Putting rocks in the balls of rubber was a form of bettering the terms of trade. Short of killing, the ultimate form of resistance was departure and search for a better *patrão*. The image of the lonely tapper and his family, bound forever to a few particular *estradas* of rubber trees, is not entirely correct. In virtually all areas tappers would switch from one *seringal* to another in search of better trees (*bom de leite*), better hunting (*bom de rancho*), a better *patrão*, a better life.[9]

The *seringalista* had several options available to see if he might get more product from his tenants. These included destruction of plots, beatings, rigorous insistence on monopoly control through any number of violent means. But here too were intermediate forms. The *seringalista* might suggest that he would give a better price for the merchandise if the *seringueiro* confined himself to tapping his trees.

The rubber boom spelled tremendous riches for a few hundred people in Manaus and Belém, but for the rubber tapper it meant only harder schedules and more violence as prices rose and *seringalistas* sought to increase their profits. In a reversal of the usual pattern, where workers suffer most when the industry collapses, the end of the boom toppled the rich in Manaus and Belém from their high estate. The *aviadores* faced slower times, but the *seringueiro* could always find a market for his balls of rubber, while in these changing conditions his agriculture, fishing and hunting kept him alive.[10]

Consigned to the oblivion of toil in a world indifferent to the producers of tropical necessities, the Amazon rubber tappers continued to supply this commodity to a national economy in which rubber barons had been able to argue effectively for trade protection and government subsidies to *aviamento* under the Rubber Credits system. Yet the attempts to establish plantations continually met with failure as leaf blight disease ravaged the stands of *Hevea*. Credits to the rubber sector rarely translated into investment in production which only eccentrics like Henry Ford attempted. Indeed the major technical advance was the introduction of the Malaysian tapping knife. Funds to the rubber sector financed *aviamento*, as *seringalistas* applied their credits to this enterprise and did nothing to increase production. These credits remained firmly in the hands of the rubber elites.

TWILIGHT OF THE BARONS

The outbreak of the Second World War once more rallied the hopes of the rubber barons. Under the accords brokered in Washington, the US financed the revitalization of rubber estates, and paid for labor recruitment – the *exército de borracha*, or rubber army – to supply the Allied effort. The export and sale of rubber became a government monopoly, with marketing credits and guaranteed prices for the barons. The new US presence introduced modern formal credit structures which enabled the barons to borrow from banks instead of commercial mercantile houses, although such funds were not invested to any great degree in the improvement of production in Amazônia. While Amazonian rubber enjoyed an increased market share for a brief period after the war, tappers carried out their tasks of collecting and processing latex in the same way that they had for almost a century, life trickling on much as rubber sap filled the cups set to catch the latex from the wounded trees. For the barons, however, the rubber economy was clearly decadent, and as Asian and African plantations expanded, their future was ever more in doubt.[11]

By 1967 the Amazon bank rubber program set up during the Second World War was largely bankrupt. Beset by international competition and the growing use of synthetic rubber, the *seringalistas* or rubber barons were unable to repay their debts. The Amazon development bank, BASA, intervened by engaging in monetary correction – restructuring the debt – and in some cases even interceded in the management of the *seringais* by using its own agents and managers. The *seringalistas* were surprised by BASA's strategy, since they largely assumed that debts acquired in the past would be worthless as inflation pressed ahead. With such restrictions on credit enforced by BASA, the debts of the smaller *seringais* were called in by larger *seringalistas*, and some like Altiver Leal, later an Acrean senator, became the *patrão* of entire watersheds.[12] *Seringalistas* in control of small- or medium-sized holdings in the Acre river valley began to abandon their interest in rubber and sold their lands to pay off debts. Smaller *seringalistas* along BR 364 tended to sell their lands to smaller self-capitalized ranchers, but the larger *seringalistas* like Leal felt that sale to enormous corporations might provide more responsible development.

Thus in the state of Acre, the *seringais* in the southern region along the road connecting Rio Branco with Assis Brasil at the Bolivian border were being bought by small ranchers, while in central Acre, near Tarauaca, enormous *seringais* were sold to Paulista investors.[13] Governor Geraldo Mesquita noted that between 1971 and 1974 that about 30 per cent of the total land in Acre was sold to only 284 proprietors.[14]

These changes also affected the nature and extent of control over the *seringueiros*. In northern Acre on the Juruá, where the ranching interests advanced very little, the smaller *seringalistas* maintained their right to control *seringueiros* as debt peons. In central Acre, the large owners shifted to a rental structure where control of the *seringueiros* and their sale of rubber was relaxed, though very marginally. In the Acre river valley where smaller *seringais* prevailed, the *seringueiro autônomo* – the independent tapper – emerged from the dissolution of the old system.

Those favoring conspiratorial explanations might suggest that BASA's strategy of squeezing the extractive sector of the Amazonian economy was designed so as to cast it in a crisis that would then lead to a "modernization" of the region's economy, basing it on capitalist forms of agriculture and ranching rather than extraction. The crisis faced by the *seringalistas* did succeed in altering the economy, away from the monopolistic control of land and commerce by *seringalistas* and their agents into an economy where independent producers and independent merchants engaged in freer exchange. In this sense, the goal of transforming the "pre-capitalist" extractive economy was partially achieved through the rise of the *seringueiro autônomo*, although not in the political context preferred by the state. It was possible for tappers and their families to begin production of subsistence crops and to sell to a burgeoning class of petty traders. A socially and ecologically viable use of the land was emerging from the ruins of debt peonage in the Acrean forests in the form of the *seringueiro autônomo*, particularly in the areas near the village of Xapuri where, since the mid-seventies, the rural workers' union had been organizing the dispersed tapper plantations.

The barons' despair lit the first glimmerings of freedom for the tappers. But just as the patron/debt peon system became enfeebled, and autonomous or free rubber tappers were able to farm and buy and sell at will, they found themselves pitted against a new enemy, the ranchers and land speculators hastening to Amazônia in response to the generals' allurements. By 1982, as we have seen, more than 100 per cent of the state had been sold, with some *municípios* boasting that 160 per cent or more of their land area had been claimed. Over 85 per cent of holdings in Acre were now classified as *latifúndia*. Forests inevitably began to fall, and tappers who had been working a particular area were evicted by stockmen. The methods varied from the classic burning down of houses and crops or the destruction of rubber and nut trees to a more decorous form in which individual tappers were invited to the patron's rooms, convivially greeted by a lawyer, rancher, and of course, the patron himself, each with gun in hand, and encouraged to sign away any claim to the lands they had worked all their lives. This is what happened at Seringal Santa Fé, one of the first, although in the end, bitter triumphs of the Acrean *seringueiro* resistance.

THE STAND-OFFS BEGIN

The youth who had gone once a week to the hut of Euclides Távora was now active in trade-union work. As Chico Mendes described it a few months before his death,[15] he and Euclides would sit by the radio listening to Radio Moscow, Voice of America and the BBC Portuguese Service. When the news of the generals' coup came over the air, Euclides told Chico that maybe twenty years of dictatorship lay ahead, but that he should become active as a trade-union organizer, even if the unions were run by the state.

Mendes began by trying to organize against the central fact of the rubber tappers' domination by the *seringalista*: the price of rubber and the price of products exchanged in return. "When I learned to read I discovered what kind of robbery it was, and I began to organize so that people could sell through a *marreteiro* – an independent petty trader." For the next seven years Mendes lived a dangerous life, always fearful of denunciation by unenlightened *seringueiros*, or the church or the mayor of the little town where he was living. He had to spend almost two years in hiding, otherwise he would have been thrown in jail, this during the peak of oppression by the military dictatorship.

In these years there were no trade unions in the state of Acre at all, but in 1975 Mendes heard that the *Confederação dos Trabalhadores*, or Confederation of Rural Workers' Union (CONTAG), was sending up an organizer from Brasília to Acre. Now CONTAG was a union brought into being by the federal government, and

Mendes, who got a job with the infant Acre branch of CONTAG in Brasiléia, on the Bolivian border, found it to be fairly conservative. Supposedly there to defend the rubber tappers, it was as Mendes said, "actually all about preserving the status quo". The reality for rubber tappers was that the status quo, as far as their lives were concerned, was ceasing to exist. While Mendes had focused his organizing battles on the price of the *seringueiros'* product, to whom and where they could sell it, the ground had been shifting. The battle was no longer over prices but over land.

It was in Brasiléia in 1976 that Mendes and his fellow rubber tappers really began to challenge the ruling order of things. They organized the first *empate*, or "stand-off". Mendes recalled,

I remember very well that day in 1976, March 10, when three rubber tappers came racing into town in great consternation because a hundred-man crew guarded by gunmen had started to clear their area of trees. For the first time ever we got together seventy men and women. We marched to the forest and joined hands to stop them from clearing.

The tactic worked. "The other thing we did," said Mendes of another *empate*,

was to try to convince the work crew to give up their chain saws. The important thing was that the whole community, men, women and children took part in the *empate*. The police knew that if they fired they would kill women and children. I also remember that on at least four occasions we were arrested and forced to lie on the ground with them beating us. They threw our bodies, covered in blood, into a truck. We got to the police station and we were a hundred people. They didn't have enough room to keep us there so in the end they had to let us go free.[16]

This direct action was crucial in slowing the clearance of forest in Acre. Soon news of the rubber tapper *empates* was spreading throughout Acre and beyond, into Rondônia and Amazonas.

In 1978 there was a big *empate* in Boca do Acre, on the border of the states of Acre and Amazonas, which showed how quickly this way of challenging the ranchers had taken hold. As one rubber tapper remembered,

It was seven o'clock on a Sunday morning on September 2, 1978. The gunmen's camp was at kilometer 38, on BR 317, just a kilometer away from the *mutirão* [gathering point for those about to conduct the *empate*]. The camp of the clearing crew was also nearby. We divided into two groups and marched towards the camps. We only had machetes and axes while the gunmen had modern arms. We shouted, "We are not criminals. We only want peace and justice and we only want what is ours." Over one hundred had come from all over the state of Acre, representatives of the

Rural Workers Unions of Brasiléia, Xapuri, Rio Branco, Feijó, Tarauaca, and Sena Madureira. Many had travelled over four hundred kilometers over rivers and difficult roads, setting an example even to their own union leadership. Most of the gunslingers ran into the forest, leaving behind their arms and ammunition, followed by forty of us. The rest of our people circled the camp, in an attempt to capture the others. The leader of the gunmen was captured and at the other camp we rounded up twenty guys along with their foreman and employer.[17]

The fact that *seringueiros* were prepared to travel these great distances showed first of all their will, but also the gravity of the situation, for the forests of Acre and Rondônia were beginning to disappear rapidly.

One enormous change, besides the increased efforts at organization, was the level of information available to the *seringueiros*. For someone trying to organize a union or a movement, the upper Amazon was particularly daunting. The organizers had to travel enormous distances on rivers and *varadouros*,[18] trails between individual families and between different *seringais*. Rubber tappers led lives of immense isolation. At the age of eighteen, Chico Mendes had never seen a newspaper; and the *seringalistas* refused to allow any schools on their lands. So when the rubber tappers' leader, Wilson Pinheiro, went to Brasília not too long before he was assassinated, and discovered that the barons were getting eighty-nine cruzeiros for each kilogram of rubber but paying fifty-nine cruzeiros to the *seringueiros*, about a third less, the resentment can easily be imagined. The *seringalistas* threatened to evict rubber tappers who pointed out the discrepancy in prices. The tappers themselves said that if they did not get the prices quoted in Brasília they would take their rubber to town.[19]

The *empates* were beginning to have their effect. According to Mendes, nearly three million acres were saved through stand-offs, and by 1989 the Indians, historically the foes of rubber tappers, were agreeing to participate. But the compromises worked out by the landowners, the land-grabbers and the rubber tappers' organizations were not particularly successful. The arrangements, worked out initially on the Seringal Santa Fé, mostly consisted of transferring rubber tappers to new plots, or giving them short-term tapping contracts until the *seringal* in question was finally cleared, or transferring tappers to much smaller areas on the same *seringal*. Finally, the rubber tappers were given some money to leave. None of these options did the rubber tappers much good, because they were unable to survive on smallholdings or to last long on the monies and hence had to migrate to the cities. The rubber tappers' leader, Wilson Pinheiro, argued that the alternatives on offer only meant the end of *seringueiros* and their forest, and that there was no possible solution except the one that kept the tappers in the forests among their trees. This steadfast position outraged ranchers, *seringalistas*, the Land Office, and state officials, all of whom thought that a wad of money or a shack on the outskirts of Rio Branco would get the tappers off the land and allow the trees to fall.

Pinheiro paid for his stand with his life. On July 21, 1980, gunmen hired by local landowners walked into his Union office in Brasiléia and shot him to death. The *seringueiros* gave the authorities an ultimatum to find the culprits, well-known about the town, within a week and bring them to justice. Chico Mendes described what happened then:

> On the seventh day the rubber tappers realized that the police weren't going to do anything and angrily went off to the *fazenda* about 80 kilometers from Brasiléia, where they seized one of the landowners, Nilo, known to have organized Wilson's assassination. It was clear that this particular landowner was part of the whole conspiracy to kill Wilson. The workers gave him a summary trial and condemned him to be shot. He got thirty bullets.
>
> The workers were prepared to leave it at that because they thought they had avenged the death of their leader. But this time the police acted really fast. In the next twenty-four hours, dozens, hundreds of rubber tappers were arrested, tortured, some of them had their nails pulled out with pliers, all because ordinary workers had reacted to a crime committed by wealthy and powerful people.[20]

One of the persons who attended Wilson Pinheiro's funeral was Inácio "Lula" da Silva, the leader of the sheet-metal workers' strike in São Paulo that altered the political map of Brazil in 1980. His presence, along with the emergence of the Workers' Party (PT) was an important influence on the union at Xapuri and indeed Mendes was one of the founders of Acre's PT. While CONTAG and the Church had fueled the early efforts in organizing the rubber tappers, they had largely promoted a strategy which encouraged tappers to accept indemnification and leave, thus tacitly endorsing the position that tappers had no claims to the areas they worked. In contrast, the Xapuri unions, along with PT and the independent national workers' organization, CUT (of whose national directorate Mendes was a member), stood firm in their insistence that tappers' *posses*, or claims, were valid.

THE CHURCH AND VIOLENCE

The pressure of the ranchers' actions in the *seringais* of Acre, and Euclides Távora's fortuitous encounter with Mendes and his father were evidently not the only organizing forces in the upper Amazon. The Catholic Church began to establish base communities throughout the western Amazon in the early 1970s, and many forest dwellers got their start in active organizing under the Church's auspices which were duly honored in the remark of one rancher: "For every land invasion, a dead priest."

The Catholic Church through its base communities, and CONTAG through its union work, set into play the initial impetus for organizing. But because of the nature of the Church and of the government-sponsored CONTAG, their initiatives tended to divert the conflicts into legal channels and especially toward resettlement. While lawyers would ponder the fine points, the cutting crews would move in and regardless of the final adjudication, the *seringueiros* would have lost. In any case the forest was being destroyed at an accelerating rate, and the *municipios* of Rio Branco, Xapuri and Brasiléia were losing population, who either fled in despair to Bolivia, or migrated to cities. Rio Branco doubled its size between 1970 and 1980 and the *favelas* were filling with dispossessed rubber tappers. Virtually all the migration was from Acre, and emblematic of the enormous dislocations that were occurring.

The same story was being told wherever one turned in the Amazon. In extractivist areas, in settler areas, the struggles which had formerly revolved around working conditions, percentages of the product given over to the landlord, the processes of exchange or the conditions of access to the resources, were transformed into a grinding struggle over the basic need for land and its resources in order to survive. While the issues of slavery and peonage, found throughout the Amazon, were not struck from memory, the real issue now, as *seringais*, *castanhais*, and other forests went up in smoke, was land. Rural workers, squatters and the landless began to agitate more and more for agrarian reform.

As the pressure for reform mounted it was accompanied by immense amounts of rural violence. The Catholic Church has tried to keep track of the kinds of ''aggressions'', taking the form of murder, violent assault, kidnapping, torture, death threats, destruction of houses and agricultural plots. Across three years in the mid 1980s the number of people involved in all kinds of land conflicts throughout the whole of Brazil rose from 566,000 in 1985 to 1,363,729 in 1987. The amount of land under violent dispute rose from almost twenty-three million acres to nearly fifty million acres in the same period. In 1987 more than thirty-two million acres in the Amazon were in dispute and 109,000 people were embroiled in these confrontations. The advocates of the least powerful were increasingly subject to violence. The most famous was Paulo Fontelles, the State Deputy of Pará, who was shot in front of his apartment in Belém for his positions on the agrarian reform. Lawyers were regularly shot, as were priests, in an attempt to limit any form of recourse available to the ranchers' foes.[21]

This eruption of rural violence accelerated in the mid-1980s for two reasons: the government had announced agrarian reform and a plan to settle 450,000 families on more than 30 million acres throughout Brazil. This kindled the hopes of those who felt that the government had now begun to recognize their basic right to land, and insisted that the lands on which occupants' rights were affirmed by the land statute and usucapion laws were as legally valid as the dubious titles claimed by large owners. In response the ranchers set up their own murderous movement to foil reform, the *União Democrática Ruralista*, the UDR.

THE RANCHERS' LEAGUE

The UDR was founded by a doctor and rancher from Goiás, Ronaldo Caiado. Many had hoped that with the rise of an industrial bourgeoisie, the *latifundistas'* day would be over forever. But Caiado's organization grew to tens of thousands (they claim to have a membership between 70,000 and 130,000) and was able to elect more than sixty members to the constitutional convention of 1986–7, funding the various lobbying activities by well-publicized cattle auctions. The rhythms of rural violence increased accordingly.

Composed mainly of cattlemen, the UDR reflected the desires of one of the most revanchist groups of the rural elite. While presented in polite society as part of the "agro-industrial" modernizing rural elite, the UDR overwhelmingly reflected the interests of livestock men. No more than 2,000 owners own more than 93 million animals, most of the Brazilian livestock herd. Among the heads of UDR was one of the most notorious speculators in Brazil, Samir Jubram, whose machinations destabilized the Brazilian stock market on several occasions.[22] The UDR holds that the small producer has no role in Brazilian agriculture. In an interview with the journal *Afinal*, Caiado stated,

> It's not enough for people to just have land. You need to have "know-how", machines, credits and things like that. Since rural workers have none of those their productivity is low, and in the end when you analyze their harvests, they didn't even produce enough to support themselves.

Thus did Caiado ignore endless studies in Brazil which repeatedly emphasized the fact that a large portion of Brazilian foodstuffs, particularly beans, manioc and vegetables were being produced on smallholdings. Brazil's smallholders occupy 12 per cent of the land and produce some 80 per cent of the food.[23] In Caiado's agrarian vision, the only committed agriculturalists were those who had the knowledge and capital to elaborate the kind of agriculture that characterized the interior of Goiás, his home state, an area increasingly given over to soybean production.

Caiado's version of Brazilian agrarian structure saw large holdings as the result of diligent toil and thrifty investment. Salvador Farina, the head of the UDR in Goiás, has pointed out repeatedly that "among men of honor, property is only the fruit of one's labor". Others might have argued that all property is theft. The entire history of *latifundia*, land-grabbing, falsification of titles, the sacking of land offices and the persistent violence seemed to have occurred outside Farina's experience. The actual land distribution in Brazil which is characterized by very few holders monopolizing the land was of little concern to him;[24] nor was the size of the holding, since "the size of the holding only reflects the courage and the competence of the producer". In Brazil, properties greater than 2,400 acres only exploit 2 per cent of their holdings.

The huge Amazonian ranches represented the most perfect expression of the ideals of the UDR whose members, like most fanatics for "free enterprise", conveniently overlooked the extent of backing for large ranches from the state which in their case exceeded one billion dollars in direct subsidies. The UDR argued that since the rural population was in decline, the only possible solution was to expand the highly capitalized model of agricultural development characteristic of the Central South. Viewing any attempt at agrarian reform as the product of café leftists and subversives like liberation theologist Leonardo Boff, the UDR saw the state's proposed land reform in 1985 as a sinister socialist initiative. To give lands to small farmers would be to socialize misery. In Conceição do Araguaia, Caiado announced that in the defense of tradition, family and property, particularly in the light of agrarian reform, a man had to do what was necessary. Caiado and his UDR associates were effective at the constitution convention, and any prospect of genuine land reform was speedily eroded by their astute lobbying for limiting the area and terms of expropriation.

The darker side of Caiado's movement more closely resembled a death squad than the elegantly dressed landowners in Brasília who so effectively castrated the agrarian reform laws. While sucessfully hampering the expropriation of land in "effective use", UDR members in Amazônia and the goons that they hire are considered to be the sponsors of a great deal of rural violence, taking as their targets rural labor and religious leaders, along with their lawyers and advocates. More than 1,000 rural organizers and workers have died in conflicts, since the emergence of the Nova República in 1985, and of these cases, less than ten have gone to trial.[25]

NEW INDIAN VOICES

Turbulence amid the changing situation in the Amazon was not just confined to Acre and to rubber tappers. Indigenous people were addressing the national society and international audiences in an entirely new way. Increasing sensitivity to environmental issues within the multilateral institutions such as the World Bank[26] and pressures from international environmental, human rights and Indian advocates, had given indigenous organizations inside Brazil new leverage, and with this leverage the desire to use these advocates in a new way, preferring to operate within their organizations, using their own voices.

Among these new indigenous organizations was the *União da Nações Indígenas* (UNI), the Indigenous Peoples' Union. Founded in 1980, UNI became highly skilled in lobbying for indigenous rights, in generating basic information about the status of Indians and their lands, and in co-ordinating advocacy groups concerned with native rights. One of the most effective campaigns by UNI and other groups came during the period of the constitutional convention, held in 1986 and 1987, when they were able to affirm their rights to land, and to demand that any development of mining or hydroelectric schemes affecting them would require congressional approval, with indigenous participation in any decision that was made. They also overthrew the concept that designated Indians as wards of the state.

The underlying push of UNI and other native groups was one of searching for ways in which to increase their autonomy and to incorporate new technologies, ideas and institutions that would not undermine their traditional societies. It became clear within the movement that it would be necessary to train indigenous experts in law, engineering, business and biology.[27]

In 1987 and 1988 North Americans were treated to newsfilm and photographs of Indian chiefs in full native war regalia as they stood in a tribunal hall in Belém, denied entrance to their trial on charges of sedition. This was but one instalment in a long saga. Over a decade earlier, a North American anthropologist, Darrell Posey, had begun research for his doctoral thesis on the use of insects by Kayapó Indians. In the course of his studies, Posey realized that the Kayapó were extra-ordinary scientists, and this led him to elaborate the Kayapó project, a research program in which scientists from a number of disciplines would study with the Kayapó and transcribe their information into the terms of First World knowledge. Posey also arranged to have Indians go to scientific congresses and thus participate as full members of the Brazilian scientific community. However, the turmoil of southern Pará in the 1980s thwarted these purely academic concerns, as Indian lands came under mounting pressure and were invaded by ranchers, miners and loggers.

In October 1988 in Belém, more than fifty-four groups, including scientists, the Workers Party' (PT) and *macumba* priests, protested the trial of two Kayapó Indian chiefs who were being prosecuted with Posey for contravening the Brazilian Foreign Sedition Act. This law forbids foreigners to interfere in the internal affairs of the Brazilian Republic. The Indians were not technically foreigners, but were charged under the designation "wards of the state" (their so-called crimes had been committed before this status was changed), in which status the two chiefs, Paiakan and Kuben-i now raised with some urgency questions about the role of local populations in determining the policies that affect them and about the dynamics of the political economy of rural development in the American tropics.

Nine months earlier these two chiefs had been invited to a conference in Florida on tropical deforestation. At the Florida meeting members of the Environmental Defense Fund and the National Wildlife Federation asked the chiefs (along with Posey as translator, neither Portuguese nor the Kayapó language being widely used in Washington) to speak to the members of the World Bank, as well as the United States Treasury and Congress, about the Xingu Dam Complex. They did so explaining that the Indians were not the only victims of these dams. Thousands of *caboclos* who made their living from fishing and forest products would find their economic base vanishing beneath the water. The government estimated that 20 million acres would be inundated after two dams were built, and if five were completed, 7,000 square miles of forest would be flooded, creating the world's largest man-made body of water.

This proposed construction was part of the larger megalomania of the Brazilian energy industry, which was seeking from multilateral banks $500 million in loans for its plans. As the banks dragged their feet on the loans, Brazil's government became convinced that the depositions made by the Kayapó chiefs were instrumental in the delay. The World Bank countered that the inefficiency and poor management that characterized Eletrobrás, the national power company, not to mention its nuclear energy plants, were to blame. Just as Brazil was being toasted for its strides towards democracy, the government's behavior toward Posey and the Kayapó chiefs demonstrated an authoritarianism as shameless as ever. The case was the first in which the Nova República was actively seeking deportation of ''foreigners'' for sedition, a practice widely used under the dictatorship to muzzle Catholic priests.[28]

In the end, efforts to stop the multilateral banks' loan for Brazil's ''2010'' energy program failed, but many environmental safeguards were incorporated in the conditions of the loan. The Xingu-Altamira dam complex was put on hold. On February 12, 1989, the court in Belém dismissed charges against Paiakan and Kuben-i, saying that the law was inappropriate in the case of indigenous peoples. Charges against Posey were also dropped.[29]

In 1979 on a two-bit cattle ranch called *Tres Barras*, Genésio Ferreira da Silva was to discover that his straggling grasses and skinny cows were astride the most important gold strike in Amazonian history. Suddenly, visitors to Marabá found the telephone office bereft of labor, clerks vanished, shops were shut and Brazil nuts rotted on the ground. The Serra Pelada, or naked hill, had seduced everyone who had no work and few prospects. The fates had suddenly smiled on Genésio and many others, as the mud of Serra Pelada yielded up nugget after nugget, *bamburro* after *bamburro*. People from all over Brazil came to try their fortunes. The people in the area followed the internal regulations of the *garimpo* culture and remained fairly autonomous from external control until 1984.

The military viewed these proceedings with alarm. The SNI (the internal security agency) worried over the potential dangers of a vast population of single men swelling an area near the great Carajás mine, which was already fraught with rural conflict and served as the site for a ''guerrilla'' uprising. In 1984 they suggested to President Figueiredo that the government ought to intervene for reasons of security. But the reasons were also economic. Under the existing situation gold smuggling was common, and the state was losing substantial sums in revenues. The rudimentary techniques of *garimpagem* extraction seemed inefficient to larger mining companies who were eager to stake their claim by arguing for a need to introduce a more ''rationalized'' system of production.

On May 1, 1984, the military occupied the Serra Pelada. As Major Curió (the nickname of Sebastião Rodrigues de Moura) alighted from his helicopter surrounded by Rambo-like guards, he pointed his Magnum into the air announcing, "the gun that shoots loudest is mine". Curió had cut his teeth on the Araguaia guerrilla movement and knew a thing or two about insurgencies. An impenetrable military cordon girded the mining area and Marabá became occupied territory. The Serra Pelada suddenly found itself with a health center, bank, post office, telephone lines and a wholesale government store – facilities that no *garimpo* had ever seen before.

Curió's plan worked. The organization of the *garimpo* and provision of social facilities, as well as Major Curió's appealing rough-and-tumble style, resulted in the unusual outcome: a local populace who appreciated the military operation. This also served as a convenient forum for organizing votes for the government's candidates. As David Cleary describes General Figueiredo's visit to Serra Pelada when he was carried on the shoulders of cheering *garimpeiros*, "Figueiredo, naturally lachrymose and unaccustomed to warm demonstrations of popular affection was moved to tears, and vowed to keep the *garimpo* open forever." Later, cooler minds prevailed. Curió was elected to Congress on the basis of his popularity in the *garimpos*, but the populist military advisor and Peronist-style local leader was soon to see harder times as the military regime grew increasingly uncomfortable about the proximity of the gold mines to the technocratically proper Carajás.

Both the *Companhía Vale do Rio Doce* and the association of Brazilian mining companies, quite used to getting their way with the government, wanted the *garimpeiros* to be expelled from Serra Pelada. Hostility between the *garimpeiros* and the large and modern mining companies was becoming increasingly intense, until in 1983, the Department of Mineral Production formulated a plan for mechanized mining at the Serra Pelada which would employ about 350 workers, as opposed to the tens of thousands already earning a living at the site. According to this plan, *garimpeiros* would be transferred from Serra Pelada to reserves specially demarcated for them in Tapajós and Cumaru. An intense debate ensued around this proposal. What was at stake was the way in which gold-mining would be carried out in Amazônia. Curió, whose political legitimacy evaporated with the announcement of the proposal, broke with the government, and carried out his political badgering through huge lobbying campaigns and demands for new legislation. As tensions increased in 1984, Curió, who knew most intimately of fears of insurrection haunting the military, declared that he alone could hold the line. Indeed, the rebellious fervor displayed in the *garimpo* was proclaimed as the sequel to the Canudos revolt. On June 7, 1984, while the first major strike of temporary workers in São Paulo's sugarcane fields was taking place, several hundred *garimpeiros* marched down the Belém-Brasília highway threatening to storm the Carajás. The *garimpeiros* won the day on June 11, when General Figueiredo acceded to their demands, signed the legislation put forth by Curió and paid out some $60 million to the CVRD as compensation for its claims. The *garimpo* at Serra Pelada was to stay open, and the *garimpeiros* had emerged triumphant against the claims made by state and private mining companies.[30]

SETTLERS AND LANDLESS FIGHT BACK

In the struggles that commenced with the mid 1960s and which became progressively fiercer as the years went by, Indians and rubber tappers held center stage. But the largest number of rural folk in the Amazon are settlers and the landless. They too began to stand up against those who threatened to turn them away from their livelihood.

The *municípios* of São Joao do Araguaia, Marabá and Xinguara form a part of the area known as the Brazil-nut Polygon, an area that includes Carajás, Serra Pelada, huge SUDAM-financed ranches, Indian lands and large areas of colonization, and that contains the most extensive development of roads and other infrastructure in all of Amazônia. Its tumultuous history has painfully intensified, growing in its reputation as a terrain of rural violence. A few of these anecdotes tell the tale:

On February 2, 1987, in Xinguara, seventy-two peasants were jailed, thirty-two tortured, two women raped and houses of owners burned. These were the result of a Disarmament Project embarked on by the military police in an attempt to control armed resistance in the Brazil-nut Polygon.

On April 4, 1987 at Fazenda Bela Vista, a 42,000-acre ranch owned by a Paulista rancher, four hundred families living on its lands as squatters resisted an attack by a group of gunmen by killing one and wounding another. The local military police arrested and tortured seven *posseiros* and took two men considered to be the leaders, to the town of Conceição do Araguaia where they were tortured intensively until they needed to be hospitalized. In addition, any movement in or out of the contested zone was prohibited by the military police, a ban which often resulted in unassisted births, and the death of a child from tetanus infection. Medical corps periodically making rounds for polio vaccinations were denied entrance, causing an immense uproar. Through legal aid from the Catholic Church (CPT) and the state deputy for the Workers' Party, an inquest was carried out. Meanwhile, three hundred families demonstrated at the Office of Colonization and Agrarian Reform (INCRA) demanding the removal of military police, freeing of their arrested members, and expropriation of the *fazenda*, which has been embroiled in conflict since 1982.

On March 27, 1987, a group of Gavião Indians whose lands had been occupied by numerous settlers blocked the Carajás railroad. This interruption and potential disruption of Carajás's economic activities brought immediate attention to the demands made by the Gaviões. The protest was against the action of GETAT, which had signed over thirty-eight titles to settlers on indigenous lands that had been part of a large *castanhal*. This had been the source of constant conflict between the Gaviões and settlers for over five years.[30]

O Liberal reported on April 10, 1987 that three landless laborers, Valdir Brito, Manoel Lustosa and Raul Batista, "disappeared" after a group of their friends had managed to escape from Fazenda Rio 18, where they had been working in slave-like conditions with no pay. This group of workers were taken to Brasília, where they denounced the existence of slave labor in large ranches under labor contractors who had recruited them in Goiás. Agents of the military police also acknowledged the existence of slave labor in the large ranches.[31]

One of the most dramatic and widely-known incidents occurred on the Fazenda Agro Pecus in Conceição do Araguaia, when seven *posseiros* were accused of shooting the son of the financial director of UDR, Tarley de Andrade, and his chauffeur. Two of these *posseiros* were found dead in a shallow grave by the roadside. Five others were taken to jail and tortured. The local judge following orders from DOPS – the dreaded Delegacy of Political and Social Order, a sort of internal CIA – incarcerated twenty-four *posseiros* living on the contested ranch. Ronaldo Caiado, president of the UDR, protested to the minister of justice that the peasant land invaders constituted a major threat to the lives of the directorship of the UDR. The case involved so many human rights abuses that Amnesty International opened a campaign called "Torture Brazil", which denounced the illegal imprisonments and tried to guarantee access to medicines and lawyers for the victims.[32]

This list of events that took place only from the first quarter of 1987 provide a sense of the range of conflicts in a region torn by civil war. The origins of these conflicts were to be found in the conversion of extractive rights, *aforamentos*, on *castanhais*, to property rights invested in land; in the building of the Belém-Brasília highway; the entrance of large ranches into the "rich and empty" expanses of Amazônia; the resettlement of populations as the Tucuruí Dam filled with water; as the Trans-Amazon failed; as gold strikes were made and mines were dug; and as GETAT coughed out titles in haste to quieten the land-hungry populace, increasingly armed in their conflicts.[33]

Jean Hebette, who has studied the process of occupation along the Belém-Brasília highway for more than twenty years, describes a gradual process of organization occurring amongst the settlers with the help of rural union workers and the Church. In Hebette's view, much of the resistance in the region has followed the "politics of claims", which the GETAT attempted to address by freely distributing 124-acre plots and hoping the tensions would fizzle out.[34]

The colonist resistance has centered on land to such a degree that it has transformed itself into an armed struggle. In the case of 1,200 settlers on BR 150 studied by Hebette, the peasants resisted successfully – they refused to leave their plots, and worked collectively so that they would be less vulnerable to threats of violence. They organized their own civilian protection so that military police and private armies would not be able to dislodge them.

In the face of such pressure the predominant tendency has always been the clearance of forest to claim land. However, several committed agronomists and researchers are working with peasant groups to incorporate extractivism with agriculture, allowing the areas such as the valuable Brazil-nut forests to exist along with securing the livelihoods of peasants. In Rondônia, the precarious economic conditions of the rural poor has resulted in many of them being involved in rubber tapping to augment their incomes. An emerging concern with the importance of extractive resources coupled with agroforestry have resulted in several small projects which involve local organizations and base communities working together to establish a system of production that would sustain the settlers. Though these are less dramatic than the government-sponsored "showcase" projects, they depend on political organizing and action to help the peasants retain possession of their lands and improve local agriculture. But without the definitive resolution of the question of land, the trees will continue to disappear,[35] as both sides fell trees to establish their claims, and as the threat of violence limits long-term investment.

BEYOND EMPATES

Throughout the early 1980s the *empates* continued and the trees fell. The rubber tappers began to look for some solution that went beyond the compromises that were being urged upon them. The *empates*, while effective, were always an ad hoc solution since every inch of *seringal* held was always liable to future attack.

The rubber tappers viewed the National Confederation of Rural Workers, CONTAG, with some reserve. Its important initial organizing had created a vibrant group of leaders, but had paid less attention to the grassroots, or mobilization of a broader constituency. Activists were not being trained, and thus the ranchers' strategy of systematic violence against leaders remained a powerful way to demoralize the rubber tappers. FETACRE, or the Federation Of Acre Rural Workers Unions, which ought to have provided some support, never provided legal assistance. Eventually Marie Allegretti's Institute for Amazon Studies, through the Ford Foundation, arranged for an excellent young lawyer to assist the rubber tappers in the range of legal battles facing them. He too came under threat of death. "Now," Mendes said, "we have a group of colleagues who are committed to the struggle. Everyday we learn something, while at the same time knowing that we could be at the receiving end of a bullet any time."

It was clear that an organization that more directly addressed the needs of the rubber tappers, not just as rural workers but as forest people, would have to be elaborated. There was much to criticize in the Brazilian Amazon development strategies, and the local, national, and international forces pushing colonization and livestock, but the rubber tappers had as yet no alternative which could be proposed to policymakers and planners. The tappers decided to arrange a meeting of Amazonian *seringueiros* to expand the organizing ability of the rubber tappers and to come up with an alternative proposal that could compete with the cattle and livestock that seemed to be the only forms of land use planners in Brasília could imagine. With the help of Marie Allegretti and the Institute for Amazon Studies, Oxfam, National Heritage Foundation and other organizations, the first rubber tapper congress was held in Brasília in October of 1985. Thus was born the *Conselho Nacional do Seringueiros* which would become the means, in Chico Mendes's words, ''of strengthening the trade-union movement''. With over one hundred tappers representing an array of unions and organizations, the meeting put forward several proposals that would orient their subsequent political action. The central points (which are printed here in Appendix E) emphasized the importance of participation of rubber tappers in the drafting and execution of all regional development programs that would affect them. All forests used by extractors should be preserved. Colonization projects in areas of rubber and Brazil-nut trees should be immediately stopped. The tappers called for a policy of regional development that could help the struggle of Amazonian workers as well as other initiatives to preserve forests and nature. ''We want,'' the rubber tappers said, ''a development policy that recognizes the rubber tappers as 'the true defenders of the forest'.'' The regional development approach of the rubber tappers was followed by very specific recommendations, the most significant of which was the demand for extractive reserves.

THE EXTRACTIVE RESERVES

With land conflicts convulsing throughout the region, it was clear to the rubber tappers that some form of land safeguard was necessary. Since virtually all land titles were open to contest, the strategy of *empate* and legal harassment could not in the end assure the livelihoods of rubber tappers, and the legal struggles over squatter rights or landlord claims would lie forever in the clogged and ineffectual courts. The source of livelihood itself had to be secured. The rubber tappers had been searching for a model giving their stretches of forest the same legal status as colonization plots or ranching lands, and in the end they used the model of the rubber estate itself, which is divided up into several *colocações* or smaller holdings managed by individual rubber tapper families.[36] The rubber tappers' *conselho* and rural unions began to press for what they called ''extractive reserves''. These reserves would recognize the use rights of the local population, but the holdings would not be privately owned. They would be collective ''condominium rights'' or long-term leases from the state. Once tenure was assured, the extractive reserves would also organize health clinics, schools and small-scale rubber-processing factories, and eventually even some manufacturing.

This proposal was profoundly radical. It discounted private ownership in favor of use rights, a way of controlling any tendency of tappers to participate in land speculation, also a way of assuring sustainable management. This model was the first formal expression of a *land* management program founded in the extractive economy and history of Amazônia. To the UDR, this emphasis on collective *ejido* types of ownership was rank socialism, for the land rights of the great would be contested, perhaps replaced by some form of communal land ownership. The extractive reserves were an attack on private property and hence capitalism.

Astute political lobbying with the aid of Allegretti's Institute for Amazon Studies, resulted in a major legislative advance. Allegretti, an anthropologist, who had done her thesis on rubber tappers in Acre, and who was in essence the political liaison for the union, co-ordinated the pressure within the Ministry of Agrarian Reform to incorporate the reserves as a new model for lawful occupation, with status equal to the more traditional livestock and colonization strategies. In July 1987, the Minister of Agrarian Reform signed into law the legislation that permitted *assentámentos extrativistas*. Two weeks later he was blown up in a suspicious plane accident over the Carajás zone of eastern Amazônia.

The legislation meant that extractive reserves could be implemented in areas that were expropriated under the agrarian reform laws. More than 84 per cent of Acre was covered by *latifundia* and characterized by land titles of extraordinarily tenuous legal status. The potential for expropriation and change in the dynamic of Amazonian development, of the area in Brazil with the largest agglomerations of *latifundia* – one that favored the poor and conserved the resource base – was now a possibility rather than a dream.

RUBBER TAPPERS AND FRIENDS ABROAD

The rubber tappers now began to find new allies. Environmentalists in Brazil and in the international community quickly recognized that the extractive reserves were among the most innovative strategies for conserving forests. While many of their constituents might have been horrified at the idea that their organizations were supporting radical union organizing efforts, the reserve was at least a step in the right direction in preserving the habitat of the overwintering birds and large felines so valued by many North American environmentalists. A major leap in how North Americans viewed conservation occurred when it began to gradually dawn on conservationists that people and forests could actually co-exist. The concerted lobbying of such North American groups as the Environmental Defense Fund, the World Wildlife Fund, the Wildlife Federation began to bring Chico Mendes and his organization to international attention. Thus it was that in 1987 Mendes was awarded a major international prize by the United Nations which honored him as one of the Global 500 (an annual citation of crusaders for the protection of the environment). This caused a certain consternation in Brazil, as few journalists or "official scientists" had any idea who this rubber tapper – whom the rest of the world was adopting as the savior of Brazil's tropical forests – actually was. Extractive reserves also caught the eye of multilateral development agencies which also began to pressure for this kind of land-use model in their Amazon development project negotiations.

Perhaps at least as important that same year, however, was the development of the Forest Peoples' Alliance where rubber tappers and indigenous peoples signed a pact which focused on defending the forests and land rights of forest people. In spite of the history of conflict between Indians and tappers, Jaime Araújo, a member of the governing board of the Rubber Tappers' Council, pointed out that "we have the same way of life, and the same enemies: the rancher and the logger. The isolation we live as tappers and Indians intensifies the solidarity among men and reinforces the bonds of family, friendship, and cordiality between people."

The *Conselho* of rubber tappers also began to explore legal challenges to deforestation. The Brazilian forestry code prohibits the cutting of Brazil-nut and rubber trees. So the *Conselho* began to pressure local forestry officials to check whether ranchers had licences even to clear the areas where the trees were falling, also to see whether rubber trees and Brazil-nut trees were being cut. Since virtually no one had licences to cut, and deforestation continued to occur rapidly, the forestry agency found itself under attack by the *Conselho*.

In February 1988, after a workshop in Rio Branco on environment, politics and development that included rubber tappers, Indians, national and international scientists, local government officials, members of political parties and non-government organizations, the governor of Acre, Flaviano Melo, announced the creation of the first extractive reserve at São Luis de Remanso. A fierce battle had ensued earlier in the week in the Agrarian Reform offices among the members of the Rubber Tappers' Council, state agencies, members of non-governmental organizations, researchers and representatives of funding agencies over the exact sites where these reserves should be established. For the rubber tappers, it was urgent that the areas of intense conflict, such as Seringal Cachoeira, be immediately protected, since these were under the immediate threat of deforestation and where, given the murderous temperament of the current landowner, Darly Alves, bloodshed was likely to occur in the summer of 1988 when the clearing season began.

SHOWDOWN AT CACHOEIRA

Cachoeira, near Xapuri where Mendes's rubber union office was located and where Mendes was born, was well organized. Tappers driven off other forest lands by the *pistoleiros* had long gathered there. It had once been held by a *seringalista*, then by a Japanese investor, then by a landowner with no stomach for land-clearing wars. Some seventy or eighty tappers' families lived there. They were not going to flee violence again.

But the government representatives were naturally interested in the situation in which the political shrapnel would be mildest. They advocated sites that could be easily expropriated, were remote and not particularly organized. The compromise was São Luis de Remanso, about two hours outside of Rio Branco, already expropriated, close, and not particularly organized.

With research for the first reserve well under way, it was clear that the summer of 1988 would be different from the others. The torrential floods that had ravaged Acre and destroyed more than 30 per cent of its agriculture had receded, to be replaced by the blazing tropical sun of the deforested zones. The contracts for land clearing were signed, the gunslingers hired. From their ranch at Seringal Cachoeira, Darly Alves and his son, owners of Fazenda Paraná, prepared to claim Cachoeira for their own. At the same time, the rubber tappers claimed Cachoeira as an extractive reserve without the benediction of the state, and the *empates* began.

Who were Chico Mendes's killers? They came from down south, from the State of Paraná. Darly and Alvorino Alves had cut their teeth on rural battles twenty years earlier in the Paraná coffee wars, which saw the same battles over forest clearing that were now afflicting Acre. The Alves brothers had finally been forced to flee Paraná. One time too many they hired some *pistoleiros* – a man had died, and the judge said that the blood-money had come from Darly and Alvorino. He had put out a warrant for Darly's arrest and imprisonment. So the brothers headed northwest through Mato Grosso and into Acre, claiming title to Seringal Cachoeira.

The Alves brothers wanted to clear-cut, sell and then move along. All deforestation in Amazônia technically requires a clearing permit. This law is virtually never enforced, but since the Alves brothers had no permit, in May 1988, 400 tappers staged a sit-in in the Xapuri offices of the Brazilian forestry service, demanding that the law be enforced on Cachoeira. The Alves brothers had already marshaled their cutting crews. *Pistoleiros* attacked the tappers by night, wounding two. The tappers were claiming Cachoeira as a *de facto* extractive reserve. The tensions were becoming so extreme that Governor Flaviano Melo expropriated Cachoeira and ratified in law the rubber tappers' claim.[37]

The father of Darly and Alvorino chatted with Chico's cousin. Not knowing the relationship, the father said that plans for Chico's murder had been laid. All over Rio Branco and Xapuri, Chico's death was being foretold. Chico Mendes knew its likelihood himself. On November 30 he wrote to Mauro Esposito, superintendent of the federal police:

Even though we are often reviled for being agitators, we were never linked to violence, and never has a drop of blood been spilled by our own initiative. In spite of this, you, my dear sir, know that today I am obliged to walk with two security guards because Darly and Alvorino Alves have said that they will turn themselves in only after they see my corpse. Their *pistoleiros* walk where they will.

He told of the meeting of the local chapter of the UDR back at the start of the year where it had been agreed that Chico Mendes had to die. Marie Allegretti had dug up the Paraná warrant for Darly's arrest, and Darly (Chico told the police superintendent) had fled to a remote portion of his ranch, announcing that he would surrender to this warrant only after he had killed Chico Mendes.

The head of the UDR chapter in Acre is João Branco, owner of the local newspaper, *O Rio Branco*. On December 5 the inhabitants of Rio Branco, studying this publication, came upon an interesting announcement. João Branco's paper predicted that soon there would explode "a bomb of 200 megatons that will have national repercussions". The same column continued with abuse of Mendes. Later that month people hanging around the post office in Brasiléia, a town near the Bolivia border down the road from Xapuri, saw Gaston Mota – landowner, Darly crony, and contractor of hired guns – claim, with extreme nervousness, a telex order of 10,400,000 *cruzados* from Rio Branco, which sum, amounting to nearly $10,000, would later be proposed by investigating officer Nelson Oliveira as the contract money being put up by the UDR to reward the first man to nail Mendes. Two days before Chico Mendes stepped for the last time off his back porch, Mota, a rancher who had been at the UDR meeting outside Xapuri, was seen chatting amiably with the head of state security in Acre, a man loath to act upon Mendes's urgings that he detain the men planning his death.

The wet season began, and everyone hoped, as one does in the Amazon, that things would cool, like the deforestation fires, with the winter rains. It is hard to move, hard to see, wet, and muddy. Under the cloak of the rainstorms that force one's vision into narrower scope, and with the shield of the rain on roofs and plant leaves, the killers were able to move into the shelter of the overhang of Chico Mendes's house. As he rose from the company of his wife, two children and two federal guards, and stepped out his back door the killers opened fire.[38]

Those in custody now are only those who gave themselves up. Justice or even rudimentary legal procedure is a rare commodity in Amazônia, especially in its rural areas. In Acre the *comarcas*, the judicial districts, usually have no presiding judges. Xapuri, for example, has not had one for more than a decade. "Extremely precarious" is how the president of Brazil's Justice Tribunal describes the Acrean legal system, with its nine hundred death threats and murders, and a jury system that hears only twenty-five cases a year. This stately pace of the law, coupled with a total inability to investigate crimes – no jeeps, no gas, no material whatsoever – permits criminals (or at least those who order crimes) to continue their actions with arrogance and impunity.

ALLIANCE IN ACRE

"Chico Mendes is dead," Osmarino Amâncio Rodrigues told a crowd in Rio Branco three months later, on Easter Sunday. "Things can't be as they were, and to dream that they could would be to drive us to ruin." Through Holy Week, in late March of 1989, Rio Branco saw a meeting, the first of its kind, between rubber tappers, Indian tribal groups and various forest dwellers. There were old hatreds still smoldering. Indians remembered relatives pushed from their lands by agents of rubber barons, with uncles killed and sisters raped. Rubber tappers remembered Indian raids.

The rubber tappers had gathered from Acre, Rondônia, Amazonas, Pará, Mato Grosso and Amapá, bordering the Atlantic Ocean 2,000 miles to the east. There were Indians from tribes as diverse as the rubber-tapping Campa and Kaxinua and the last remnant of the Krenak, exiled from their lands in the south by Brazil's largest state-owned corporation. From Tefé, two days upriver from the Amazon city of Manaus, came the *ribeirinhos* – fisherfolk, harvesters of gum, latex and wild medicines. Flanking them were advisers ranging from an Irish Holy Ghost father to prominent Brazilian eco-activists to international environmental groups.

In the same week, the Inter-American Development Bank met in Amsterdam and listened to the Brazilian Minister of Finance plead for credit concessions as the bankers, themselves being lobbied by environmentalists from Western Europe and the United States, pressed him on his government's plans for the Amazon. Back in Brasília, Ruben Bayma Denys, chief of the Military Cabinet and National Security Council, was putting final touches to the official environmental policy document *Nossa Natureza*, to be promulgated by President José Sarney. And in the upper Acrean forests west of Rio Branco, ninety families were under threat of being driven from their land, with 3,500 acres of forest starting to fall to chainsaws even before the rainy season had come to an end.

There are moments in the always ambiguous dialectic between First World conscience and Third World conditions when the former's concerns reach a critical mass. The murder of Chico Mendes had caught the attention of North America and Western Europe, and presented the plight of the forest like a Passion play. And indeed, the Good Friday crowds following the statue of the Virgin through the candlelit streets of Rio Branco listened on their transistor radios as Moacir Grecchi, Archbishop of Acre and himself under threat of death, compared the fate of Chico Mendes to Christ's passion, and the persecution of forest workers to that of the early Christians.

In the wake of Mendes's assassination, the Brazilian government and the murderers themselves had been stunned by the international outcry over what they regarded as the very ordinary termination of an obscure labor leader. Members of the US Congress, well aware of the interests of their own constituents, headed south.

The meeting wound up against a backdrop of salvos in the newspaper from members of the landowners' vigilante organization, the UDR. João Branco, the former local UDR president, and a man regarded as having instigated the assassinations of rubber tappers, returned in time to scream abuse in the Rio Branco airport at Fernando Gabeira, head of Brazil's Green Party. Equally vitriolic was an Acre Assemblyman, João Batista Tezza, who compared extractive reserves to concentration camps and called the participants in the Easter meeting "theoretical Nazis". João Branco, representative of UDR opinion, announced in his newspaper that if he had his way, 95 per cent of the Amazon's forest would be cleared and nuclear reactors implanted. Brazilian newspapers were full of concern about the "internationalization of the Amazon" and the threat that this and any new form of land use might imply to national sovereignty and security.

Amid these provocations the rubber tappers and Indians worked out a program that gave forest peoples the prime role in formulating their regional development. They saw the vital principles in agrarian reform as recognition of rubber-tapper and Indian land rights, establishment of extractive reserves, and an end to their debt peonage on traditional rubber estates. They demanded local authority in the reserves over health and education, now the province of the state, urged co-operatives and demanded public investment in the processing of forest products. In other words, they called for popular control over the means of production and distribution of forest commodities, along with the provision of financial credits to producers rather than to middlemen. They also called for justice and legal protection of their rights to land and life. These are the concrete elements of a socialist ecology – the only strategy that can save the Amazon and its inhabitants.

NOTES

1. An estimate of Artus Ramos, quoted by Darcy Ribeiro, *The Americas and Civilization* 1971. Estimates of the total number of Africans transported have varied from 18 million to 3.3 million.

2. Vincente Salles, *O Negro no Pará* 1971.

3. See Robin Anderson, "The Caboclo as Revolutionary: The Cabanagem Revolt: 1835–1836", in *Studies in Third World Societies* No. 32, 1985.

4. For an excellent account of the revolt, see Pasquale di Paolo, *Cabanagem* 1986. Also see Gustavo Morães Rego Reis, *A Cabanagem* 1965.

5. Quoted by Barbara Weinstein in "Capital penetration and problems of labor control in the Amazon rubber trade", *Radical History Review*, Vol. 27, 1983.

6. Quoted by Barbara Weinstein 1983.

7. M. Almeida, "Seringais e Trabalho na Amazônia: o caso do Alto Juruá", manuscript, 1988.

8. See James C. Scott, *Weapons of the Weak: Everyday Forms of Peasant Resistance* 1986; also T. Aston and C. Philpin, *The Brenner Debate* 1985.

9. For internal migration see Hecht and Schwartzman, "Internal Migration in the Seringal", in preparation. It should be said here that there was also a great deal of return migration to the Northeast after the boom ended.

10. For the economic consequences of the end of the boom, see Barbara Weinstein, and Oliveira, *Encontros Com da Civilização Brasiliera*.

11. See S. Schwartzman and M. Allegretti 1989; L. A. Oliveira, *O Sertanejo, o Brabo e o Posseiro* 1985; M. Almeida 1988; A. Reis, *O Seringal e O Seringueiro*; J. Galey 1977.

12. In Leal's case, these were the Gregório, Taurauacá and Riozinho da Liberdade. See T. Aquino, *Indios Caxinua: De Seringueiro Caboclo a Peao Acreano* 1982.

13. *O Varadouro*, May 19, 1980, cites the following corporations and the areas (in hectares) of the holdings they bought:

Coloama	1,000,000
Coperacucar	600,000
Viação Garcia	600,000
Agipito Lemos	520,000
Bradesco	500,000
Atlantica Boa Vista	500,000
Paranacre	450,000

14. G. Mesquita, Evidence given to the Brazilian Congress, *Diário do Congresso Nacional*, December 1977.

15. An English version is printed with a commentary in the excellent booklet, *Chico Mendes in his Own Words: Fight for the Forest*, edited with commentary by Tony Gross, Latin America Bureau (Research and Action) Ltd., 1 Amwell Street, London EC1R 1UL; adapted from *O Testamento do Homem da Floresta*, edited by Candido Grzybowski, FASE, São Paulo 1989. Another version of the interview can be found in *Chico Mendes*, a booklet, published by the Sindicato dos Trabalhadores Rurais de Xapuri, Conselho Nacional dos Seringueiros (CSN) and the Central Unica dos Trabalhadores (CUT), January, 1989.

16. See *Chico Mendes in his Own Words: Fight for the Forest*.

17. Quoted from the alternative newspaper, *Varadouro*, published in Rio Branco, in Keith Baks, *Peasant Formation and Capitalist Development: The case of Acre*, Ph.D. Thesis, University of Liverpool 1986.

18. No one has ever expressed the significance of the *varadouro* better than Euclides da Cunha in his book of essays on the Amazon, *Um Paraíso Perdido*:

Between one water course and the next, the forest's expanses are isolating as though they were mountains. [The forest] is an isolator. It separates and subdivides .... One sees then ... this inversion: Man instead of mastering this land has become enslaved by the river. The populations never expanded outward, but merely stretched themselves. They proceeded in long files, and returned always on the same route they started out on ... thus immobilizing themselves by the appearances of an illusory progress, in the retreats and advances of the adventurer who sets out, goes to the end of the earth, but explores and returns on the same trail, or renews, monotonously the same itineraries.... In their short but very active history, the new staging points in the region, except for a few minor variants, continue to press aridly along those already unraveled routes to the South West: three or four risks, three or four river voyages, tottering, undefined in a desert.

This discouraging social aspect, created primarily by the conditions, in the beginning so favorable, of the rivers, corrects itself by the transversal linkages of its great valleys. The idea was neither original nor new. In the past, with admirable intuition, those rough frontiersmen of those distant corners implemented the opening of the first *varadouro*.

The *varadouro*, a legacy of the heroic Paulista, is today shared by the people in Amazonas, in Bolivia, in Peru. It is the path, the short cut which goes from one fluvial slope to the next. At first tortuous and short, suffocating, down in the forest thickness, the *varadouro* reflected the indecisive steps of an emerging vacillating society which abandoned the comforting laps of the rivers, and chose instead to walk for itself ... Today the narrow one-meter wide trails of this society, trails cut out with machetes stretch everywhere, diverting themselves in numerous directions and crossroads, and linking the various affluents of all the headwaters: of the Acre river for that of the Purus, thence to the Juruá river, and then to the Uyacali, they trace the contemporary history of the new territory in a way totally counter to the primitive, impotent, fatal submission to the great natural lines of communication ... Taking to the trails, man in fact is not submissive. He is an insurgent against affectionate and treacherous nature which enriches and kills him.

19. Farmers in the North American mid-west have tickers in their offices or barns telling them the hour-by-hour cost of farm commodities. By the analogy of the isolation of the upper Amazon, it is as though they never got news of prices, only getting quotation once a year from grain companies refusing to tell them their selling prices.

20. See Gross.

21. The church's figures are given in *Conflitos No Campo Brasil/87*, Commisão Pastoral da Terra, Brazil.

For a sense of the texture of everyday violence in the Amazon, in this case on BR 364 just east of Porto Velho, consider two stories which appeared in the *Estadão* on March 20, 1989:

A LATE DEBT RESULTS IN TRAGEDY ON 364 – A laborer, José Aureliano de Conceição, 46, father of 6, killed on Tuesday Valderi Anselmo da Silva, 41 known as Gaúcho, in his house in Beja Flor – k. 60, near the district of Itipoa. The criminal recounted how he had known Valderi for three years, bought 2000 coffee seedlings at an agreed price of 700 cruzados each, promising to pay one week later when his daughter returned from a journey to collect a debt. "By May she had not returned, but sent a message saying she had no money, and I explained this to Gaúcho. He didn't like it a bit. I urged patience."

At the end of last year José Aureliano met Gaúcho at a tavern on BR 364 where he was abused and reviled and called a sleazebag and a thief. "I couldn't strike back because I was indebted to him." On another occasion Gaúcho went to José's house. "I was not at home, but he abused Josepha, 39, and threatened to destroy the seedlings." On the day of the crime José Aureliano left his house early and went to Itapura to buy tobacco and basic products. As he had some money he resolved to stop off at Beja Flor and stay forever misunderstandings and abuse. As he approached Gaúcho's house, Gaúcho took advantage of the presence of his brother-in-law Antônio de Souza, just in from Paraná three days earlier, to humiliate José Aureliano. "He said I could keep the money as alms because he didn't want to get money from an untrustworthy sleaze, and I should shove off, otherwise I would get my face smashed in. There were two other workers with me who asked why I didn't react and I answered that I would take vengeance as the opportunity offered."

In his house José Aureliano called his wife and children into the kitchen to explain to them what had happened and made clear to them that as a man and head of a family he had to sustain the honor of the family name. "I remember I went out and got my rifle and I walked in the direction of the house of Gaúcho. I avoided walking on the road, and went on the rough terrain between the trees. I saw him talking to his brother at the table, and then I found a good spot and I waited there for my chance." Continuing to detail the crime, José Aureliano remembered, "The first chance I had was after about 20 minutes. The victim got up to go to the door. I made ready. But at the last minute his wife asked him a

question and Gaúcho once again sat down and went on talking. The second chance came ten minutes later. I was already getting uncomfortable with insect bites, and then I saw Gaúcho come and look out of the window. This was the position I needed. I cocked my gun, pointed it and fired. He reeled and fell heavily, calling to his brother, who I'd also wounded, and his wife and saying he was going to die. I went home and I was sure I'd killed at least Gaúcho. I told my wife that I had had my revenge and had cleansed my honor."

José Aureliano's house was surrounded by civil police. He says it had been his intention to give himself up just as long as he was not caught *in flagrante*. He lamented only that he had wounded the brother, who had nothing to do with the affair, and that it had all been to cleanse his honor.

Gaúcho's harsh reaction to José Aureliano's attempt to repay the debt will be better understood if it is remembered that inflation had probably made the offer of repayment almost worthless.

On the same day, in the same newspaper, another story stated that

Rancher João Bahiano hired contract gunmen to kill twelve families of colonists concentrated in an unclaimed area on the river Jamary. It was more grave than mere threats. He was accused of entering the sub-delegacy of Itapoa and advising policeman Armindo da Silva that he was going to kill these agriculturalists. The policeman did nothing, but went on drinking coffee. This accusation was made by Albertinho Nascimento, president of the rural association of Itapoa, defender of the interests of workers in the district, to Commissioner Claudio Ribeiro of the 5th police district. He said that João Bahiano wanted to conquer by bullets. In the complaint made to the police delegate, Albertinho told of trying to come to an agreement with Bahiano who has a *fazenda* at k. 104 on BR 364 and to explain to him that laws protected families on state lands. According to the coordinator of the land office of Upper Madeira, known only as George, Bahiano didn't listen to him, and on the twentieth day last month at around 11 am he entered brusquely, suddenly telling Albertinho he was going to kill three agriculturalists who had entered his land.

22. The Central Bank of Brazil views him as one of the most dangerous speculators in Brazil, *Jornal do Brasil*, May 10, 1986. In 1989 he was able to cause total chaos in the exchange.

23. These results are from J. Graziano da Silva, *A Modernização Dolorosa* 1982.

24. About 87,000 owners (in a Brazilian population of over 120 million) own about 57 per cent of all Brazilian landholdings. In areas

that have come to be dominated by livestock, such as Conceição do Araguaia, Santana and Marabá, large landowners control nearly 85 per cent of the land. See Hecht 1985.

25. Amnesty International.

26. Such sensitivity was the result of several forces, among them the persistent pressure of the World Bank environmental officer, Robert Goodland, and other Brazil specialists who had become horrified at the consequences of Brazil's development programs and the World Bank's role in them. The "Multilateral Banks Campaign" organized by Bruce Rich of the Environmental Defense Fund, mobilized political pressure and public opinion in the US, and these pressures gave local Indian advocacy organizations more room for maneuver, with their knowledge of a resourceful lobby supporting them at the international level. This attention also brought the everyday disasters of indigenous peoples on to the everyday news agenda.

27. An innovative program at the University of Goiás was set up to train Indians selected from different tribes. As Posey described it in May 1989, there were

five positions for Indian students to study biology and five to study law. The idea is to secure for native peoples a space within a university which they've never had, and at the same time to promote traditional knowledge and set up experimental stations on native reserves and bring traditional knowledge-holders to the university and there work with indigenous and non-indigenous students; then take ideas back and try to apply them in the village, to come up with alternative crop systems, and alternatives for sustainable economic development, utilizing resources that are traditional to the tribe, and try and figure an income that allows some native people to have some independence. So there are a number of elements: 1. train native people in a white man's university, but have a separate structure so they can think, work and share together and not just be lost in this enormous university structure, and also at the same time to integrate through their traditional knowledge sharing ideas with elders and university professors, so they can see how transfer of traditional knowledge can be put into practice. It's a great idea, should be easy as a pie to fund, but it isn't, because people really don't want alternatives.

With the help of the university, but under the control of the Xavante and UNI, a program was set up to recuperate degraded agricultural lands and to carry out reforestation on savannah lands. After extensive consultations with elders and shamans, the group decided that what they wanted most was to have better hunting and this could only be achieved through the planting of fruit trees to attract and maintain game animals. These fruits would also be sold as luxury flavorings on the international market. In 1988 a West German company agreed to buy these flavorings through a co-operative organized by the Xavante.

28. Who gains from these mad development projects? Brazil's construction companies. These, in conjunction with their governments and multilateral lending agencies, underpin the political economy of tropical devastation. Such Third World Bechtels make the most money with least risk, are powerful lobbies and have been able to capture the benefits of indebtedness brought on by Brazil's stratospheric borrowing. With much of the rest of its population crammed into hovels, these corporate groups cavort in *Fortune*'s International 500, emblems of the aqua-military-industrial complex.

In any tropical development the luscious trove is "infrastructure": the Machu Pichus, the Tikals, the Monte Albans of today's tropical world, pharaonic reveries conceived by their sponsors as monuments to their will. Infrastructure development – roads, hydropower, other forms of civil construction – absorbs 50 to 60 per cent of regional development funds, the rest going to government bureaucracies, graft, and some services and credits for the "target" populations. These infrastructure deals, involving hundreds of millions of dollars in transfers to construction companies, now represent the major rural employment strategy in tropical America, as local populations are marginalized and extensive livestock operations spread across the landscape.

29. Posey has escorted Kayapó chiefs such as Paiakan on trips around the United States, raising money for Kayapó projects. For his views on anthropologists, outside experts

and other topics, see Appendix B.

At a conference in Altamira in February 1989, organized by the Kayapó Indians who invited native peoples from North America and from Brazil beyond the Amazon region, the participants at the conference agreed that one of the central issues in Amazonian development was now the participation of affected peoples in discussions about development projects. They urged that these projects become part of a larger national debate, addressing itself to both increased democratization and greater environmental sensitivity.

30. D. Cleary. The uprising we describe is based on this thesis and newspaper articles.

31. *A Provincia do Para*, July 7, 1987.

32. *O Liberal*, January 4, 1987.

33. The introduction of charcoal production into the scenario is likely to exacerbate this extremely fraught situation as huge numbers – at least 25,000 laborers – pour back from the areas influenced by the Carajás iron deposits, to cut trees and make charcoal for the pig-iron factories. The profitability of these pig-iron factories depends, as mentioned in earlier chapters, entirely on the interference with and destruction of a "free" forest. CVRD, "Centrais de Aço ao Longo da E.F. Carajás", Documento Interno 1987.

34. M. Schmink 1982. Also see Alfredo Wagner, "O Intransitivo da Transição Conflito Agrário e Violência na Amazônia", manuscript 1988. There are about 615 associations or rural workers' unions, but about two-thirds of these are considered as "pelegos", compromising and accommodating.

35. Studies on the land question in this region can be found in J. Hebette, "Resistência dos Posseiros no Grande Carajás", Cadernos do CEAS #104, 62–75. *Para Agrario* #2 Jan/Jun 1987, which is entitled *A Tensao no Polígono*. Also see Alfredo Wagner, "Estructura Fundiaria e Expansão Camponesa", in J.M. Almeida, *Carajás: Desafio Político, Ecológico e Desenvolvimento* 1986.

36. See M. Allegretti 1989; S. Schwartzman and M. Allegretti, for a description of rubber-tapper holdings.

37. Governor Melo came from the Acrean elite which had no love for rubber tappers in general, but which was worried about the challenge to its sway by the new ranchers who already triumphed in Rondônia and now threatening to do so in Acre. Also Melo was well aware of the interest of such bodies as the World Bank and the Inter-America Development Bank in environmental controls on development in the Amazon and therefore hoped to attract "green" multilateral funding for his state. Melo was also viewed as a skillful political operator. While working with the *seringueiros* he would also develop schemes opposed to their interest.

38. That same night, just an hour and a half after Chico fell, two reporters from *O Rio Branco* arrived to cover the "200-megaton bomb" (i.e. Chico's murder) foretold in their paper eighteen days earlier. They had been well enough briefed to be on the scene of the crime just ninety minutes after it happened, though it takes two and a half hours (four when the roads are bad, as indeed they were) to drive from Rio Branco, which is where they supposedly were when news of Chico's death came through. The day after the murder João Branco thought it prudent that the head of the Acre chapter of the UDR step aboard his private plane and leave Acre for a season.

The Alves brothers were nowhere to be found. Then, two days later, Darly's son Darcy gave himself up. He said he was the man who had organized Chico's death. In mid-January Darly surrendered. Alvorino, they say, is across the frontier in Bolivia. In São Paulo the university's crime lab now says that human hairs inside the hood of a rain cape abandoned near where Chico's killers stood in wait most likely belong to Darcy.

The UDR was unabashed. Its national leader, Ronaldo Caiado, said in the aftermath of the murder, "The Amazon is ours to do what we want with."

NINE

The Ecology of Justice

The forest is one big thing; it has people, animals, and plants. There is no point saving the animals if the forest is burned down; there is no point saving the forest if the people and animals who live in it are killed or driven away. The groups trying to save the race of animals cannot win if the people trying to save the forest lose; the people trying to save the Indians cannot win if either of the others lose; the Indians cannot win without the support of these groups; but the groups cannot win without the help of the Indians, who know the forest and the animals and can tell what is happening to them. No one of us is strong enough to win alone; together, we can be strong enough to win.

PAIAKAN, Kayapó leader

From the moment the Amazon was opened to the Old World, it was embraced with widely varying expectations. As we saw at the start of this history, some nourished hopes for the Amazon as an Eden under glass; some as a treasure-house of gold and kindred blessings; others as the invitation to a march of national destiny.

We have tried to show that there are many dreams of the Amazon but the reality is often forgotten. The struggle over the region's future is fundamentally about justice and distribution; whether the Amazon becomes both a literal and moral desert – a land of exterminated Indians, evicted forest people, swollen urban slums and million upon millions of acres of degraded pasture and poisoned rivers.

The forces propelling this destruction are not irrational. Explanations that focus on the supposed ignorance of the actors or on short-sighted planning miss the reality: there was money to be made; survival to be sustained in clearing forest. These have been processes with a logic and trajectory deeply embedded in the region's political and economic history. Despair has also fed these processes of environmental destruction – the small peasant desperate for land who clears his five acres a year; the goldminer who leaches mercury into the streams as he refines out his nuggets – and this despair must be set in the context of agrarian and political history, and the wild swings of Brazil's economy over the last twenty-five years, which have systematically increased the already vast distance between the relatively few rich and the innumerable poor.

When the generals began their project of "flooding the Amazon with civilization", as General Golbery put it, they had no idea of the environmental holocaust they were about to unleash. They viewed their enterprise as an orderly military occupation – indeed General Castello Branco described it in just those terms. When crises peaked, as they often did, the military were close at hand with short-term solutions ranging from repression to ad hoc agrarian reform in order to appease the increasingly intractable rural populations. But, as we have described in episode after episode of Amazonian history, both the social and the natural terrain have rarely respected such orderly ambitions. The region's structures and resources have encouraged the forays of short-term despoilers who then enjoyed their riches elsewhere – whether the royal court in Lisbon, the *bandeirantes* or ranchers in São Paulo, or the rubber barons in Paris.

The Amazon's history is not a closed option, doomed to repeat with accelerating viciousness the cycles of the past. People learn from history. Each era of destruction also engendered resistance, and sent to later generations the memory of that resistance. Old Kayapó Indians can recall vividly the battles they won against the invaders as well as those they lost. Rubber tappers remember the Acrean revolution, think that without the rubber they sent to the Allied armies the Second World War could not have been won, mourn their fallen leaders like Wilson Pinheiro and Chico Mendes, but carry the lesson of the *empates* in their heads and hearts.

In the battles over the Amazon's future there have already been victories. Just as the great Amazonian rebellion of the 1830s threw up leaders from the humblest shacks beside the Amazon, so now the struggles have thrown up authentic leaders, whether it be Paiakan or Chico Mendes or hundreds of others – rural union leaders, the clergy, lawyers, advocates who see the struggle for justice as the primary concern, defense of the whole as the key to triumph.

TUTELAGE AND THE DISNEY VERSION

One of the victories they have won, but which not all in the First World concede, is the victory against tutelage. In the past, tutelage has meant the government of Brazil giving Indians the status of children. It has meant anthropologists speaking on behalf of "their" tribes. It has meant development experts – whether from Brasília or Washington – devising for the region "appropriate" plans, which have so far been almost invariably disastrous. In Latin the word *tutela* means guide, and the paradigms of tutelage have run very deep in the minds of outsiders deciding what the Amazon needed. Maury thought the Amazon would be improved by grain fields stretching from the Bolivian frontier to Belém. Coudreau supposed that Aryan colonists would save the region. Farquhar thought that railroads (all owned by him) would turn the tide. But native peoples of the region now have a voice and speak with passion in a language that most people understand better than the patois of the environmentalists, developers or technocrats. On any street corner in any part of the world one can listen to native peoples talking about how destruction and injustice tear at their existence, at their health, at the integrity of their families; and what is being lost, in terms of food, medicinal plants and good soils; how these material losses reflect the more intangible losses in their lives. The strategies evolved by Amazon peoples are more innovative than anything outsiders can devise, and range from planting techniques to regional development. They make arguments that anyone can understand, and this makes their voices in the end more powerful and more moving.

Today there are prescriptions by the hundred for the Amazon's future, ranging from an exclusionary Eden, to Ronaldo Caiado's call for an Amazon half untouchable and half given over to mechanized, large-scale agriculture. Some of the counsel from the First World has an arrogance that is ludicrous if one imagines the terms of advice being reversed. In 1988 the French President, François Mitterrand, proposed that some countries should renounce portions of their sovereignty if the environmental stakes were sufficiently high, and thus large areas of the Amazon should be placed under the supervision of the United Nations. This was effectively the resurrection of an early postwar scheme and the proposal was greeted with enormous indignation by the Brazilians. Some US senators and American politicians were eager to make the same sort of suggestion for "internationalizing" the Amazon – so that Brazilians irritably recalled North American plots at the turn of the century to take over the territory of Acre, at that point the jewel of the Amazonian rubber economy.

One can hardly blame Brazilian politicians for chafing at demands for the "internationalization" of the Amazon. What reception would they get if they headed for Ukiah to denounce the clear-cutting of the redwoods, calling them the common heritage of all mankind, or mustered outside Sellafield, reviling Margaret Thatcher for making the Irish Sea into a nuclear waste dump?

The First World politicians, technocrats, representatives of private voluntary organizations, rock stars and film-makers rush south to Brazil just as a few years ago they rushed east to Ethiopia. This is a reflection of real as well as opportunistic concern, and real as well as illusory contributions are made. There are now concerts and fund-raisers for the forest, as previously for the starving. The interest attains the thunder and velocity of an avalanche but, alas, an avalanche that drops into the void between solicitude and political reality.

It was easy to see, even a few hours into the Easter 1989 meeting of forest peoples in Rio Branco, that the assorted participants had very different views on an appropriate political strategy – and indeed, perception of the fate of the forest varies sharply, depending upon the latitude on which the observer dwells. US Congressmen see an Amazon trip as perhaps a low-risk way of demonstrating ecological sympathies: no messy battles with large corporations back home, with

timber companies, utilities companies, construction firms and other powerful den-
izens of the fund-raiser's Rolodex. Their preferred strategy usually involves
turning the Amazon into a national park, in which so-called primal forest is
secluded by law, force, and cash bribe (the debt-for-nature swap) from the pred-
ations of man.

The rubber tappers, the Indians and the petty extractors who live in the forest
see things less romantically – no doubt like the Miwok Indians, driven out of
Yosemite when it was made into a national park, or like the Ute and Navajo,
expelled from Bryce and Zion. Where the First World sees only nature under
threat, they see the forest as the integument in their own elemental struggle to
survive.

Others seek to expand the reserve system – native, extractive, and ecological,
with people living within them – and ponder ways of funneling international
funds into these types of projects. This approach often involves raising funds in the
home country with urgent pleas and then their magisterial delivery to the appropriate project carried out by the appropriate group of rubber tappers or Indians.
Not all organizations take this approach: the Ford Foundation, the Canadian
Embassy and Oxfam have found it possible to release monies directly to the rural
unions and activist organizations, and do so without the need to gloss over the
struggle for human rights to life and land with a Disneyized version of forest
peoples. It is well to remember that Disney's nature films began with the careful
documentation of live animals, and ended up as sentimental fables.

Mendes was murdered in the far western reaches of the Amazon, and the
international press was at least there to cover his murder, however limited the
terms in which they described it. But throughout the whole of Amazônia people
repeatedly die as they try to defend their ways of life and bits of land, and the dead
are not just labor organizers, but also women, children and anyone who gets to the
wrong side of superior firepower.

The Catholic Church keeps rudimentary statistics on human rights violations
and conflicts in rural areas. It also characterizes the kinds of conflicts that take
place: whether these revolve around the struggle for land, are workplace conflicts,
conflicts within the *garimpos* that now cling to the banks of all the major tributaries,
or political murders. The statistics also note monthly incidents of torture or threats;
the burned houses and fields. Although less than 3 per cent of all these episodes –
including land expulsion and robbery – end up in murder, the overall picture is
one of savage and continuous pressure by landlords, the violence finally mirrored
in resistance but ignored by the state. This is the "normalcy" that is almost never
described to North Americans and Europeans.

In fact Brazil's status in the imagination of First World news organizations is
curious. In the category of travelogue and feature story it has mostly been displayed as the home of Carnival, of psychedelic religious cults like *santo daime*, of
soccer, of beach life. But it is also the Third World country most indebted to First

World banks and hence incurs the traditional taxonomy of journalists discussing economically frail countries with the capacity to menace the stability of First World banks. Here the approach is one of truly astounding uniformity: the need of the beleaguered economy to be opened to "market forces", to increase its exports, to cut back on public services and other wasteful expenditures by the state. The admonitions to austerity are ubiquitous, as though Brazil abounded with debauched profligates. There are stories about the slums, deforestation, and decimation of native populations, but none about the class structure that permits capital flight, which has now risen to about $12 billion a year, or about the state and business elites that probably recycle more than half of all the aid received into North American and European bank accounts.

THE SEDUCTION OF MODELS

In a widely read paper, the anthropologist Mac Chapin greatly annoyed many in environmental circles by suggesting that many of the promising approaches to problems of environmental degradation suffered from a poor fit with social realities: "technicians overlooked the wider social, economic and political context in which farmers lived and therefore had no notion of how their model might adapt within that context." His central point was that so-called solutions often "break free of the constraining grip of the tangible world to take on a life of their own. The curious thing is that [this] is not the exception, but that confusions of this sort are normal. They ... can be found occupying prominent parts of development literature. This is especially there in the subfield of ecodevelopment. We become blinded by the beauty of the conceptual model, mistaking it for reality itself."[1]

There are many people with good intentions, but in their commitment and dedication to a particular conception of the world they may overlook the issues at hand, or their visions may be entirely undermined by the local context. To quote Ailton Krenak and Osmarino Amâncio Rodrigues, "We don't have a proposal, but rather principles to inform the development of the region's possibilities."[2]

Many of those worried about deforestation think mainly of the extinction of animals or the erosion of their habitats, taking the development of national parks as one of the central issues for conservation. They set aside large areas on maps and put a few forest guards on the ground, perhaps with a local environmental education program lauding the virtues of forests. The institutional frailty of most park systems and the forestry agencies in Latin America is well known. Their failure is usually attributed to lack of finances and to the common problem of poorly trained, poorly paid forest guards who look the other way as colonists or loggers cleave their way through the protected terrain. The national parks in most of Latin America constitute what Fearnside has called "the Paper Parks".[3] They represent good intentions, but after the people living there have been expelled and armed guards put in place, these areas are prime targets for incursions.

Parks of this sort do not pretend to address the social context from which they have been theoretically excised. Their justification is usually that of "buying time" (and space) while others supposedly address the social problems that prompted the need for the parks in the first place. So the parks are set up under credentials remote from social and political reality, and these realities subsequently intrude – usually in the form of settlement within the parks and degradation of the assets.

Many people in the Third World find it an ironic proposition that such beautiful areas, rich in resources, are set aside for occasional and wealthy visitors carrying elaborate photographic or scientific equipment. In areas where land distribution is immensely skewed, the setting aside of such bountiful expanses of land is viewed with skepticism, if not deep hostility. The rubber tappers and other resource extractors fenced out from nature parks and preserves north of Manaus[4] regard such acts of expulsion as little different from the evictions by the owners of large ranches or of big Brazil-nut groves who have been lobbying, on ecological grounds, for the creation of enormous reserves for *castanhais*.

Resistance to the classic national park has generated a modified approach, exemplified in the Biosphere Reserve where a core area is maintained in its natural state while a buffer zone around it involves local peoples. This version of conservation – the untrammeled "set-aside" – lies at the very heart of the idea of many debt-for-nature swaps.

BAD DEBTS, GOOD DEEDS

Behind debt swaps was the search for a way to fund environmental initiatives in countries ravaged by debt, austerity programs and lurching economies, where conservation concerns are swiftly extinguished by budgetary emergencies. The US banks, vastly overexposed by lending policies in the early 1970s, found that the variable interest rates on loans due made it unlikely that the loans would be repaid. The secondary debt market, where debt is discounted down from its face value, was seen as one way that banks could recoup their losses. Legislation passed by the US Congress in December of 1987 allowed banks to receive a tax write-off for 40 per cent of the face value of the debt so long as they offered the debt to private voluntary organizations. These bodies would buy the debt in hard currency, with a commitment from the indebted countries that they will invest an equivalent sum of the national currency in environmental programs. A commercial bank is owed $100 by, say, Bolivia. The bank then offers this debt on the secondary debt market at ten cents on the dollar. Conservation groups can then buy the $100 obligation for $10. The bank takes the $10 and the $40 tax write-off. Conservation International, or any other interested environmental group, then makes an agreement that Bolivia commit $100 in local currency to environmental projects. The bank pockets the tax write-off and some cash, the conservation agencies have helped in turning "bad debts to good deeds" for relatively few dollars. The country has reduced its debt and supposedly its environmental degradation.

The debt-for-nature mechanism is a reformulation of some ideas developed by Osvaldo Sunkel and his group at CEPAL/ECLA, the Economic Commission on Latin America at the United Nations offices in Chile. In their formulation they focused on "debt for development" to address the funding problems faced by social programs in Latin America, in which they included environmental initiatives ranging from potable water-supply systems and sewage systems to the provision of parks. Sunkel and colleagues initially devised the scheme as a means of compensating those who were repaying the debt – accrued in many cases under military regimes – through the hardship and poor quality of their daily lives.

Most Latin American populations understand that a few hundred thousand dollars of secondary debt has little impact on multibillion-dollar obligations owed by these countries. They realize that a far more comprehensive approach is necessary to address the real needs and problems faced in Latin America.

Of the Bolivian debt swap the $250,000 in local currency in part supplied by the government of Bolivia represents a substantial portion of the budget for the national park system. The buffer zone is not a wilderness preserve, as it has been presented in the US press, but an area where cattle production (for export) and lumbering are being promoted – part of the very export-oriented development that many environmentalists reject.[5]

Left Business Observer, the New York monthly, in an article in its issue for December 20, 1988, saw it the same way:

> In return, the country [Bolivia] agreed to spend $250,000 (most of its conservation budget) protecting the Chimanes forest – or so the PR had it. Actually the forest will continue to be exploited, for export of course, by the same logging companies and cattle ranchers from which the swap was supposed to rescue it, now only in a "controlled" fashion. The Chimanes Indians weren't consulted, nor was the Bolivian Congress. The government had made the deal without telling them."[6]

Not surprisingly, debt-for-nature proposals in this form have been hailed from both the left and the right in Brazil as an affront to national sovereignty, and a manifestation of the country's "internationalization". Many politicians used these terms opportunistically to stir up nationalist sentiment, but the underlying concerns are genuine, and thus Brazilian organizations in favor of using some kind of debt swap usually insist that it come without strings. After initial resistance to the idea, Sarney and General Denys have suggested that swaps might be a way to finance the environmental fund set up for *Nossa Natureza*, thus reducing the eventual need to allocate funds from the national treasury. Refinements of the debt swap idea focus on the use of swaps as a means of generating funds for scientific institutions, co-operatives, extractive reserves, native communities and environmental education, and funneling these monies through the agencies that have traditionally been responsible for such activities. These agencies range from organizations with impeccable credentials such as the Institute for Amazon Studies in Manaus, INPA (whose research funds were slashed a few days after the announcement of *Nossa Natureza*), to the forestry agencies traditionally charged with corruption. Some of the debate about debt swaps has focused on the "political will", since Brazil's good environmental legislation is routinely ignored. As Robert Chambers has pointed out succinctly, "lack of political will just means that the rich and powerful have failed to act against their interests. 'Political will' is a way of averting eyes from the ugly facts. It is a convenient black box."[7]

The idea of indigenous reserves has had a long history, but the idea of cultural parks such as the Kuna in Panama and the Cuyabeno reserve in Ecuador are recent. These are managed by Indians, and represent one way by which income is generated by the exoticism of the natives themselves, in a manner that allowed people to continue living there.[8] While natural parks had kept all people but visitors at bay, Indian reserves have traditionally taken the opposite tack. The dawn of "cultural parks" put the two concepts together and helped "prepare the path" for the idea of conservation units in which there were actual people, albeit seemingly folkloric ones, living their lives.

PARKS, RESERVES, RESERVATIONS

The idea of reserves for forest people, for placer miners, and peasants has become a major topic in international and Brazilian development circles.[9] Jean Hebette has acidly argued that when some pre-existing economic form gets in the way of Brazil's approach for development of the Amazon, the problem population is shunted into enclaves, while the "real world" outside these protected zones continues as before. Extractive reserves, *garimpo* reserves, and native reserves have all been shaped by the intense political efforts of local people and their allies. They represent a space where livelihood can be secured while people press for transformation of their lives and economies under their own terms. But recently the idea of reserves, particularly the extractive reserve, has taken on a life of its own.

When rubber tappers and Indians discuss the idea of reserves, they see them primarily as social and political spaces as well as physical entities. But the zealous enthusiasm of development agencies in adopting this new model itself necessitates caution, for all the reasons Chapin mentions in his critique of models. With the land demarcated and permanent title awarded, access to, and economic use of, the trees is then controlled by the traditional elites. After expropriating Indian and public *castanha* forests and transforming their leases from the state to landed property, the stance of such oligarchs echoes the earlier cries of livestock promoters who invoked ecological arguments against peasants to further their own ends.[10] In the case of the Brazil-nut Polygon of Amazonas, these represent "extractive reserves" for large landowners, and Mac Chapin's admonition holds good. The United Nations Environment Program, UNEP, is prepared to fund dozens of extractive reserves in the Amazon. But without social content, the reserves become mere lines on a map, and not necessarily more secure than any other parcel in Amazônia. Without thorough organizing at local levels (which for many reasons is politically unpalatable to the local, if not national, elites), the reserves on their own cannot survive. They will only have a cartographic reality.

Extractive reserves are vulnerable to incursions from the powerful, also to sabotage by planners themselves. Philip Fearnside depicted one case where the planners aimed to settle extractive reserves with more than ten times the number of families recommended by rubber tappers and local people.[11] The leases themselves can be rescinded by the state if the activities are viewed as being no longer economically justifiable. Finally, the Amazon has a forbidding history of turning resource leases into landed property which is then sold. Without political ballast these reserves could just end up as one more slogan on the fund-raising circuit, advertising the true salvation for the Amazon, or cynically used by large landowners as another means of consolidating holdings.[12]

Indigenous reserves have been subject to constant incursions, as one might expect. Apart from the straightforward theft of territory and redrawing of boundaries, it is well to remember that the agile military land agency GETAT (Grupo Executivo das Terras do Araguaia-Tocantins) handed titles out to settlers on Indian territories without a second thought. Even the much lauded *Nossa Natureza* of the civil-military government of José Sarney redefined large areas, previously designated as indigenous reserve lands of the Yanomami, as national forest. Indeed, to an increasing degree, it is no longer necessary to steal Indian lands in order to claim their resources. The official Indian protection agency, FUNAI, brokers timber and goldmining contracts which continue to offer private enterprises all the freedom they enjoyed in rougher days, now cloaked in the drapery of legal sanction. The ensuing environmental degradation is attributed to the tripartite co-operation between government, private enterprise and indigenous peoples: in the end it becomes an "Indian Problem" and less likely to appear on the agenda of any review of processes that destroy the Amazon.

More than 85 per cent of Brazil's gold is found and extracted by artisanal miners. As we have seen in the case of the Serra Pelada, private mining companies with mechanized techniques have yearned to take over the deposits scoured by these placer miners, and indeed during the crisis of the Serra Pelada, they were able to push President Figueiredo to open up mining claims for these very companies on indigenous lands. Popular resistance at Serra Pelada thwarted attempts to resettle tens of thousands of mineworkers into the areas of Cumaru and Tapajós, but the idea of reserve-as-dumping-ground had understandable allure for government planners and their corporate allies. They saw the utility of a concept – the reserve – bearing credentials that seemed unimpeachably progressive, but which could easily be transformed into an instrument that would shake thousands of small miners from valuable real estate; herding them into reserves where they could be conveniently left to their own devices while the larger mining companies made off with their booty. To anyone familiar with the fate of North American Indians whose land rested on valuable resources, the lesson is clear.

Rubber tappers have not risked their lives for extractive reserves so that they can live on them as debt peons. Indians, as Darrell Posey observes (see Appendix B in this book), do not wish to live out some fable by Chateaubriand. *Garimpeiros* understand as well as anyone that mines play out. The Kayapó of Gorotiré sell their timber because they find it a reasonable way of raising funds, providing them with some autonomy from a corrupt and weak FUNAI. The basic concerns occupying all these peoples are: what can they do, within the existing system, to receive fair remuneration for their labor; how can they diversify their economies; and how can they achieve the basic rights to health, education, political recognition, freedom and autonomy.

One solution is through the expansion of co-operative structures so that they lose less to middlemen. An important part of the programs set forward by the Forest Peoples' Alliance focuses on ways to improve the payment they receive for their products as well as the price they pay for goods, to expand the markets for their products, and to create more economic opportunities by processing these products locally. The efforts made by the Indian organization, UNI, and by organizations like Cultural Survival towards eliminating intermediaries for selling their products are therefore of singular importance.

How are people to be compensated for their knowledge and skill? Pharmaceutical companies test plants for their medicinal value and trail the footsteps of shamans in order to profit from centuries of accumulated knowledge. In like manner, geneticists pluck up native cultivars to improve the genetic stock of their plants. Products evolved from these cultivars are patented and marketed while the tribe receives nothing in return. It may seem mundane, but one of the prime tasks for forest peoples and their allies lies in developing mechanisms that ensure adequate compensation for knowledge, resources and products that are translated elsewhere into billions of dollars in commercial trade. Forest peoples' knowledge and their plants are heralded as "common heritage" while being translated into commodities in the First World.[13] This is what "internationalization" has meant in practice.

Reserves that focus on the folkloric attributes of forest inhabitants overlook the desperate need of these people to improve their economic condition. Extractive reserves and their products will face increasing competition from producers in plantation systems. Extractors face the difficult questions of how to maintain existing resources and how to diversify their economic base.[14]

Robert Chambers, who has long pondered issues of rural development, has pointed out that most outsiders – particularly funders – prefer prescriptions and solutions that they find gratifying, and these tend to be projects that yield quick and conspicuous results acceptable both to the board members of charitable First World foundations and to local Third World elites. The fund-raisers' circuits are now tumid with talk of debt swaps, and reserves of every description, but the issues surrounding deforestation have been dropped from the agenda.

The reserve system is taking on the characteristics of the *ejido* system of Mexico – state- or community-owned lands – where resources and social services were a fraction of those given to other sectors in the rural economy, particularly large farms. The orientation and training of most researchers in forestry and agronomy are unlikely to permit much appreciation of the contributions of native sciences or to use those as a starting point. Will they in consequence turn to techniques elaborated outside the reserves which may prove unstable and destabilizing within them? The development and refining of native sciences to deal with the problems that increasingly face them will take many years to accomplish. Knowledge systems are systems of domination – the question of who defines a situation is crucial. To be fair, there is a young cohort of agronomists today that are willing to address this challenge, but they represent only a small minority.

To the Brazilian authorities at the federal and state level as well as the large entrepreneurs, the challenge of tens of thousands of militant *garimpeiros*, extractors and peasants, backed by public opinion and international concern, has been something to be taken very seriously. After all, loans can be frozen, negotiations rendered more arduous, Brazil's reputation impugned, and – most serious of all – the authority of the government itself contested. In this hour of peril the concept of the reserve offers a handy sanctuary against such problems and often does so without calling into question actually existing social and political arrangements. Moreover the reserve can demobilize an aroused population which has been vehemently pressing for larger structural change.

Here we come to the pitfalls that lie in the line of march staked out by the "green" movements in the First World. By de-emphasizing "old-fashioned" concerns with political economy, property relations and distribution, they extoll the reserves as environmentally sound solutions where the good rural life can continue. But all reserves are far more precarious than their current popularity would suggest. "New social movements" as they now exist have focused on the politics of short-term claims where pressures bear on the topic of the moment –

once the claims are met, the movement evaporates. The Amazon forest inhabitants will not be well served or saved by short-term success if the longer-term structural problems are not also addressed.

THE NEW JARGON

While the term "extractive reserve" trips from the lips of development functionaries with ever greater frequency, there is a parallel term that has gained prominence: "agro-ecological zoning". The idea behind such zoning is simple enough. Planners would use the natural resource surveys now available to determine areas apt for particular uses of land according to soil or other resources. The areas would then be committed to appropriate activities (such as ranching and agriculture), and Amazonian occupation would proceed in an orderly manner. The popularity of reserves, and the incessant discussion of agro-ecological zoning suggests that there may well be convergence in the implementation of both, with the political content excised, thus condemning Amazônia to a continuation of its present path: sanctions against the infringement of zoning "codes", under the imperatives of high market value and political clout.

In the week *Nossa Natureza* was announced, General Bayma Denys, the architect of Sarney's Amazonian Plan, gave an interview to the prominent Brazilian daily, *Estado de São Paulo*. The General suggested that the problem with Amazonian development had been its consistent history of deficient planning, and that "the absence of initial general planning brought about the well-recognized problems of integrating sectoral plans (in Rondônia and southern Pará) and as a result a very disorganized process of occupation". Thus was a generation of struggle for land and justice reduced to poor techniques. General Denys was not alone in his views that conflicts over land and resources could be handily avoided by better planning. The former head of the Association of Amazonian Entrepreneurs, and the Brazilian Stockmen's Association argued that

> conflicts that result from a lack of planning, whether it is of a social nature, like the invasion of native lands, or of an ecological nature ... like the occupation of areas inappropriate for livestock can no longer be justified ... we have the information and technology to permit definition of permanent areas of preservation: Indian reserves, ecological reserves and national parks.[15]

Increasingly, landowners crave a final demarcation of the lands destined to lie forever outside of land markets because, they argue, once these are established, the clearer will be their fairway on the lands in private domain.[16] And, as the head of the Association of Amazonian Entrepreneurs once complained: "we're tired of

CHICO MENDES
UMA HISTÓRIA DE LUTA E RESISTÊNCIA

"É minha lei
É minha questão
Virar este mundo
Cravar este chão
Não importa saber se é terrível demais
Quantas guerras terei que vencer
Por um pouco de paz
E amanhã,

Se este chão que eu beijei
For meu leito e perdão
Vou saber que valeu delirar e morrer de paixão
E assim, seja lá como for
Vai ter fim a infinita aflição
'E o mundo vai ver uma flor
Brotar
Do impossível chão"

Poster of the rubber tapper leader Chico Mendes after his assassination on
December 22, 1988.

Degraded land: once forested, now unproductive.

*Poster at the Easter 1989 meeting in Rio Branco of Forest People. It reads,
"These are the members of the UDR in Acre. We demand punishment of the
UDR for their involvement in the murder of Chico Mendes."*

The Seringal Remanso, west of Rio Branco, in 1905. Notice balls of rubber in foreground. In 1988 Remanso became the first extractive reserve.

São Luis de Remanso, 1989. Home of a rubber tapper and his family, who had gone off that day to an Easter party.

Blocks of pre-fab houses on the edge of Rio Branco for rubber tappers driven out of the forest.

A trial house built by the Fundação Tecnológica do Acre (FUNTAC) for a rubber tapper and his family. Constructed entirely out of local products, it is scheduled to cost $1,000 to build.

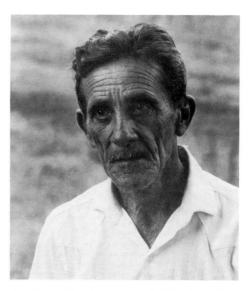

Rubber tapper originally recruited out of the Northeast for the rubber war, financed by the US.

Another rubber tapper recruited for the rubber war. Both men were in Rio Branco for the Forest Peoples' meeting.

Satirical book cover referring to João Alberto, the veteran of the Prestes column who was in charge of mustering labor for the rubber war.

Settler winnowing rice. Most settlers fail, driven out by lack of credit, or by violence.

"Appropriate technology": Testing local products at FUNTAC's station outside Rio Branco. Four outhouses; four different roofs, of barrel tile, aluminum v-crimp, shingle and corrugated iron. But appropriate technology is not enough.

The problem of the Amazon is also the problem of Brazil: relatively few rich, relatively many poor. Here is a view in Rio de Janeiro from the window of an elegant highrise down on to the Favela Rosinha, one of the largest slums in Latin America. In periods of unrest the favelados throw rocks down and block the tunnels (see lower right) that carry commuters from the rich suburbs to downtown.

always having to play the villain. Get native lands demarcated so that we can get on with business.''[17]

In this light, the fervor for reserves and agro-ecological zoning could be seen as a process where ''set-asides'' with and without people are demarcated, serving the function of diminishing pressures for social justice, providing substantial areas for conservation, and opening up the remaining area to destruction. One might view in this light the *Companhía Vale do Rio Doce* (CVRD), the Brazilian parastatal mining company whose careful environmental planning for the area under control of the Carajàs mine was exemplary and included large reserve areas. Widely commented upon in development circles it is viewed as the model of tropical environmental planning. Outside the closed gates, however, more sinister forces prevailed as speculation raged, land conflicts exploded, peasants were systematically expelled from their lands, and shanty-towns swelled.

Environmental planning in Amazônia has had a venerable history. Earlier versions of environmental assessment and environmental zoning suggested that more than 150 million acres were apt for the production of livestock, and document after document based on RADAM results have backed up whatever land-use strategy was politically favored at the time. These summary designations were based on radar images which are likely to provide the foundation for the current agro-ecological forays, and whose scale is not considered adequate for the fine-scale planning proposed in the zoning models. Agro-ecological zoning is one way in which large and expensive resource assessment programs will be set up within large bureaucratic structures. With politics, distribution and history excised from the Amazon question, the turmoil that reigns there will be reduced to some kind of geographic fantasy that draws lines on maps while ignoring the economic forces that have washed over the region and shaped its people and land uses. The Amazon landscape is not the outcome of a few planning errors.

It was for the Araguaia-Tocantins area, fraught with land conflict and deforestation, that some of the most assiduous planning documents were prepared. These excellent volumes sit undusted on their shelves, testimonies to the planner's art and life's cruelties.[18] The other area of careful planning was in Rondônia. The current euphoria over some supposed change of environmental outlook on the part of the Brazilian government reveals a touching faith in the efficacy of monitoring, maps, and new environmental infrastructure. Even with the best plans, the forces loose in the region simply gallop over the lines drawn in Brasília. Thus the fine *terra roxa* soils in some parts of Rondônia next to BR 364 are mantled in degraded pasture even when all the land-use plans for the region invoked settler agriculture as the desired goal.

Nowhere can this be seen more clearly than in the opportunity created by the Grande Carajás. Beyond its borders, the CVRD had taken a political decision that would in the end make the livelihood of peasants more arduous and which in the process overlooked a historic opportunity in the one area where peasant agriculture might have had strong enough local markets to make it more economically viable. Although there was a huge local market for foodstuffs – because of the various *garimpos*, large mines and cities, and a fairly large peasant population strung along the length of the railway which produced food for markets in São Luis – the choice focused on the pig-iron plants whose local effects can include expulsion of peasants and accelerated deforestation. Reserves abound in the region, in the form of invaded native areas or indigenous reserves where mining and logging can be done through contracts without the vexatious aspects of landownership in such a region. The local elites are quite in favor of extractive reserves for Brazil nuts, but under their own terms and for their own gain.

With debt swaps, agro-ecological zoning, the expansion of reserves, and emphasis on technological solutions, the process of deforestation has been systematically removed from the context that created it, and thus the environmental question is viewed as a problem of planning mistakes, faulty technologies and a problem of boundaries. By defining the questions in these ways, the solutions that follow are primarily technocratic. International alliances between environmental groups, and scientific and technical agencies are elaborated through "counterpart agencies" or "counterpart NGOs". The objectives of many First World environmental organizations focus primarily on resource conservation and the technical means through which this can be achieved. But the agrarian question that produces the environmental degradation remains largely undiscussed, at least in US environmental circles. Their plans have a timbre that is usually technocratic and politically "neutral" – that is, conservative in content.

It would be unfair to paint all organizations and allies with a uniformly critical brush. Within development agencies there are those who press for basic rights of local peoples to determine their fate along with that of the forest. Environmental groups, fierce in their advocacy, have hammered at bureaucracies in Washington and Brasília to change their ways of approaching these problems. Scientists have devoted themselves to understanding native knowledge, and to showing how complex indigenous wisdom really is, and how it can guide and inform development. The world does change. But in the end these allies will not decide the Amazon's future. It is not an imperial world, and the forest's fate will depend on the vision and the political sagacity of the people who live in it.

This task requires a coalition of people who have hated each other to move generously to a common ground where their resistance can transform the world. There are burgeoning alliances among forest people of all kinds, as well as peasantries, to carve out solutions that address their different plights. Settlers viewing the 720-acre *colocação* from the vantage point of a 50-acre plot do not entirely share the extractors' perspective. However, with the increasingly spontaneous incorporation of extractivism into the settler economy, in the south of Pará and in areas of Rondônia, their common concerns are more visible. Settlers, Indians, and extractors do not have entirely congruent interests, but they do have enough in common to begin forging an alternative history for the region, one that challenges the bias towards the wealthy, that invents a way of development whose theory and practice come out of local experience and knowledge.

Indians, *garimpeiros*, rubber tappers, extractors of all kinds have eagerly pressed for reserves. These have been among their foremost demands and without these reserves their fate would resemble that of the settlers, chased off their lands by ranchers and *pistoleiros*, in a process with which the aforementioned groups are very familiar anyway. But these forest people put the reserves in a wider political context. Chico Mendes's career as an environmentalist cannot be divorced from his active life as an extremely radical political militant.[19] While welcoming alliances with those prepared to share common ground, the larger agenda of the rubber tappers, Indians and kindred groups seeks the transformation of existing property relations. To grasp the concrete implications of a phrase like "socialist ecology" consider the implications of the manifestoes promulgated by the rubber tappers and the Forest Peoples' Alliance (as published in Appendix E). They emphasize that plans for the development of the region should be based on the culture and traditions of forest peoples. They take as axiomatic the preservation of the environment and improvement of the quality of life. Rubber tappers and Indians are by no means hostile to development, nor are they anti-technology. Their idea is to use local knowledge as a springboard for elaborating ways to use the forest, remembering that those who have made the forest their home are also its most accomplished masters. By the same token they also insist on speaking for themselves, through their own organizations.

The right of forest peoples and those on the spot to know what is being planned, to have a role in the formulation of those plans, and to be involved in bringing them to pass, is also fundamental. As projects and programs washed over the Amazon, its inhabitants were often the last to know. The first time Kuben-i, the Kayapó chief, saw projections for dams in the Amazon was in Washington DC, long after the environmentalists had begun to lobby against them.

Any program for the Amazon begins with basic human rights; an end to the debt bondage, violence, enslavement, and killings practised by those who would seize the lands these forest people have occupied for generations. Forest people seek legal recognition of native lands and extractive reserves held under the principle of collective property, worked as individual holdings with individual returns. They seek a coherent agrarian reform for the region. The model of the Institute for Colonization and Agrarian Reform, INCRA, imposed a 100-hectare (240-acre) "module" for forest lands, which bore no relation to the terrain or the needs of the people who would inhabit these bureaucratic blueprints. Forest people thus argue for a land unit based on the *colocação* – a more coherent regional unit. They oppose a political economy that favors large owners who impose social and ecological ruin on the region. Once seen through the eyes of local people, the schemes of development agencies and functionaries based in Brasília or Washington take on a very different aspect.[20] At the level of everyday life forest people demand control of the relations of production and of the distribution of the fruits of their labor. They look to a redistribution of resources and power, and invoke a vision of development that uses their knowledge, their culture and their ideas.

If there is one word that is the keystone to their demands and hopes for the future, it is the single word on which all hopes for the Amazon rest: justice.

NOTES

1. M. Chapin, "The seduction of models", in *Grassroots Development* 12(1), 1988.

2. One can easily see the very mixed blessings of the First World culture industry seeking to cash in, no doubt for the most laudable of motives, on a moral commodity, the martyr Chico Mendes.

    What would be the effects of a movie production descending on Mendes's village of Xapuri or even on Rio Branco for six to eight months? Up to one million dollars a month could be injected into the local economy producing effects similar to the eruption of a coca company although far briefer in duration: high inflation, flocking job seekers of all stripes, increases in cattle purchases even within extractive reserves as rubber tappers hired as extras stored their cash windfalls in the securest investment they know.

    And as the movie came to First World theatres, no doubt launched with lavish benefits to "save the forest", the net effect back in Acre would be likely to be deforestation, as not only rubber tappers but restaurateurs, attorneys, air taxi pilots, and so forth, all deployed their earnings in land and livestock. If there ever was a case for a movie project to be forced to file an environmental impact statement, this was it.

3. P. Fearnside and G. Ferreira, "Roads in Rondônia: Highway Construction and the Farce of Unprotected Reserves in Brazil's Amazonian Forest", in *Environmental Conservation*, 11 1984.

4. J. Araujo, *Relatorio*, CNS 1988.

5. According to a Congressional Research Service report for the US Congress entitled *Debt-for-Nature in Developing Countries*, dated September 26, 1988, "The Bolivian government contributed $100,000 of the $250,000 set aside for operations. The US Agency for International Development (USAID) contributed the remaining $150,000."

6. In an article for *Around the World* titled "Bolivia's Debt Swap: Not only Birds and Trees", Amanda Davila reported that the "swap agreement was signed at the highest level and did not consider the needs and rights of the original settlers of the area: Mojenos, Yacareses, Movinas, Chimanes, and other groups." Bolivian journalist Erick Foronda reported in *Latinamerica Press* for October 20, 1988 that "opposition labor leaders claim the move is only a smokescreen for hiding the sale of some of the country's richest land to transnationals." According to Bolivian labor leader Andrés Solíz Rada, "the CI swap was just a publicity stunt because if today land can be sold for environmental protection, tomorrow it can be sold under another cover but with the same end: accepting the dictates of the centers of political and economic power." The article concludes: "For a year now, the following lumber companies are legally working in the Chimanes under the supervision of conservation groups: Fatima Ltda, Hervel Ltda, Monte Grande, Bolivian Mahogany, Bosques del Norte, Madre Selva and San Ignácio. These companies must now abide

by Conservation International's norms for preserving the environment or lose their licenses.'' Other issues revolve around whether the agencies who administer these activities – the usual forestry institutes, park services, etc. – are institutionally weak, often with histories of corruption because they lack funds or the political will. The second question is whether the debt-swap-style set-asides really address the question of deforestation. Another question often raised in Brazil, is whether the debt itself is legitimate. It was, after all, incurred under the authoritarian military regime. Is it just to have to repay the excesses of a regime that overindulged in cheap credits that became more expensive with the gyrations of financial markets in the 1970s and 1980s? On the whole, debt swaps appear to address First World conservation concerns, but if this type of set-aside model and its form of implementation are an indication of future patterns, then there is much to rue.

7. R. Chambers. *Rural development: Putting the Last First* 1982, New York.

8. ''Compared with racism, exoticism is merely decorative and superficial. It doesn't exterminate. Exoticism cares mostly about its own amusement, and tends to find difference amusing where racism finds it threatening.... Exoticism grew up rich, and a little bored. The racist is hedged by dangers, the exoticist by used-up toys.'' Quoted from Phillis Rose, *Jazz Cleopatra: Josephine Baker and Her Time* 1989.

9. See Jean Hebette, ''Reservas indigenas hoje, reservas camponesas amanha?'' in *Para Desenvolvimento*, 20/21, 1987.

10. O. Vello, 1974, UK.

11. P. Fearnside, ''A prescription for slowing deforestation in Amazônia'', *Environment* 31(4), 1989.

12. See P. Fearnside, ''Forest Management in Amazônia: The Need for New Criteria in Evaluating Economic Development Options'', in *Forest Ecology and Management*, forthcoming 1989.

13. For a discussion of the political economy of plant commerce see J.R. Kloppenberg, *First the Seed* 1989. If native peoples had been as zealous for patent as First World entrepreneurs they would be receiving substantial royalties for their crop genetic work on corn, beans, sweet potatoes, manioc, peanuts, potatoes and bananas.

14. You can look at alternative management systems, taking agriculture and integrating it into agroforestry systems, and create a long-term management system for large areas, maintaining ecological and biological diversity, and at the same time maintain a high number of useful plants. But to use these plants economically you have to do market research and laboratory research. So while there are many options, nobody talks since there is no money. Extractive reserves get money, but other options need to be considered.

15. J.C. Souza Meirelles, ''Ecologia e Desenvolvimento'', *Folha de São Paulo*, October 1, 1984.

16. A. Wagner, *Areas indigenas e o mercado de terras: Povos Indígenas no Brasil* 1986.

17. Lunardelli, quoted in A. Wagner, ''As areas indígenas e o Mercado de terras'', *Povos Indígenas no Brasil* 1986.

18. The PRODIAT, *Projeto de Desenvolvimento Integrado da Bacia do Araguaia-Tocantins*, involved exhaustive analysis that produced eighteen large and detailed volumes.

19. A note Mendes jotted down shortly before his death read as follows:
''Attention youth of the future:

6th September of the year 2120 Anniversary of first centenary of the World Socialist Revolution, that unified all the people of the planet. Not just an ideal, and not just a thought of socialist unity....

Excuse me
I was dreaming when I wrote this Occurrences that I really never will see, but which I have the pleasure of having dreamed.''

20. Appendix E contains the complete version of the various policy statements by the Rubber Tapper Council and by the Forest Peoples' Alliance. Also see M. Melone, *Rubber Tappers and Extractive Reserves: A Development Alternative for the Amazon* 1988.

Interview with Ailton Krenak

Ailton Krenak, 34, belongs to a small tribe of the Krenak Indians who lived in the Vale do Rio Doce at the frontier of Minas Gerais and Espírito Santo. This group is also known generically as the Botocudos. In 1920 the Krenak people were estimated to have a population of about 5,000, and lived in an area of 200 square miles. Today they are reduced to 150 Indians who live on an area of some 15 square miles which has been almost entirely invaded by ranchers.

Ailton Krenak has lived in the city since he was about eighteen which was when he learned to read. He has worked as a journalist and in public relations. Since 1980 he has placed his skill, and knowledge of the press at the disposition of Indian peoples. In recent years he has co-ordinated the Indian Program of the radio of São Paulo distributed by about five networks in Brazil.

When talking of native science it's impossible to separate it out of its context. If I pull one of the shells off a bracelet, the entirety is less beautiful, and the shell itself, however beautiful, has less meaning. We can miss so much of what a shell actually is if we cut it away from myths, practices, the people who discovered and named the shell and other similar shells, and the rituals and stories and secrets of that shell. That's only one part of the bracelet, and that shell – let's say it's agriculture – is only one part of the special knowledge we have about nature. There are strands of life and history and nature and what it means to be an Indian that tie that shell to the others.

In the indigenous cycle of things, when we stayed too long in an area we would see that the game fled and that people's dreams were no longer good, and so we would leave, and let the *maloca* collapse. But that place was not lost to us or abandoned because sometimes we had our dead there, and we knew that we would always return, and so for this reason we would plant fruits, medicines and magic plants for this life and for the other forest lives that would follow us. We saw that forest not as a wild bunch of trees, but as a place in which our history and our future was written; the trees planted to remember the dead or to provide someday for our sons and daughters. The forest is not a wild thing to us. It is our world.

At the Altamira meeting, a Kayapó woman in full regalia raced up to the head of Eletronorte, brandishing her machete, and with a scream raised it and brought it down just short of each of his shoulders. She swore at him, full of bitter contempt: "Do you think that we're so stupid, do you think that we don't know what your plans are for us, what your plans are for this forest? Here we have been for millennia and you think that your silly plans are beyond our understanding. If you are a person of so much courage, knowledge and understanding, why don't you come and say what you have to say there and we'll kill you for once and all. Come with all your ministers and we'll take care of you once and for all. But for godsake don't think for a moment that we are somehow going to disappear between now and 1995 when you plan to flood these lands."

Well, yes, they are theatrical gestures. There are moments when theatrical gestures are very necessary. But because we occasionally engage in such gestures, people think that when we don't do them all the time we are adapting ourselves to the plans the Brazilian government has in mind for us. That's not really the case. One must choose the moments in which theatrical gestures will be most effective, and everything is achieved by dramatic presentation. But just because things are calm and quiet doesn't mean that we're quiescent. All of these things show that we are vibrant and living cultures and we won't be undone by what the Brazilian government has in mind for us.

For a long time the press was taken with a certain exotic and romanticist view of what Indians were. So when someone managed to contact a tribe that had never been heard of before, this was heralded with much applause for the great "indigenists" – the Villas-Boas brothers or whoever – and those Indians were viewed as residue of some stone-age past, whether this bore any relation to the cultural reality or not. On the other hand, magazines like *Manchete* would photograph bucolic scenes of Indian kids diving into beautiful forest ponds, with headings like "Brazil preserves its native heritage", noble warriors, or beautiful women. So what one saw was the savage and the exotic.

For a long time the spokesmen about Indian affairs were people from FUNAI, that is to say the government itself, who would speak of the lost innocence of the world, the Rousseauian idea. Then we had anthropologists who studied us and spoke for us for a while. For a long time only the anthropologists were able to get into the Indian areas and describe what was going on. Since the 1970s this has all changed. This is due to changes in the government policy itself. As they penetrated more deeply into Amazônia, any time they cut a road Indians would leap out of the way. Thousands of Indians would be running out of the way of bulldozers. People didn't realize that the area was full of Indians. Another factor is technological. The level of communication improved and people could hear what was going on and began to realize that all over the region Indian groups were experiencing the same problems. What began to happen was the emergence of a true indigenous voice. We had our own analysis and point of view that we ourselves could articulate. We didn't want to be represented only by anthropologists. Before the 1970s, few Indians were off the reservations, and an Indian off the reservation was a dead

Indian. With the 1970s, Indians began to move into other parts of Brazil as Indians rather than half-breeds, and to participate as an autonomous political force, to send people down to Brasília.

The big thing is to turn Brazilian history on its head, the history of colonization. You are a forest person, from some tribe, and then some "civilizing agent" enters the region, whether it's the Church, a political party, or an association of whites. Then they go "discover" this tribe of Indians in the same way they have done with other tribes. Once the contact is made, then begins the progressive, actually repressive infection, "civilizing" the tribe. Each day the tribe becomes less of the forest, of the rural zones, and more of the city. This is a progressive story – one day the tribe will be absolutely integrated. They will have learned how to talk Portuguese, to buy clothes, gasoline and a series of products that they don't produce. This obliges them to migrate from the land, or to apply a type of economy which will turn them into a village, town, and so forth. This is the history of the world.

Extractive reserves bring into play part of the population which came to the Amazon to "civilize" it along with the Indians, but who instead learn from them a new way of living with nature. Rubber tappers learn how to humanize nature and themselves. Thus the reserve brings a new form of social culture, and economic character. Migrants to this region came in search of land, but the property of the people cannot be commercialized. An extractive reserve is not an exchange item, and it isn't property. It is a good that belongs to the Brazilian nation, and people will live in these reserves with the expectation of preserving them for future generations. This is tremendously innovative.

Imagine if all the people in Amazônia decided in the next decade that they didn't want to treat the places they lived in as a commodity but rather as a sacred place! How does one guarantee a reserve's effective occupation? A fruit as it ripens goes through several different processes. I think that the first step is to get the reserves established. We are determined now to do a survey of the practices of rubber tappers and Indians in reference to real economic dynamics. From this inventory we are going to observe which activities are being done in a form in which resources are underutilized, and what their potential is. If there is a process in extractivism that can be mechanized, then let's see if we can develop a structure to use it.

Of course there are a lot of people waiting for the hour in which they can proclaim the whole thing a failure. We have to view this as normal. There are days when things are cloudy but the sun is shining above it all. The wind comes and blows these clouds away. It's entirely normal that there are other intentions about how to occupy the Amazon. One cannot in any way treat with disrespect and violence the thoughts of others. I think that this is the most generous aspect of the Forest Peoples' Alliance – to unite people who've been killing each other for a century. Do you think that back then rubber tappers wanted to throw in their lot with Indians? Let's just suppose that the people who are today against this most reasonable form of land occupation perceive that they can make money; that municipalities, potential producers supplying large markets bring large taxes. We have to convince them of this. The alliance has to show its fruits, we cannot only keep talking.

I think that the paving of the road BR 364 is an emergency. The task of establishing a link between various centers of productive populations is an emergency. But it needs to be planned. It shouldn't be a threat to local populations, because there is no sense in linking no one with nothing. The Trans-Amazon should have been built, but it shouldn't bring financial costs to Brazil and to nature and decimate tribes. Brazil needs energy but it doesn't need the Balbina Dam which will create a lake of 1,700 square kilometers of rotten water, threatening life in Manaus. Those who live in a ten-kilometer radius of that lake are suffering now from fly-transmitted leprosy. Soon they will need a hospital to attend to the diseased, and this represents real financial costs.

So if that road takes into account the needs of local peoples it will be an enormous success. But if it doesn't it will be an immense disaster. We don't want to be understood as being against development. I would never feel happy to say that the road should not be built. I would be quite happy, on the other hand, to sit with the government and say how one might do it in another way . . .

Interview with Darrell Posey

Darrell Posey, a North American anthropologist, has been living and working with the Kayapó since the 1970s, and is an active advocate for Kayapó rights.

A few anthropologists have been involved in the indigenous movements, but the great majority of them do in fact exploit their people, run off and never do anything more, using as an excuse the necessity of science to be "objective". But there is a certain percentage – a small one – who have become intimately involved with the people that they've studied. The accusation from the other side was – is – that they were going "native", which for some reason or other was meant to be bad. As soon as you got involved in native peoples' issues you were losing your anthropological objectivity. There has always been a bias against such involvement. The idea is that you remain detached, that you don't affect the society under study and if you do so you are making decisions you don't have the right to make.

Such thinking used to be very dominant in anthropology. One of the people who helped change it most was Margaret Mead – she, along with others, popularized the application of anthropology and legitimated it within the academic profession. So that gave anthropological involvement a bit more space. There have been other problems. Native peoples have been manipulated by anthropologists to side with governments or political movements or revolutions or parties or whatever. In other words it's been a rocky history and anthropologists getting involved with native movements were taking a risk in their own profession.

But some said to hell with it, we have to become involved, native people are who we make our livelihood out of, and it's unethical and unprofessional not to get involved. There were very few over the years, some in Brazil. There's another irony here, in that anthropologists get very paternalistic about native peoples, in the sense of being their great protectors. They have taken on such a role to the degree of not allowing them to speak out. There have been exceptions, like David Mayberry-Lewis, who established a very sound academic reputation, then realised that wasn't enough, and set up Cultural Survival as a way of aiding native peoples. He also gave support to native peoples organizing around the world. There were others, from the Brazilian Anthropological Association, who were instrumental in setting up the *Comissão pró Índio*. They worked for many years trying to represent such peoples, then came to see that representing them was not enough, and that what had to be done was to help them organize so they could represent themselves. And so the Union of Indigenous Nations got going with the help of the *Comissão pró Índio*, and also with the help of CEDI, the most active, well-grounded, academically-based group working in Brazil. They have a very balanced view of political, economic and social realities and have over the years worked very closely *with*, not *for*, native leaders. They perform a very important service, documenting what's happening with native people. It's a source of information about which films, which books, which monographs, which newspaper articles have been published on Indians. They have also effected a very important survey of native groups in Brazil. We simply didn't know until very recently how many groups, how many Indians there were in Brazil. It's hard to defend peoples when you don't know how many there are or where they are.

One of the most important things they recently published was on mining, showing how the government had sold off native peoples' rights to national and multinational interests. This came just as they were holding the constitutional convention and studying the future of indigenous lands and mineral rights, and was a great shock to the Brazilian people. So it gave a critical push towards a more progressive and public policy about mining in indigenous areas.

So we had changing anthropological attitudes, and an emerging leadership. We had Mario Juruna, who became a notable leader, very much with the help of an anthropologist, Darcy Ribeiro. He showed that native peoples could have a voice, even within the Brazilian Congress. That was the political side, which always has its disadvantages, in that people who don't know how to move within a national system of politics which is very complicated may have a difficult time in maintaining links to their own people and land. Physically they have to be in a city, and far from their own extended family. So it's hard for native peoples to straddle two worlds, both white and Indian.

Indians are communally organized, and they have to formalize that, which they can in fact do under the new constitution. The new constitution provides that native peoples can have independent representation, whereas previously they had to be represented by the federal government, by FUNAI. It remains to be seen how this will proceed. Getting this kind of juridical standing hasn't even occurred with the Kayapó, where I thought it would take place very quickly.

The sale by Indians of their own resources, and the destruction of their resources, is a very touchy subject. What are the rights of native peoples to do what they want on lands that are theirs? Under Brazilian law, Indians only have use-rights to the land, with the land belonging to the federal union. Federal lands are protected under the ecological articles in the constitution as well as the indigenous ones. Under the latter, destructive exploitation of the environment does have to be approved by the Congress. So taken literally, the constitution does not give native peoples the right to exploit their lands destructively without congressional approval. They could probably do sustainable resource exploitation of their lands under the constitution and this would be perfectly commensurate with their rights as native peoples and the articles that govern ecological preservation.

The case of goldmining on Kayapó lands, which I do know about, was basically provoked by unwanted goldminers who invaded Kayapó lands. There was no way the Kayapó could get them off. The more they threw off, the more came back. It got to a point where there was no way they could be held at bay. There was at that point just two small villages, Gorotiré and Kratum, which together have 900 people out of which you can muster maybe 300 warriors. They couldn't use traditional arms, a rifle with .22 bullets or a shotgun; there's no way you can go against 4,000 armed *garimpeiros*, many of them with automatic weapons shipped in there clandestinely. So the Indians had to deal with reality, and the reality was, ''If we go against these people they are going to wipe us out''. Of course there was no protection for them from the federal government at that time, and anyway there just aren't physically enough federal agents to stop that occurring. So the Kayapó were forced to put up with the goldmining, and it was very controversial, because the old people didn't want it and still don't want it. It brought them a lot of diseases, a lot of pollution, and questionable goods. It created many more problems than it resolved. There had to be redistribution of things coming in, and this redistribution was in the hands of two of the chiefs who didn't know how to go about it, so a lot of it got stuck in their houses, not because they were greedy but they didn't know how to sort it out without causing friction in the village. So there were enormous crises provoked by the gold, and the Kayapó didn't want mining and really don't now. This doesn't mean that the money generated from mining hasn't in a sense gotten under their fingernails and they will have a hard time getting it out.

Lumbering is a very different matter, first because the lumbering of 10,000 mahogany trees, when you're talking to people who can't count to ten, doesn't make a lot of sense. What they did know is that 10,000 mahogany trees would bring them a road and they'd wanted a road because the village of Gorotiré did want contact. Certainly the younger people did and also the chiefs. And the reason for that, you know, was the Kayapó like change as well. This idea that native peoples hung around and were always in some stagnant state before they were contacted by white people is just not true. They like change, they like things that are new, they want to see what's going on. Here, from their point of view, was a chance to get a free road to their village – they could get cars and trucks, go out to the town, buy what they wanted and come back. It was a neat idea, like going to the moon: Let's see what's up there and then we'll worry about what the after-effects are. It's just part of the human endeavor and they're no different from us in that sense.

* * *

Once integrated into capitalist society, will Indians lose all features of the traditional society, with rifts within the tribe and all sorts of cultural erosions? Well, we've got all sorts of cultural erosions as a result of the drastic depopulation which came from lack of immunity against European diseases. These people have already been reduced to a very small proportion of what they used to be, so they've already undergone enormous change. They'll continue to undergo a lot of change. In analyzing these cases one has to ask, what are the questions of history: were the changes in Tribe A forced upon them or did they in fact have the right to choose the things they wanted? In North America most of the changes among American Indians were forced upon them, including the speed of the changes, and where and how they occurred. The Indians were controlled by the government, the Bureau of Indian Affairs and the general circumstances of the time. In Brazil now, where the Indians are in fact guaranteed their rights and their lands, they can pick and choose what they want from white men's society – TVs, video-cameras – and they'll find out what they want and what they may reject. They might like video-tapes with which villages can communicate to each other what is going on, or the planes to take chiefs to have councils; which they couldn't have done ten years ago because they didn't have the money and the income to buy the planes and video-cameras. In other words, native peoples, if given economic independence and stability of land and resources, will make some errors and some good choices, just as any other society would do.

We have a legacy which is dangerous. One romantic Rousseauian view is that native peoples have lived in perfect harmony with nature and don't have any problems. The other one is that they are primitive. Somehow these fuse together to make an even larger myth, which is that primitive peoples are in harmony with nature and should stay there and never change. These are just not true, so we'll have to see what will happen.

APPENDIX C

Interview with Osmarino Amâncio Rodrigues

All through the Easter Week meeting in March, 1986 in Rio Branco, one of the most visible rubber tappers was an energetic and humorous young man called Osmarino Amâncio Rodrigues. He hails from Brasiléia, a small town southwest from Rio Branco, almost on the Bolivian border. Osmarino is the secretary of the Rubber Tappers' Union. Schooled in organizing by the Catholic Church and a longtime associate of the late Chico Mendes, he is one of the most dynamic of the forest's activists. He talked to us the evening of Easter Sunday, as his bodyguards paced about somewhat unconvincingly in the shadows.

I was born in 1957 on a rubber estate called Hummingbird. At the time it was really a traditional *seringal*, where the rubber baron forced everyone to sell at a lousy price only to his middlemen, and to buy supplies from his agents. It's far back in the forest, and the guy would only send his middleman out once a year with merchandise, and rubber tappers would be out there starving, waiting for supplies and unable to sell or buy from anybody else. And we still had to pay rent on our holding! We were in debt slavery because no matter how much rubber you got, the supplies always cost more. So, when I was a teenager, the struggle began out there simply because it was impossible to live in such conditions.

In 1970, when Wanderley Dantas was Governor of Acre, he began a big propaganda campaign about how Acre should advance and have progress, and the only way that would do that would be ranching. He arranged land concessions, bank financing and fiscal incentives for people from the south, all the things he never gave to the actual workers of his state. Ranchers began to come here, and after telling the poor guys out in the *seringal* that the Governor had sold them the land, they'd threaten rubber tappers or burn their houses and buildings. And then began the expulsions and the killings, as ranchers' gunmen – *jagunços* – came into the rubber plantations and forced people to leave. They did this with thousands of people. Right now there are 10,000 Brazilians living in Bolivia because they were forced out of Acre.

Well, this strategy of expulsion and killing worked up to a certain point, but only as long as people didn't realize that it was going on all over. They didn't yet know about the deaths in other places. We were all very isolated. In 1973 there began the organization of base communities by the Catholic Church, and this is where I really got going. I started to go to these Church meetings. And there they talked of human liberation, of freeing oneself from slavery. Lots of people were interested in this, because the conditions were really awful and we had to do something.

In 1975 we began to work on union development. When I started to get involved, I went because I wanted to learn. I didn't realize then that I would be in this till the end. Anyway, in 1976 we started the first *empates*, the stand-offs to the ranchers. These *empates* really gave us hope. Here's how it was done. The leader of the union in a place like Boca de Acre or Xapuri, Brasiléia or Assis Brasil, would learn that tappers were being thrown off their land. A leader in, let's say, Boca de Acre would then get on the phone or radio to Xapuri or Brasiléia and ask people there to travel so that these guys in Boca de Acre wouldn't be kicked off their lands. Truckloads of people would show up. It was really great.

The first *empate* occurred in Brasiléia, where I'm from, on an *seringal* called Carme, which still is a standing rubber forest. The ranchers kicked everybody off, but we really battled it out. We had to face down the army, the police, but we had right on our side. After all, we were struggling for the land we had lived and worked on all our lives. State officials worked out a deal where they gave each tapper from 25 to 125 acres so that they wouldn't have to migrate to the city. This system didn't work out all that well, which was why we want to go with reserves.

Well, *empates* became a regular thing, and each year there were more, so rubber barons and ranchers began to go after the union leadership. I was getting involved more, especially after 1980, when they killed Wilson Pinheiro, then the Rubber Tappers' Union leader. The secretary of my union, who was Chico Mendes, had to go to Xapuri to organize the union there, and the few people who could work away from the *seringal* went from municipality to municipality trying to make sure that unions were in touch with each other. I didn't know how to read then, but I had to learn because I'd go to meetings and I'd come back and have to read things to people in my union. There I was, a director of a base community and a union leader, and I didn't know how to read. It was awful.

In 1985 we set up the first Rubber Tappers' Council meeting to get people organized on a national level, to get extractive reserves going and also to talk about the systematic murder of the union members and leaders. From then until now it's only been this work. I don't even have time to play soccer. I used to like to go to parties, to dance, to bum around a bit. But all my time was taken. There were killings and killings and killings. They were murdering the lower leadership, but I told Chico at that time that they are going to keep killing until they get to us. They're breaking the legs of the union now, but they won't stop until they get to the heart. We have to prepare people so that when we're shot there will always be others to take our places.

Nobody believed that people lived in the forest. Even as recently as 1985 the Census Bureau said there were no people out here in spite of the fact that these forests are full of tappers, Indians and *ribeirinhos*. We may be illiterates isolated in the middle of the forest, but we do know what's going on. We know that livestock doesn't work here, and we know which other things will, but we don't have the technical ways of explaining it. So the authorities never give much importance to what we have to say. The only time they give us any credit is when they're crying crocodile tears after one of us has been shot.

In a seminar on the environment and development in 1988, things took on a different rhythm because we finally had some technical information that we could use to wrangle with the government officials. The government was more concerned, and began to have meetings with us. That was also when they declared the first extractive reserve at São Luis de Remanso.

Today we see that a lot of people are concerned with our struggle, but basically Brazilian justice doesn't give a shit about us. And we're worried; all this international attention doesn't make the Brazilian nation do anything about the systematic murders. Brazilian authorities have done nothing to calm this violence. I, for example, have about a 2 per cent chance of getting through this year. The same night they went to get Chico they also passed by my house in Brasiléia. There's just no way I'm going to get through this alive. There are organized death plans, and everybody knows it. Out in the Juruá a rubber baron, Camili, says that there is no doubt that Macedo – who organized people not to pay rent – is going to die. He says, "I'm going to order it; I'm going to kill him." Meanwhile, in the judicial district of Brasiléia there are more than two hundred cases that haven't got a public prosecutor or even a police detective on them. The Governor doesn't appoint prosecutors, or people simply won't take these jobs on. Each year the University of Acre coughs out forty new lawyers, but you can't get a lawyer out here for public service or for rural workers' rights. If people kill and are never punished, they just keep on murdering.

Today, for example, I'm not permitted to carry a firearm, but every goddamn rancher out here is armed to the teeth, as are all their minions. They've circled my house various times; wrecked my house on some occasions. One time it was just luck that a car came by and they fled. We sent letters to the Governor, to the head of the federal police, Romeu Tuma. We've sent letters and telegrams about the nature of the organized violence, and the only thing that happens is yet another one of us gets blown away. We don't really have immense options. We have to think of ways to live a bit longer. I have those bodyguards over there from the government. The guns that they have mostly don't work.

I have to pay for those guards – travel, meals, lodgings, even their bullets. Look, I don't have any money. I sent a letter to the Justice Department explaining that I understood the importance of security, but I don't have any way to support four men. I live with my parents, I don't have the wherewithal to set up my own household. The government isn't interested in my safety. They want me to sign a document saying that I dismissed these guys. The thing is I simply can't pay for them. What will happen is that once the document is signed, the government will say, ''Look, we assigned guards to him, and he dismissed them; it's not our fault if he gets killed.''

What are the things foreigners can do? They can do a lot. We need people who can help us evaluate natural resources, marketing the products so we can get a better price; ways to get better co-operatives going. We know that rubber and other extractive products can sustain a community without destroying the forest. We need market development and basic economic infrastructure. We're not anti-development; you only need to see how poor we are to know that. What we need is to develop the organizational techniques so that these things can move into the market in some kind of serious way, so that we can keep some of the value of the products we produce. We also need things like good historians, who will tell history the way it happened, and not develop a history from some fantasy. We need serious and honest scientists. We want this alliance with other forest dwellers to go forward, and to develop ways of doing this kind of work. We want you to do what you do best, and use this knowledge in solidarity with us.

Interview with Father Michael Feeney

Fther Feeney started working in Tefé, on the Solimões, in Amazonas in 1982. He is a member of the Holy Ghost Fathers, a Catholic order which originated in France.

I come from Ballintra, halfway between Ballyshannon and Donegal town, near Rossnowlagh, which has one of the nicest beaches in Ireland. I first came to Brazil in January of 1972, and spent nine years in the interior of the state of São Paulo, in an ordinary parish, talking to day laborers – *diaristas* – who get up at 4 a.m. to work all day in coffee or agriculture. They work for small farmers, of whom there were lots in our area. Lots of people took down their coffee and planted sugarcane for alcohol for cars – it caused a big change in the lives of the people; they had to change to different types of work. They hadn't much of a consciousness then of land prices and exploitation; but slowly but surely through our meetings they were beginning to realize they were an enslaved nation. The whole land question was still going on, with people camping on the side of the roads. Big landowners won't give in; the poor invade big estates, to force the government to give them land. If that didn't work, people were forced to move north – to Rondônia, Acre and then Amazonas, the last frontier. They'd suffer all sorts of diseases; it was a cultural shock. People don't know how to work the land there: it's poorer soil. But I believe that these poor people have the power to defend the forest.

I passed through Tefé in July 1982 on the Solimões river. I had left Brazil in 1980, spent a year in Denver, then to Ireland where I did work on justice and peace. Then, back in Brazil with a friend from Tipperary; we had a list where the Holy Ghost Fathers were working. We went to Rio, to Recife, Fortaleza, Manaus, Tefé, Rondônia, Mato Grosso, São Paulo. I met a group of young people in Tefé, who were interested in the indigenous question. So I decided perhaps this type of work would help me as a person and be of some use to Indians in and around Tefé. I started going upriver. The area I work in is 256,000 square kilometers. (Ireland, for example, is 70,000 square kilometers.) It's a big area, with twelve Indian groups in it. We invited young people from the South to come in to support the Indians, live the life of Indians in their villages, get involved in education, help them to read and write history and mythology in their language, and then get working on the land question. Land is not demarcated; you have to work with Indians, get them conscious of what their area is. Then health: it's a very precarious business for us. We have been trying for four years to get medical people to help in our area. The young people there have no medical training. In one area of ours, there's lots of tuberculosis; normally the Indians get diseases from white men, and have no plants to combat these illnesses. With tuberculosis, it's a six-month treatment; but they have no idea of medication; they take it all in one go. So we tried to get this medical team but we can't get them, because Brazilians becoming doctors and nurses don't want to go back to the interior. There's better money in towns. The whole mindset is against Indians. If you're called Indian in our place it's a terrible insult. It means the lowest of the low. We have been working in Tefé, where there are white *caboclos*, white Indians, 22,000 in all. It's growing. So-called education helps them not to become better persons, but to become functioning cogs in the capitalist system.

We try to work with white society, questioning their attitude towards Indians. Up to 1984 they didn't even know Indians were in the area. Indians hid their identity because of fear. Tribes called the Kokama, Tikuna, Mayoruna, Irana, Maku, Panamari, Catocina, Kawishana – about 5,000 – in small, very small, groups settled. Just remnants, really, of much bigger groups.

I didn't come to Brazil to save the Indians. They are the ones who will look after themselves. We are here to accompany them, to help them look at the society around them, to try and analyze this type of society, what it does to people, and the values they have as an Indian community. They have the ability to take the initiative in their field, and in their lives, to defend themselves and also to think of the future generations. You say it is just a defensive thing. That might be the first step, in terms of building up their defenses, but it's also a matter of finding other ways and means of leading their lives in future. Of course you have the pressure from the big companies and the government; because the bottom line of the government of Brazil is to do away completely with the Indians, to wipe them out. That has been the bottom line all over the world. These people are looked upon as being obstructive of capitalist progress, if you like. They're only in the way, and the quicker you get them out of the way the better, so that capitalist progress and development can take place.

All this talk about the Brazilian government being worried about its borders, it's a bluff. They want to push ahead with projects. They're pushed by big companies, who want to make their dams and roads, make their money and get out. Mendes showed the non-violent way to stand up against big farmers. That idea will have to expand through Amazonas, so these small people realize they have power.

Our area is relatively quiet. You have invasions of Indian land – but this would be local. In our area the big movement is to preserve lakes. Local communities build up stocks of fish; then big fishermen from Manaus invade the lakes. They come in, fill up their boats with fish, then when they find better fish, they heave out the first lot. Some people in each community are over-fond of money; they get paid off by big fishermen, who fish out lakes. So small groups of people in each community take on the responsibility to guard it and tell boats they are not allowed to fish.

On the Juruá and the Jutaí river there are tappers. A lot of them are leaving their areas and coming into towns for education. They feel they are *burros* and know nothing, having given their lives to rubber tapping (*burro* meaning a mule and a dope in Portuguese). Then you talk to them. What does it mean to be educated? They have a whole education and way of life they've picked up in the forest, but they don't regard that as education. So they want to get their kids to school. They feel they're going up in the world if they can afford a TV and a fridge. That's the way they look at it. These rivers, the Juruá, the Jutaí – talk about green hell! It really is murder. You have little insects that torture you all day long. About 6:30 they leave, then you have mosquitoes all night long. Without a net it's hell really. These little insects hit you on the back of the hand, get under your chin or your throat, leave you completely black, get on your nerves. People there develop skin against it. People in that area have a tough time. The physical thing is rough. Lots say they have no alternative: that's all they know. A lot of these rubber tappers, apart from fishing, they're not into planting; if these people want to stay, they'll have to get into agriculture. Otherwise they depend on boat shops which are very expensive and exploit these tappers. The co-ops are not very successful.

I believe in the force that the Indians and the *seringueiros* and the *ribeirinhos* have, if they can get together to defend the forest. They can put up a hell of a fight. I went to São Paulo with a film of the situation of Indians in the Javari valley; twelve tribes being culturally massacred, timber being taken out in loads, no one stopping the big timber companies. We showed the thing to people in the *favelas*, and they suddenly realized their struggle to get land and houses was similar to the struggle of Indians; that there would be need for alliances not just with people in the forest but towns as well.

The young people who come to Tefé and get involved with the Indians – sometimes there's a problem. They get so bogged down in the Indian question they think they are going to save Indians, and then they get the Messiah complex, which is very dangerous. You have a young couple living with a certain tribe. They think they are the only ones to save the Indians. If anyone else comes along to join the team they are ostracized by means of various subtleties, so the couple become the owners of that particular tribe. Anthropologists? They come and go. One of the problems we have with anthropologists is the following: you have an anthropologist coming into an area; they get their material; they leave, write their book, their thesis; it's published. That's it. There's no return to the Indians for what the anthropologist did in that area – there's nothing the Indians can use to help them in their struggle in terms of their health and education.

What can a person of conscience in Europe or in the States do to help? Some time ago the whole thing was that the Brazilian government was doing this and that to the jungle. Then someone said, these bastards in Europe, what did they do? They killed off their Indians, cut down their forests and now they're looking to the Amazon. Pollution for example: how are they in Europe affecting the atmosphere? Survival International has the idea of letter campaigns, putting pressure on governments. There's a lot people can do.

Forest Peoples' Manifesto

PLATFORM OF THE NATIONAL RUBBER TAPPERS' COUNCIL

We the rubber tappers representing the states of Rondônia, Acre, Amazonas, and Pará united in Brasília October 11-17, 1985 for the first Amazonian Rubber Tappers' Meeting take the following resolutions:

Amazonian Development

1. We demand a development policy for the Amazon that addresses the interests of rubber tappers and respects our rights. We do not accept an Amazonian development policy that favors large entrepreneurs who exploit and massacre workers and destroy nature.

2. We are not against technology if it is there to serve us and does not ignore the knowledge we possess, our experience, our concerns and our rights. We want our culture and way of life to be respected as that of inhabitants of the Amazon forest.

3. We demand that we participate in all the development projects and plans for the region (Planacre, Polonoroeste, paving BR 364 and others) through our own organizations in both the stages of formulation and implementation.

4. We demand that all projects and plans include the preservation of forests occupied and used by us *seringueiros*.

5. We no longer accept colonization projects for rubber tappers and nut collectors.

6. We want a development policy that helps the struggle of Amazonian workers who are involved in extractivism, and other types of production of interest to us, and that preserve forests and natural resources. We demand a development policy that favors workers and not *latifundistas* and multinationals. We rubber tappers demand to be recognized as producers of rubber and as the true defenders of the forest.

Amazon Reform

1. Natural rubber stands should be expropriated.

2. *Colocações* occupied by rubber tappers should be demarcated by them conforming to their traditional rubber *estradas* – paths.

3. Land should not be divided in colonist lots.

4. Areas occupied by rubber tappers should be placed in extractive reserves, secured for their use by tappers.

5. The number of areas disappropriated should be indemnified, transferring these costs to tappers.

6. The decisions of the 4th National Congress of Rural Workers should be respected which argues for a specific model of agrarian reform for Amazônia that guarantees a minimum of 300 hectares and a maximum of 500 hectares per *colocação* obeying the reality of extractivism in the region.

7. Rubber tappers should have the right to send their delegates to the constitution convention to defend forest and agrarian legislation in accord with the specific needs of rubber tappers.

1989

The National Rubber Tappers' Council in this its second national meeting affirms its desire to establish the broadest possible alliances with traditional peoples in Amazônia, with workers' unions, with environmental organizations, with movements in alliance with forest peoples.

Since our first meeting in 1985 we can today affirm that we have won the first extractive reserves, through which the workers want to demonstrate that it is possible to have development without destruction.

We know that our path has been tragic, and marked by resistance to our proposals, and to the programs of traditional peoples, by the already established model of development for this region.

This second national meeting offers its homage to all those in the struggle who gave their lives for the principles affirming our regional cultures. Especially we remember our most illustrious comrade Chico Mendes.

The most generous fruit of this struggle is embodied in the Alliance of Forest Peoples which, from this moment on, proposes to advance policies informed by the knowledge and aspirations of these communities.

To recognize this initiative is the first step in reducing the stain that covers the history of occupation of this region of Brazil, where one can still find disgraceful debt peonage, where one can see with indignation the practices of humiliation, the spurning of the most basic rights of human beings, destruction of habitats, the assaults on the sources of wealth represented by the forest composed of rubber and

Brazil-nut trees. We look for permanent support, not just for our economies, but for our traditions and culture.

An understanding of the local and regional realities of our communities served as the basis for elaborating the following program. The National Rubber Tappers' Council affirms the resolution to struggle for the following program:

Policies for Development for Forest Peoples

1. Models of development that respect the way of life, cultures and traditions of forest peoples without destroying nature, and that improve the quality of life.

2. The right to participate in the process of public discussion of all the government projects for forests inhabited by Indians and rubber tappers as well as other extractive populations, through the associations and entities that represent these workers.

3. Public guarantees to scrutinize and curb the disastrous impacts of projects already destined for Amazônia, and the immediate halt of projects that damage the environment and Amazonian peoples.

4. Information on policies and projects for Amazônia and any large projects to be subject to discussion in Congress, with the participation of the organizations that represent those people affected by these projects.

Agrarian Reform and Environment

1. The immediate implementation of extractive reserves in Amazônia in areas indicated by extractive workers and their associations.

2. The immediate demarcation of indigenous lands, placing them under direct control of native populations.

3. Immediate recognition by summary process of all the *colocacões* of rubber tappers, giving them immediate land rights.

4. Immediate expropriation of forest areas which are occupied by extractive workers, or of extractive potential.

5. Resettlement in national territory of those of our population thrust into foreign lands by *latifundias*.

6. The end to the payment of rent and to the social relations that enslave *seringueiros* on the traditional *seringais*.

7. A policy of zoning that identifies areas inhabited by extractors from areas appropriate for colonization, and a policy of recuperation of degraded areas.

8. A revision of the policy that seeks to transform indigenous areas into indigenous colonies as proposed by the *Calha Norte* project.

Development, Education and Health

1. Administration and control of reserves directly by the extractive workers and their organizations.
2. Training and improvement of the technologies of rubber tappers and other extractive workers in order to guarantee their position in the economic and technical development of extractive reserves.
3. The introduction of health posts in forests containing rubber tappers who will be given the training and resources appropriate to the characteristics of the region.
4. Introduction of schools in *seringais* and forests, with *seringueiro* teachers trained in programs that adequately reflect the region's reality.
5. Introduction of co-operatives and systems of commercialization that develop and make viable economic independence, and raise the incomes of extractive populations.
6. The realization of research that recognizes the economic potential of forests and the ways of using them in a balanced and sustainable way.
7. Investment in the areas of processing and industrialization of extractive products.

Pricing Policy and Marketing

1. A pricing policy should be maintained that is compatible with maintaining extractive workers in their areas.
2. Direct credits for extractive producers.
3. The implementation of marketing and supply systems that are adapted to Amazonian conditions.
4. An end to fiscal incentives for livestock or agriculture in forest areas, and direction of such financial resources to the benefit of forest people instead.

Violence and Human Rights

1. An immediate end to all the forms of oppression of forest peoples, in particular debt peonage.
2. Immediate investigation by the police of crimes against rural workers and an end to the violence against the defenders of the Amazon forest. Accelerated legal cases against murderers of Indians, tappers and union leaders.
3. The punishment of all acts of land-grabbing in areas inhabited by Indians, colonists, rubber tappers, and Brazil-nut collectors.
4. A police inquiry into all the forms of private militias raised by landowners, in order to assure the principles of social justice in rural areas.

Seven Beliefs, True and False, about the Amazon

The Amazon is the lungs of the world and if the forest disappears there will be less oxygen produced.

This is false, though it is a widely held belief about the Amazon. What is true is that destruction of the rainforest has already added large amounts of carbon in various forms to the atmosphere, thus assisting in the "greenhouse" effect, which is heating up the earth's atmosphere. For detailed discussion, see chapter 3.

The Amazon could be the bread basket of the world.

This view, promoted as early as the mid nineteenth century, is false. Amazon soils are mainly poor and without quantities of fertilizer and insecticides, cannot deliver high yields under monocultural systems. Hopes for the Amazon as a potentially vast producer of short-cycle crops over large areas are misplaced. But the Amazon and its forests can sustain a large population, using an array of different agricultural techniques and forms of production including agroforestry, exploitation of areas of fertile soil, and manipulation of native forests.

Logging is to blame for the forest's destruction.

Most deforestation in the Amazon is not caused by logging, but rather by the expansion of pasture for cattle and colonist agriculture. Logging is often linked to these two, but it is not the driving force behind the deforestation that we see today. Clearance of forest for cattle ranching is unquestionably the most important factor in current deforestation.

Deforestation in the Amazon has occurred because fast-food chains in North America need cheap tropical beef.

While clearing for pasture is the main reason the forests are cut down, cattle ranching in the Amazon has nothing to do with North American fast food. In fact the Amazon is a net beef importer. Cattle are used primarily as an excuse for claiming land, for clearing it and for economic purposes that have little to do with producing commodities. For a full discussion of the role of cattle, see chapter 7.

Small settlers and peasant pyromania are to blame for the disappearing Amazonian forest.

This is one of the most widely held beliefs about the Amazon and it is wrong. The culprits in setting fires to clear forest are overwhelmingly large-scale landowners and land-grabbers. Settlers tend to clear relatively small areas and they cultivate them far more intensively. With the influx of about a million people in the last decade, the Amazonian state of Rondônia has had some of the highest rates of deforestation in the Amazon. But large ranching areas in Rondônia under less scrutiny also showed extremely high rates of deforestation and in absolute terms these ranches covered a much larger area. In areas outside the Brazilian Amazon, such as the Peruvian Amazon, deforestation is carried out by smallholders but again, a proportionately larger area is given over to cattle ranching rather than crops.

The Amazon rainforest has almost disappeared.

The Brazilian government stated at the start of 1989 that only 5 per cent of the rainforest had been cleared. Other studies have argued that by the end of 1988 as much as 20 per cent of the forest had gone. The variations in estimate stem from differences in satellites, and in analysis of the photographs; in uncertainty over what is cleared or secondary forest; and other methodological uncertainties. The extent of deforestation is part of the dispute about Amazonian development. Rates of deforestation vary enormously according to geographical area and proximity to roads. On a prudent estimate, by 1988 about 8 to 10 per cent of the rainforests of the Amazon had been cleared. For more discussion see chapter 3.

The Amazon basin has large mineral reserves.

The Amazon basin is rich in minerals: 97 per cent of Brazil's bauxite reserves, 48 per cent of its managanese, 77 per cent of its astanho, 60 per cent of its kaolin. The Amazon produces gold, oil and has the largest deposit of iron ore in the world. The mining of gold is producing a major catastrophe for human health and the environment, by mercury poisoning. For further discussion, see chapter 7.

Glossary of Plant Names

English	Portuguese	Scientific Name
acai	açaí	*Euterpe oleracea Mart.*
babassu palm	babaçu	*Orbignya phaterata Rodr.*
bacaba	bacaba	*Oenocarpus Bacaba M.*
bacuri	bacuri	*Platonia insignis Mart.*
banana	banana	*Musa Sp.*
buriti	burití	*Mauritia flexuosa L.*
cashew	cajú	*Anacardium occidentale L.*
castilla (castilla rubber)	caucho	*Castilla ulei Warb.*
cedrela (tropical cyprus)	cedro	*Cedrela odorata L.*
Brazil nut	castanha	*Bertholletia excelsa Humb.*
chicle	chiclo	*Achras sapota L.*
cidra	cidra	*Citrus Medica L.*
coca	coca	*Erythroxylon coca Lam.*
cocoa	cacau	*Theobroma cacao L.*
copaiba, copal	copaíba	*Copaifera multijuga Hayne*
cotton	algodão	*Gossypium hirsutum L. var.*
cupuacu	cupuaçu	*Theobroma grandeflorum W & Sp., Sch*
curare	curare	*Lonchocarpus Sp.*
datura	estramônio	*Datura insignis B. Rodr*
flag gras	brachiaria quiquyo da Amazon	*Brachiaria decumbens Brachiaria humidicoa*
guava	goiaba	*Psidium guayava L.*
ginger	gengibre	*Zingiber officinale Rosc.*
guarana	guaraná	*Paullinia cupana HBK*
inga	inga	*Inga Sp.*
ipecac	ipecac	*Cephaelis ipecacuanha Rich. Uragoga ipecacuanha (Rich.) Baill.*

English	Portuguese	Scientific Name
jenipap	jenipapo	*Genipa Americana L.*
mahogany	mogno	*Swietenia (Meliaceae) Sp.*
mango	manga	*Mangifera Indica L.*
manioc	mandioca	*Manihot escultenta Rodr.* *Manilkara balata*
orange	laranja	*Citrus sinensis Osbeck*
palmito	palmito	*Euterpe edulis Mart.* *Euterpe oleracea*
papaya	mamão	*Carica papaya L.*
passionfruit	maracuja	*Passiflora edulis Sims.* *(Alata L. et ALT.)*
pineapple	abacaxi	*Ananas comosus (L.) Merril.*
piqui	piqui	*Caryocar guinanensis*
peach palm	pupunha	*Guilielma Gasipaes HBK, Bailey*
rice	arroz	*Oryza sativa L.*
rosewood	pau-rosa	*Aniba rosaeodora Ducke.*
rubber (Seringa rubber)	borracha	*Hevea brasiliensis M. Arg.*
tucuma	tucumá	*Astrocaryum tucuma Mart.*
umari	umarí	*Poraqueiba paraensis Duke.*
urucu, annato	urucú	*Bixa orellana L.*
vanilla	baumilha	*Vanilla planifolia Andr.*
yage	caapi	*Banisteria caapi*

Glossary of Portuguese Terms

aforamento: A lease from the state for extractive rights. The boundaries of *aforamentos* were notoriously imprecise, but these usufruct rights were later transformed into *de facto* land rights as large owners began to sell *aforamento* areas for ranching.

apuração: Legal process.

aviador: an intermediary linking the export houses with the direct producers. The aviador advanced the credit to *seringalistas* or other merchants and received rubber in return.

aviamento: The credits system by which producers were connected via various intermediaries to the export houses, and hence to the European and American markets.

bandeirantes: Explorers and adventurers, literally flag bearers, who swept over Brazil in search of wealth in the name of the Portuguese crown.

barracão: The store and administrative office of the *seringalista* on the rubber estate.

bóias frias: Temporary wage-labor.

Cabanagem: Popular rebellion of the 1830s.

caboclo: The term refers to Amazonian backwoodsmen. Initially it was used to refer to detribalized Indians and various racial mixtures that included Indian blood.

castanhal: Brazil-nut grove

castanha: Brazil nut

caudillo: These are strong men, usually with their own private armies.

colocação: Area used and maintained by rubber tapper and family.

drogas do sertão: Literally, this means drugs of the backlands. These included a range of

extractive products and not just "drugs" or medicinals. Flavorings like cacao and vanilla, spices like clove bark, dyes such as indigo, oils like copal or balsa oil were included in the *drogas do sertão.*

empreiteiro: Labor contractor.

empate: A stalemate, or stand-off. In Acre it refers to the show of force to interfere with deforestation on land occupied by *seringeiros.*

estrada de seringa: The is the route followed by a tapper connecting the trees that he bleeds, and usually has about two hundred trees. A *colocação* usually has three *estradas.* The term also implies the tappers' dwelling-place and area where the rubber is processed.

favela: Slum.

fazenda: Ranch, large holding or plantation.

flagelados: Those desperate and impoverished by the Northeastern droughts.

garimpo: Placer mine.

garimpeiro: Artisanal placer miner.

gaúcho: Brazilian from the far south.

grileiro: Land-grabber. Their basic strategy is to clear forest, thus claiming it, and then to sell the land as quickly as possible. *Grileiros* use land purely as a speculative enterprise.

igarapé: Stream or small river.

juquira: Secondary brush that invades pastures and agricultural lands.

latifundio: Large estate.

marreteiro: A local mobile trader.

patrão: The patron, the person to whom one sells and from whom one might be able to ask for favors every once in a while.

pela or *pelle:* A ball of rubber produced in the smoking process.

planalto: Usually refers to savannah areas on the Brazilian Shield.

pistoleiro: Gunslinger

posseiro: Squatter; someone who lives on land without legal title.

quilombo: A community of escaped slaves

regatão: Literally it is the name of the river trader boat. It is used to refer to petty traders.

ribeirinhos: People who live in *várzeas.*

sesmaria: Land grant from the Portuguese crown.

seringal: The area, or "estate" in which natural rubber groves are claimed. Plural: *seringais.*

seringalista: Owner of a rubber estate, and master of its commerce.

seringueiro: Rubber tapper.

sertão: Backlands.

terras devolutas: Unsurveyed lands of the state. These can be lands that were never leased, or can be lands whose leases or claims have not been renewed.

várzea: Amazonian floodplain.

Bibliography

Ab'Saber, A.N. (1982), "The paleoclimate and paleoecology of Brazilian Amazônia", in G. Prance ed. *Biological Diversification in the Tropics*, New York: Columbia University Press, pp. 41–59.

Absy, M.L. (1986), "Palynology of Amazônia: the history of the forests as revealed by the palynological record", in G. Prance, and T. Lovejoy eds. *Amazônia*, Oxford: Pergamon Press, pp. 72–82.

Acosta, J. de (1977), *Historia Natural y Moral de las Indias*, Valencia: Valencia Cultural. (Orig. 1590).

Acuna, F.C. (1641), *A New Discovery of the Great River of the Amazons, 1639*, Madrid: Royal Press.

Adalbert, Prince of Prussia (1849), *Travels of His Royal Highness Prince Adalbert of Prussia, in the South of Europe and in Brazil, with a Voyage up the Amazon and Xingu, Now First Explored*, 2 vols. trans. by R.H. Schomburgk and J. E. Taylor, London: D. Bogue.

Aeschylus (1932), *Prometheus Bound*, ed. and trans. by G. Thomson, Cambridge: Cambridge University Press.

Agassiz, J.L.R. and Mrs. (1888), *A Journey in Brazil*, Boston: Houghton Mifflin.

Alcorn, J.B. (1984), *Huastec Mayan Ethnobotany*, Austin: University of Texas Press.

Alden, D. (1965), "The growth and decline of indigo production in colonial Brazil: a study of comparative economic history", *Journal of Economic History* 25: 135–60.

—— (1969a), "Black robes versus white settlers: the struggle for 'Freedom of the Indians' in colonial Brazil", in H. Peckham and C. Gibson, eds. *Attitudes of Colonial Powers Toward the American Indian*, Salt Lake City: University of Utah Press.

—— (1969b), "Economic aspects of the expulsion of the Jesuits from Brazil: a preliminary report", in H. Henry and S. Edwards, eds. *Conflict and Continuity in Brazilian Society*, Columbia, S.C.: University of South Carolina, pp. 25–26.

—— ed. (1973), *Colonial Roots of Modern Brazil: Papers of the Newberry Library Conference*, Berkeley and Los Angeles: University of California Press.

Alencar, J.M. (1965), *Iracema*, lenda do Ceará, 1865–1965, Rio de Janeiro: J. Olympio.

Allegretti, M. (1989), "Extractive reserves and development", in A. Anderson, ed. *Alternatives to Deforestation*, New York: Columbia University Press.

Almeida, A., Sprandel, M., Victor, A. and Correa, C. (1986), "Os garimpos na Amazônia como zona crítica de conflito e tensão social", *Pará Desenvolvimento* 19: 3–10.

Almeida, F.J.L. (1841), *Diário da viagem pelas Capitanias do Pará, Rio Negro, Mato-Grosso, Cuyaba e S. Paulo, nos annos de 1780 a 1790*, São Paulo.

Almeida, M. (1988), "Seringais e trabalho na Amazônia: o caso do Alto Juruá", manuscript.

Altieri, M. (1987), *Agroecology: The Scientific Basis of Alternative Agriculture*, Boulder: Westview Press.

Altieri, M. and Hecht, S.B. eds. (1989), *Agroecology and Small Farm Development*, New York: CRC Press.

Alves, M.H.M. (1985), *State and Opposition in Military Brazil*, Austin: University of Texas Press.

Alvim, P.T. (1980), "Agricultural production potential of the Amazon region", in F. Barbira-Scazzocchio, ed. *Land, People and Planning in Contemporary Amazônia*, Cambridge: Cambridge University Press, pp. 27–36.

Amazon Steam Navigation Co. Ltd. comp. (1904), *The Great River*, London: Simpkin, Marshall, Hamilton, Kent & Co.

Anderson, A.B. (1981), "White sand vegetation of Amazônia", *Biotropica*, 13(3): 199–210.

— (1987), *Consultancy Report to the Ford Foundation*.

— (1988), "Use and management of native forests dominated by acai palm in the Amazon estuary", *Advances in Economic Botany* 6: 144–54.

— (1989), "Smoke stacks in the rainforest", submitted to *World Development*.

— ed. (1989), *Alternatives to Deforestation*, New York: Columbia University Press.

— and Anderson, S. (1983), *People and the Palm Forest*, Washington: U.S. MAB Publication.

— and Posey, D.A. (1985), "Manejo do campo e cerrado pelos indios Kayapó", *Boletim do Museu Paraense Emilio Goeldi*, Belém, Brazil: MPEG.

— and Posey, D.A. (1987), "Reflorestamento indígena", *Ciência Hoje* 6(31): 44–51.

— and Ioris, E.M. (1989), "The logic of extraction: resource management and income generation by extractive producers in the Amazon estuary", paper presented at the International Workshop "Traditional Resource Use in Neotropical Forests", University of Florida, Gainesville, 19–22 January.

—, Gely, A., Strudwick, J., Sobel, G.L., and Pinto, M.C. (1985), "Um sistema agroforestal na varzea do estuario Amazonico", *Acta Amazonica*, Supl., 15: 195–207.

Anderson, R. (1976), "Following Curupira: colonization and migration in Pará, 1758 to 1930 as a study of settlement in the humid tropics", Ph.D dissertation, University of California, Davis.

— (1985), "The caboclo as revolutionary: the Cabanagem Revolt: 1835–1836", *Studies in Third World Societies* 32: 51–113.

Aquino, T. (1982), *Indios Caxinua: De Seringueiro Caboclo a Peao Acreano*, Rio Branco: Empresa Grafica Acreana.

Aragon, L. (1978), "Migration to northern Goiás", Ph.D. dissertation, Michigan State University.

Aramburu, C.E. and Garland, E.B. (1986), "Poblamiento y Uso de los Recursos en la Amazônia Alta: El caso del Alto Huallaga", in CIPA-INANDEP, ed. *Desarrollo Amazonico: Una Perspectiva Latinoamericana*, Lima: CIPA-INANDEP.

Araujo, J. (1988), *Relatorio*, CNS.

Aspelin, P.L. and Dos Santos, S.C. (1981), *Indian Areas Threatened by Hydroelectric Projects in Brazil*, Copenhagen: International Workgroup for Indigenous Affairs (IWGIA), Document 44.

Asselin, V. (1982), *Grilagem: Corrupção e Violência em Terras do Carajás*, Petrópolis: Vozes.

Aston, T.H., and Philpin, C.H.E., eds. (1985), *The Brenner Debate: Agrarian Class Structure and Economic Development in Pre-Industrial Europe*, Cambridge: Cambridge University Press.

Azevedo, F.A. (1982), *As Ligas Camponesas*, Rio de Janeiro: Paz e Terra.

Azevedo, T. (1901), *O Acre: O Discurso do Sr. Dionysio*, Rio de Janeiro: Rodrigues.

Baker, H. (1972), "Diversity in the tropics", *Biotropica* 1: 1–12.

Bakx, K.S. (1986), "Peasant formation and capitalist development: the case of Acre, southwest Amazônia", Ph.D. dissertation, University of Liverpool.

Balandrin, M., Klocke, J., Wurtele, F.E., and Bollinger, W. (1985), "Natural plant chemicals: sources of industrial and medicinal materials", *Science* 228: 1154–60.

Baldus, H. (1960), *The Tribes of the Araguaia Basin and the Indian Service*, New Haven: Human Relations Area File Source. (Orig. 1948).

Balée, W. (1986), "Análise preliminar de inventário florestal e a etnobotânica Ka'apor", *Boletim do Museu Paraense Emilio Goeldi*.

Balick, M. (1985), "Useful plants of Amazônia: a resource of global importance", in G. Prance and R. Lovejoy, eds. *Key Environments—Amazônia*, Oxford: Pergamon Press, pp. 339–68.

Barata, M. (1915), *A Antiga Produção e Exportação do Pará*, Belém: Livraria Gillet.

Barbira-Scazzocchio, F., ed. (1980), *Land, People and Planning in Contemporary Amazônia* (Proceedings of the Conference on the Development of Amazônia in Seven Countries, Cambridge, 23–26 September 1979), Cambridge: Cambridge University Press.

Barrow, C. (1988), "The impact of hydroelectric development on the Amazonian environment with particular reference to the Tucuruí project", *Journal of Biogeography* 15: 67–78.

Bates, H.W. (1910), *The Naturalist on the River Amazon*, London: J.M. Dent.

Baum, V. (1943), *The Weeping Wood*, Garden City, N.Y.: Doubleday, Doran & Co.

Baxter, M. (1975), "Garimpeiros of Poxoréo: small-scale diamond miners and their environment in Brazil", Ph.D. dissertation, University of California, Berkeley.

Becker, B.K. (1982), *Geopolítica da Amazônia*, Rio de Janeiro: Zahar Editores.

Beckerman, S. and Kiltie, R.A. (1980), "More on Amazon cultural ecology", *Current Anthropology* 21(4): 540–46.

Berg, M.E. van den (1982), *Plantas Medicinais na Amazônia: Contribuição ao seu Conhecimento Sistemático*, Belém: CNPq/PTU.

Berredo, B. P. de (1749), *Annaes historicos do Estado do Maranhão, em que se dá notícia do seu descobrimento e tudo o mais que nelles tem succedido desde o anno em que foy descoberto ate o de 1718*, Lisbon: Francisco Luiz Ameno.

Binswanger, H. (1987), *Fiscal and Legal Incentives with Environmental Effects on the Brazilian Amazon*, Washington, D.C.: World Bank.

Black, J.K. (1977), *United States Penetration of Brazil*, Philadelphia: University of Pennsylvania Press.

Blank, L. and Bogan, J., eds. (1984), *Burden of Dreams*, Berkeley: North Atlantic Books.

Boxer, C. (1962), *The Golden Age of Brazil 1695–1750*, Berkeley: University of California Press.

Bramwell, A. (1989), *Ecology in the 20th Century: A History*, New Haven and London: Yale University Press.

Branford, S. and Glock, O. (1985), *The Last Frontier: Fighting Over Land in the Amazon*, London: Zed Books.

Browder, J.O. (1986), "Logging the rainforest: a political economy of timber extraction and unequal exchange in the Brazilian Amazon", Ph.D. dissertation, University of Pennsylvania.

—— (1987), "Brazil's export promotion policy (1980–1984): impacts on the Amazon's industrial wood sector", *The Journal of Developing Areas* 21: 285–304.

—— (1988a), "The social costs of rainforest destruction", *Interciencia* 13(3): 115–20.

—— (1988b), "Public policy and deforestation in the Brazilian Amazon", in R. Repetto and M. Gillis, eds. *Public Policies and the Misuse of Forest Resources*, Cambridge: Cambridge University Press, pp. 247–97.

—— (1988c), "Colonists in Rondônia", paper presented at the Latin American Studies Association meeting, New Orleans, March.

—— ed. (1989), *Fragile Lands of Latin America*, Boulder: Westview Press.

Brown, J.H. (1981), "Two decades of homage to Santa Rosália", *American Zoologist*, 21: 877–88.

Bryce, J. (1912), *South America: Observations and Impressions*, London: Macmillan.

Buarque de Holanda, S. (1936), *Raízes do Brasil*, Rio de Janeiro: José Olympio Editora, Documentos Brasileiros.

—— (1960-), *História Geral da Civilização Brasileira*, São Paulo: Difusão Européia do Livro.

Bunker, S.G. (1982), "The impact of deforestation on peasant communities in the Media Amazonas", *Studies in Third World Societies* 13: 45–61.

—— (1985), *Underdeveloping the Amazon: Extraction, Unequal Exchange, and the Failure of the Modern State*, Urbana: University of Illinois Press.

—— (1986), "Extração e tributação: problemas de Carajás", *Pará Desenvolvimento* 19: 11–12.

—— (1989), "The eternal conquest", *Report on the Americas* 23(1): 27–35.

Burke, E. ed. (1988), *Global Crises and Social Movements: Artisans, Peasants, Populists, and the World Economy*, Boulder: Westview Press.

Buschbacher, R. (1986), "Tropical deforestation and pasture development", *Bioscience* 36(1): 22–8.

Butler, J. (1985), "Land, Gold and Farmers: Agricultural Colonization in the Brazilian Amazon", Ph.D. Thesis, Gainesville: University of Florida.

Carneiro, G. (1965), *História das Revoluções Brasileiras*, 2 vols. Rio de Janeiro: Cruzeiro.

Carpentier, A. (1968), *The Lost Steps*, Harmondsworth: Penguin Books.

Carvalho, J. (1904), *A Primeira Insurreição Acreana*, Belém.

Casement, R. (1912) *Correspondence Respecting the Treatment of British Colonial Subjects and Native Indians Employed in the Collection of Rubber in the Putamayo District, Presented to Both Houses of Parliament by Command of His Majesty, July 1912*, London.

Castelnau, F. de (1850), *Expedition dans les Parties Centrales de l'Amerique du Sud*, 6 vols. Paris: P. Bertrand.

Castro, F. (1954), *A Selva, Romance*, 15th ed. Lisboa: Guimarães.

Cavalcante, P. and Frikel, P. (1973), *A Farmacopéia Tiriyo: Estudo Etno-Botânico*, Belém, Museu Paraense Emilio Goeldi.

Chambers, R. (1983), *Rural Development: Putting the Last First*, New York: Longman Scientific & Technical.

Chapin, M. (1988), "The seduction of models: Chinampa agriculture in Mexico", *Grassroots Development* 12(1): 8–17.

Chernela, J. (1985), "Indigenous fishing in the neotropics: the Tukanoan Uanano of the Blackwater Uaupes River Basin in Brazil and Columbia", *Interciencia* 10(2): 78–86.

—— (1986), "Os cultivares de mandioca na área do Uaupés", *Suma Etnológica Brasileira*, São Paulo: Vozes.

—— (1987), "Environmental restoration in SW Colombia", *Cultural Survival Quarterly* 11(4): 71–3.

Clay, J.W. (1988), *Indigenous Peoples and Tropical Forests: Models of Land Use and Management from Latin America*, Cambridge, Mass.: Cultural Survival, Inc.

—— ed. (1989), "Brazil: Who Pays for Development", *Cultural Survival Quarterly* 13(1): 1–47.

Cleary, D. (1987), "An anatomy of a gold rush: Garimpagem in the Brazilian Amazon", Ph.D. thesis, St. Antony's College, University of Oxford.

Cochrane, T.T. and Sanchez, P.A. (1982), "Land resources, soils and their management in the Amazon region: a state of knowledge report", in Hecht, S.B. ed. *Amazônia: Agriculture and Land Use Research*, pp. 137–209, Cali, Colombia: CIAT.

Coelho, M. and Cota, R. (1986), "Relações entre o garimpo e estrutura fundiária: o exemplo de Marabá", *Pará Desenvolvimento* 19: 20–24.

Colinvaux, P. (1987), "Amazon diversity in light of the paleoecological record", *Quaternary Science Reviews*, 6: 93–114.

Collier, D. ed. (1979), *The New Authoritarianism in Latin America*, Princeton, N.J.: Princeton University Press.

Collier, R. (1968), *The River that God Forgot*, New York: E.P. Dutton.

Collins, J. (1986), "Small holder settlement of tropical South America", *Human Organization* 45(1): 1–10.

Collins, J.L. (1988), *Unseasonal Migrations: The Effects of Rural Labor Scarcity in Peru*, Princeton, N.J.: Princeton University Press.

Comaroff, J. (1985), *Body of Power, Spirit of Resistance: The Culture and History of a South African People*, Chicago: University of Chicago Press.

Comissão Pastoral da Terra (1988), *Conflitos No Campo Brasil/87*, São Paulo: CPT.

Comité International de la Croiz Rouge (1970), *Report of ICRC Medical Mission to the Brazilian Amazon (May-August 1970)*, Series D1168-b, Geneva: Comité International de la Croiz Rouge.

Condamine, Ch-M. de La (1981), *Voyage sur l'Amazone*, Paris: François Maspero.

Connell, J. (1987), "Diversity in tropical rain forests and coral reefs", *Science*, 199: 1302–10.

Connell, J. and Souza, W.P. (1983), "On the evidence needed to judge ecological stability", *American Naturalist*, 3: 1119–44.

Cooper, J.F. (1928), *Technique of Contraception*, New York: Day-Nichols.

Coudreau, H.A. (1886), *Voyage au Rio-Branco, aux Montagnes de la Lune, au Haut Trombetas*, Rouen.

—— (1897), *Voyage au Tocantins-Araguaia*, Paris: A. Lahure.

Coy, M. (1987), "Rondônia: Frente pioneira e programa Polonoroeste", in G. Kohlhepp and A. Schrader, eds. *Homem e Natureza na Amazônia*, Tubingen: Geographisches Inst., pp. 253–70.

Craig, N.B. (1907), *Recollections of an Ill-fated Expedition to the Headwaters of the Madeira River in Brazil*, Philadelphia: J.B. Lippincott.

Craveiro Costa, J. (1940), *A Conquista do Deserto Ocidental*, São Paulo: Companhía Editora Nacional.

Crocker, C. (1985), *Vital Souls*, Cambridge: Harvard University Press.

Cunha, E. da (1944), *Rebellion in the Backlands*, trans. from *Os Sertões*, Chicago: University of Chicago Press.

—— (1946), *À Margem da História* (6th edition), Porto: Lello and Irmão. (Orig. 1909).

—— (1986), *Um Paraíso Perdido*, Rio de Janeiro: José Olympio Editora.

Cunha, M.C. da (1989), "Native realpolitik", *Report on the Americas* 23(1): 19–22.

Davis, S.H. (1977), *Victims of the Miracle: Development and the Indians of Brazil*, Cambridge: Cambridge University Press.

—— and Mathews, R.O. (1976), *The Geological Imperative: Anthropology and Development in the Amazon Basin of South America*, Cambridge: Anthropology Resource Center.

Dean, W. (1987), *Brazil and the Struggle for Rubber: A Study in Environmental History*, Cambridge: Cambridge University Press.

De Courcy, V.E. (1889), *Six Semaines Aux Mines D'Or Du Bresil*, Paris: Librairie Générale.

De Janvry, A. (1981), *The Agrarian Question and Reformism in Latin America*, Baltimore: Johns Hopkins University Press.

—— and Garcia, R. (1988), "Rural poverty and environmental degradation in Latin America", paper presented at the International Consultation on Environment, Sustainable Development, and the Role of Small Farmers, Rome: International Fund for Agricultural Development.

Denevan, W.M. (1966), "A cultural ecological view of the former aboriginal settlement in the Amazon basin", *The Professional Geographer* 15(6): 346–51.

—— (1970), "Aboriginal drained-field cultivation in the Americas", *Science* 169: 647–54.

—— (1976), "The aboriginal population of Amazônia", in W. Denevan, ed. *The Native Population of the Americas in 1492*, Madison: University of Wisconsin Press, pp. 205–34.

—— ed. (1976), *The Native Population of the Americas in 1492*, Madison: University of Wisconsin Press.

——, Treacy, J.M., Alcorn, J.B., Padoch, C., Denslow, J., and Flores P. (1984), "Indigenous agroforestry in the Peruvian Amazon: Bora Indian management of swidden fallows", *Interciencia* 9(6): 346–57.

Denevan, W.M. and Padoch, C. (1987), *Swidden Agroforestry*, New York: New York Botanical Garden.

Denslow, J.S. and Padoch, C. (1988), *People of the Tropical Rain Forest*, Berkeley: University of California Press.

Dias, A.G. (1860), *Cantos: Collecção de Poesias de A. Gonçalves Dias*, Leipzig: F.A. Brockhaus.

Dias, M.N. (1967), "Colonização da Amazônia (1755–1778)", *Revista de História* 34: 471–90.

—— (1970), *Fomento e Mercantilismo: a Companhía Geral do Grão Pará e Maranhão (1755–78)*, Belém: Universidade Federal do Pará.

Dickinson, R.E. ed. (1987), *The Geophysiology of Amazônia: Vegetation and Climate Interactions*, New York: John Wiley & Sons.

Di Paolo, P. (1986), *Cabanagem: A Revolução Popular da Amazônia*, Belém: Edições CEJUP.

DNER (1987), "A experiência nacional no desenvolvimento Rodoviário da Amazônia", in *Seminário Sôbre transporte Rodoviário na Amazônia*, Amazon Pact/OAS.

Ducke, A. and Black, G. (1983), "Phytogeographical notes on the Brazilian Amazon", *Anais da Academia Brasileira de Ciencias* 25(1): 1–47.

Edmundson, G. (1904), "Dutch trade in the basin of the Rio Negro", *English Historical Review* 123: 1–25.

Edwards, W.H. (1847), *A Voyage up the River Amazon*, London: John Murray.

Ehrenreich, P. (1965), *Contributions to the Ethnology of Brazil*, New Haven: Human Relations Area File Source. (Orig. 1891).

Elisabetsky, E. and Setzer, R. (1985), "Caboclo concepts of disease, diagnosis and therapy", *Studies in Third World Societies* 32: 243–78.

Emmi, M.F. (1987), *A Oligarquia do Tocantins e o Domínio dos Castanhais*, Belém: Centro de Filosofia e Ciências Humanas /NAEA/UFPA.

Erwin, T.L. (1982), "Tropical forests: their richness in Coleoptera and other Arthropod species", *Coleopterists Bulletin* 36(1): 74–5.

—— (1988), "The tropical forest canopy: the heart of biotic diversity", in E.O. Wilson, ed. *Biodiversity*, Washington, D.C.: National Academy Press, pp. 123–9.

Etzel, E. (1976), *Escravidão Negra e Branca: O Passado Através do Presente*, São Paulo: Global.

Evans, P. (1979), *Dependent Development: The Alliance of Multinational, State and Local Capital in Brazil*, Princeton: Princeton University Press.

Falcão, E. ed. (1907), *Álbum do Rio Acre, 1906–1907*, Pará, Brasil: E. Falcão.

FAO (1987), *Projetos Agropecuários Polonoroeste: Exame Técnico*, Rome: FAO/World Bank.

FAO (1987), *Production Yearbook*, Rome: FAO.

FAO-CP/World Bank (1987), *Brazil: Northwest I, II, and III Technical Review: Final Report*, 141/86, CP-BRA 30(E), Rome: FAO Cooperative Program.

FAO/WRI (1988), *Tropical Rain Forest Action Plan*, Washington, D.C.: World Resources Institute.

Fearnside, P.M. (1982), "Deforestation in the Amazon Basin. How fast is it occurring?" *Interciencia* 7: 82–8.

—— (1984), "Brazil's Amazon settlement schemes", *Habitat International* 8: 45–61.

—— (1985), "Environmental change and deforestation in the Brazilian Amazon", in J. Hemming, ed. *Change in the Amazon Basin, Vol.1*, Manchester: Manchester University Press, pp. 70–90.

—— (1986), *Human Carrying Capacity of the Brazilian Rainforest*, New York: Columbia University Press.

—— (1987a), "Rethinking continuous cultivation in Amazônia", *Bioscience* 37(3): 209–13.

—— (1987b), "Causes of deforestation in the Amazon basin", in R.E. Dickinson, ed. *The Geophysiology of Amazônia: Vegetation and Climate Interactions*, New York: John Wiley & Sons, pp. 37–61.

—— (1988), "Extractive reserves in Brazilian Amazônia: an opportunity to maintain tropical rain forest under sustainable use", manuscript.

—— (1989a), "A prescription for slowing deforestation in Amazônia", *Environment* 31(4): 16–20, 39–40.

—— (1989b), "Forest management in Amazônia", in *Forest Ecology and Management* 26, forthcoming.

—— and Ferreira, G. (1984), ''Roads in Rondônia: highway construction and the farce of unprotected reserves in Brazil's Amazonian forest'', *Environmental Conservation* 11(4): 358–60.

Fernandez de Oviedo y Valdes, G. (1851–55), *História General y Natural de las Indias*, Madrid: Impr. de la Real academia de la historia.

Ferrarini, S.A. (1979), *Transertanismo: Sofrimento e Miséria do Nordestino na Amazônia*, Petrópolis: Vozes.

Ferreira, A.R. (1907), *Viagem filosófica às Capitanias do Grão-Pará, Rio Negro, Mato Grosso e Cuiabá*, E.C. Falcão, ed. 2 vols. São Paulo: Graficas Brunner.

Ferreira, M.R. (1987), *A Ferrovia do Diabo, História de uma Estrada de Ferro na Amazônia*, São Paulo: Melhoramentos. (Orig. 1959).

Fittkau, E.J., Junk, W., Klinge, H., and Sioli, H. (1975), ''Substrate and vegetation in the Amazon Region'', in H. Dierschke, ed. *Vegetation und Substrat*, Vaduz J. Cramer, pp. 73–90.

Foweraker, J. (1981), *The Struggle for Land*, Cambridge: Cambridge University Press.

Frikel, P. (1971), ''A técnica da roça dos índios Mundurucu'', in C. Rocque, ed. *Antologia da Cultura Amazônica* 6: 132–6. São Paulo.

Fritz, Fr. S. (1922), *Journal of the Travels and Labours of Father Samuel Fritz in the River of the Amazons between 1686 and 1723*, London: Hakluyt Society, Series 2, No. 51.

Furtado, C. (1963), *The Economic Growth of Brazil: A Survey from Colonial to Modern Times*, Berkeley: University of California Press.

Galey, J. (1977), ''The politics of development in the Brazilian Amazon, 1940-1950'', Ph.D. dissertation, Stanford University.

—— (1979), ''Industrialist in the wilderness: Henry Ford's Amazon venture'', *Journal of Inter-American Studies* 21: 264–89.

Gallais, E-M. (1942), *O Apóstolo do Araguaia: Frei Gil de Vilanova, Missionário Dominicano*, São Paulo.

—— (1954), *Uma Catequese Entre os Índios do Araguaia*, Salvador.

Gasques, J.G., and Yokomizo, C. (1986), ''Resultados de 20 anos de incentivos fiscais na agropecuária da Amazônia'', *Proceedings ANPEC*: 47–84.

Gauld, C.A. (1964), *The Last Titan: Percival Farquhar, American Entrepreneur in Latin America*, Stanford: Institute of Hispanic America & Luso-Brazilian Studies, Stanford University.

Glacken, C.J. (1967), *Traces on the Rhodian Shore: Nature and Culture in Western Thought from Ancient Times to the End of the Eighteenth Century*, Berkeley: University of California Press.

Gomez-Pompa, A., Vazquez-Yanes, C., and Guevara, S. (1972), ''The tropical rainforest: a non-renewable resource'', *Science* 177: 762–5.

Gonçalves, M. (1961), ''O índio do Brasil na literatura portuguesa dos séculos XVI, XVII e XVIII'', *Brasília* 11: 97–209, Coimbra.

Gonçalves Jr., J.M. ed. (1986), *Carajas: Desafio Político, Ecologia e Desenvolvimento*, São Paulo: Brasiliense.

Goodland, R.J.A. (1978), ''Environmental assessment of the Tucuruí hydroelectric project Rio Tocantins, Amazônia,'' *Survival International Review* 3(2): 11–14.

—— (1980), ''Environmental ranking of Amazonian development projects in Brazil'', *Environmental Conservation* 7(1): 9–26.

—— (1982), *Tribal Peoples and Economic Development*, Washington, D.C.: World Bank.

—— (1985), ''Brazil's environmental progress in Amazonian development'', in J. Hemming ed. *Change in the Amazon Basin, Vol.1*, Manchester: Manchester University Press, pp. 5–35.

Goodland, R.J.A., and Irwin, H.S. (1975), *Amazon Jungle: Green Hell to Red Desert?* Amsterdam: Elsevier.

Goodman, E. (1972), *The Explorers of South America*, New York: Macmillan.

Gottleib, O.R. (1981), ''New and underutilized plants in the Americas: solution to problems of inventory through systematics'', *Interciencia* 6(1): 22–9.

Goulding, M. (1980), *The Fishes and the Forest*, Berkeley: University of California Press.

Gradwohl, J. and Greenberg, R. (1988), *Saving the Tropical Forests*, Washington, D.C.: Island Press.

Graham, D. et al. (1987), "Thirty years of agricultural growth in Brazil: crop performance, regional profile, and recent policy review", *Economic Development and Cultural Change* 36(1): 1–34.

Greenbaum, L. (1989), "Plundering timber on Brazilian Indian reservations", *Cultural Survival Quarterly* 13(1): 23–6.

Grilli, E.R., et al. (1980), *The World Rubber Economy: Structure, Changes, and Prospects*, Baltimore: Johns Hopkins University Press.

Gross, S.E.A. (1969), "The economic life of the Estado do Maranhão e Grão Pará, 1686–1751", Ph.D. dissertation, Tulane University.

Guenther, K. (1931), *A Naturalist in Brazil*, Boston: Houghton Mifflin.

Haffer, J. (1982), "General aspects of the refuge theory", in G.T. Prance, ed. *Biological Diversification in the Tropics*, New York: Columbia University Press, pp. 6-24.

Hames, R.B. and Vickers, W.T., eds. (1984), *Adaptative Responses of Native Amazonians*, New York: Academic Press.

Hancock, T. (1857), *Personal Narrative of the Origin and Progress of the Caoutchouc or India-Rubber Manufacture in England*, London: Longman, Brown, Green, Longmans, & Roberts.

Hardin, G. (1968), "The tragedy of the commons", *Science* 162: 1243–8.

Hartshorn, G. (1980), "Neotropical forest dynamics", *Biotropica* 12(Supp.): 23–31.

Hays, S.P. (1987), *Beauty, Health, and Permanence: Environmental Politics in the United States, 1955-1985*, New York: Cambridge University Press.

Hebette, J. (1986), "A resistencia dos posseiros no Grande Carajás", *Cadernos do CEAS* 102: 62–75.

—— (1987a), "Reservas indigenas hoje, reservas camponesas amanha?" *Pará Desenvolvimento* 20/21: 26–9.

—— (1987b), "A tensão no poligonio", *Pará Agrario* 2.

Hecht, S.B. (1981), "Deforestation in the Amazon Basin: magnitude and dynamics and soil resources effects", *Studies in Third World Societies*, 13: 61–101.

—— (1982a), "Cattle ranching development in the Eastern Amazon: evaluation of a development policy", Ph.D. dissertation, University of California, Berkeley.

—— (1982b), "Agroforestry in the Amazon Basin", in S.B. Hecht, ed. *Amazônia: Agriculture and Land Use Research*, Cali, Colombia: CIAT, pp. 330–71.

—— (1982c), "Deforestation in the Amazon Basin: magnitude, dynamics and soil resource effects", *Studies in Third World Societies* 13: 61–101.

—— ed. (1982), *Amazônia: Agriculture and Land Use Research*, Cali, Colombia: CIAT (Centro Internacional de Agricultura Tropical).

—— (1985), "Environment, development and politics: capital accumulation and the livestock sector in eastern Amazônia", *World Development* 13(6): 663–84.

—— (1986a), "Regional development: some comments on the discourse in Latin America", *Environment and Planning D: Society and Space* 4: 201–9.

—— (1986b), *Development and Deforestation in the Amazon: Current and Future Policies, Investment and Impact on Forest Conversion*, Washington, D.C.: World Resources Institute.

—— (1989a), "Rethinking colonist attrition in the Amazon Basin", submitted to *World Development*.

—— (1989b), "Chico Mendes: Chronicle of a Death Foretold", *New Left Review* 173: 47–55.

—— (1989c), "The sacred cow", *Report on the Americas* 23(1): 23–6.

——, Norgaard, R., and Possio, G. (1988), "The economics of cattle ranching in eastern Amazon", *Interciencia* 13(5): 233–40.

——, Andersond, A. and May, P. (1988), "The subsidy from nature: shifting cultivation, successional palm forests and rural development", *Human Organization* 47(1): 25–35.

—— and Schwartzman, S. (1989), "The good, the bad and the ugly: extraction, colonist agriculture and livestock in comparative perspective", submitted to *Interciencia*.

—— and Schwartzman, S. (1989), "Internal migration in the seringal", in preparation.

—— and Posey, D. (1989), "Preliminary results on soil management techniques of the Kayapó Indians", *Advances in Economic Botany* 7: 174–88.

—— and Nations, J.D. eds. *Deforestation: Processes and Alternatives*, forthcoming.

Hemming, J.H. (1978a), *Red Gold: the Conquest of the Brazilian Indians*, Cambridge: Harvard University Press.

—— (1978b), *The Search for El Dorado*, New York: Dutton.

—— ed. (1985), *Change in the Amazon Basin: Vol.1, Man's Impact on Forests and Rivers, Vol.2, The Frontier after a Decade of Colonisation*, Manchester: Manchester University Press.

—— (1987), *Amazon Frontier: The Defeat of the Brazilian Indians*, Cambridge: Harvard University Press.

Herndon, W.L. (1952), *Exploration of the Valley of the Amazon*, New York: McGraw-Hill. (Orig. 1854).

Himes, N.E. (1970), *Medical History of Contraception*, New York: Schocken Books.

Hiraoka, M. (1985), "Cash cropping, wage labor and urban migration in the Peruvian Amazon," *Studies in Third World Societies* 32: 199–242.

Hitz, W. (1989), "Debt for nature, meeting conservation needs in Costa Rica?", M.A. thesis, University of California, Los Angeles.

Hopper, J.H. ed. (1967), *Indians of Brazil in the Twentieth Century*, Washington, D.C.

Hudson, W.H. (1944), *Green Mansions: A Romance of the Tropical Forest*, New York: Random House.

Hugh-Jones, S. (1987), *The Palm and the Pleides*, Cambridge: Cambridge University Press.

Humboldt, A. von and Aime-Bonpland (1815), *Personal Narrative of Travels to the Equinoctial Regions of the New Continent during the Years 1799–1804*, Philadelphia: Carey.

Inglis, B. (1973), *Roger Casement*, London: Hodder & Stoughton.

Irvine, D. (1989), "Succession management and resource distribution in an Amazonian rain forest", *Advances in Economic Botany* 7: 223–37.

Janzen, D.H. (1974), "Tropical blackwater rivers and mast fruiting by the dipterocarpaceae", *Biotropica* 6: 69–103.

Jarvis, L. (1986), *Livestock in Latin America*, New York: Oxford.

Jeffrey, L.H. (1987), *Natural Resources and Economic Development in Central America*, New Brunswick, N.J.: Transaction Books.

Johnson, A. (1982), "Ethnoecology and planting practices in a swidden agricultural system", in D. Brokensha, D. Warren, O. Werner, eds. *Indigenous Knowledge Systems and Development*, Washington, D.C.: USA Press, pp. 49–67.

Jordan, C.F. (1985), *Nutrient Cycling in Tropical Forest Ecosystems*, Chichester: Wiley Press.

—— ed. (1987), *Amazonian Rain Forests: Ecosystem Disturbance and Recovery*, Ecological Studies, No. 60, New York: Springer-Verlag.

—— , and Uhl, C. (1978), "Biomass of a 'tierra firme' forest of the Amazon Basin", *Oecologia Plantarum* 13: 387–400.

—— , Golley, F., Hall, J.B., and Hall, J. (1980), "Nutrient scavenging of rainfall by the canopy of an Amazonian rain forest", *Biotropica* 12: 61–6.

Julião, F. (1972), *Cambao – The Yoke: The Hidden Face of Brazil*, Harmondsworth: Penguin Books.

Kaufman, L. and Kenneth, M. eds. (1986), *The Last Extinction*, Cambridge: MIT Press.

Kaufman, Y.J., Tucker, C.J., and Fung, I. (1989), "Remote sensing of biomass burning in the tropics", unpublished manuscript. NASA/ Goddard Space Flight Center.

Keith, H.H. and Edwards, S.F. eds. (1969), *Conflict and Continuity in Brazilian Society*, Columbia, South Carolina: University of South Carolina Press.

Kidder, D.P. (1939), *Sketches of Residence and Travels in Brazil*, 2 vols. Philadelphia: Sorin & Ball. (Orig. 1845).

Kieman, M. (1954), *The Indian Policy of Portugal in the Amazon Basin, 1614–1693*, Washington D.C.: Catholic University Press.

Kiernan, M. (1989), ''From forest to failure near the Carajas Mines: salvaging sustainability and land-use zoning in the impact area'', M.A. thesis, University of California, Los Angeles.

Kitamura, P. (1982), *Análise Econômica de Algumas Alternativas de Manejo de Pastagens Cultivadas*, Belém: EMBRAPA.

Klinge, H. (1967), ''Podzol soils: a source of blackwater rivers in Amazônia'', in H. Leut, ed. *Atas do Simpósio Sobre a Biota Amazonica* Vol. 3, Rio de Janeiro: CNPg, pp. 117–25.

Kloppenburg, J.R. (1988), *First the Seed: The Political Economy of Plant Biotechnology, 1492–2000*, Cambridge: Cambridge University Press.

Kuehl, S.A., Nittrouer, C.A., and DeMaster, D.J. (1982), ''Modern sediment accumulation and strata formation on the Amazon continental shelf'', *Marine Geology* 49: 279–300.

Labre, A.R.P. (1887), *Itinerário da Exploração do Purus ao Beni*, Pará.

Lange, A. (1912), *In the Amazon Jungle*, New York: Knickerbocker Press.

Leite, L.L. and Furley, P.A. (1985), ''Land development in the Brazilian Amazon with particular reference to Rondônia and the Ouro Preto colonization project'', in J. Hemming, ed. *Change in the Amazon Basin Vol.2*, Manchester: Manchester University Press, pp. 119–39.

Leonard, H.J. (1987), *Natural Resources and Economic Development in Central America*, New Brunswick, N.J.: Transaction Books.

Lévi-Strauss, C. (1970), *The Raw and the Cooked*, New York: Harper and Row.

—— (1974), *Tristes Tropiques*, New York: Atheneum.

Lima, C.A. (1973), *Plácido de Castro um Caudilho contra o Imperialismo*, Brasília: Civilização Brasileira.

Lisansky, J.M. (1980), ''Santa Terezinha: life in a Brazilian frontier town'', Ph.D. dissertation, University of Florida.

Lopes, O.C. (1906), *O Acre e O Amazonas*, Rio de Janeiro: Jornal do Commercio.

Luz, N.V. (1968), *A Amazônia para os Negros Americanos*, Rio de Janeiro: Editora Saga.

Lyon, P.J. ed. (1974), *Native South Americans: Ethnology of the Least Known Continent*, Boston: Little, Brown and Company.

Macdonald, Jr., T. (1986), ''Anticipating colonos and cattle in Ecuador and Colombia'', *Cultural Survival Quarterly* 10(2): 33–6.

MacLachlan, C. (1972), ''The Indian directorate: forced acculturation in Portuguese America (1757–1799)'', *The Americas* 28: 357–87.

—— (1973), ''The Indian labor structure in the Portuguese Amazon, 1700–1800'', in D. Alden, ed. *The Colonial Roots of Modern Brazil*, Berkeley: University of California Press, pp. 199–230.

—— (1974), ''African slave trade and economic development in Amazônia'', in R. Toplin, ed. *Slavery and Race Relations in Latin America*, Westport, Conn.: Greenwood Press, pp. 112–45.

Mahar, D.J. (1979), *Frontier Development Policy in Brazil: A Study of Amazônia*, New York: Praeger Publishers.

—— (1988), *Government Policies and Deforestation in Brazil's Amazon Region*, Washington, D.C.: World Bank.

Malingreau, J. and Tucker, C. (1988), ''Large-scale deforestation in the southwestern Amazon Basin of Brazil'', *Ambio* 17(1): 49–55.

Martine, G. (1980), ''Recent colonization experiences in Brazil: expectations versus reality'', in F. Barbira-Scazzocchio, ed. *Land, People and Planning in Contemporary Amazônia*, Cambridge: Cambridge University Press, pp. 80–94.

Martinello, P. (1988), *A ''Batalha da Borracha'' na Segunda Guerra Mundial e suas Consequencias para o Vale Amazônico*, São Paulo: UFAC.

Martins, A.L. (1984), ''Historia dos Garimpos de Ouro no Brasil'', in G. Rocha, ed. *Em Busca do Ouro*, São Paulo: Editora Marco Zero.

Martins, J. (1981), "Lutando pela Terra: Indios e posseiros na Amazônia", in *Os Camponesas e a Politica no Brasil*, Petrópolis.

Martins, J. de S. (1984a), *A Militarização da Questão Agrária no Brasil*, Petrópolis: Vozes.

—— (1984b), "The state and the militarization of the agrarian question in Brazil", in M. Schmink and C.H. Wood, eds. *Frontier Expansion in Amazônia*, Gainesville: University of Florida Press, pp. 463–90.

—— (1987), "O poder de decidir no desenvolvimento da Amazônia: conflitos de interesses entre planejadores e suas vitimas", in G. Kohlhepp and A. Schrader, eds. *Homem e Natureza na Amazônia*, Tubingen: Geographisches Inst., pp. 407–13.

Marx, K. (1973), *Grundrisse*, New York: Vintage Books.

Matthiessen, P. (1965), *At Play in the Fields of the Lord*, New York: Random House.

Mattos, C.M. (1980), *Uma Geopolítica Pan-Amazônica*, Rio de Janeiro: J. Olympio.

Maury, M.F. (1853), *Valley of the Amazon: The Amazon and the Atlantic Slopes of South America*, Washington D.C.: Franck Taylor.

May, P. (1986), "The tragedy of the non-Commons", Ph.D. dissertation, Cornell University.

Meade, R.H., Dunne, J.E., Richey, U., Santos, M., and Salati, E. (1985), "Storage and remobilization of suspended sediment in the lower Amazon River of Brazil", *Science* 228: 488–90.

Medina, J.T., ed. (1988), *The Discovery of the Amazon*, New York: Dover. (Orig. 1934).

Melon, M. (1988), "Rubber tappers and extractive reserves: a development alternative for the Amazon", M.A. thesis, University of California, Los Angeles.

Mendes, A.D. (1985), "Major projects and human life in Amazonia", in J. Hemming ed. *Change in the Amazon Basin, Vol.1*, Manchester: Manchester University Press, pp. 44–57.

Mendes, C. (1989), *Fight for the Forest: Chico Mendes in His Own Words*, London: Latin America Bureau.

Mendes, C. (1989), *Chico Mendes*, São Paulo: Sindicato dos Trabalhadores Rurais de Xapuri, Conselho Nacional dos Seringueiros and the Central Unica dos Trabalhadores.

Mendonca, B. (1989), *Reconhecimento do Rio Juruá, 1905*, Acre: Fundação Cultural do Estado do Acre, Belo Horizonte: Itatiaia, Coleção reconquista do Brasil, 2 serie, v.152.

Miller, D. (1985), "Replacement of traditional elites: an Amazon case study", in J. Hemming, ed. *Change in the Amazon Basin Vol.2*, Manchester: Manchester University Press, pp. 158–71.

Millikan, B.H. (1988), "The dialectics of devastation: tropical deforestation, land degradation, and society in Rondônia, Brazil", M.A. thesis, University of California, Berkeley.

Moog, V. (1956), *Bandeirantes e Pioneiros*, Rio de Janeiro: Editora Globo.

Moran, E.F. (1974), "The adaptive system of the Amazonian caboclo", in C. Wagley, ed. *Man in the Amazon*, Gainesville: University of Florida Press, pp. 136–59.

—— (1981), *Developing the Amazon*, Bloomington: Indiana University Press.

—— ed. (1983), *The Dilemma of Amazonian Development*, Boulder: Westview Press.

—— (1985), "An assessment of a decade of colonisation in the Amazon Basin", in J. Hemming, ed. *Change in the Amazon Basin Vol. 2*, Manchester: Manchester University Press, pp. 91–102.

Morner, M. (1965), *The Expulsion of the Jesuits from Latin America*, New York: Knopf.

Mors, W.B., and Rizzini, C.T. (1966), *Useful Plants of Brazil*, Rio de Janeiro: Holden-Day.

Morse, R.M. (1965), *The Bandeirantes: the Historical Role of the Brazilian Pathfinders*, New York: Knopf.

Mozeto, A.A., Stone, T.A. et al. (1988), "Avaliação do impacto ambiental através do uso de sistema geográfico de informação e de sensoreamento remoto na área de proteção ambiental da UHE Samuel, Rondônia, Brasil," submitted to *Interciencia*.

Murphy, R. (1960), *Headhunter's Heritage*, Berkeley: University of California Press.

Myers, N. (1979), *The Sinking Ark*, Oxford: Pergamon Press.

— (1984), *The Primary Source: Tropical Forests and Our Future*, New York: W.W. Norton & Co.

Myers, T. (1981), "Aboriginal trade networks in Amazônia", in P. Francis, F. Kense, and P. Duke, eds. *Networks of the Past: Regional Interaction in Archaeology*, Calgary, Canada: Chacmool, pp. 19–28.

Nelson, R. et al. (1989), "Determining rates of forest conversion in Mato Grosso", *International Journal of Remote Sensing*, in press.

Nigh, R.B., and Nations, J.D. (1980), "Tropical Rainforests", *Bulletin of the Atomic Scientists* 36(3): 12–19.

Norgaard, R.B. (1981), "Sociosystem and ecosystem coevolution in the Amazon", *Journal of Environmental Economics and Management*, 8: 238–54.

Norton, B.G. ed. (1986), *The Preservation of Species: The Value of Biological Diversity*, Princeton, N.J.: Princeton University Press.

O'Donnell, G. (1979), *Modernization and Bureaucratic Authoritarianism*, Berkeley: University of California Press.

Odum, H.T. and Pigeon, R.F. (1970), *Tropical Rainforest: A Study of Irradiation and Ecology at El Verde, Puerto Rico*, Washington, D.C.: United States Atomic Energy Commission.

Oliveira, A.U. de (1987), *Amazônia: Monopolio, Expropriação e Conflitos*, Campinas, SP: Papirus.

Oliveira, J.J.M. (1861), "Os Cayapós", *Revista do Instituto Histórico e Geographico Brasileiro* 24: 491–524.

Oliveira, L.A.P. (1985), *O Sertanejo, O Bravo e O Posseiro*, Rio Branco: Fundação Cultural do Acre.

Pacheco de Oliveira Filho, João (1979), "O caboclo e o brabo: notas sobre duas modalidades de forca-de-trabalho na expansão da fronteira Amazônica no século XIX", *Encontros com a Civilização Brasileira* 2: 101–40.

Pacific South West Experiment Station (1987), *Fire in Mediterranean Ecosystem*, Berkeley: University of California Press.

Padoch, C., Inoma, C., Jong, J. and Unruh, Ju. (1985), "Amazonian agroforestry: a market-oriented system in Peru", *Agroforestry Systems* 3(1): 47–58.

Page, J. (1972), *The Revolution that Never Was: Northeast Brazil, 1955–64*, New York: Grossman.

Parker, E.P. (1985), "Caboclization: the transformation of the Amerindian in Amazônia: 1615–1800", *Studies in Third World Societies* 32: 1–49.

— ed. (1985), "The Amazon caboclo: historical and contemporary perspectives", *Studies in Third World Societies* 32: 1–317.

Parker, P.R. (1979), *Brazil and the Quiet Intervention, 1964*, Austin: University of Texas Press.

Pastor, M. (1987),"The effects of IMF programs in the Third World: debate and evidence from Latin America", *World Development* 15(2): 249–62.

Pearce, R.H. (1965), *Savagism and Civilization: A Study of the Indian and the American Mind*, Baltimore: Johns Hopkins Press.

Pearson, H.C. (1911), *The Rubber Country of the Amazon*, New York: The India Rubber World.

Pepper, D. (1984), *The Roots of Modern Environmentalism*, London: Croom Helm.

Pinto, L.F. (1980), *Amazônia: No Rastro do Saque*, São Paulo: Editora Hucitec.

Pinto, N.P.A. (1984), *Política da Borracha no Brasil*, São Paulo: Editora Hucitec.

Pires, M., and Prance, G. (1977), "The Amazon forest: a natural heritage to be preserved," in G. Prance, ed. *Extinction is Forever*, New York: New York Botanical Garden, pp. 158–213.

Pliny the Elder (1938–63), *Natural History*, trans. by H. Rackham, 10 vols. Cambridge: Harvard University Press.

Pomer, V. (1980), *Araguaia: O Partido e a Guerrilha*, São Paulo: Brasil Debates.

Pompermeyer, M.J. (1979),"The state and frontier in Brazil", Ph.D. dissertation, Stanford University.

Posey, D.A. (1981), "Ethnoentomology of the Kayapó Indians of central Brazil", *Journal of Ethnobiology* 1(1): 165–74.

— (1983a), "Indigenous knowledge and development: an ideological bridge to the future", *Ciencia e Cultura* 35(7): 877–94.

— (1983b), "Indigenous ecological knowledge and development of the Amazon", in E. Moran, ed. *The Dilemma of Amazonian Development*, Boulder: Westview Press, pp. 225–57.

— (1983c), "Folk apiculture of the Kayapó Indians of Brazil", *Biotropica* 15(2): 154–8.

— (1985a), "Indigenous management of tropical forest ecosystems: the case of the Kayapó Indians of the Brazilian Amazon", *Agroforestry Systems* 3(2): 139–58.

— (1985b), "Native and indigenous guidelines for new Amazonian development strategies: understanding biological diversity through ethnoecology," in J. Hemming ed. *Change in the Amazon Basin, Vol.1*, Manchester: Manchester University Press, pp. 156–81.

— (1989), "From warclubs to words", *Report on the Americas* 23(1): 13–18.

— and Santos, P.B. dos (1985), "Concepts of health, illness, curing and death in relation to medicinal plants and the appearance of the Messianic King on the Island of Lencois, Maranhão", *Studies in Third World Societies* 32: 279–313.

— and Balée, W., eds. (1989), *Resource Management in Amazônia: Indigenous and Folk Strategies (Advances in Economic Botany Vol.7)*, New York: New York Botanical Garden.

Potter, G.A. (1988), "Debt swaps: buying in means selling out", *IDOC Internazionale* Vol. 1.

Prance, G.T. (1982), *Biological Diversification in the Tropics*, New York: Columbia University Press.

— (1985), "The increased importance of ethnobotany and underexploited plants in a changing Amazon", in J. Hemming, ed. *Change in the Amazon Basin, Vol.1*, Manchester: Manchester University Press, pp. 129–36.

— ed. (1986), *Tropical Rain Forests and the World Atmosphere*, Boulder: Westview Press.

Prance, G.T., and Elias, T.S. eds. (1977), *Extinction is Forever: The Status of Threatened and Endangered Plants of the Americas*, New York: New York Botanical Garden.

Prance, G. and T. Lovejoy, eds. (1986), *Key Environments–Amazônia*, Oxford: Pergamon Press.

Quandt, C. (1987), "Evaluation of spatially discontinuous social impacts: the case of Itaipu, a major resource-based project in Brazil", M.A. thesis, University of California, Los Angeles.

Ramos, A.R. (1984), "Frontier expansion and Indian peoples in the Brazilian Amazon", in M. Schmink and C.H. Wood, eds. *Frontier Expansion in Amazônia*, Gainsville: University of Florida Press, pp. 83–104.

Redford, K. and Richards, J. (1987), "The game of choice", *American Anthropologist* 89(3): 650–67.

Redford, K., Klein, B., and Murcia, C. (1989), "The incorporation of game animals into small scale agroforestry systems in the neotropics", paper presented at Man and Environment Program Conference, Gainesville, February 1989.

Rego Reis, G.M. (1965), *A Cabanagem: Um Episódio Histórico de Guerra Insurrecional na Amazônia (1835-1839)*, Manaus: Edições Governo do Estado do Amazonas, Série Torquato Tapajós.

Reichel-Dolmatoff, G. (1971), *Amazonian Cosmos: The Sexual and Religious Symbolism of the Tukano Indians*, Chicago: University of Chicago Press.

— (1976), "Cosmology as ecological analysis: a view from the rain forest", *Man* 11(3): 307–18.

Reis, A.C.F. (1931), *História do Amazonas*, Manaos: Officinas Typographicas de A. Reis.

— (1944), *O Processo Histórico da Economia Amazonense*, Rio de Janeiro.

— (1953), *O Seringal e O Seringueiro*, Rio de Janeiro: Servico de Informação Agrícola, Ministerio da Agricultura.

—— (1956), *A Amazônia Que os Portugueses Revelaram*, Rio de Janeiro: Ministério da Educação e Cultura, Serviço de Documentacão.

—— (1968), *Amazônia e a Cobiça Internacional*, Manaus.

Ribeiro, B.G. (1986), *Suma: Etnologica Brasileira, 1 Etnobiologia*, Petrópolis: FINEP.

Ribeiro, D. (1970), *Os Indios e a Civilização*, Rio de Janeiro: Civilização Brasileira.

—— (1971), *The Americas and Civilization*, trans. by L. Barrett and M. Barrett, New York: Dutton.

—— (1984), *Maíra*, New York: Aventura.

Ribeiro, N. (1930), *O Acre e Os Seus Heroes*, Maranhão: Rabello.

Rippy, J.F. (1944), *Latin America and the Industrial Age*, New York: G.P. Putnam's Sons.

—— (1959), *British Investments in Latin America, 1822–1949*, Minneapolis: University of Minnesota Press.

—— and Nelson, J.T. (1936), *Crusaders of the Jungle: The Origin, Growth and Decline of the Principal Missions of South America during the Colonial Period*, Chapel Hill: University of North Carolina Press.

Rocha, G. (1984), *Em Busca do Ouro*, São Paulo: Editora Marco Zero.

Rodrigues, L.A. (1947), *Geopolítica do Brasil*, Rio de Janeiro: Edição da Biblioteca Militar.

Rose, P. (1989), *Jazz Cleopatra: Josephine Baker in Her Time*, New York: Doubleday.

Ross, E.B. (1978), "The evolution of the Amazon peasantry", *Journal of Latin American Studies* 10: 193–218.

Salati, E. (1987), "The forest and the hydrological cycle", in R.E. Dickinson, ed. *The Geophysiology of Amazônia*, New York: John Wiley & Sons, pp. 273–96.

Saldarriaga, J.G., and West, D.C. (1986), "Holocene fires in the northern Amazon basin", *Quaternary Research* 26: 358–66.

Salles, V. (1971), *O Negro no Pará*, Belém: Fundação Getúlio Vargas.

Salo, J., Kalliola, R., Hakkinen, L., Kakinen, Y., Niemela, P., Phakka, M., and Coley, P.D. (1986), "River dynamics and the diversity of Amazon lowland rain forest", *Nature* 322: 254–8.

Sanchez, P.A. (1985), "Management of acid soils in the humid tropics", paper presented at Acid Soils Network Inaugural Workshop, Brasília, Brazil.

—— and Benites, J. (1987), "Low input cropping systems for acid soils of the humid tropics", *Science* 238: 1521–7.

Sanford, R.L., Saldarriaga, J., Clark, K.E., Uhl, C., and Herrera, R. (1985), "Amazon rainforest fires", *Science* 227: 53–5.

Santa-Anna Néry, Baron de (1901), *The Land of the Amazons*, London: Sands & Co. (Orig. 1885).

Santilli, M. (1988), *Madeira-Mamoré*, São Paulo: Mundo Cultural Editora.

Santos, A.P. et al. (1979), *Relatório final do Projeto INPE/SUDAM.INPE- 1610-RPE/085*, São José dos Campos: Brazilian Institute of Space Studies.

Santos, R.A.O. (1980), *História Econômica da Amazônia: 1800–1920*, São Paulo: T.A. Queiroz, Biblioteca Básica de Ciências Sociais, Serie 1, v. 3.

Santos, R. (1984), "Law and social change: the problem of land in the Brazilian Amazon", in M. Schmink and C.H. Wood, eds. *Frontier Expansion in Amazônia*, Gainesville: University of Florida Press, pp. 439–62.

Sawyer, D. (1989a), "The effects of the Brazilian economic crisis on migration to the Amazon", manuscript prepared for the Annual Meeting of the Population Association of America, Baltimore, March 30–April 1, 1989.

—— (1989b), "Migration and ecological upheaval in the humid tropics: patterns and prospects for Brazil's western Amazon", manuscript.

Sayad, J. (1984), *Crédito Rural no Brasil*, São Paulo: Pioneira.

Schickel, R. (1968), *The Disney Version*, New York: Simon & Schuster.

Schidrowitz, P., and Dawson, T.R. eds. (1952), *History of the Rubber Industry*, Cambridge: Heffer & Sons.

Schmink, M. (1982), ''Land conflicts in Amazônia'', *American Ethnologist* 9(2): 341–57.

—— (1985), ''Social change in the Garimpo'', in J. Hemming ed. *Change in the Amazon Basin, Vol.2*, Manchester: Manchester University Press, pp. 185–99.

—— (1989), ''The rationality of tropical forest destruction'', in S. Hecht and J. Nations, eds. *Deforestation: Processes and Alternatives*, forthcoming.

—— and Wood, C.H. eds. (1984), *Frontier Expansion in Amazônia*, Gainesville: University of Florida Press.

—— and Wood, C.H. (1987), ''The 'political ecology' of Amazônia'', in P.D. Little, M.M. Horowitz, and A.E. Nyerges, eds. *Lands at Risk in the Third World*, Boulder: Westview Press, pp. 38–57.

Schneider, S.H. (1989), ''The greenhouse effect: science and policy'', *Science* 243: 771–9.

Schwartzman, S. and Allegretti, M. (1987), ''Extractive Reserves: a sustainable development alternative for Amazônia'', manuscript, Washington D.C.: World Wildlife Fund.

Schwartzman, S. and Allegretti, M. (1989), ''Extractive production in the Amazon and the rubber tappers' movement (1)'', in S. Hecht and J. Nations, eds. *Deforestation: Processes and Alternatives*, forthcoming.

Scott, J.C. (1976), *The Moral Economy of the Peasant: Subsistence and Rebellion in Southeast Asia*, New Haven: Yale University Press.

—— (1986), *Weapons of the Weak: Everyday Forms of Peasant Resistance*, New Haven: Yale University Press.

—— and Kerkvliet, B.J.T., eds. (1986), *Everyday Form of Peasant Resistance in South-East Asia*, London: Frank Cass.

Seeger, A. (1981), *Nature and Society in Central Brazil: The Suya Indians of Mato Grosso*, Cambridge: Harvard University Press.

SEPLAN. (1988), *Plano Diretor da Estrada Ferroviária Carajás*, Brasília.

Serrão, E.A. and Toledo, J.M. (1988), ''Sustaining pasture-based production systems in the humid tropics'', paper presented in the MAB Conference on Conversion of Tropical Forests to Pasture in Latin America, Oaxaca, Mexico, October 4–7.

Sharp, R.H. (1945), *South America Uncensored*, New York: Longmans Green & Co.

Silva, A.L., Santos, L.A., and Manzoni Luz, M., eds. (1985), *A Questão da Mineração em Terra Indígena*, São Paulo: Cadernos da Comissão Pro-Indio/SP no. 4.

Silva, A.T. da (1986), ''Grandes Projetos em implantação na Amazônia'', *Pará Desenvolvimento* 18: 23–5.

Silva, A., Lima, I., Hebette, J., Braga, J., Gastal, M., and Macambira, M. (1986), ''Como repensar o garimpo na Amazônia?'' *Pará Desenvolvimento* 19: 25–6.

Silva, G.C. (1967), *Geopolítica do Brasil*, Rio de Janeiro: J. Olympio.

—— (1981), *Conjuntura Política Nacional: O Poder Executivo e Geopolítica do Brasil*, 3rd ed. Rio de Janeiro: Livraria José Olympio Editora.

Silva, J.G. da (1982), *A Modernização Dolorosa*, Rio de Janeiro.

Silva, R. da, Souza, M. de, and Bezerra, C. (1988), *Contaminação por Mercúrio nos Garimpos Paraenses*, Belém: DNPM.

Simon, P. (1861), *The Expedition of Pedro de Ursua and Lope de Aguirre in Search of El Dorado and Omagua in 1560–1561*, ed. and trans. by W. Bollaert, London: Hakluyt Society, no. 28 (1st series).

Simpson, B.B., and Haffer, J. (1978), ''Speciation patterns in the Amazonian forest biota'', *Annual Review of Ecology and Systematics* 9: 497–518.

Skidmore, T. (1967), *Politics in Brazil 1930–1964: An Experiment in Democracy*, Oxford: Oxford University Press.

Smith, N.J.H. (1974), ''Destructive exploitation of the South American river turtle'', *Yearbook of the Association of Pacific Coast Geographers* 36(c). Oregon State University Press.

—— (1980), "Anthrosols and human carrying capacity in the Amazon," *Annals of the American Association of Geographers*, 70: 553–66.

—— (1981), *Man, Fishes, and the Amazon*, New York: Columbia University Press.

—— (1982), *Rainforest Corridors: The Transamazon Colonization Scheme*, Berkeley: University of California Press.

Snethlage, E. (1910), "A travessia entre o Xingu e o Tapajoz", *Boletim do Museu Goeldi (Museu Paráense) de História Natural e Ethnográphia* 7: 49–92. Belém.

Soares, L.E. (1981), *Campesinato: Ideologia e Política*, Rio de Janeiro: Zahar Editores.

Soule, M.E. ed. (1986), *Conservation Biology: The Science of Scarcity and Diversity*, Sunderland, Mass.: Sinauer.

Souza, J.A.S. (1852), *Pro Memória de Duarte Ponte Ribeiro*, Rio de Janeiro.

—— (1952), *Um Diplomata do Império*, São Paulo: Companhía Editora Nacional.

Souza, M. (1977), *A Expressão Amazonense: do Colonialismo ao Neocolonialismo*, São Paulo: Alfa Omega, Biblioteca Alfa-Omega de Cultura Universal, Serie 1. Esta América, v.5.

Spix, J.B. (1823–31), *A Grande Aventura de Spix e Martius*, (translated to Portuguese in 1938) Brasília: Instituto Nacional do Livro.

Spruce, R. (1908), *Notes of a Botanist on the Amazon and Andes*, 2 vols. London: Macmillan.

Steinen, K. von (1940), *Entre os Aborígenes do Brasil Central*, São Paulo. (Orig. 1886).

Stepan, A. (1971), *The Military in Politics: Changing Patterns in Brazil*, Princeton, N.J.: Princeton University Press.

Sternberg, H.O. (1975), *Amazon River of Brazil*, New York: Springer Verlag.

Stone, R.D. (1985), *Dreams of Amazônia*, New York: Viking Penguin Inc.

Stone, T.A. and Woodwell, G.M. (1988), "Shuttle imaging radar: an analysis of land use in Amazônia", *International Journal of Remote Sensing* 9(1): 95–105.

SUDAM (1986), *Problemática do Carvão Vegetal na Área do Grande Carajás*, Belém.

Sweet, D.G. (1974), "A rich realm of nature destroyed: the Middle Amazon Valley, 1640–1750", Ph.D dissertation, University of Wisconsin, Madison.

—— and Nash, G.B. eds. (1981), *Struggle and Survival in Colonial America*, Berkeley: University of California Press.

Taunay, A.E. (1954), *História das Bandeiras Paulistas*, São Paulo.

Taussig, M. (1987), *Shamanism, Colonialism, and the Wild Man*, Chicago: University of Chicago Press.

Telles, C. (1946), *História Secreta da Fundação Brazil Central*, Rio de Janeiro: Editora Chavantes.

Tocantins, L. (1961), *Formação Históriçá do Acre*, 3 vols. Rio de Janeiro: Conquista.

—— (1984), *Estado do Acre: Geografia, Historia e Sociedade*, Rio de Janeiro: Philobiblion.

Tomlinson, H.M. (1920), *The Sea and the Jungle*, New York: E.P. Dutton & Co.

Tucker, C.J. et al. (1984), "Intensive forest clearing in Rondônia, Brazil, as detected by satellite remote sensing," *Remote Sensing Environment* 15: 255–64.

Uhl, C. and Murphy, P. (1981), "A comparison of productivities and energy values between slash and burn agriculture and secondary succession in the upper Rio Negro region of the Amazon Basin", *Agro-Ecosystems* 7: 63–83.

Uhl, C. and Jordan, C.F. (1984), "Vegetation and nutrient dynamics during the first five years of succession following forest cutting and burning in the Rio Negro region of Amazônia", *Ecology* 65: 1476–90.

Uhl, C. and Buschbacher, R. (1985), "A disturbing synergism between cattle ranch burning practices and selective tree harvesting in the Eastern Amazon", *Biotropica* 17: 265–8.

Uhl, C. and Vieira, I. (1989), "Impacts of logging in Parágominas", manuscript submitted to Biotropica.

Velho, O.G. (1972), *Frentes de Expansão e Estrutura Agraria*, Rio Janeiro: Zahar Editores.

Vickers, W.T. (1979), "Native Amazonian subsistence in diverse habitats: the Siona-Secoya of Ecuador", *Studies in Third World Societies* 7: 6–36.

Villas Boas, O. and Villas Boas, C. (1973), *Xingu: The Indians, Their Myths*, New York: Farrar, Straus & Giroux.

Von Hagen, V.W. (1948), *The Green World of Naturalists: A Treasury of Five Centuries of Natural History in South America*, New York: Greenberg.

Wagley, C. ed. (1974), *Man in the Amazon*, Gainesville: University of Florida Press.

—— (1976), *Amazon Town: A Study of Man in the Tropics*, Oxford: Oxford University Press. (Orig. 1953).

Wagner, A. (1986a), "As areas indigenas e o mercado de terras" in *Povos Indigenas no Brasil*, São Paulo: CEDI, pp. 53–9.

—— (1986b), "Estrutura fundiaria e expansão camponesa", in J.M. Gonçalves, Jr. ed. *Carajas: Desafio Político, Ecologia e Desenvolvimento*, São Paulo: Editora Brasiliense, pp. 265–93.

Wallace, A.R. (1853), *Narrative of Travels on the Amazon and Rio Negro, with an Account of the Native Tribes*, London: Ward, Lock & Co.

Walle, P. (1911), *Au Pays de l'Or Noir: le Caoutchouc du Bresil*, Paris: Guilmoto.

Watt, M. (1983), *Silent Violence*, Berkeley: University of California Press.

Weinstein, B. (1983a), *The Amazon Rubber Boom, 1850–1920*, Stanford: Stanford University Press.

—— (1983b), "Capital penetration and problems of labor control in the Amazon rubber trade", *Radical History Review* 27: 121–40.

—— (1986), "The persistence of precapitalist relations of production in a tropical export economy: The Amazon rubber trade, 1850–1920", in M.P. Hanagan and C. Stephenson, eds. *Proletarians and Protest: Studies in Class Formation*, Westport, Conn.: Greenwood Press.

Whitesell, E.A. (1988), "Rubber extraction on the Jurua in Amazonas, Brazil: Obstacle to progress or development paradigm?" M.A. thesis, University of California, Berkeley.

Wickham, H.A. (1872), *Rough Notes of a Journey through the Wilderness, from Trinidad to Pará, Brazil by way of the Great Cataracts of the Orinoco, Atabapo and Rio Negro*, London: W.H.J. Carter.

—— (1908), *On the Plantation, Cultivation, and Curing of Pará Indian Rubber*, London.

Wilbert, J. ed. (1984), *Folk Literature of the Gê Indians*, Los Angeles: UCLA Latin American Center Publications, University of California, Los Angeles.

Wilkes, C. (1858), *Exploring Expedition During the Years 1838, 1839, 1841, 1842*, New York: G.P. Putnam.

Wilson, E.O. ed. (1988), *Biodiversity*, Washington, D.C.: National Academy Press.

Wolf, E.R. (1982), *Europe and the People Without History*, Berkeley and Los Angeles: University of California Press.

Woodroffe, J.F. and Smith, H.H. (1915), *The Rubber Industry of the Amazon, and How its Supremacy can be Maintained*, London: J. Bale, Sons & Danielsson.

Woodwell, G.M. et al (1987), "Deforestation in the tropics: new measurements in the Amazon Basin using Landsat and NOAA AVHRR Imagery", *Journal of Geophysical Research*, 92: 2157–63.

Woodwell, G.M., Stone, T.A., and Houghton, R.A. (1988), "Deforestation in Pará, Brazilian Amazon Basin: measurements using Landsat and rader imagery – a report: August 31, 1988", manuscript.

Worster, D. (1985), *Nature's Economy: A History of Ecological Ideas*, Cambridge: Cambridge University Press.

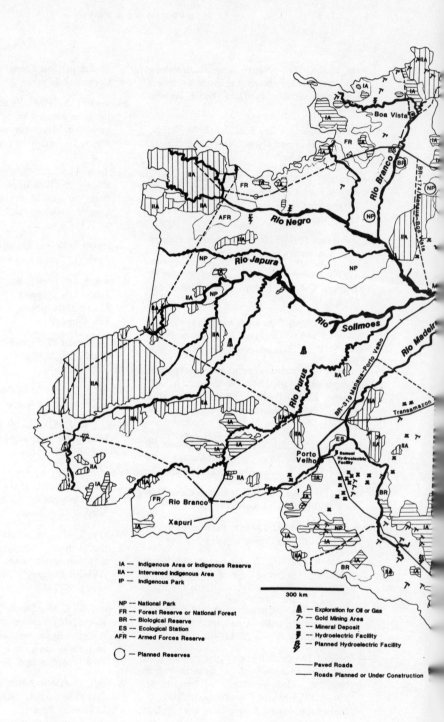

IA — Indigenous Area or Indigenous Reserve
IIA — Intervened Indigenous Area
IP — Indigenous Park

NP — National Park
FR — Forest Reserve or National Forest
BR — Biological Reserve
ES — Ecological Station
AFR — Armed Forces Reserve

◯ — Planned Reserves

300 km

🛢 — Exploration for Oil or Gas
↗ — Gold Mining Area
✕ — Mineral Deposit
⚡ — Hydroelectric Facility
⚡⚡ — Planned Hydroelectric Facility

——— Paved Roads
- - - - Roads Planned or Under Construction

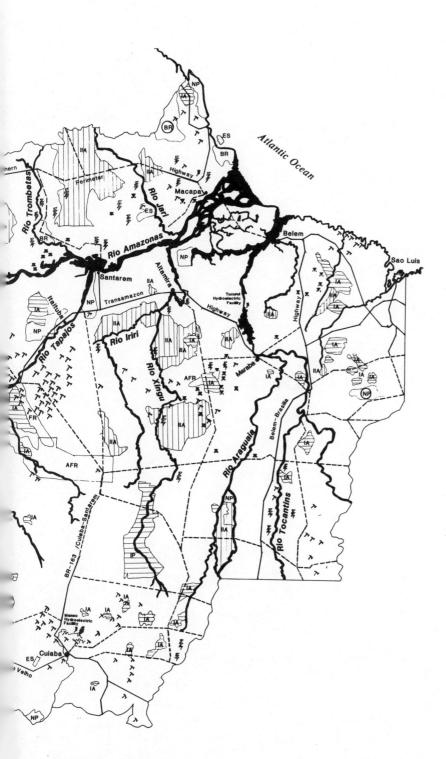

The Amazon, early 1989

Index